"This outstanding book is a compelling read for all early childhood educators offering a vibrant and engaging insight into the visual arts as essential and vital languages of young children. It is a book which raises the profile of the visual arts, the quality of practice and its impact on young children's learning by empowering its reader to reflect on their pedagogy, practice and provision. It is a book woven with theoretical perspectives and expert practical guidance which will become a constant reference for all working in early childhood education."

Debi Keyte-Hartland, *Pedagogical Early Childhood Consultant & Artist-Educator, UK*

"*Art Play and Inquiry* makes an invaluable contribution to early childhood literature, offering a rich theoretical understanding of the value of early childhood arts practice and providing in-depth knowledge to support adults to confidently embed engaging visual art practices. Playful inquiry is central. Children expressing their ideas and feelings, making decisions and choices and in turn finding their voice, generating new ideas and making sense of their world. This book will directly impact practice leading to more children taking delight and flourishing through the visual arts. Highly recommended reading."

Pete Moorhouse, *Early Childhood Creative Consultant, UK*

"This book is an essential resource for every early childhood methods class. It seamlessly bridges theory and practice, making it the perfect guide for both preservice and experienced educators. For teachers hesitant about introducing art to young children, it offers empowering strategies and builds confidence. Packed with practical insights and easy-to-implement ideas, it equips educators with strategies to inspire creativity in the classroom. Whether you're just starting out or have years of experience, this book will be invaluable in fostering a dynamic, engaging learning environment for young learners."

Kathy Danko-McGhee, PhD, *First Encounters: An Art Studio for Little Ones, USA*

"This volume offers visionary and hopeful support for early childhood educators. Rich with pedagogical and artistic guidance it's a valuable companion in creating and engaging in meaningful art experiences together with children and for ensuring the arts have a central place in children's daily lives. The authors encourage educators to be fully present and nurture their own artistries while opening joyful, playful, vibrant and expansive spaces for children's curiosity, creativity, and artistic expression. It's a beautiful invitation for adults and children alike to see the arts as sites of personal and relational flourishing."

Sylvia Kind, PhD, *Capilano University, Canada*

"This is a 'must read' text for every early childhood educator. It is a comprehensive, accessible and inspirational account of the 'why, what and how' of visual art in early childhood. It takes the reader by the hand and walks them through the theories and practices that underpin the magic of making art. It finishes with a treasure chest of art materials, activities and techniques; the 'how' of teaching the visual arts. This text is guaranteed to empower educators to embrace the visual arts as a leading activity for learning."

Margaret Brooks, *Associate Professor Early Childhood Education (retired), Australia*

"The authors offer a varied set of lenses through which to understand the inestimable value of Art with young children. Students of education, teachers, and college educators will find a unifying thread weaving the practice of art activity with major theoretical trends in the field from around the world. This book represents a major contribution to the field of early childhood education."

Sylvia Chard, *Professor Emeritus at the University of Alberta, Canada*

"This exciting new book provides comprehensive coverage of all the things that are needed to provide high quality art education for young children. Backed up with current education theory and research, and illustrated with beautiful examples of good practice, this book is essential reading for practicing teachers as well as students in training. Parents of young children and people with an interest in art education will also find it helpful for understanding the importance of art education in an ever changing world."

Lisa Terreni, PhD, *Arts advocate and adviser, New Zealand*

Art Play and Inquiry

Combining theoretical inspiration, practical guidance, and visual examples, this book empowers educators to implement rich visual arts experiences and foster joyful, art-centered learning environments with children.

Drawing upon decades of experience and research, the authors offer rich, practical, plain English information alongside inspiring images, reflection points, and visual examples to support educators to understand the WHY, WHAT, and HOW of designing and delivering a rich visual arts curriculum for and with young children. Making no assumptions about prior visual arts knowledge or experience, this informative, visually beautiful book connects theory and practice, while providing guidance to inspire and inform interactions with children and visual arts materials in meaningful ways.

This is an essential resource for educators, teachers, parents, students or academics aiming to enhance their teaching practices and enrich children's learning through visual arts. Whether you are new to visual arts education or looking to deepen your practice, this book will inspire and equip you to support children's creative and expressive potential.

Gai Lindsay is passionate about art and early childhood education, with long-term experience as a preschool teacher, academic, consultant, and art-maker. Her work focuses on visual arts pedagogy and educator self-efficacy, aiming to inspire children and educators alike to embrace lifelong joy through arts-inspired learning and play.

Sarah Probine is an academic and early childhood researcher based in Aotearoa New Zealand. Her work examines visual arts pedagogy and collaborative inquiry approaches, highlighting their capacity to foster intersubjectivity and interconnectedness in early childhood education.

Rachel Denee is a teacher and academic who is interested in visual arts in early childhood contexts. Her research is grounded in her experience in the early childhood sector as a teacher, leader, facilitator, and co-researcher. Rachel studies visual arts pedagogy, leadership, curriculum, and professional learning for teachers.

Denise Savins is an Early Childhood Teacher from Northern New South Wales, Australia. Denise also holds a degree in Visual Arts and has worked for a number of years as an art educator/atelierista with children aged 2–6 years. She is passionate about fostering children's learning, creativity, and self-expression through meaningful visual arts pedagogy.

Art Play and Inquiry

The Why, What and How of Visual Arts Education with Young Children

Gai Lindsay, Sarah Probine,
Rachel Denee and Denise Savins

Routledge
Taylor & Francis Group
LONDON AND NEW YORK

Designed cover image: Mural created by a group of 4-year-old children at Sophia Preschool who had been on an excursion to their local Ōakura Beach to explore ways to protect the ocean and its creatures [Image: Adrienne Wilkins, Sophia Preschool].

First published 2026
by Routledge
4 Park Square, Milton Park, Abingdon, Oxon OX14 4RN

and by Routledge
605 Third Avenue, New York, NY 10158

Routledge is an imprint of the Taylor & Francis Group, an informa business

British Library Cataloguing-in-Publication Data
A catalogue record for this book is available from the British Library

Library of Congress Cataloging-in-Publication Data
Names: Lindsay, Gai author
Title: Art play and inquiry : the why, what and how of visual arts education with young children / Gai Lindsay, Sarah Probine, Rachel Denee, and Denise Savins.
Description: Abingdon, Oxon ; New York, NY : Routledge, 2026. | Includes bibliographical references and index. | Identifiers: LCCN 2025012232 (print) | LCCN 2025012233 (ebook) | ISBN 9781032911977 hbk | ISBN 9781032911960 pbk | ISBN 9781003561835 ebk
Subjects: LCSH: Art--Study and teaching (Primary)
Classification: LCC N361 .L56 2026 (print) | LCC N361 (ebook) | DDC 372.5--dc23/eng/20250516
LC record available at https://lccn.loc.gov/2025012232
LC ebook record available at https://lccn.loc.gov/2025012233

ISBN: 9781032911977 (hbk)
ISBN: 9781032911960 (pbk)
ISBN: 9781003561835 (ebk)

DOI: 10.4324/9781003561835

Typeset in Avenir LT Std
by KnowledgeWorks Global Ltd.

To our families and friends, thank you for your love and support.

To our many colleagues dedicated to visual arts-centred pedagogies, your commitment to creating meaningful art experiences for children is truly inspiring.

A special thanks to the "Possums," a remarkable group of early childhood academics and practitioners. Your enthusiasm and friendship motivate us to elevate visual arts within early childhood education.

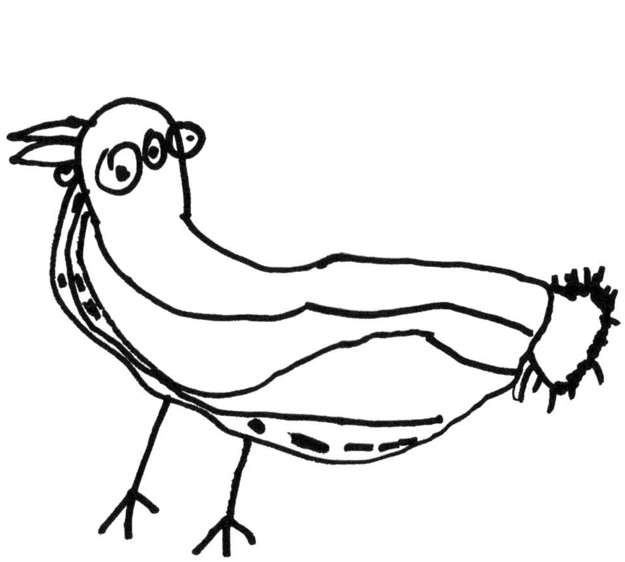

Contents

Foreword

The first time I saw images of children at work with materials from the municipal pre-primary schools of Reggio Emilia, I cried. I know now that my response is not unique, but at the time, the tears surprised me. I hadn't known it was possible to have my own aesthetic sensibilities moved so deeply by still images of children working with the languages of the arts. But nor had I seen children working in this particular way before – in process, in collaboration with others, beautiful materials in hand. Even now, 25 years later, rarely are children photographed in process. Much more frequently we see them smiling at the camera, holding up their product in hand. In those photos, you can almost hear the adult behind the camera demanding – "show me what you made!" glad to have new content to share but already griping about the clean-up. The child is dutiful, cute, and messy.

These images that so provoked my thinking, shared by Louise Cadwell and Chuck Schwall at a conference, depicted children actively engaged in their creative work. The images, which I later understood to be part of a process called pedagogical documentation, were framed by the adult photographer around what the children were doing, not what they had made. The images captured the children lost in the flow of their own expression, often in collaboration with other children, and, as I'd soon come to learn, in dialogue with the materials as well as their learning environment. Loris Malaguzzi, founder of the Reggio Approach, has said that it is a kind of "nostalgia for the future" that can feel so moving to adults who see children deeply engaged in the process of making and doing. It reminds us of what we are all capable of: we meaning makers, storytellers, playful animals; we the social, creative, and wondering. These images seemed to capture the best in our shared humanity, and the unique gifts of children, still part of us all, even in spite of some fairly inevitable atrophy. These images ignite a longing.

This book you hold is oxygen for the flame.

In the tradition of teachers, researchers, and visionaries like Louise Cadwell and Chuck Schwall, Lella Gandini, Carolyn Edwards, Ann Pelo, Margie Carter, Ann Lewin-Benham, Karen Gallas, Cathy Topal, Ursula Kolbe, Dee Smith, Jeanne Goldhaber, Miriam Beloglovsky, and those who create resources for Reggio Children, we have a rich new volume that takes on the complex and beautiful world of children, art, and artists. Dr. Gai Lindsay, Dr. Sarah Probine, Dr. Rachel Denee, and Denise Savins have given us a volume that goes deep and wide, providing practitioners with a wealth of possible entry points, reflection points, and reference points - tools to support work with children, to deepen their own practices and strengthen courage, and to advocate for the rights of all human beings to their creative birthright.

This is the kind of book I wish I'd had when I was beginning to explore what would become the story workshop structure I created with colleagues and the children we taught over many years. The founder of our school, Judy Graves, had invited the teachers to research, if it was of interest to them, the relationship between literacy and the arts. It was of great interest to me! Like many teachers of young children, I strongly valued the opportunity I had to support creativity, social and emotional development, and habits of mind that would strengthen vigorous intellectual and cognitive growth. However, although I had a hunch the arts were central to that process, I did not see myself as an artist. How would I overcome my own lack of competence and confidence in order to get out of the way of the children building theirs? Without a supervisor and mentor such as I had in Judy, I would have been too intimidated to experiment with the practices that helped us develop theories that became the foundation of our approach to playful inquiry and the story workshop structure. I would have benefitted from a book like this one. Without creating new scripts to follow or methods to replicate, this book provides the kind of synthesis of much of the exciting and beautiful terrain that grounds a rationale for prioritising experiences with the arts. It is solid footing for adults who feel an urgency to engage in the arts despite the negative messages they likely remember from their own experiences in school.

To take action that responds to our nostalgia for the future, we need courage, but also we need imagination. To long for a world that is guided by the unique gifts of childhood – a sense of wonder, a desire to play, a need to belong that can neutralise conflict – adults must preserve them, prioritise them, advocate for them as human rights. These actions are the only way to bring that world into being. The authors of the book you hold in your hands are committed to connecting the work of artmaking to the kinds of expression, compassion, inquiry, culture, community, and ideas that are central to the work of freedom. They are intentional about including the work of our very youngest citizens and supporting adults to become more comfortable with their own creative arts practice.

They include a wealth of imagery that will put new memories in your mind - new memories that will embolden your courage for new possibilities and help you work with others who share that vision.

Once you've read this book, I'm confident that it will take its place on your bookshelf as a valued resource to revisit again and again as you continue to learn and grow. Reading this book, I felt like I was being invited and immersed gently in the world of art – able to examine it from multiple angles, supported as an educator, but also as a maker and a beholder of art. These are practices that take time and benefit from ample amounts of reflection, practice, and wonder. What if children saw more of their hearts and minds expressed through their own hands? What if they saw more of their classmates' hearts and minds? Or other artists? How might they feel more in relation to the things that make us human? What if the arts sustained our capacity for joy and play well into adulthood? What if the arts supported a mindset that prioritised multiple perspectives and perseverance and humor and resilience? What if our work as teachers was the work that mattered most to the creation of a just and sustainable future? And what if that future relied on the arts? What would you find the courage to do?

Let's wander our way together towards that future.

Susan Harris MacKay
The Center and Studio for Playful Inquiry

Acknowledgements

To our colleagues and friends who have provided images and case studies for this book, we sincerely thank you for sharing your work with us and our readers. Your contributions enrich and bring life to our words. Warm thanks to the following organisations, educators and artists for sharing their stories and images in this publication:

Adrienne Wilkins, Sophia Preschool, Ōakura, Aotearoa New Zealand
Aurora International School Of The Arts, Ho Chi Minh City, Vietnam
Blue Gum Community School, Canberra, Australia
Bomaderry Community Preschool, Bomaderry, Australia
Bundanon, Shoalhaven, Australia
Daisies Early Education & Care Centre, Wellington, Aotearoa New Zealand
Dripstone Children's Centre, Darwin, Australia
Explore and Develop Castlereagh Street, Sydney, Australia
Frances Forshlager, The Nature of Creativity
Joke den Haese, Erasmus Brussels University of Applied Sciences and Arts, Brussels, Belgium
Judith Urry, Northland School, Te Kura o Orangi Kaupapa, Wellington, Aotearoa New Zealand
Kathy Danko-McGhee, Fort Wayne, United States of America
Lyrebird Preschool, Nowra, Australia
Maitland East Preschool, Maitland, Australia
Pete Moorhouse, Bristol, United Kingdom
Saigon Kids Early Learning Centre, Ho Chi Minh City, Vietnam
Sherry Polley, Indianapolis, United States of America
The Friends Long Day Childcare Centre, Lismore, Australia
The Point Preschool, Oyster Bay, Australia
UOW Pulse Kids' Uni, Wollongong, Australia

And, most importantly, our heartfelt thanks to the many children whose artworks have brought this book to life!

PART 1

WHY the visual arts are important for young children's education and for educator's work with children

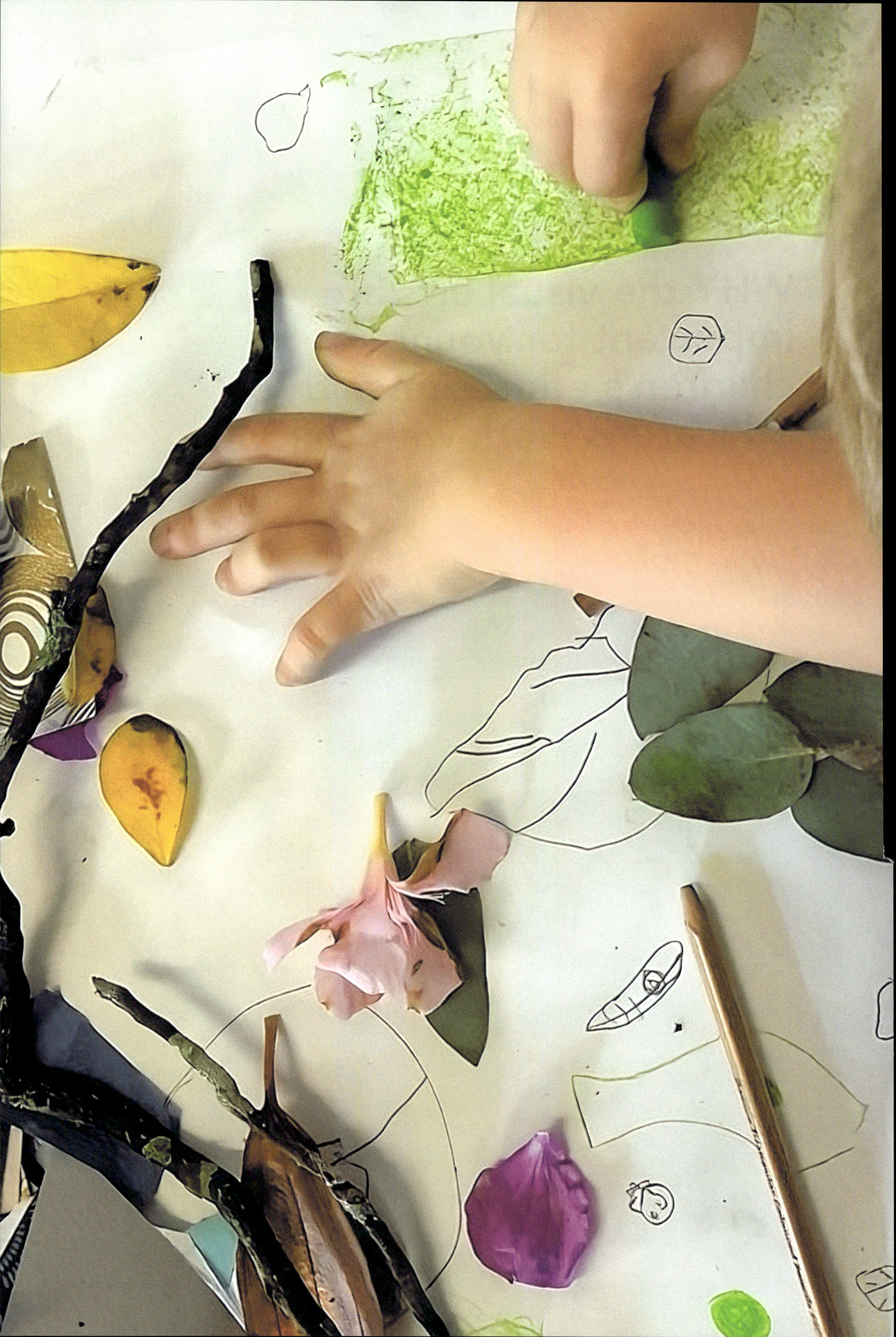

1 Introduction

The desire to communicate and express ideas visually is fundamentally human. Without art, we would have no records of ancient societies and few insights into the beliefs, customs, and cultures that define us. Artmaking is not just about creating; it is the expression of ideas, exploration of issues, and a process of wondering that involves both the hands and minds. The joy of creating and appreciating art invites us to see the world through each other's eyes. Recognising this, the United Nations Convention on the Rights of the Child (UNCRC) affirms that all children must be afforded the right to "freedom of expression" including "freedom to seek, receive and impart information and ideas...in the form of art or through any other media of the child's choice" (Article 13), and to "engage in play and recreational activities appropriate to the age of the child and to participate freely in cultural life and the arts" (Article 31). The visual arts enrich our lives and have the potential to enrich children's education, play, and learning experiences.

Visual arts learning can be positioned as the "glue" which holds together holistic and playful inquiry, connecting children's interests, rights, and development. Visual arts learning experiences equip children with skills and dispositions that will support them to flourish, not only in their education but throughout life. In our own work as early childhood teachers, art-makers, and researchers, we have experienced the profound joy, curiosity, learning, and growth that visual arts bring into the lives of young children and educators. We want readers of this book to discover the same magic!

However, perceptions about children's artmaking, and what quality visual arts practice looks like, vary greatly in early education settings, resulting in varied experiences and outcomes for children (Lindsay, 2023). While educators value the potential of visual arts learning for children, some express uncertainty about how to plan for and implement quality visual arts experiences (Denee et al., 2024). In some contexts, this can result in art activities that lack opportunities for children's creative expression. If educators see art as a form of entertainment or busy work or regularly use templates to create cute seasonal products, children's ideas, thinking, and decision-making opportunities are limited. The predetermined outcomes of such "close-ended" arts experiences undermine children's innate creativity and innovation.

Figure 1.1 Rich visual arts materials and provocations invite children to express their ideas, make choices, and engage deeply with their creativity, honouring their right to explore, wonder, and create in meaningful ways [Image: Maitland East Preschool].

DOI: 10.4324/9781003561835-2

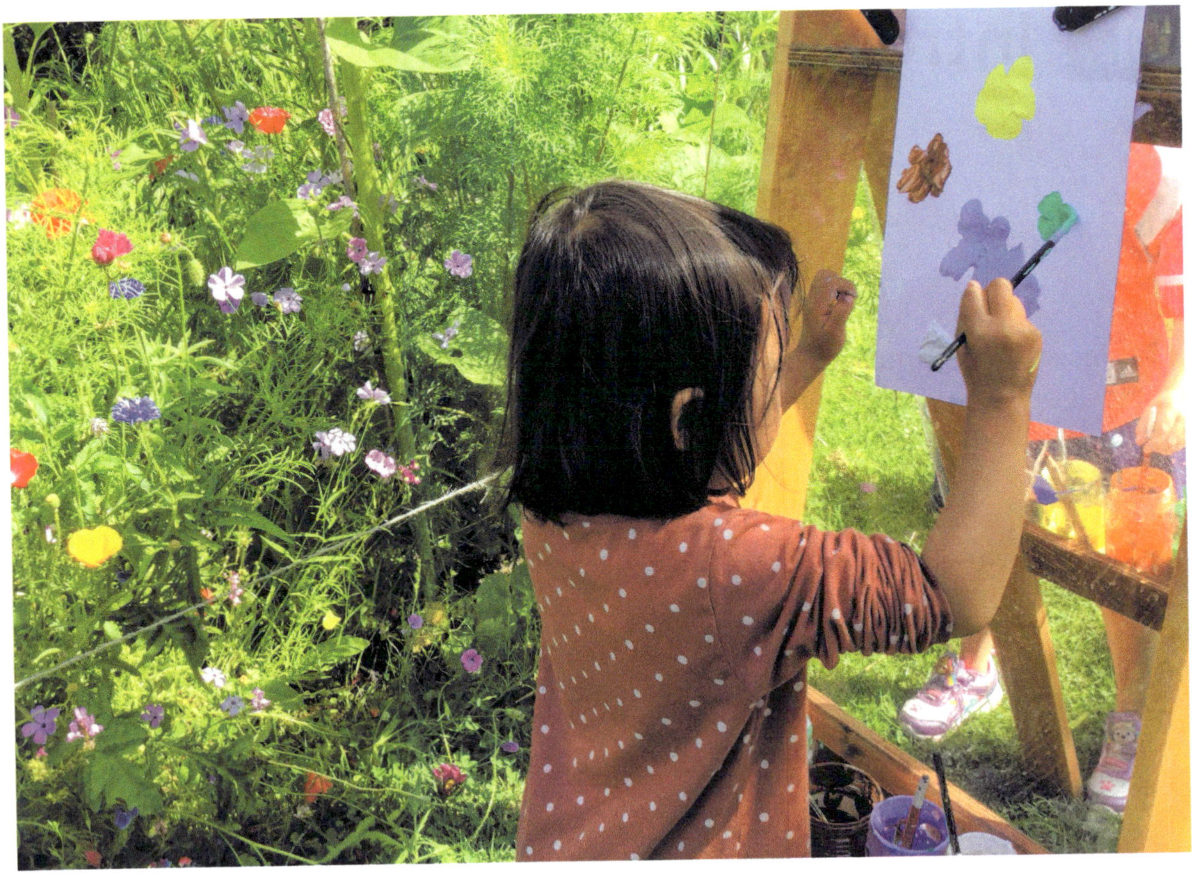

Figure 1.2 Inspiring environments support children to connect their world and their art. Educators play a vital role by encouraging curiosity, nurturing confidence, and embracing the creative process alongside them [Image: Adrienne Wilkins, Sophia Preschool].

Some educators are uncertain about whether they should actively engage in artmaking with children or should stand back to observe as children experiment and explore. Some choose not to participate in visual arts learning experiences at all, leaving this responsibility to colleagues seen as more "arty" or creative than themselves. Adding to this, pre-service training doesn't automatically empower educators to build their visual arts self-efficacy and knowledge due to existing beliefs and "baggage" that constrain learning and practice (Lindsay, 2021). Curriculum frameworks, and even creative arts textbooks, often lack pedagogical guidance for visual arts teaching and learning. There is confusion about whether the processes or the products of children's artmaking should be valued. Because of such uncertainties, too many children experience very structured, adult-centred activities, while others are left with minimal art materials and no interaction or extension at all. This is what we hope to change!

The aim of this book

Our main aim in writing *Art Play and Inquiry: The Why, What and How of Visual Arts Education with Young Children* is to equip adults who work with children with the knowledge and confidence to implement rich visual arts experiences. Whether you are a leader, teacher, educator, student-teacher, or parent, this book is designed to empower and inspire quality teaching practices to enrich children's play, inquiry, and learning through encounters with the languages of the visual arts.

This book is presented in three sections, focused on the why, what, and how of visual arts education with young children. In this, we were inspired by McArdle's (2012) reminder that before learning *what* to do (to implement visual arts learning experiences) and gathering ideas about *how* to implement a range of arts processes and methods, it is necessary to appreciate *why* the visual arts are important for young children.

Our decision to use the words "play" and "inquiry" in the book title is not limited to children's play and inquiry-based learning. Our intentional use of these words highlights the value of playful inquiry required of adults who work with children to create meaningful visual arts learning experiences. An attitude of play and inquiry is essential for educators if they are to foster their own knowledge and capacity for visual arts-centred pedagogies. Malaguzzi (interviewed by Gandini, 2012, p. 58) reminds us that teachers must be learners in collaboration with children:

> Learning and teaching should not stand on opposite banks and just watch the river flow by; instead, they should embark together on a journey down the water. Through an active, reciprocal exchange, teaching can strengthen learning and how to learn.

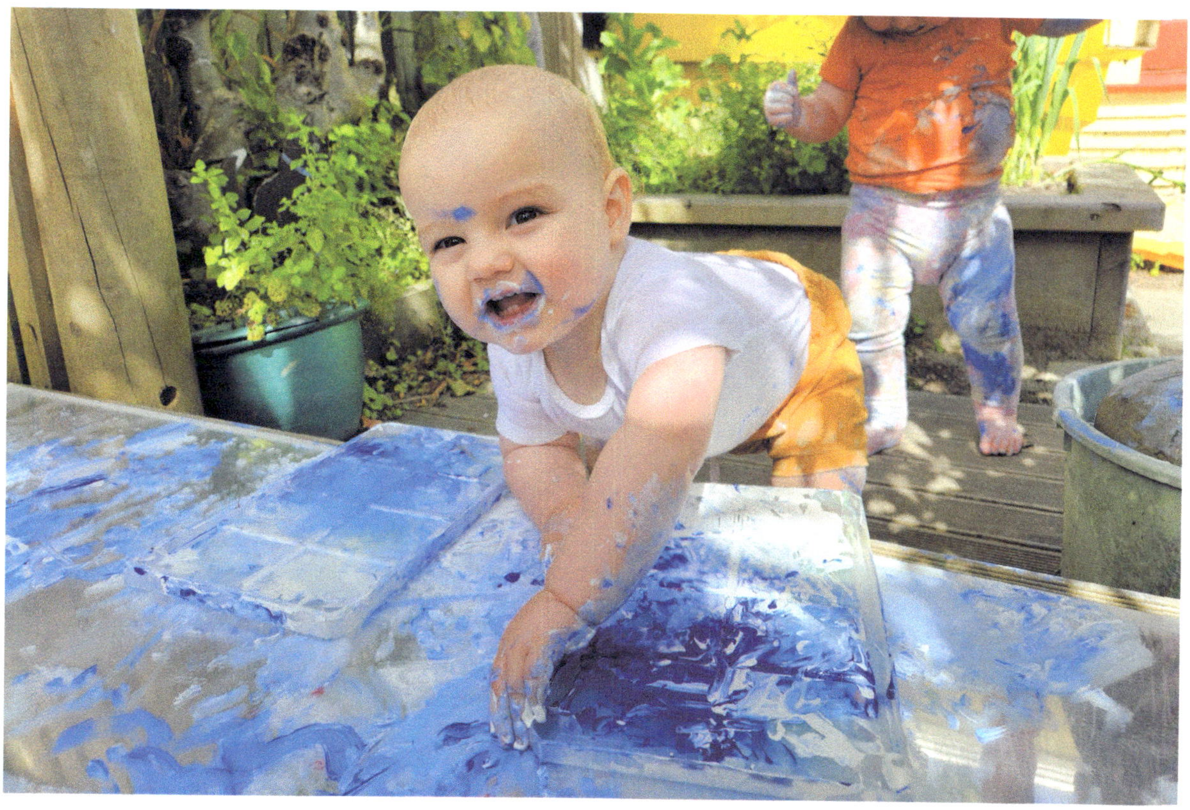

Figure 1.3 Delight and discovery begin with playful exploration. To nurture such moments, educators must embrace their own sense of curiosity and inquiry—learning alongside children and fostering meaningful, relationship-based encounters with the visual arts [Image: Daisies Early Education & Care Centre].

If children are to experience the many benefits of visual arts, the adults in children's lives must also learn (or perhaps re-learn) how to play with visual arts expression and engage in research and inquiry to inform practice. We urge everyone working with children to grapple with the ideas, theories, and philosophies presented in this book to provoke inquiry, action research, and deep reflection about visual arts pedagogy and curriculum choices. It is vital to move visual arts education beyond the provision of formulaic activities and instead facilitate rich relationship-based encounters between children, materials, tools, and processes.

Building visual arts confidence

While educators may feel uncertain about how to translate their value for the visual arts into daily practice with children, they do not need to be art experts to create rich experiences for children. However, it is critical for educators to reflect deeply about their own visual arts self-efficacy and pedagogical content knowledge and intentionally develop their own visual arts skills and knowledge. By adopting a mindset of lifelong learning and reflection, educators can support and enhance children's visual arts learning, leading to engaging, playful experiences and a richer artistic and cultural life (Article 31, United Nations Convention on the Rights of the Child, UNICEF, 1989). To support these aims, it is helpful to position visual arts pedagogy and practice as a visual language.

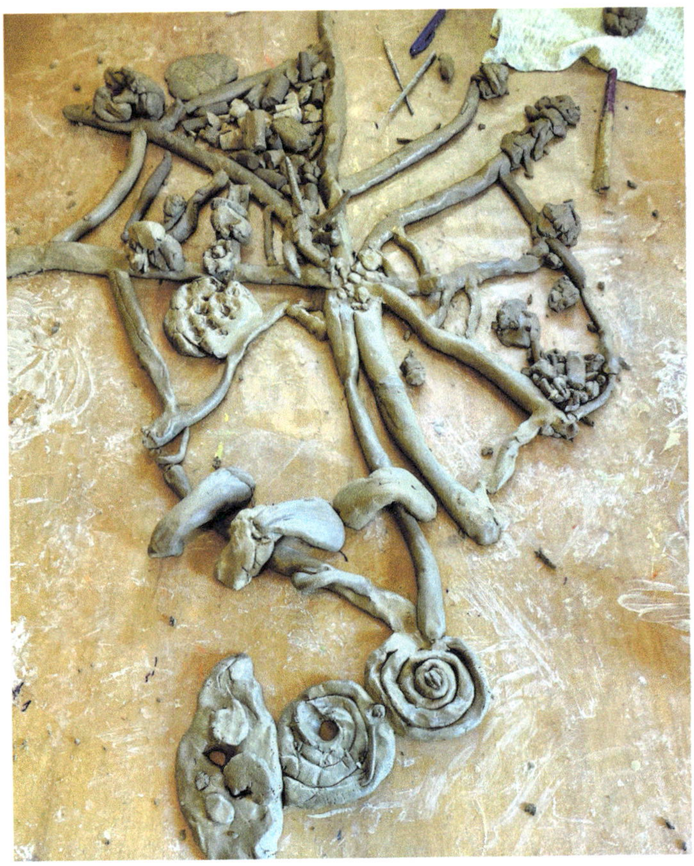

Figure 1.4 This intricate clay spider web emerged from a collaborative investigation with four-year-olds exploring spirals, spiders, and their homes. Such projects show how educators, by fostering curiosity and open-ended exploration, can create opportunities for children to develop their ideas and express them through the visual arts [Image: Adrienne Wilkins, Sophia Preschool].

Valuing the visual arts as a language

In early education settings, the visual arts are ideally positioned as expressive languages by which young children can make sense of the world and express their thinking, inspired by Loris Malaguzzi's conception of the "hundred languages of children" (Edwards et al., 2012). Malaguzzi led the development of the Reggio Emilia Approach in post-World War II Italy, collaborating with parents and community members to create progressive early childhood education programs. Rooted in constructivist and socio-cultural theories, this approach emphasises children as capable citizens, democratic participation, and the arts as a central language for learning and expression.

Positioning the visual arts mediums as languages, extends them well beyond traditional artmaking to recognise how visual, poetic, and symbolic languages support both children and adults to collaboratively build knowledge, facilitate learning, and make thinking visible (Edwards et al., 2012). Consequently, Vecchi (2010, p. 132) notes educator's professional responsibility to recognise "the extraordinary, beautiful and intelligent things" children know and to avoid learning experiences where children's role is marginal and adult minds and hands are central. Underpinning these ideas, Dewey (1934, p. 291) reminds us that art products bear witness to the voice, heart, and mind of the artist as a "medium of expression" (Dewey, 1934, p. 291). By involving children in creative processes similar to those of an artist, the educators in Reggio Emilia foster exploration, inquiry, communication and meaning-making (Vecchi, 2010). These values underpin the heart and intentions of this book.

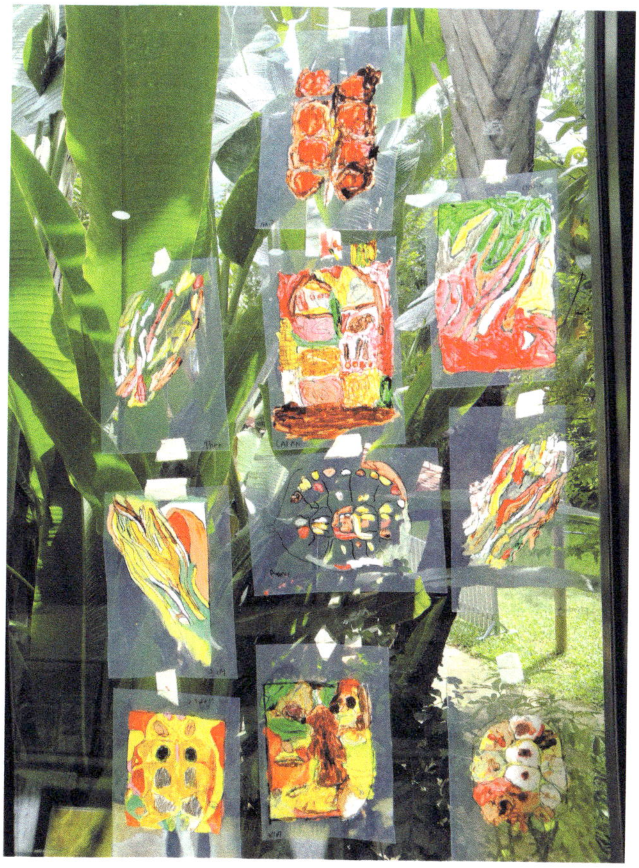

Figure 1.5 When visual arts are valued as a language, children can explore and express their thinking in profound ways [Image: Carolyn Prawius, Saigon Kids Early Learning Centre].

About this book

This book is woven together from our combined years of experience as early childhood teachers and visual arts advocates, as well as our research and passion for the visual arts. We gratefully acknowledge the research and practice champions who have informed our shared understanding about children's visual arts learning. In our desire to foster capability and confidence in adults who design and deliver children's visual arts learning, we draw on the collective knowledge of generations of educators and artists around the world. We thank our inspiring community of academic colleagues for their contributions, encouragement, and guidance.

Overview

The early years are a formative time when children develop interests, skills, dispositions, and an image of themselves as learners that will likely stay with them throughout their lives. During this critical period, children can be supported to access the rich potential of the visual arts, and to learn to see themselves as people who can create, communicate, innovate, and problem-solve through artistic expression. However, for this to happen meaningfully requires those working with children to be equipped and inspired for the task.

This book aims to inspire educators and those working with young children to prioritise high-quality visual arts opportunities in their practice. It offers encouragement to make the visual arts a joyful, integral part of early childhood education, enriching teaching practice and enhancing children's lives through engagement with the world of art. We support educators to appreciate the importance of their role in children's visual arts learning, and the importance of upholding children's right to express themselves through mark-making, cultural engagement, and visual communication. When educators understand the many values and benefits of visual arts learning, they are more able to provide meaningful and effective open-ended visual arts experiences with children. We therefore offer both theoretical inspiration and practical guidance to design, deliver, delight, and participate in visual arts play and inquiry with children.

Part 1 focuses on WHY the visual arts are important for young children's education and for educator's work with children.

Following the current introduction chapter, in Chapter 2, *Why visual arts education matters*, we discuss the importance of visual arts in early education contexts, examining its unique role as a language for cognition and expression. The chapter highlights the wide-ranging benefits of visual arts pedagogies, including fostering imagination, creativity, and key learning dispositions, while supporting identity development, cultural understanding, inclusion, and social learning. We also outline the many potentials for a rich visual arts curriculum to contribute to children's cognition and brain development, promote children's well-being and self-regulation, enhance physical skills, and provide rich opportunities for educators to engage in meaningful, collaborative learning experiences alongside children. This chapter presents educators with research-informed information to be able to advocate for rich and meaningful visual arts learning.

Chapter 3, *Theories, philosophies, and approaches to inspire visual arts pedagogy*, introduces foundational theories and philosophical ideas that inform, shape, and enrich visual arts education. The chapter offers an overview of key theoretical worldviews and presents the ideas of influential theorists and educationalists. Each section includes provocations and reflective questions to build awareness about theoretical implications and applications for visual arts practice with children. By engaging with Constructivist, Socio-Cultural, Critical, Post-modern, Practice, Social Learning, and Developmental theories, we offer multiple perspectives that enable and extend critically informed choices in visual arts education. This theoretical grounding will empower you to advocate for the role of visual arts and the role of the educator in supporting children's learning, while adopting practices that enhance children's creative and developmental growth through meaningful, art-centred experiences.

Chapter 4, *Examining and building a personal visual arts identity*, delves into the influences that shape educator self-beliefs about the visual arts and discusses how these perceptions impact pedagogy and practice with children. The chapter presents reflective and practical exercises that invite you to explore your personal backgrounds and attitudes toward art, encouraging you to engage or reconnect with mark-making and art materials. Key topics include embracing one's inner artist, fostering a growth mindset, and overcoming low visual arts self-efficacy. Additionally, this chapter offers strategies to build personal visual arts content knowledge, equipping educators to confidently create opportunities for children's art learning.

Part 2 focuses on WHAT to do and think about when developing rich visual arts curriculum with children. This section takes a more detailed look at the role adults play in facilitating meaningful visual arts learning experiences with children. Ideas for resources, language, teaching strategies, and the set-up of the learning environment will inspire you to plan for success, wonder, and joy.

Chapter 5, *Artful Pedagogy: The role of the educator*, focuses on developing a personal philosophy for teaching the arts. Central to this philosophy is a belief in the child as competent, creative, and capable. The chapter highlights the importance of intentional teaching, inviting educators to reflect on their beliefs and knowledge about how children learn. Key strategies include planning, organising the environment, creating engaging invitations for learning, and actively engaging with children during artmaking. Guidance is provided for talking with children about their creative work, as well as documenting and evaluating children's visual arts learning. The chapter emphasises the importance of being a reflective practitioner to continuously enrich teaching practices.

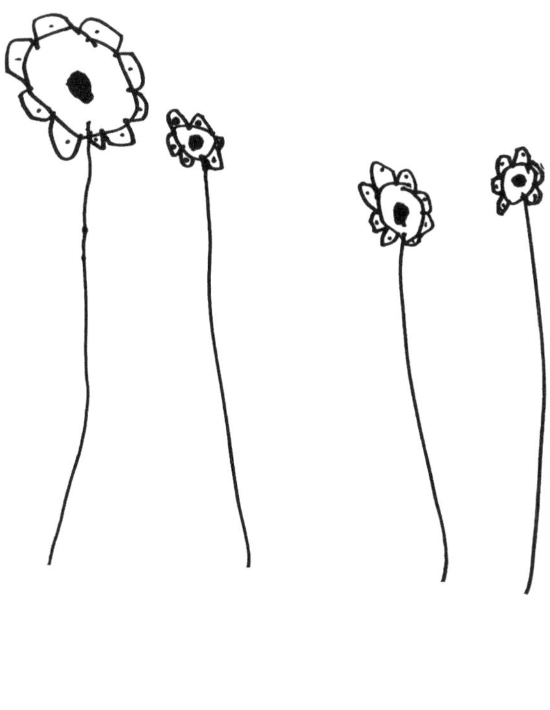

Chapter 6, *Aesthetic encounters and material research*, explores the vital role of aesthetic encounters and material research in visual art curricula for young children. It emphasises the importance of providing children with sensory-rich environments and supporting them to engage with the beauty and wonder of everyday things. We discuss the importance of children's encounters with rich materials, offering guidance for fostering material encounters for very young children and children who are meeting materials and processes for the first time. Educators are encouraged to act as co-researchers alongside children within collaborative art experiences, helping them build meaningful relationships with materials and nurturing skills for expressing their ideas, creativity, and thoughts. The chapter also offers practical strategies for aesthetic encounters and material research to enrich children's educational experiences and foster a deeper appreciation for the visual arts.

Chapter 7, *The visual arts in children's projects of inquiry*, highlights key aspects of inquiry-based projects with young children, centred around the potential of the visual arts to support children's robust investigative learning experiences and processes. It emphasises the importance of creating environments where experimentation and collaboration are fostered. The chapter defines inquiry projects and outlines how to begin an inquiry by using provocations, carefully selected materials, and environments that stimulate engagement. It also discusses the role of documentation in recording and enhancing children's investigations and in supporting the assessment of children's engagement, learning and future possibilities. Specific attention is given to the ways infants and toddlers can be supported to participate in inquiry. The chapter also outlines issues of inclusion and the need to ensure that all children, regardless of development, age or ability, can engage and contribute to rich, holistic learning experiences.

Chapter 8, *Art in and with the community*, explores how the visual arts help children connect to their communities, local environments, and cultural traditions. It discusses how making connections with local artists and community artworks can inspire wonderful learning experiences, enhancing children's engagement with cultural and community life. Illustrated through several case studies about community arts connections, the chapter emphasises fostering curiosity through art and learning about the history, culture, and stories of the community and the local environment. It also highlights the value of traditional crafts and observational drawing to deepen children's connection to nature, environmental education, communities, and cultures.

Chapter 9, *Engaging with the world of art, artists, and galleries*, focuses on the value of art appreciation and arts-inspired learning experiences to foster children's thinking, imagination, and interactions with art. It presents strategies for developing children's visual literacy such as visiting galleries and museums, viewing and discussing art, selecting diverse and meaningful artworks, and using art as inspiration for practice. The chapter also highlights the intentional use of games, storytelling, and technical questions to foster and provoke children's observations, appreciation, and responses to artworks, art materials, and tools.

Chapter 10, *Creating inspiring visual arts spaces*, explores how a thoughtfully designed environment can enrich children's learning experiences in the visual arts. The chapter discusses the importance of creating inviting, inclusive spaces where children feel free to create, investigate, and collaborate. It emphasises the need to balance practicality with aesthetics, selecting high-quality, flexible materials that encourage creativity without overwhelming children. The importance of documenting and displaying children's work to both communicate respect for children's efforts and enhance educator's reflective learning processes is also presented. Guidance for setting up an inspiring visual arts studio space includes advice about the selection of furniture, lighting, and materials. The chapter also discusses the sustainable use of materials, the inclusion of various media, and the significance of open-ended resources.

Part 3 focuses on The HOW of visual arts education, providing guidance about how to choose and use visual arts materials. This section of the book offers clear information about how to engage with the broad range of visual arts tools and techniques that make up the vocabulary of visual arts "languages" for young learners. It details clear, practical guidance about selecting, presenting and storing visual arts materials, along with ideas and techniques for open-ended learning experiences. Additionally, we offer strategies for clean-up and maintenance of materials to ensure they remain in good condition. Sustainable practices are highlighted to support environmentally conscious choices. Part 3 provides in-depth guidance about the specific art materials most suitable for early education contexts in relation to drawing and mark making, painting, printmaking, clay play and sculpture, ephemeral art and loose parts design, collage and assembly, traditional crafts and artisan processes, and photography, light, and lenses. By engaging with this detailed practical information, educators can develop their confidence to use new materials and skills, embracing a playful, experimental approach that brings freedom and enjoyment to artmaking with children.

Our greatest desire in writing this book is to offer an informative and inspirational collection of theory and practice. Whether it is read from cover to cover, or referred to as the need arises, we hope those who partner with, educate, and honour children will find it useful as they embrace their important role in nurturing children's creativity and expressive potential through art play and inquiry.

Yours in art,

Dr. Gai Lindsay, Dr. Sarah Probine, Dr. Rachel Denee, and Denise Savins

References

Denee, R., Lindsay, G., & Probine, S. (2024). Visual arts self-efficacy: Impacts and supports for early childhood teachers. *Early Childhood Education Journal, 52*(6), 1035–1045. https://doi.org/10.1007/s10643-023-01489-5

Dewey, J. (1934). *Art as experience*. Penguin Group (USA) Inc.

Edwards, C., Gandini, L., & Forman, G. (Eds.). (2012). *The hundred languages of children: The Reggio Emilia experience in transformation* (3rd ed.). Praeger.

Gandini, L. (2012). History, ideas, and basic principles: An interview with Loris Malaguzzi. In C. Edwards, L. Gandini, & G. Forman (Eds.), *The hundred languages of children: The Reggio Emilia experience in transformation* (3rd ed., pp. 27–71). Praeger.

Lindsay, G. (2021). Visual arts pedagogy in early childhood contexts: The baggage of self-efficacy beliefs, pedagogical knowledge and limited pre-service training. *Australasian Journal of Early Childhood, 41*(6), 80–92. https://doi.org/10.1177/1836939120979061

Lindsay, G. (2023). Visual arts in early childhood settings. Everyday Learning Series. 21(1). Early Childhood Australia.

McArdle, F. (2012). The visual arts: Ways of seeing. In S. Wright (Ed.), *Children, meaning-making and the arts* (2nd ed., pp. 30–56). Pearson Australia.

UNICEF. (1989). United Nations Convention on the Rights of the Child (UNCRC). https://www.unicef.org/child-rights-convention/convention-text

Vecchi, V. (2010). *Art and creativity in Reggio Emilia: Exploring the role and potential of ateliers in early childhood education*. Routledge.

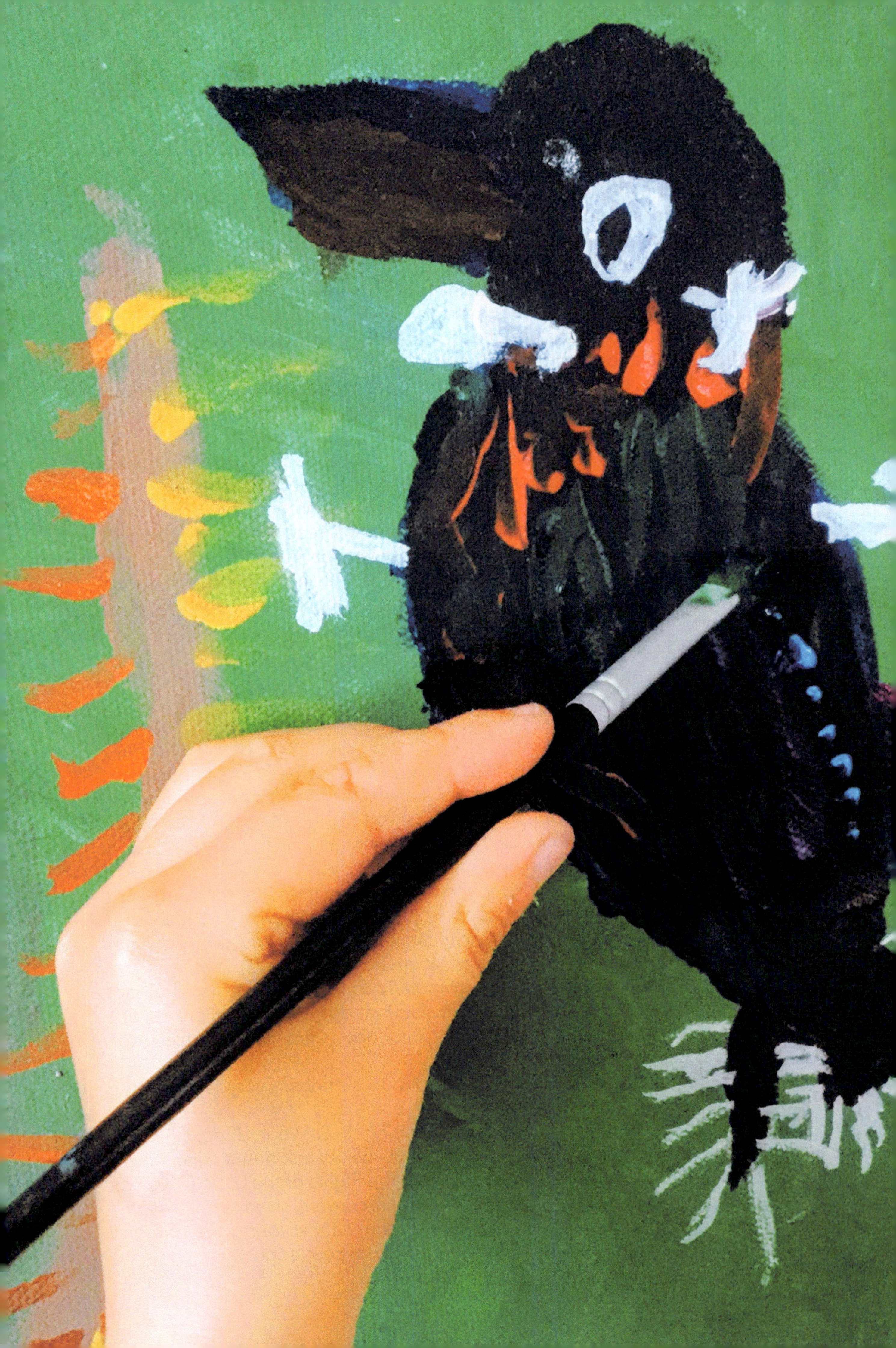

2 Why visual arts education matters

The visual arts offer children, and the adults who partner with them, rich opportunities to wonder and collaborate. There is an innate human desire to construct and communicate meaning using aesthetic materials, integrating play, aesthetic awareness, and cognition (Dewey, 1915). Recognising the visual arts as a language for exploring and expressing ideas lays a strong foundation for the many potential learning benefits we outline in this chapter. However, the rich benefits of visual arts are more likely when the curriculum is transformed by educators who reject habitual practice to reimagine and deliver high-quality experiences that support children's learning with visual arts materials and processes (Cunningham & Gibson, 2023). For this reason, this book aims to equip educators to appreciate the varied and holistic ways that visual arts learning can benefit children and enrich pedagogy and practice.

This chapter will outline how visual arts experiences support aesthetic learning and cognitive, physical, social, and emotional development. Visual arts pedagogies also play a crucial role in developing communication skills, identity formation, cultural awareness, inclusion, and the development of dispositions for lifelong learning. We also note a range of important benefits for educators and teachers who centralise the visual arts within holistic, inquiry-based curriculum approaches.

Early artistic experiences foster the healthy development of the whole child by creating rich opportunities for sensory exploration, inquiry, and relationship-building, integrating emotional, cognitive, and social dimensions of learning (Churchill Dower, 2019; Dinham & Chalk, 2018). Arts-rich educational settings enhance school readiness, particularly benefiting children impacted by inequity (Brown et al., 2018). By encouraging collaborative inquiry, visual arts support children to ask questions, imagine possibilities, and experiment with techniques, nurturing critical thinking, creativity, and problem-solving skills (Churchill Dower, 2019). Such experiences enhance educational outcomes and provide children with meaningful ways to connect with others and build critical dispositions for lifelong learning (Ewing, 2013; Magsamen & Ross, 2023).

Figure 2.1 This tūī bird was observed during weekly excursions in the local park. A 4-year-old child was supported to work on the painting over many days, developing observational skills, perseverance, and strengthening connections to place [Image: Adrienne Wilkins, Sophia Preschool].

DOI: 10.4324/9781003561835-3

Alongside the educational benefits and improved learning fostered through visual arts engagement, the arts must be valued for their unique capacity to offer ways of thinking and knowing unavailable in other disciplines (Hetland & Winner, 2001). Rather than justifying the arts only for their measurable benefits, the arts offer pedagogical alternatives that are focused on the complex interplay of relationships, environment, and cultural influences (Churchill Dower, 2019). By valuing the arts for their own sake, educators can harness their potential to offer transformative and meaningful learning experiences. These experiences not only contribute to holistic development but also help shape children into reflective, creative, and empathetic individuals ready to thrive in a complex and interconnected world.

Aesthetic learning

Aesthetic learning nurtures children's ability to engage with sensory, emotional, and artistic experiences, helping them develop an appreciation for beauty, form, and expression. It encourages children to become more attuned to the visual, tactile, auditory, and emotional aspects of the world, allowing them to interpret meaning in objects, environments, and artistic creations. This type of learning goes beyond factual knowledge to foster creativity and imagination, promoting holistic development and a deeper connection to the surrounding world and cultural heritage.

Children experience delight, wonder, and aesthetic awareness through relational encounters with materials and spaces. These encounters help them cultivate an appreciation for beauty and its emotional impact (Danko-McGhee, 2023; Dinham & Chalk, 2018; Gibson & Ewing, 2020). The development of aesthetic sensibility empowers children to recognise and engage with the sensory and emotional resonance of different forms of art (Dinham & Chalk, 2018; Gibson & Ewing, 2020). Furthermore, aesthetic experiences can have transformative effects on children's mental health, holistic well-being, and mindfulness. Environments enriched with colours, textures, light, and natural materials encourage children's active and mindful engagement, promoting healthy development and well-being (Magsamen & Ross, 2023). In addition, arts experiences contribute to community-building, highlighting the important role of the arts in fostering meaningful social connections and a sense of belonging (Magsamen & Ross, 2023).

Cognitive benefits

Engagement with the visual arts during childhood fosters significant cognitive and brain development benefits. During the early years of life, when neural pathways form rapidly, sensory-rich arts experiences enhance memory, communication, and cognitive flexibility while also supporting social-emotional growth and adaptability

(Churchill Dower, 2019; Danko-McGhee, 2023; Lewin-Benham, 2023). Arts activities strengthen executive functions like working memory and self-regulation, fostering critical thinking, problem-solving, and the ability to adapt to challenges (Dinham & Chalk, 2018; Korn-Bursztyn, 2012). Additionally, curiosity and intrinsic motivation are fostered, encouraging collaborative inquiry and reflective practices that deepen learning (Korn-Bursztyn, 2012). Research highlights the correlation between long-term arts participation and improved literacy, numeracy, and academic readiness, particularly benefiting children experiencing disadvantage (Brown et al., 2018; Churchill Dower, 2019; Danko-McGhee, 2023). By integrating emotional, cognitive, and social development, visual arts lay a foundation for lifelong learning, creativity, and adaptability (Magsamen & Ross, 2023).

The arts are a powerful tool for inquiry and meaning-making, enabling children to explore, construct knowledge, and represent ideas visually. In summary, engagement in visual arts play and inquiry processes fosters the following cognitive benefits and potentials:

- **Thinking and Inquiry:** Visual arts processes support children to investigate and test ideas, fostering concentration, and building strategies for problem-solving and aesthetic inquiry through focused material exploration (Christensen & Kirkland, 2009; Knight, 2008).
- **Visual Thinking:** Drawing and artmaking, closely linked to cognitive processes, help children clarify ideas, sort thoughts, and retain new information as they simultaneously represent and refine their thinking (Brooks, 2022).
- **Curiosity and Meaning-Making:** The arts provide diverse entry points into learning, enabling children to reflect on their experiences, explore collaboratively, and develop shared and personal meaning (Churchill Dower, 2019; Korn-Bursztyn, 2012).
- **Executive Function:** Visual arts processes support the development of cognitive flexibility, working memory, and self-regulation, fostering problem-solving, decision-making, and adaptability skills (Dinham & Chalk, 2018; Korn-Bursztyn, 2012).
- **Skills for Learning:** Arts-based learning improves skills such as memory retention, concentration, and observation while addressing educational equity and inclusion, particularly for children who experience economic disadvantage (Brown et al., 2018; Danko-McGhee, 2023).

Early visual arts engagement fosters critical cognitive development, enhancing memory, executive functions, and problem-solving skills. Such cognitive benefits enhance foster capacity for imagination and creativity.

Imagination and creativity

Visual arts experiences offer significant benefits in developing children's imagination, critical thinking skills, and potential for creative thinking (Ewing, 2013). Arts practices encourage deliberate decision-making, adaptability, and metacognitive

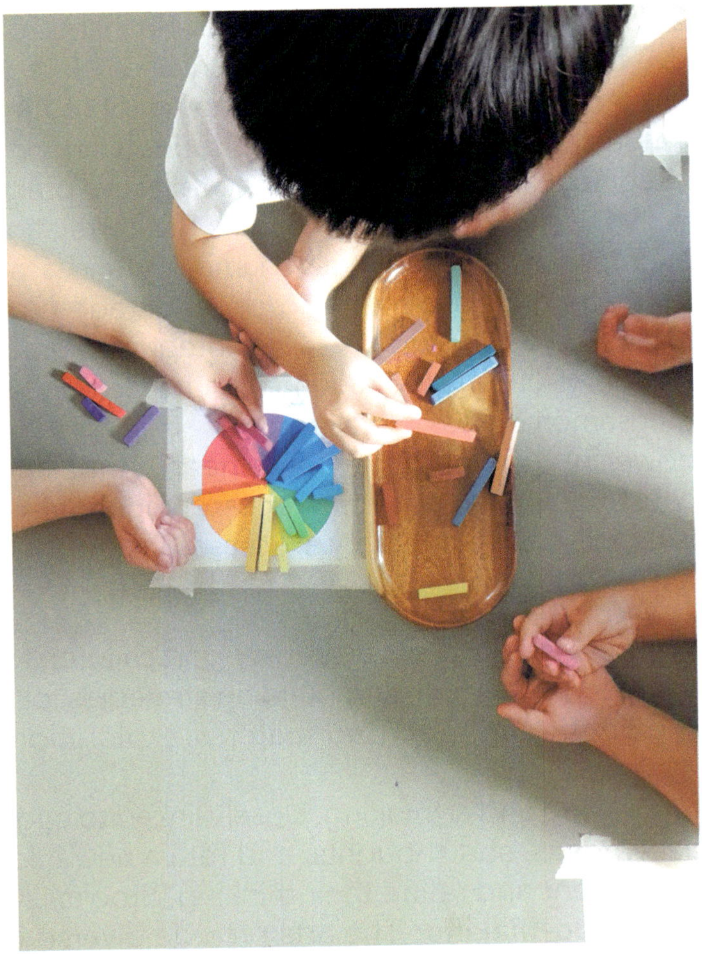

Figure 2.2 Children explore colour variations matching chalk pastels to a colour wheel. This experience was part of a long-term investigation into colour, including art appreciation, discussions, colour-mixing and art-making [Image: Carolyn Prawius, Saigon Kids Early Learning Centre].

awareness, helping children gain new insights and refine their creative processes (McArdle, 2012). Creativity itself is a dynamic process involving the generation, experimentation, and refinement of ideas, which promotes resilience, flexibility, and critical decision-making (Kim et al., 2019). In this context, risk-taking and embracing mistakes become integral to building confidence and adaptability (Hetland & Winner, 2001; McArdle, 2012). Importantly, artmaking also facilitates states of immersive "flow," which are linked to enhanced joy, focus, and experimentation, further supporting creative exploration (Danko-McGhee, 2023; Magsamen & Ross, 2023). Through material knowing, children align conceptual understandings with tangible outcomes, reinforcing their grasp of abstract concepts through hands-on learning (Pacini-Ketchabaw et al., 2024; Wright, 2012). Such experiences promote cross-disciplinary skills, including scientific reasoning and mathematical measurement (McArdle, 2012), while symbolic and reflective practices within the arts cultivate dispositions for learning that extend to a wide range of contexts beyond the arts.

Fostering dispositions for learning

While many people assume that artmaking guarantees the development of creativity, this is not the case. We believe that to foster the conditions which may lead to creative skills development, it is imperative to foster learning dispositions, attitudes, and habits that shape how individuals engage with new experiences and challenges. For example, a child feeling challenged by an art process may demonstrate perseverance, a trait that a perceptive educator can recognise and highlight, reinforcing its importance for learning (Dinham & Chalk, 2018; Gibson & Ewing, 2020). Engaging in visual arts learning experiences offers children opportunities to develop dispositions such as curiosity, persistence, problem-solving, resilience, and imagination, all of which lay the groundwork for creative thinking in the future.

- **Curiosity and Wonder:** Arts experiences inspire intrinsic motivation, encouraging children to explore, ask questions, and seek solutions to problems in creative and innovative ways (Dinham & Chalk, 2018; Vecchi, 2010).
- **Perseverance and Resilience:** Artmaking teaches children to persist through challenges and overcome frustration, fostering emotional resilience and a growth mindset (Hetland & Winner, 2001; McArdle, 2012).

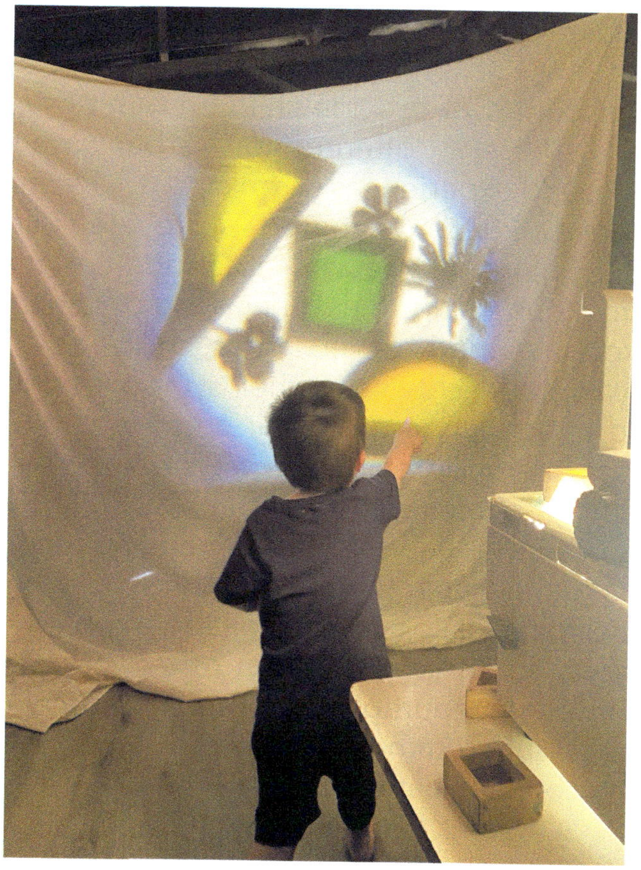

Figure 2.3 Open-ended materials such as objects on a projector empower children to imagine, collaborate and create [Image: Daisies Early Education & Care Centre].

- **Problem-Solving and Critical Thinking:** Inquiry-driven visual arts experiences help children navigate complex problems with flexibility, reflect on their ideas, and make thoughtful decisions (Dinham & Chalk, 2018).
- **Imagination and Experimentation:** Creative processes encourage children to imagine possibilities, experiment with materials, and innovate, laying the groundwork for future creative thinking (Dinham & Chalk, 2018; Vecchi, 2010).
- **Collaboration and Responsibility:** Through shared art experiences, children develop skills in collaboration and learn to care for their work, focus on tasks, and see projects through to completion (Gibson & Ewing, 2020).
- **Love of Learning:** The joyful discovery inherent in arts engagement fosters intellectual curiosity and a love of learning that extends into adulthood (Ellen Galinsky, in Magsamen & Ross, 2023).

Visual arts experiences not only nurture creativity but also equip children with the adaptability, critical thinking, and curiosity needed to navigate an ever-changing, highly visual world. By fostering these essential dispositions, the arts ensure that children are prepared to embrace lifelong learning and growth in meaningful and impactful ways (Robinson & Robinson, 2022; Churchill Dower, 2019).

Communication

Visual arts learning experiences provide children with powerful tools for communication and self-expression, offering non-verbal ways to visually express their ideas, emotions, and experiences (Brooks, 2017; Pacini-Ketchabaw et al., 2024; Richards & Terreni, 2022). Art materials provide children with tangible and practical ways to explore abstract concepts and translate their understandings into visual form, connecting their immediate experiences with symbolic representation. Through guided conversations, children translate these reflections-in-action into language, enhancing their symbolic thinking, visual literacy, self-regulation, and understanding of their creative choices (Korn-Bursztyn, 2012). Such processes offer children unique ways to express complex thoughts and make their thinking visible (Edwards et al., 2012). Engaging with art also fosters symbolic and visual language development, helping children represent and interpret their experiences through shapes, colours, and forms (Churchill Dower, 2019). Art facilitates dialogue and collaboration as children and adults engage in discussions about artmaking and the work of artists. Educators play an important role in encouraging children to articulate their thoughts, while respecting their visual communication preferences. The following points summarise the many communication and visual literacy benefits of visual arts engagement:

- **Artistic Perspectives:** Visual arts foster unique ways of seeing and interpreting the world, helping children engage with abstract ideas and make sense of their experiences through personal expression (Vecchi, 2010).

- **Creativity and Play:** Artmaking combines creativity and play, offering children dynamic, flexible ways to approach problem-solving, take risks, and explore various communication methods (Palmer et al., 2021).
- **Language Development and Literacy:** Viewing and creating art play a foundational role in children's language development by fostering dialogic exchanges and building connections between visual and verbal expression. Through artmaking and discussions about their work, children also learn how images, symbols, and representations relate to words and concepts, supporting their literacy skills and development (Brown et al., 2018; Palmer et al., 2021; Vecchi, 2010; Wright, 2012).
- **Symbolic Thinking and Representation:** Engaging with visual arts helps children develop symbolic systems, linking visual representation to language and meaning-making. Through interpreting visual symbols, children recognise their role in influencing thoughts, emotions, and desires, fostering critical thinking and cognitive growth (Danko-McGhee, 2023; McArdle, 2012; Wright, 2012). By using visual, physical, and embodied forms to represent ideas, children strengthen symbolic thinking, which is essential for abstract reasoning. The arts connect visual forms of meaning with linguistic expression, expanding children's capacity for metaphorical expression and enhancing critical thinking skills (Korn-Bursztyn, 2012).
- **Connecting Visual and Linguistic Representation:** Engaging with visual arts helps children bridge visual and verbal communication, enabling them to navigate complex ideas and messages. By blending visual and verbal elements, art also allows children to express their thoughts, emotions, and experiences in diverse, multimodal ways (Korn-Bursztyn, 2012; Wright, 2012).
- **Interpreting Visual Messages:** Children learn to analyse visual content, recognising the intentionality behind images and their ability to convey ideas, values, and perspectives, enriching their communication skills, critical thinking abilities and fostering analytical and interpretative skills (Danko-McGhee, 2023; Korn-Bursztyn, 2012; McArdle, 2012).
- **Collaboration and Dialogue:** Discussions about art encourage reflection, critical thinking, and opportunities to revisit previous learning to consolidate skills and knowledge and make new plans for learning (Brooks, 2017; Richards & Terreni, 2022).
- **Narrative Skills:** Art supports the development of storytelling and multimodal communication by combining visual elements, graphic signs, body actions, and verbal dialogue, helping children create stories and share meaning (Vecchi, 2010; Wright, 2012).
- **Expanding Communication Skills:** Exposure to art-specific terminology, such as colour, shape, and texture, enhances children's ability to discuss and articulate ideas about visual content (McArdle, 2012).

The visual arts offer young children a dynamic platform for communication and self-expression. Whether non-verbal expression, collaboration, or the development of symbolic systems, art plays a vital role in helping children communicate their thoughts, emotions, and ideas. By integrating art into early childhood education, educators can support the growth of children's communication skills, providing them with the tools to express themselves in creative and meaningful ways.

Physical benefits

Engaging with the visual arts offers children task-driven opportunities to support, challenge, and extend their physical development. Rather than using structured templates and skills-focused activities (e.g. cutting along dotted lines on a stencil), we advocate for the application of complex and authentic arts processes to develop physical skills in meaningful, purposeful, and process-oriented ways. Practical use of art tools and materials enhances both fine and gross motor skills and develops children's broader kinaesthetic awareness about how their body moves in space to coordinate the use of materials and tools. Experiences such as drawing, painting, construction, and clay sculpting require the precise use of small muscles in the hands and fingers, while also engaging the arms, shoulders, and neck as children position themselves in relation to their artwork. Tools like paintbrushes, markers, and construction tools such as hammers, enhance coordination and dexterity, while supporting children to explore sensory learning through tactile interactions with materials and the purposeful application of tools (Churchill Dower, 2019; Dinham & Chalk, 2018).

For larger-scale activities, such as working on big surfaces such as rolls of paper or large boards, children engage their gross motor skills, using arms, legs, and torso. These experiences, often conducted outdoors or on the floor, promote

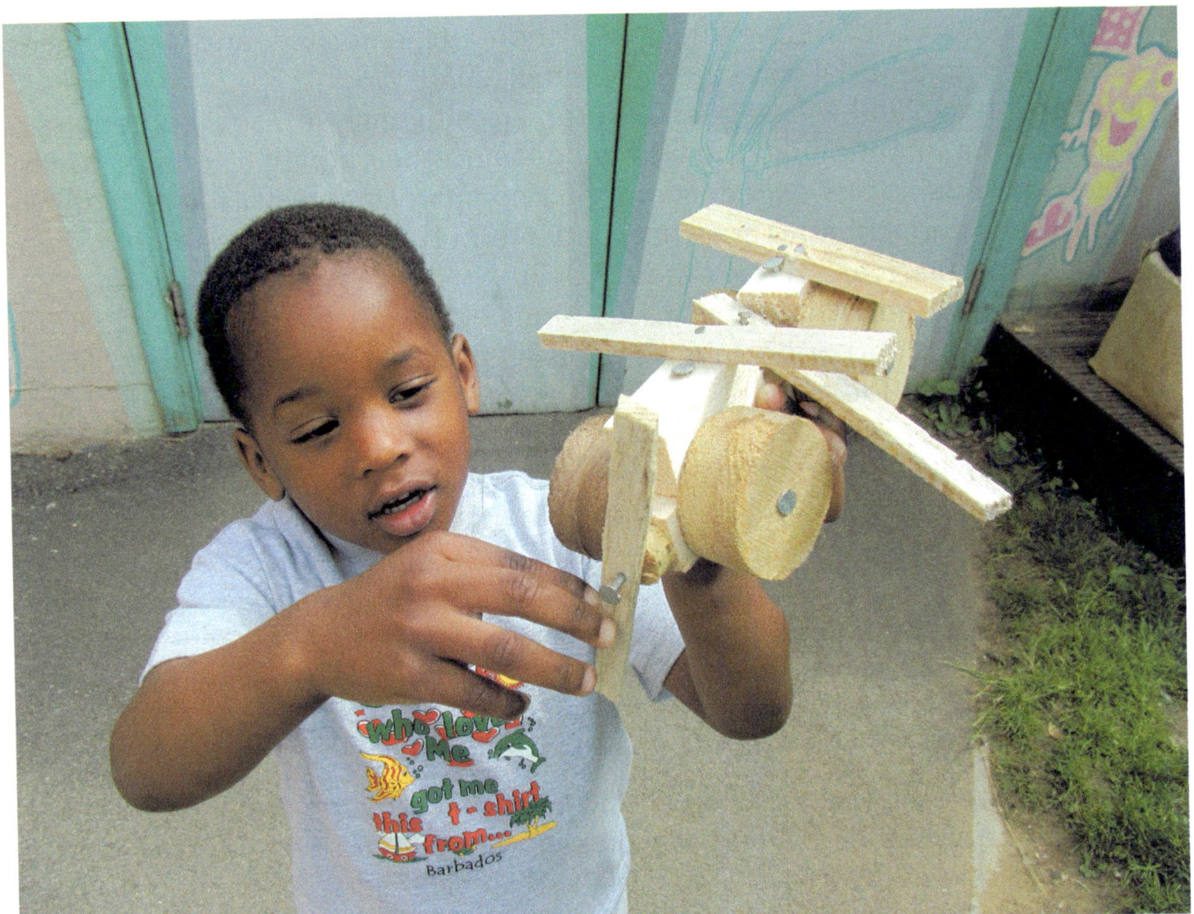

Figure 2.4 Hands-on, purposeful visual arts experiences foster fine and gross motor development, enhance children's coordination and builds skills and personal confidence [Image: Pete Moorhouse, Irresistible Learning].

physical strength and flexibility, while also fostering awareness of their bodies in space, improving balance, coordination, and overall body confidence (Dinham & Chalk, 2018). Such meaningful experiences not only provide children with the chance to practice gross motor skills but also make the process enjoyable, while contributing to children's overall coordination and physical skills development (Churchill Dower, 2021; Dinham & Chalk, 2018; McArdle, 2012).

Through play and manipulation of visual arts materials, children not only develop essential motor skills but also build a positive sense of self and confidence in their abilities. The integration of physical and sensory experiences supports holistic growth, benefiting children's physical, emotional, and cognitive development in a unified way. By offering opportunities to exercise both fine and gross motor skills, visual arts experiences help foster not just physical capacity but also the kinaesthetic awareness essential for broader life skills.

Identity development

Visual arts experiences support identity development during childhood by supporting children to explore and express who they are in relation to the world around them (Brown et al., 2018; Korn-Bursztyn, 2012).

As children begin to develop their individual identity, artmaking becomes a powerful tool for making sense of their experiences, relationships, culture, and environment. Through the process of creating, children start to ask questions such as "Who am I?" and engage in a deeper exploration of their own self-image. Self-portraits and family narratives, for example, offer meaningful ways for children to provide a visual representation of their personal identity, fostering conversation, self-reflection, and expression of their developing sense of who they are (Brown et al., 2018; Korn-Bursztyn, 2012). Identity development benefits include:

- **Identity and Agency:** Through art play, children develop their personal voice by expressing their thoughts and feelings, building confidence and a sense of agency. By making process decisions and developing awareness about the impacts of their choices, children not only strengthen their self-expression but reinforce their sense of responsibility and contribution within a shared learning environment (Dinham & Chalk, 2018; Hetland & Winner, 2001; McArdle, 2012).
- **Sense of Belonging:** Art provides children with a safe space to explore emotions and experiences, building a sense of pride and connection to their individual identities (Dinham & Chalk, 2018; Gibson & Ewing, 2020).

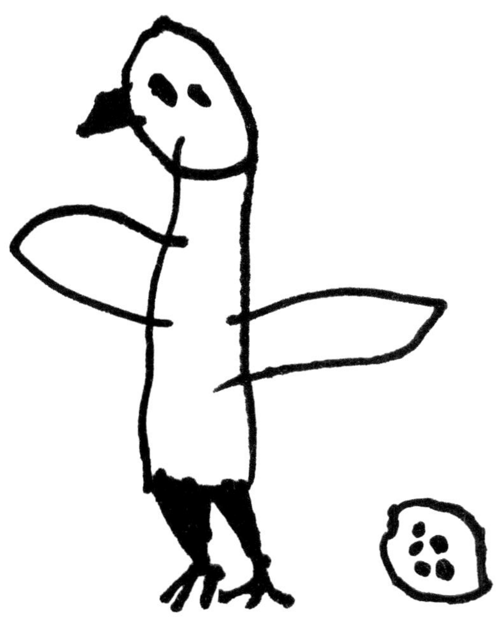

- **Confidence and Skill-Building:** Creative expression fosters confidence and resilience, while helping children develop skills to manage emotions (Brown et al., 2018; Churchill Dower, 2019).
- **Body Awareness and Self-Esteem:** Through interaction with various materials and movements, children develop a positive relationship with their bodies, boosting their physical confidence and emotional well-being (Dinham & Chalk, 2018).

Visual arts provide a space for children to explore their emotions, assert their individuality, and develop a deeper understanding of themselves and others. By expressing their unique perspectives, children build a sense of belonging and pride, which contributes to their overall emotional well-being and self-esteem.

Social and relational learning

Engagement with visual arts plays a crucial role in fostering children's social and relational learning. Art activities provide rich opportunities for children to collaborate and communicate. By working alongside peers and educators, children develop empathy and an appreciation for the diverse strengths, ideas, and perspectives of others, learning to interpret the world and value the many ways people think, create, and express themselves (Dinham & Chalk, 2018; Gibson & Ewing, 2020; Chapman & O'Gorman, 2022). Additionally, collaborative visual arts learning experiences help children to recognise there is no one "right way" to make art, encouraging them to embrace multiple viewpoints and solutions. Exposure to diverse cultural and social contexts, such as visiting art galleries, community cultural sites, or engaging with media, further supports children's exposure to multiple perspectives (Dinham & Chalk, 2018; Gibson & Ewing, 2020). Through shared creative experiences, children learn to navigate social encounters and develop strong social skills that are foundational for positive relationships and emotional well-being. Key social and relational benefits include:

- **Empathy and Social Imagination:** Through art, children explore themes like family, friendships, and community, enhancing their ability to empathise with others and understand diverse emotional experiences (Dinham & Chalk, 2018; Korn-Bursztyn, 2012).
- **Cooperative Learning:** Arts engagement with peers and educators promotes cooperation, communication, taking turns, sharing, and conflict resolution, helping children build social-emotional skills and a sense of community (Brown et al., 2018; Dinham & Chalk, 2018).
- **Exploring Humanity and Building Relationships:** Art helps children explore complex social themes such as family, friendships, gender, and community, fostering a broader understanding of themselves and others (Korn-Bursztyn, 2012). Early childhood arts activities lay important foundations for the development of social competencies (Dinham & Chalk, 2018), while also enhancing parent-child relationships and encouraging intergenerational connections (Churchill-Dower, 2019; Magsamen & Ross, 2023).

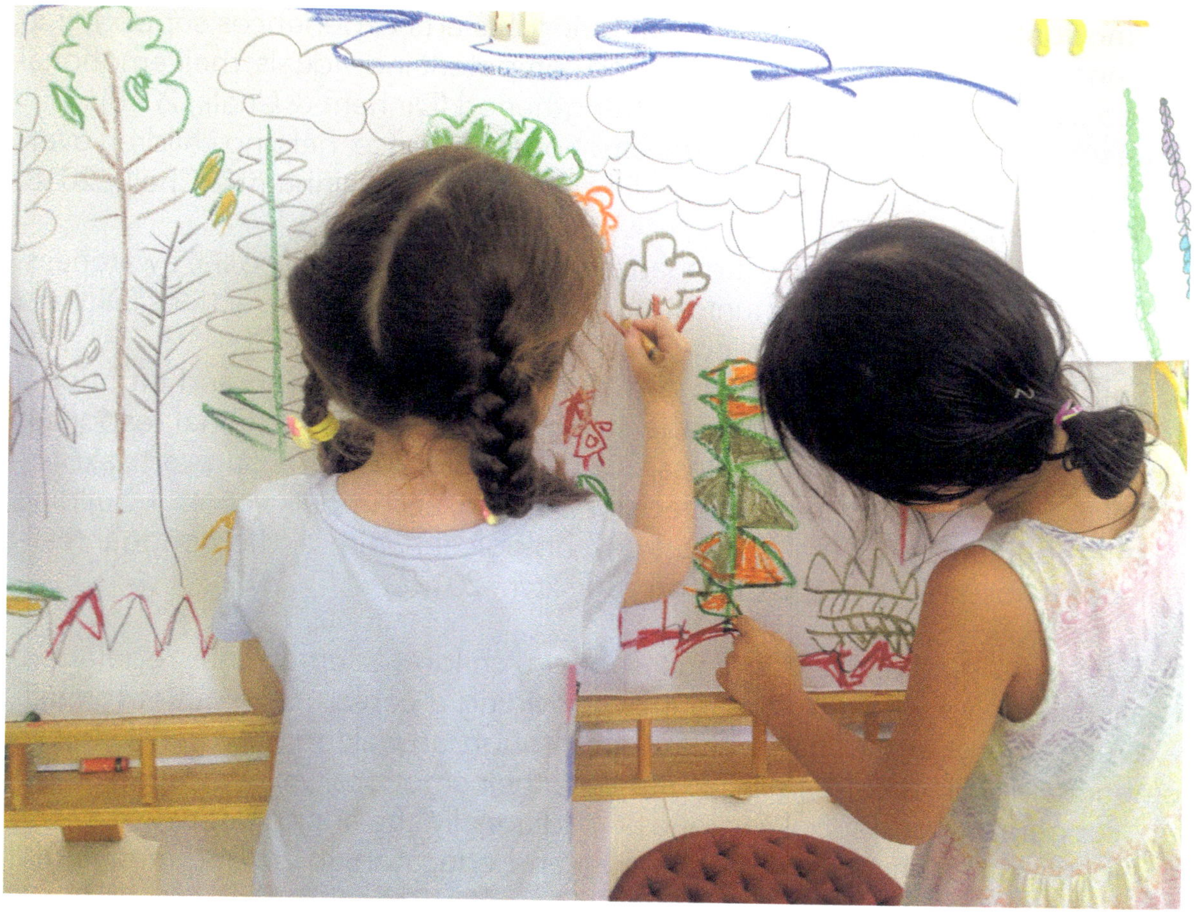

Figure 2.5 As children imagine and create together, they practice generosity, negotiation, and shared thinking [Image: Denise Savins, Saigon Kids Early Learning Centre].

Emotional well-being

Engagement with visual arts materials and tools offers children opportunities to build emotional well-being. Additionally, arts experiences offer opportunities for children to learn about sharing resources and taking turns, helping them to learn to regulate their emotions and impulses. Artmaking provides a safe space for children to express their emotions, process, and manage complex feelings. Such experiences encourage emotional regulation, as children learn how to navigate social interactions constructively and develop a sense of community, which helps build both individual and collective emotional well-being (Brown et al., 2018; Dinham & Chalk, 2018). By engaging in art, children learn to navigate their emotional responses, build resilience, and improve their emotional intelligence; all crucial for both personal growth and academic success (Dinham & Chalk, 2018; Magsamen & Ross, 2023). Emotional well-being and self-regulation benefits include:

- **Emotional expression:** Visual arts offer children a way to communicate feelings they may struggle to express verbally, promoting emotional release (Brown et al., 2018; Korn-Bursztyn, 2012).

- **Emotional and psychological well-being:** As arts experiences support children to view themselves as capable and competent individuals, their emotional and psychological well-being are strengthened (Dinham & Chalk, 2018).
- **Resilience:** Engaging in art fosters emotional resilience, helping children overcome challenges and cope with difficult emotions (Dinham & Chalk, 2018; Magsamen & Ross, 2023).
- **Emotional intelligence:** Art enhances self-awareness and social awareness, promoting empathy, communication, and positive social interactions (Dinham & Chalk, 2018; Gibson & Ewing, 2020).
- **Self-Regulation of Emotions:** Artmaking fosters relaxation and emotional stability, helping children manage stress and complex emotional responses constructively (Magsamen & Ross, 2023; McArdle, 2012). Through arts experiences, children practice focus, decision-making, and impulse control, building self-regulation skills that support psychological health and emotional resilience (Gibson & Ewing, 2020; Korn-Bursztyn, 2012).

Visual arts play and experience support children's emotional regulation, resilience, and social development by providing a constructive outlet for self-expression and emotional regulation. Through artmaking, children cultivate emotional intelligence, learning to navigate their emotions while fostering empathy, cooperation, and social awareness. Additionally, the arts promote well-being and human flourishing, offering children and educators joyful and meaningful opportunities to connect with their emotions, others, and the world around them.

Cultural identity

Visual arts experiences play an important role in fostering cultural awareness and supporting the development of children's cultural identity. Thoughtfully planned and culturally responsive visual arts curricula offer children opportunities to explore their heritage, express their individuality, and build connections to diverse cultural traditions. These experiences not only affirm children's sense of belonging but also cultivate respect for the diverse cultural practices that shape our communities (McArdle, 2012; Richards & Terreni, 2022). By engaging with both their own cultural traditions and those of others, children gain a deeper appreciation for cultural diversity, strengthening their personal and collective identities. The visual arts serve as powerful tools for promoting inclusion, empathy, and a nuanced understanding of cultural values and practices, enriching children's learning and their ability to navigate an interconnected world (Dinham & Chalk, 2018; Gibson & Ewing, 2020). Potential cultural learning benefits include:

- **Fostering Cultural Identity:** Visual arts provide children with opportunities to explore their own cultural heritage, fostering a sense of belonging and affirming the value of their traditions within their communities (Richards & Terreni, 2022).

- **Culturally Responsive:** Thoughtfully designed art experiences that reflect children's familial and cultural contexts, send powerful messages about the value of their backgrounds and foster encouraging an inclusive environment (Harris et al., 2020; McArdle, 2012).
- **Cultural Diversity:** Engaging with diverse cultural artworks broadens children's understanding of the world and nurtures sensitivity and respect for cultural differences (Dinham & Chalk, 2018).
- **Cultural Heritage:** Visual arts experiences support the exploration and appreciation of indigenous traditions and cultural practices, fostering deeper connections to historical and cultural legacies (Churchill Dower, 2019; McArdle, 2012).
- **Community and Belonging:** Collaborative art activities promote a sense of shared identity and social cohesion, helping children build relationships and feel a strong connection to their peers and communities (Magsamen & Ross, 2023).
- **Cultural Exploration:** Visits to galleries and museums provide children with authentic learning opportunities to engage with diverse art forms, fostering their appreciation for local and global cultures and histories (Danko-McGhee, 2023; Palmer et al., 2021).

The cultural benefits of visual arts engagement naturally extend to fostering inclusive pedagogy and practice. By valuing and reflecting the diverse cultural identities of children, visual arts create opportunities for meaningful representation, ensuring that every child feels seen, respected, and included within the learning environment.

Inclusion

Visual arts engagement enhances inclusive learning environments by providing accessible and equitable opportunities for children with diverse abilities. For children with delayed development, disability, or neurodivergent thinking, visual arts experiences offer alternative pathways for communication, emotional regulation, and social interaction. By embracing creative expression as an intelligence, the arts provide a broad view of learning that recognises diverse abilities, fosters acceptance of varied learning styles, and enables all learners to thrive (Magsamen & Ross, 2023).

Potential arts engagement benefits include:

- **Non-Verbal Communication:** Visual arts provide children with powerful alternative ways to express emotions, ideas, and experiences, fostering positive interactions and understanding (Korn-Bursztyn, 2012).
- **Support Neurodivergent Learners:** Arts engagement can support children with ADHD, autism, and other developmental conditions to enjoy times of focus, emotional regulation, and positive social experiences (Korn-Bursztyn, 2012; Magsamen & Ross, 2023).
- **Therapeutic Benefits:** Art provides a safe and transformative space for emotional healing and regulation, helping children express difficult feelings and boosting self-esteem, particularly for those in therapy or with disabilities (Korn-Bursztyn, 2012).

- **Enhanced Social Interaction:** Collaborative art activities foster social connections, helping children work together, explore new ideas, and build relationships through shared creative experiences (Korn-Bursztyn, 2012).
- **Learning Equity:** By embracing diverse abilities and intelligence, visual arts promote a broad, inclusive approach to education that values creativity, emotional expression, and varied learning styles (Korn-Bursztyn, 2012; Magsamen & Ross, 2023).

The arts help children of all backgrounds and abilities access education that values and supports diverse ways of being. Additionally, visual arts encourage collaborative and reflective teaching, helping educators enrich their professional growth and understanding of children's development. By incorporating the arts into education, we can create equitable and respectful learning environments for all children.

Benefits for educators

Integrating visual arts into the curriculum offers numerous benefits for educators, enhancing their teaching practices and fostering deeper connections with children. By embracing their role in nurturing children's artistic experiences,

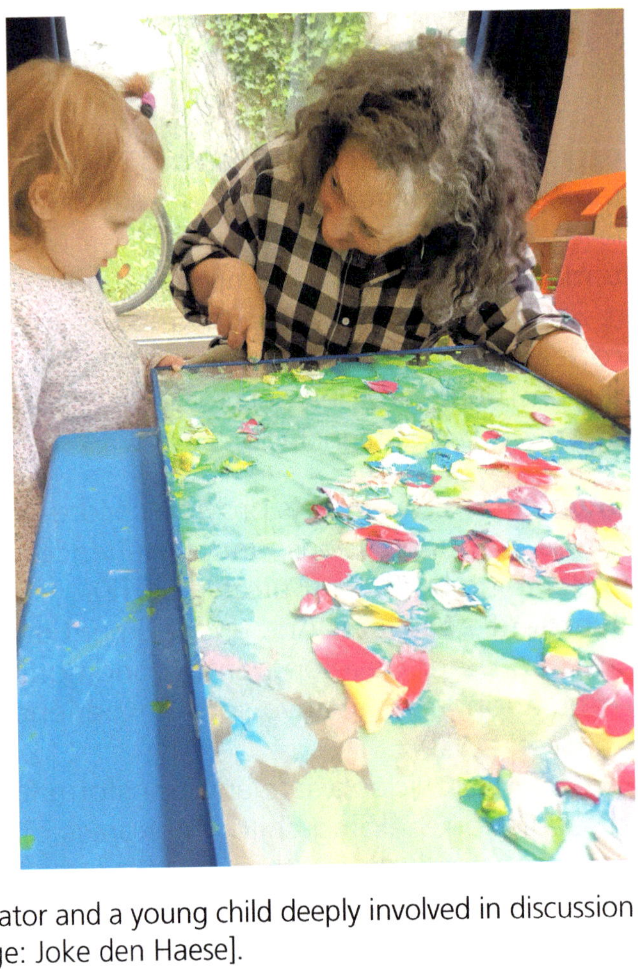

Figure 2.6 An educator and a young child deeply involved in discussion about a collaborative art experience [Image: Joke den Haese].

educators gain valuable insights into children's thinking, which allows them to adapt their teaching methods to children's individual development and preferences (Gibson & Ewing, 2020). The arts also encourage critical thinking and support curriculum flexibility as educators gain a deeper understanding of how children approach problem-solving, fostering more flexible and innovative curriculum approaches (Korn-Bursztyn, 2012). Additionally, intentionally providing time to develop artistic skills helps educators and children to build stronger relationships with art materials and techniques to enrich teaching and learning (Denee, 2024; McArdle, 2012). Collaborative art activities also strengthen relationships, fostering mutual respect and shared meaning-making (Korn-Bursztyn, 2012). Finally, the arts provide educators with rich opportunities to reflect on their own visual arts confidence and knowledge to extend their professional growth and self-efficacy (Denee, 2024; Korn-Bursztyn, 2012).

Conclusion

Incorporating visual arts play and inquiry across the curriculum benefits both children and the adults who work with them in profound and multifaceted ways. The visual arts foster holistic child development, enhancing cognitive, social, emotional, and physical capacities while nurturing creativity, communication skills, and cultural awareness. For educators, integrating the arts into teaching promotes reflective practice, professional growth, and deeper connections with children. The arts also provide opportunities for educators to cultivate their own confidence and skills, creating an environment where shared exploration and joy in learning thrive. Ultimately, the arts provide a powerful tool for building deeper connections between yourself as an educator and children, enriching educational experiences and fostering joyful, play-based, and artful learning experiences.

References

Brooks, M. (2017). Drawing to learn. In M. Narey (Ed.), *Multimodal perspectives of language, literacy, and learning in early childhood* (pp. 25–44). Springer.

Brooks, M. (2022). *Drawing to learn.* Pademelon Press.

Brown, E. D., Garnett, M. L., Velazquez-Martin, B. M., & Mellor, T. J. (2018). The art of head start: Intensive arts integration associated with advantage in school readiness for economically disadvantaged children. *Early Childhood Research Quarterly, 45*(1), 204–214. https://doi.org/10.1016/j.ecresq.2017.12.002

Chapman, S. N., & O'Gorman, L. (2022). Transforming learning environments in early childhood contexts through the arts: Responding to the United nations sustainable development goals. *International Journal of Early Childhood, 54*(1), 33–50. https://doi.org/10.1007/s13158-022-00320-3

Christensen, L. M., & Kirkland, L. D. (2009). Early childhood visual arts curriculum: Freeing spaces to express developmental and cultural palettes of mind. *Childhood Education, 86*(2), 87–91. https://doi.org/10.1080/00094056.2010.10523119

Churchill Dower, R. C. (2019). *Creativity and the arts in early childhood: Supporting young Children's development and wellbeing* (1st ed.). Jessica Kingsley Publishers.

Cunningham, M., & Gibson, R. (2023). Rethinking curriculum: A pandemic opportunity for re-engagement with the arts? *Curriculum Perspectives, 43*(1), 3–12. https://doi.org/10.1007/s41297-022-00170-y

Danko-McGhee, K. (2023). *Viewing art with babies:* First encounters. Routledge.

Denee, R. (2024). Visual arts with infants and toddlers: Developing respectful and intentional pedagogy. *The First Years Ngā Tau Tuatahi: New Zealand Journal of Infant and Toddler Education, 26*(1), 5–10.

Denee, R., Lindsay, G., & Probine, S. (2024). Visual arts self-efficacy: Impacts and supports for early childhood teachers. *Early Childhood Education Journal, 52*(6), 1035–1045. https://doi.org/10.1007/s10643-023-01489-5

Dewey, J. (1915). *The school and society* (2nd ed.). The University of Chicago Press.

Dinham, J., & Chalk, B. (2018). *It's arts play: Young children belonging, being and becoming through the arts.* Oxford University Press.

Edwards, C., Gandini, L., & Forman, G. (Eds.) ((2012). *The hundred languages of children: The Reggio Emilia experience in transformation* (3rd ed.). Praeger.

Ewing, R. (2013). *Creative arts in the lives of young children: Play, imagination and learning.* ACER Press.

Gibson, R., & Ewing, R. (2020). *Transforming the curriculum through the arts* (2nd ed.). Springer. https://doi.org/10.1007/978-3-030-52797-6

Harris, P., Brock, C. H., McInnes, E., Diamond, A., Neill, B., Carter, J., & Giannakis, E. (2020). Co-constructing culturally sustaining practices for fostering young children's literacy in Fiji. *Journal of Research in Childhood Education, 34*(1), 127–152. https://doi.org/10.1080/02568543.2019.1692105

Hetland, L., & Winner, E. (2001). The arts and academic achievement: What the evidence shows. *Arts Education Policy Review, 102*(5), 3–6. https://doi.org/10.1080/10632910109600008

Kim, S., Raza, M., & Seidman, E. (2019). Improving 21st-century teaching skills: The key to effective 21st-century learners. *Research in Comparative and International Education, 14*(1), 99–117. https://doi.org/10.1177/1745499919829214

Korn-Bursztyn, C. (2012). *Young children and the arts: Nurturing imagination and creativity* (1st eds.). Information Age Publishing, Incorporated.

Lewin-Benham, A. (2023). *Infants and toddlers at work: Using Reggio-inspired materials to support brain development* (2nd ed.). Teachers College Press.

Magsamen, S., & Ross, I. (2023). *Your brain on art: How the arts transform us.* Canongate Books.

McArdle, F. (2012). The visual arts: Ways of seeing. In S. Wright (Ed.), *Children, meaning-making and the arts* (2nd ed., pp. 30–56). Pearson Australia.

Pacini-Ketchabaw, V., Kind, S., & Kocher, L. M. (2024). *Encounters with materials in early childhood education* (2nd ed.). Routledge.

Palmer, A., Britt, C., Davis, B., Shepherd, W., Barakat, N., Macleod, C., & Morgan, B. (2021). *Art and wonder: Young children and contemporary art: A collaboration between the Museum of Contemporary Art Australia, Mia Child and Family Study Centre and Macquarie University*. Museum of Contemporary Art Australia.

Richards, R. D., & Terreni, L. (2022). Intentionally supporting and extending young children's learning about and through the visual arts: Suggestions and strategies for early childhood education teachers. *Curriculum Matters, 18*(1), 88–106. https://doi.org/10.18296/cm.0061

Robinson, K., & Robinson, K. (2022). *Imagine if...: Creating a future for us all*. Penguin Books.

Vecchi, V. (2010). *Art and creativity in Reggio Emilia: Exploring the role and potential of ateliers in early childhood education*. Routledge.

Wright, S. (2012). *Children, meaning-making and the arts* (2nd ed.). Pearson Australia.

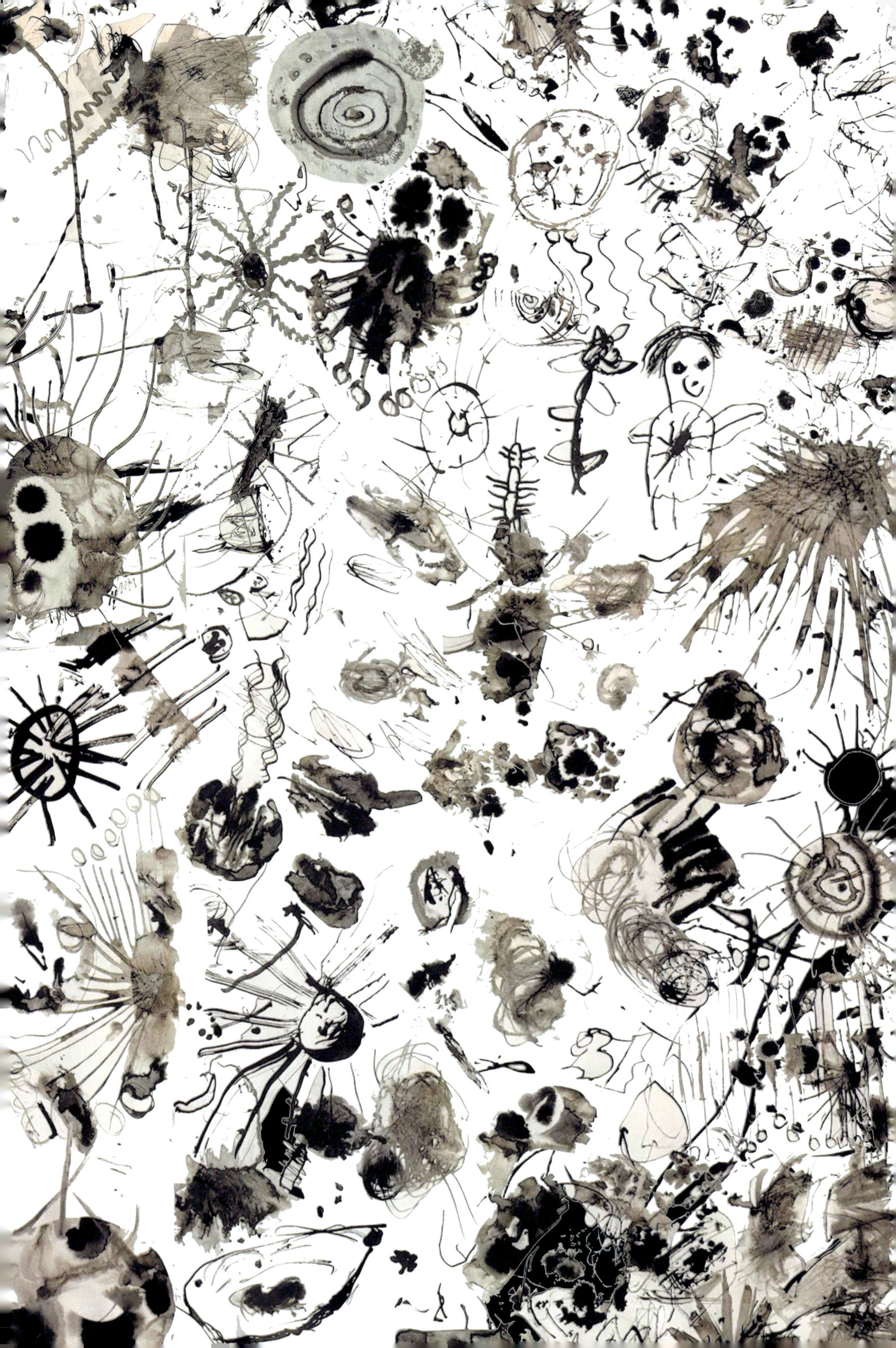

3 Theories, philosophies, and approaches to inspire visual arts pedagogy

The ways we position childhood, education, and the role of educators impact how we design and deliver visual arts learning experiences with children. Our pedagogical beliefs and practices, whether informed by theory or not, directly impact the kinds of visual arts learning experiences children will experience. Learning about and reflecting on theories, philosophies, and well-regarded approaches to early childhood education can powerfully inform, provoke, and inform rich visual arts learning experiences for children. Theories help us to question personal beliefs, assumptions, and habitual pedagogical choices. They help us to consider other perspectives to extend and enrich our visual arts planning and practice. In this chapter, we explore a selection of theories to provoke critical reflection about visual arts pedagogy and practice. For each group of theories, we offer a brief summary of the theoretical worldview and explore the key ideas of several influential theorists and philosophers. Each section offers provocations and reflective questions to enrich visual arts practice with children.

Constructivist and socio-cultural theories

Constructivist and socio-cultural theories both position children as active learners who develop social, cognitive, emotional, and physical skills and knowledge through tangible, relational, and play-based experiences. These theories are grounded in the assumption that development and learning are socially and culturally constructed within the learning environment. Learning through experience, and in relationship with people, places, and materials, leads children's development and extends upon their prior learning and understandings. This is broadly positioned as constructionism by Vygotskian scholars and as constructivism by

---

Figure 3.1 Learning to think about visual arts pedagogy through different theoretical lenses can feel messy and overwhelming, much like the many lines and shapes on this ink drawing compilation. However, theories support educators to question beliefs, assumptions and pedagogical habits [Image: Georgia Cleanthous, Dripstone Children's Centre].

DOI: 10.4324/9781003561835-4

Dewey, Malaguzzi, Bruner, and others (Brooks, 2022a; Malaguzzi, 1993). Whether labelled constructionist or constructivist, the important distinction to make is that socio-cultural theories appreciate that knowledge is constructed through relationships with people, places, and materials.

John Dewey is known for his philosophies of art, education, and democracy and his value for aesthetic and democratic education, children's home contexts, and culture. He noted that:

- Experience and active play foster authentic and meaningful learning.
- Cross-disciplinary, inquiry-led learning projects inspire learning engagement.
- Rich learning experiences should be designed to lead children to further experience and learning rather than disconnected "one off" experiences (Dewey, 1934).
- Visual arts learning (in art laboratories) should be positioned at the centre of both the curriculum and the design of the school (Lindsay, 2016).
- Arts expression unifies children's cognition, action, emotion, and thought (Dewey, 1915).
- Visual arts and crafts (the work of artisans) should be equally valued and accessible in both education and society (Dewey, 1915; 1934).

The **Reggio Emilia approach** is not a theory but a theory-informed approach to early childhood education that is strongly informed by constructivist and socio-cultural theories. Loris Malaguzzi, the founding director of the project, drew upon a range of theories to work collaboratively with community members, educators, and visual artists to establish and enact the values that underpin the Reggio Emilia approach (Edwards et al., 2012; Lindsay, 2015). In the Reggio Emilia approach:

- Visual art is positioned as a language (one of the many "Hundred Languages of children").
- Children are valued as capable citizens with human rights to be upheld.
- Children, parents, and teachers are valued as equal partners in teaching and learning.
- The environment is positioned as the third teacher.
- Democratic and aesthetic education is viewed as a form of political advocacy and activism.
- Teaching and learning are positioned as co-learning and co-researching.
- Time, reciprocity, aesthetics, beauty, and inquiry are valued.
- The atelier (art studio) is valued as a place for inquiry.
- The expertise of visual artists (Atelierista) informs and provokes pedagogy.
- Inquiry-based learning approaches (Progetazzione) provide opportunities for problem-solving as well as pedagogical research.
- Documentation is a process of research and advocacy.
- Children's learning is made visible through the arts.

Lev Vygotsky is known for his **socio-cultural theory** of cognitive development, which highlights the role of social interaction, culture, and language in shaping a child's learning and thinking processes (Carter, 2018). He noted that:

- Children acquire knowledge and beliefs through social collaboration and problem-solving with more capable or knowledgeable peers (known as the zone of proximal development).
- Individual development must be understood within social and cultural contexts.
- Knowledge is co-constructed through relationships with others and through cultural tools, the environment, and materials.
- Social learning drives development.

Bioecological systems theory, conceptualised by Urie Bronfenbrenner (1979), positions children's development as influenced by the interplay of individual, social, and environmental systems. Bronfenbrenner suggests that five interrelated systems influence child development and impact their growth. The systems

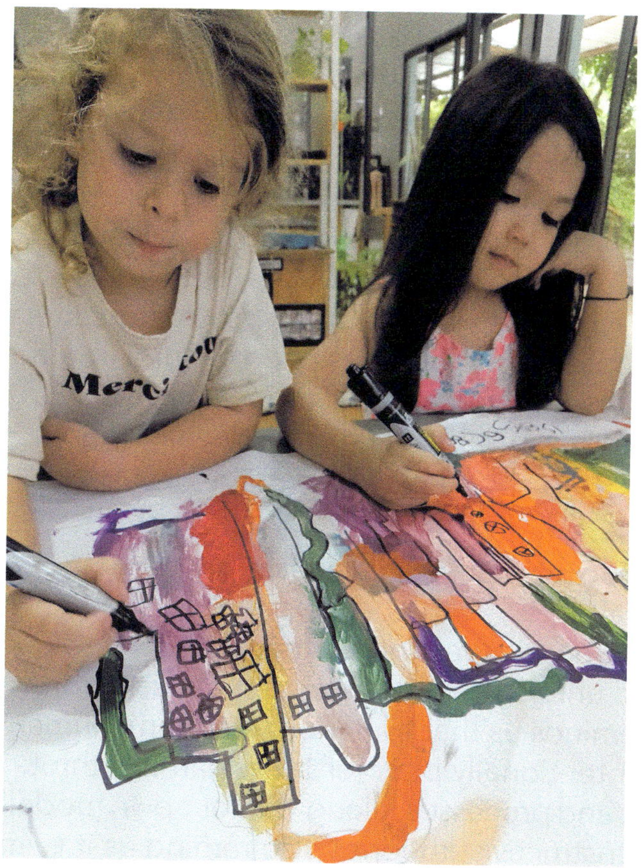

Figure 3.2 Meaningful collaboration in long-term projects helps children co-construct and scaffold shared knowledge and skills within a zone of proximal development [Image:Carolyn Prawius, Saigon Kids Early Learning Centre].

range from direct influences on the child to broader cultural and societal impacts on the systems that surround and support the child, including:

- **Microsystem:** direct environments such as family and education settings.
- **Mesosystem:** captures the connections between these environments, such as the relationship between home and school.
- **Exosystem:** external factors indirectly impacting the child, like parents' workplaces.
- **Macrosystem:** encompasses wider societal, cultural, and political contexts that shape beliefs and values.
- **Chronosystem:** considers the role of time, including a child's developmental stage and historical influences.
- The model also incorporates the role of biological factors, recognising the child as an active participant in their own development (Bronfenbrenner & Ceci, 1994).

The Process-Person-Context-Time (PPCT) model, developed by Bronfenbrenner (1994), identifies four dimensions of development: Process, involving bidirectional interactions or "proximal processes" as the "engines of development" (Bronfenbrenner & Morris, 2006); Person, representing individual traits like biology and genetics; Context, comprising nested systems influencing development; and Time, reflecting changes in individuals and environments over the lifespan.

Proximal processes, emphasised by Bronfenbrenner (1979), highlight bidirectional interactions where children influence and are influenced by their environment. Relationships play a central role, requiring mutual adaptation between children and their settings. Bioecological systems theory offers a holistic lens for early childhood education, advocating for integrated, relationship-based learning. The visual arts can act as a bridge between systems, such as home (microsystem) and school (mesosystem), by fostering cultural connections and continuity. For example, art projects based on cultural traditions strengthen links between family values and educational settings. Proximal processes are integral to supporting cognitive, social, and creative development.

Reflection and provocations for visual arts practice

Socio-constructivist theories remind us that learning in and through the visual arts is not a "magic unfolding" of inborn arts capacity for the "lucky" few. This theory paradigm reminds us that to honour children's human right to engage in the arts, we must intentionally plan for their learning through encounters with visual arts materials and processes, along with our own modelling and active participation. Socio-constructivist theories also remind us it is important to choose good quality, aesthetic materials and set up beautiful environments that invite children to wonder and delight in active learning, problem-solving, and inquiry.

While the immediate enjoyment of an arts experience is easy to observe, the longer term effects of the experience, and therefore children's learning, are not immediately evident (Dewey, 1938). Brooks (2022b) suggests it takes time, work and intention to be pedagogically active. Interrogating practice through a constructivist and socio-cultural lens invites us to re-imagine and re-ignite intentional visual arts teaching with children. When children and adults play with visual arts materials in a shared zone of proximal development (ZPD) knowledge is co-constructed (Brooks, 2022a). This empowers educators to remain present and involved during children's visual arts experiences; to observe, scaffold, and support children's learning.

While recognising that children learn in relationship with materials, educators play a critical role in supporting and guiding children's learning and exploration. Individual learning is richly enhanced and extended by the engagement of both child and adult co-partners in artful play, learning, teaching, and research. Proximal processes (the interactions between an individual and their environment that drive development and learning), and repeated meaningful interactions, nurture children's cognitive, social, and creative growth when shared artmaking creates opportunities to build relationships, foster problem-solving and extend social-emotional skills. Collaborative art making experiences also present opportunities for observational and bi-directional learning. Therefore, to nurture and scaffold children's capacity to "speak" visual arts languages, it is necessary to express your own value for visual languages and intentionally build your own visual arts knowledge, skills, and confidence.

When planning and implementing arts experiences informed by Constructivist and socio-Cultural theories:

- Set up aesthetic environments that communicate value for children as capable and active learners.
- Design the environment and select materials as provocations and invitations to offer rich encounters for learning.
- Provide many opportunities for children to engage in hands-on exploration with rich, high-quality arts materials and processes.
- Intentionally create social zones of proximal development (both between children and educators).
- Adopt an active and intentional role in scaffolding arts skills and techniques.
- Support children to reflect and build upon prior knowledge and experience.
- Intentionally make connections to children's family, community, and culture within your visual arts curriculum.
- Exposure children to diverse cultural and historical art forms to promote artistic awareness, global citizenship, and cultural empathy.
- Connect home (microsystem) and education settings (mesosystem) through culturally inspired visual arts and traditional crafting projects that foster belonging and connection.
- Embrace your personal and professional capacity to develop visual arts skills and knowledge.
- Use visual arts to extend and provoke further experience, learning, and growth in the (cognitive, social, emotional, and physical domains).
- Document children's work to make children's learning visible for children, families, and the broader community.

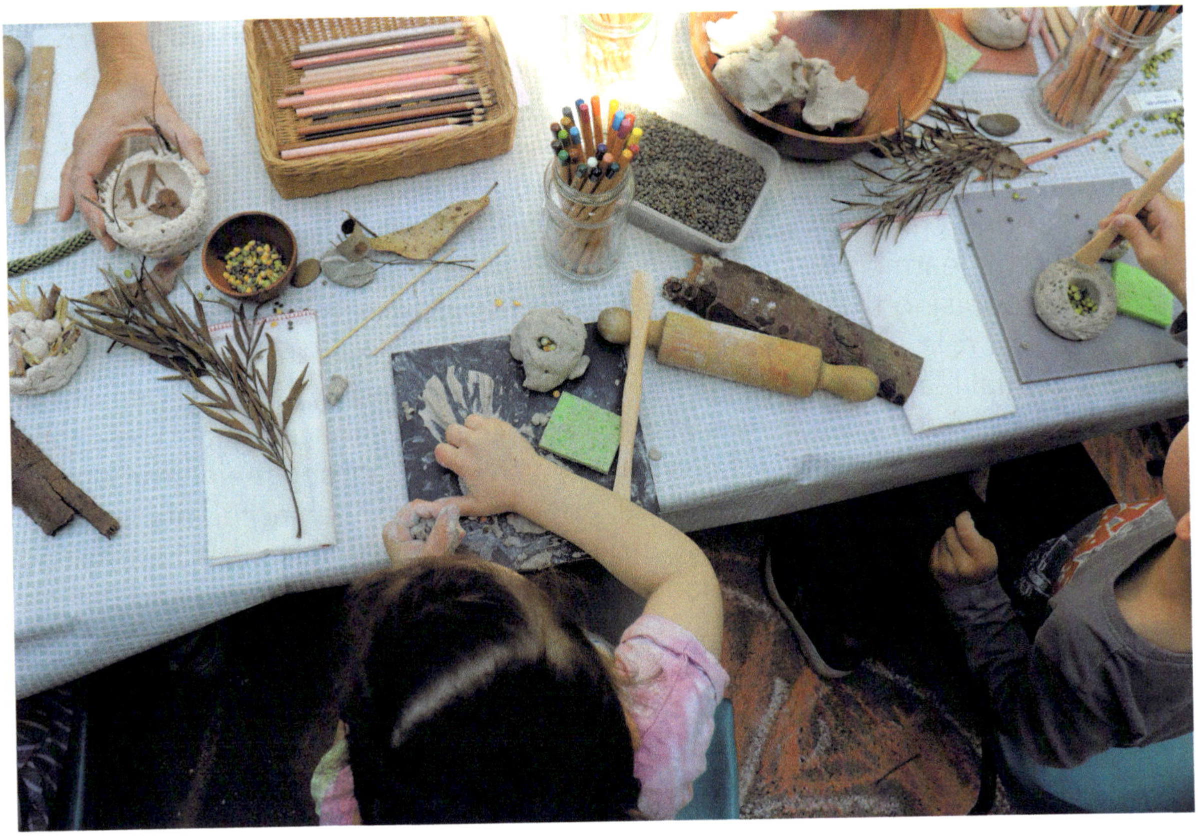

Figure 3.3 Intentionally select material provocations and design invitations to offer rich learning encounters through supported hands-on exploration with high-quality arts materials and processes [Image: Bomaderry Community Preschool].

Critical and postmodern theory perspectives

Critical theories are social theories that aim to improve society by critiquing and highlighting biases and assumptions that create barriers to full participation (Irving & Carter, 2018). In educational contexts, critical theories provoke deep reflection and examination of the personal and professional assumptions that influence pedagogy and practice. Similarly, Postmodern (also known as post-structuralist) perspectives encourage critical engagement with notions of truth, knowledge, power, and control to interrogate how some people (and some kinds of knowledge) are privileged over others (Irving & Carter, 2018). Critical and postmodern theorists remind us it is important to engage in critical reflection about how the visual arts may be empowered or marginalised in the curriculum.

Critical and postmodern theoretical perspectives are grounded in the following assumptions:

- All people are born with rights (individual, family, community, and culture).
- Inequalities (poverty, racism, sexism, and exclusion) compromise a sense of belonging.
- Social transformation is supported through education for a more just and equal world.

- Human identities are complex and shift as they transition between and participate in different cultural groups and across time.
- Unless examined and critiqued, assumptions and certainty can foster biased and exclusionary pedagogical practices.
- How "success" is perceived in relation to a field or domain of learning (such as the arts) is dependent on how cultural capital is valued and examined.
- There are many forms of knowledge, and the notion of "truth" is contested.

Pierre Bourdieu's theory of cultural capital and particularly his discussions about habitus and field (Longhofer & Winchester, 2023) provoke reflection about how an educator's personal cultural capital and habitus (ingrained beliefs, skills, and attitudes) can positively or negatively influence children's learning experiences.

Paulo Freire's focus on adult education theory also offers inspiration for educators to critique their own current assumptions and approaches and to be open to new pedagogical ideas through self-criticism, critical thinking, dialogue, and reflection (Schugurensky, 1998).

Deleuze and Guattari's rhizome theory and lines of flight theory provoke us to embrace the messiness of "not knowing" and consider the hidden elements of the situation as well as the obvious and visible (Deleuze & Guattari, 1987). This means that as educators respond to children's interests, dispositions, and playful inquiry, it is not possible or desirable to predetermine the path children's learning will take. Like the tangled growth of a rhizome (a tangled organic root that grows in multiple, unpredictable directions), or like the unexpected twists and turns of a flock of birds in flight, visual arts pedagogy and practice can evolve in multiple directions and celebrate the multiple possibilities that emerge in relationship with the environment, materials, and children.

Reflection and provocations for visual arts practice

Critical and postmodern theories challenge us to embrace uncertainty, reject binary thinking, and reflect on the existence of multiple truths and perspectives. They remind us to empower children by rejecting the binary assumption that there is a "right" and "wrong" way to teach children in the visual arts domain. Instead of positioning visual arts learning as a linear progression from free exploration to intentional expression, Kind (2010, p. 114) explains that artistic practice is grounded in "failure, struggle, uncertainty, and not knowing."

These theories provoke examination about whether children are afforded equal rights to experience visual arts learning. We must engage in deep critical reflection about the hidden meanings and assumptions embedded in unexamined and habitual approaches to visual arts pedagogy and practice. For example, question habitual practices by critically examining how celebrations, such as Christmas, are enacted in arts learning experiences. When cardboard fireplaces or snowmen products are produced in settings where children experience Christmas in warm climates, critical theories demand reflection about the potential lack of relevance to children's cultural capital and knowledge of Christmas traditions. Adults facilitating children's learning experiences must question whether the provision of activities with predetermined, stereotyped outcomes affords children the freedom and self-expression to apply art materials to express their own cultural knowledge and traditions. When selecting the work of artists to inspire visual arts experiences, consider the cultural and gender assumptions maintained when famous European male artists are chosen ahead of local, multi-gendered, and multi-cultural exemplars. When educators embrace open and honest discussions about fairness, justice, and power, even in relation to visual arts pedagogy, an anti-bias curriculum is fostered.

The joy in visual arts practice includes freedom from rules and conventions, reminding us it is not necessary to follow formulas or templates. And yet, if educators avoid embracing the uncertainty of "not knowing" all of the answers, outcomes, and potentials of visual arts pedagogies, children will experience what Elliot Eisner called the "null curriculum" (Eisner, 2002); that is, the curriculum children miss out on because it was not delivered at all. When we engage in arts learning experiences with children, it is important to value children's agency and processes of inquiry and avoid adult-imposed, structured activities which enact adult power and control. On the other hand, when teachers view children as capable, it is more likely they will be empowered to access the multiple affordances of rich arts materials and arts processes that empower child-led learning.

When planning and implementing arts experiences informed by critical and postmodern theory perspectives:

- Question, challenge, and examine your everyday visual arts pedagogy and practice
- Think about how your personal assumptions and beliefs might advantage or disadvantage the children you work with
- Reflect on possible adult agendas and biases when planning arts learning experiences
- Reflect on who is empowered or marginalised in your visual arts curriculum
- Ensure every child's human rights are promoted through visual arts experiences

Practice theories

Practice theories focus on the learning affordances offered by the environment. James Gibson's (1979, p. 127) ecological approach to visual perception suggests the "values" and "meanings" of things in the environment can be directly perceived." Further to this, Eleanor Gibson highlights that children's perceptions of the environment guide their responses and actions (Adolph & Kretch, 2015). Kemmis' theory of practice architectures offers a framework for understanding how education practices are produced, reproduced, and transformed in settings (Kemmis, 2023). Rönnerman

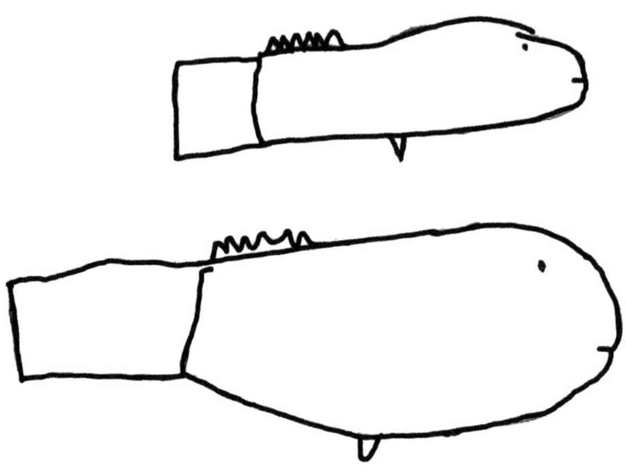

et al. (2017, p. 6) note that practices are formed socially through the interrelated characteristics of *sayings* (forms of understanding expressed through language and discourse), *doings* (modes of action or activity), and *relatings* ("ways in which people relate to one another and the world"). Additionally, practices are constrained or enabled by the "cultural-discursive, material-economic, and social-political arrangements found in, or brought to, the site where the practice occurs" (Kemmis, 2023, para 1).

Reflection and provocations for visual arts practice

Children's interactions, practices, and engagement are influenced by the invitations and affordances offered within the environment. When setting up visual arts learning spaces, consider how the environmental design invites and guides children's interactions with the materials and with each other. Ask yourself, "what messages does the environment convey about how children's visual arts work is valued?"; "Are materials presented in ways that foster social learning?"; "Are visual arts experiences presented in ways that encourage children to maintain care and respect for both the space and the materials?" When planning visual arts experiences, aim to intentionally respond at the intersections of children's understandings and prior experience with materials (sayings), their individual activity preferences and capabilities (doings), and their material and personal relationships (relatings).

When planning and implementing arts experiences:

- Consider the activity and learning potentials suggested by the physical environment and materials.
- Set up the environment and materials in ways that communicate your expectations about the physical location and movement, care for materials and the space, cleaning responsibilities, and affordances for social and material interactions.
- Evaluate your pedagogical intentions when setting up visual arts learning experiences.
- Critically evaluate how an experience invites engagement, relationships, and learning.
- Consider your role in supporting children's relationships with materials.

New materialism

While Practice Theories emphasise the environmental affordances and relational dynamics that shape children's interactions and engagement, New Materialism extends this understanding by positioning materials themselves as active agents in these processes. Together, these frameworks offer a more expansive lens to analyse how children, materials, and their environments co-create learning experiences, highlighting the dynamic interplay between social, cultural, and material forces in early childhood visual arts practices.

Reflection and provocations for visual arts practice

New Materialism repositions materials as active participants in children's creative learning, challenging traditional views of materials as passive tools for manipulation or self-expression (Penfold, 2019). This framework, rooted in the works of theorists such as Barad (2003), Bennett (2004), and Braidotti (2006), emphasises the dynamic, reciprocal relationships between humans and materials. Central to New Materialism is Barad's (2003) concept of intra-action, which suggests that meaning and agency are not located solely in humans but emerge through mutual transformations between human and non-human entities. This perspective acknowledges materials as vibrant forces that shape and influence learning processes rather than objects subordinated to human intent. New Materialism positions:

- **Materials as Active Agents**: Materials are not passive but are vibrant and dynamic and as such, are active participants in learning through their physical properties and transformations (Barad, 2003; Bennett, 2004).
- **Intra-Action**: Agency and meaning emerge through the interplay between human and material forces, rather than existing solely within one or the other (Barad, 2003).
- **Collaboration with Materials**: Children and materials co-create knowledge and learning experiences. For example, how materials like clay fold, stretch, or adhere directly influences children's thinking and actions.

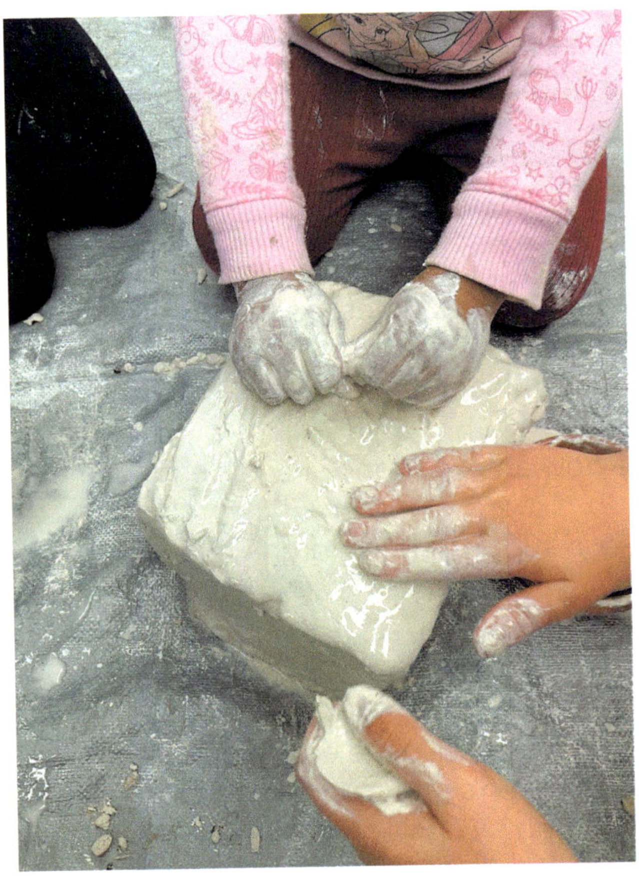

Figure 3.4 Materials are not passive but are vibrant and dynamic. Children create meaning through the interplay between human and material forces [Image: Maitland East Preschool].

- **Unpredictability and Emergence**: New Materialism challenges linear notions of cause and effect, suggesting that learning emerges from the interplay of multiple systems and forces.
- **Dynamic Pathways of Discovery**: Sensory-rich, open-ended materials such as water, cellophane, or tissue paper offer opportunities for divergent, emergent learning pathways based on material transformations.

When planning and implementing arts experiences informed by New Materialism, consider the following strategies:

- Reframe the role of materials as collaborators in the creative process.
- Plan learning experiences that support dynamic exchanges between children and materials, emphasising open-ended exploration which value unexpected outcomes.
- Encourage children to investigate physical properties such as transparency, weight, or motion using materials such as tissue paper or cellophane to foster deeper connections with the physical world.
- Embrace unpredictability, allowing materials to guide the learning process and recognising materials as active participants.
- Create learning environments where children, materials, and educators all work together in a continuous process of discovery.
- Support the development of creativity, agency, and a deeper understanding of the interconnectedness between people and their material worlds.

Social learning theories

Theories about behaviour originally focussed on "managing" or "conditioning" children's behaviour using rewards and punishments; a concept rejected by contemporary views of children as capable, competent learners. However, restrictive behaviour-control attitudes continue to undermine respectful teaching practices; demanding ongoing examination of our attitudes toward children's "behaviour," and rejection of strategies that contradict child-honouring pedagogical values. For example, are visual art experiences offered as a reward for *"good behaviour"* or even removed as a punishment? Are children denied access to some materials because *"children can't be trusted to use the materials properly"* or because *"children will just make a mess"*?

Contemporary theorists have moved beyond traditional behaviourism to consider the social and cognitive impacts on behaviours and learning. Social learning theorists value the influence of social relationships and relational attachments to consider the cognitive processing children undertake as they respond to environmental experiences. The impact of social relationships on behaviours helps educators to consider alternate interpretations and responses. **Albert Bandura's** social learning theory extended on behaviourism to propose that children's learning and behaviours are reinforced through both environmental observations and cognitive processing (Irving & Carter, 2018). Children learn by observing, critically evaluating (cognitive mediation processes), and imitating behaviour modelled by others. When behaviour, including positive engagement with visual arts, is reinforced by people a child identifies with, the behaviours are more likely to be repeated. **John Bowlby's** attachment theory promotes the notion that responsive and supportive interactions with significant people support children to regulate their behaviour and create a context for emotional wellbeing. **Mary Ainsworth's** "strange situation" experiment showed that caregiver sensitivity and behaviour directly influence children's attachment style, whether secure, insecure avoidant, or insecure resistant, highlighting the responsibility to foster responsive relationships as a foundation for all learning (Irving & Carter, 2018).

Reflection and provocations for practice

Thinking about social and relational influences on behaviour supports deep reflection about children's experiences, choices, and responses in the learning environment, including the visual arts experiences presented to children. When children are immersed in visual arts learning experiences that are intrinsically motivating and rewarding, they are more likely to engage positively in rich learning and play and to demonstrate focused and engaged behaviours. Additionally, when the significant people in children's lives actively engage with children, collaboratively role-modelling visual arts skills, techniques, and dispositions, children are able to co-learn and co-partner with others in and through the visual arts.

Behaviours that some may label as "negative" or "disruptive" must instead be interpreted as communication. Children yearn to feel secure, valued, and heard. They also respond positively to complexity and challenge. When children are underestimated, or when adults doubt their capabilities, it is not surprising that some children communicate their frustration. The provision of high-quality, responsive visual arts materials and experiences offers a climate of complexity and challenge and communicates positive belief in, and respect for, children's strengths and capabilities. Positive contexts are created when educators foster secure and trusting attachments, actively engage in and interpret children's play, and respond to children's needs and strengths.

When planning and implementing arts experiences informed by Social learning theory, consider how you:

- Role-model positive attitudes towards the visual arts.
- Listen and respond to children's non-verbal communication.
- Plan experiences that align with children's dispositions, attachment styles, interests, and motivations.
- Plan processes that respect and foster children's capabilities.
- Remain present during arts experiences to support self-regulation and maintain focused engagement.
- Critically reflect on your own fears and attitudes. How often do children miss out on wonderful learning opportunities because educators doubt children's abilities or readiness and fear "destructive play," "mess-making," or "silly behaviour"?

Developmental theories

Developmental theories explain cognitive, language, physical, and emotional development from birth to adulthood within progressive or continuous stages that are positioned as predictable and universal (Irving & Carter, 2018). Developmental theories are grounded in the assumption that development results from a combination of genetic and biological foundations and environmental influences (nature and nurture). Theorists who focus on children's development acknowledge that children learn and develop through experience, exploration, and play with concrete materials. However, unlike the constructivist belief that experience fosters development, developmental theory proposes that learning will only occur when a child is developmentally ready.

In relation to visual arts development, post-war scholars focused on the stages of children's drawing (see, for example, Rhoda Kellogg, Herbert Reid, and Victor Lowenfeld). Although it is interesting to consider children's progression from early mark-making to representative drawings and symbols, we caution that developmental stage theories, developed from Western perspectives, are potentially limiting and narrow in focus. We propose it is much more valuable to appreciate the social mark-making and artful play children engage in, rather than attempting to define or limit children within a drawing or conceptual "stage." At the same time, well-known developmental theorists offer important points for reflection about visual arts experience planning.

Jean Piaget is well known for cognitive constructivism theory and the notion that language acquisition and cognitive development occur in stages. These stages are understood to occur as children engage in active play, experience, experiment, research, and interact with their environments (Piaget, 1973). Piaget proposed that children build new knowledge by adapting their prior knowledge to accommodate new information. In doing this, children seek equilibrium by assimilating and accommodating new information into their existing schemas (categories that organise knowledge about the world). The experience of disequilibrium and cognitive conflict leads to higher mental functioning (Piaget, 1973).

Howard Gardner, known for Multiple Intelligence theory, suggests that intelligence is located and expressed in multiple ways and should not only be measured by linguistic and logical-mathematical measures. Gardner identified a range of specific intelligences, including naturalist, intrapersonal, interpersonal, visual-spatial, bodily-kinaesthetic, verbal-linguistic, musical, and logical-mathematical intelligence (Gardner, 1983).

Reflection and provocations for visual arts practice

Developmental theories offer a useful guide to ensure planned experiences take children's individual development into consideration so that learning experiences respond to children's current developmental capabilities. If learning experiences require children to engage in processes beyond their current capabilities, development, and dispositions, children may be disempowered and become frustrated. A grounding knowledge of the stages of children's development, as well as the phases of children's mark-making and drawing development, are useful when evaluating the kinds of visual arts learning experiences that will be effective for children. However, the notions of developmental readiness and developmentally appropriate practice can also restrain visual arts practice with children if educators determine that children are "not ready" to use particular materials or processes. While developmental awareness is an important consideration to ensure arts experiences are aligned with children's physical and cognitive capacities, this must be balanced with our belief that children are capable and always ready to learn and be introduced to visual arts materials.

When you intentionally use visual arts terminology and introduce new techniques and processes, you are supporting children to assimilate and accommodate new visual arts knowledge and schemas. Additionally, it is important not to rush to solve the problems children encounter when engaged in visual arts experiences. Children will seek solutions and in doing so will learn and develop in ways that are meaningful for them and aligned with their capabilities. It is important to remember that developmental theories are not the only lens by which to plan for and evaluate practice. Malaguzzi articulated this when he urged educators to "know your Piaget and think for yourself" (Moestrup & Eskesen, 2004, p. 4).

Gardner's theory encourages educators to intentionally expand learning experiences by valuing the multiple ways children learn. His theory reminds us to value the whole child and to provide opportunities for children to express their

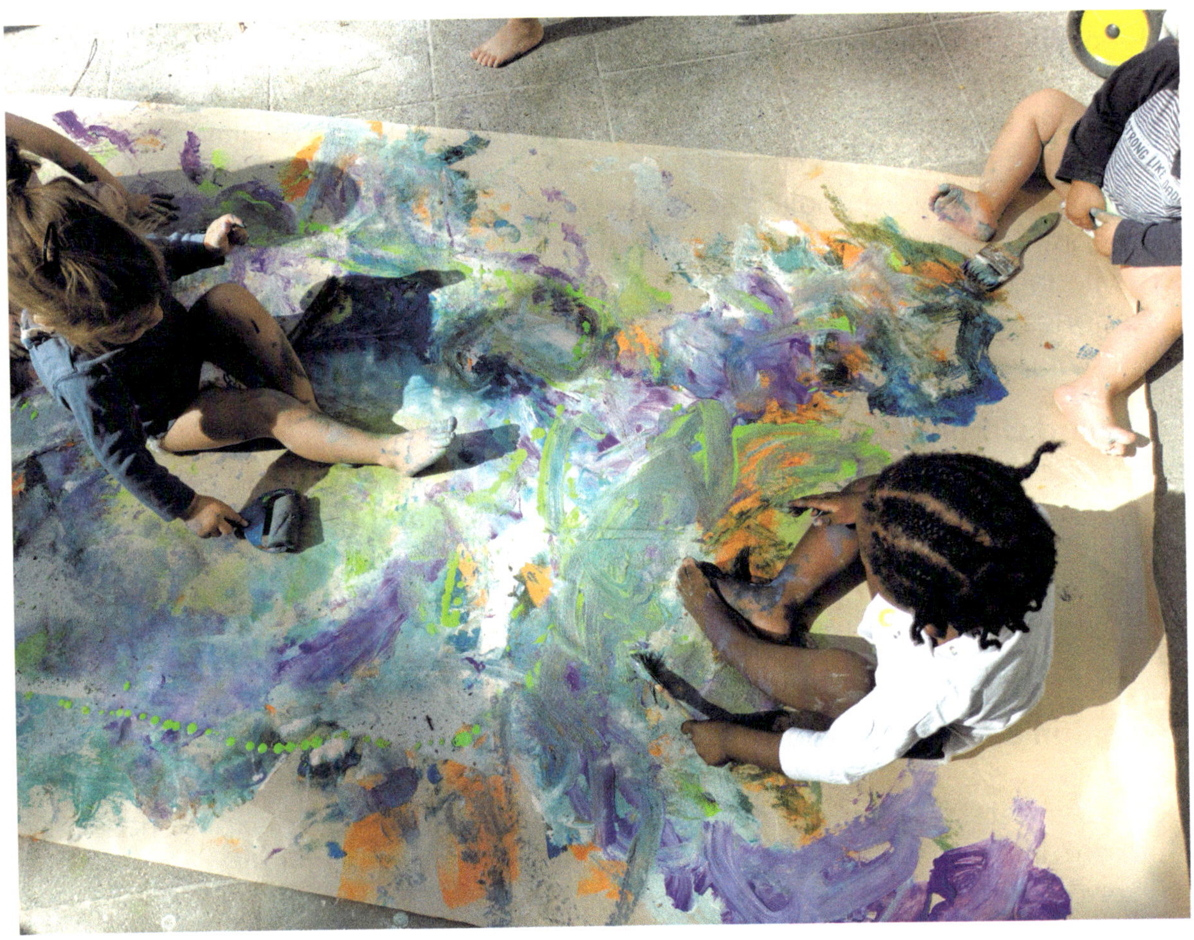

Figure 3.5 Developmentally suitable art processes supports children's inclusion and engagement, regardless of their experience, development, or abilities [Image: Joke den Haese].

intelligence in many ways across a range of learning domains. For example, educators can facilitate rich, holistic learning by combining bodily-kinaesthetic movement (dance and music) with visual-spatial mark-making. Gardner's theory can also support educators to advocate for an expanded view of intelligence by showing families and the broader community how visual arts learning celebrates and demonstrates children's diverse capabilities.

When planning and implementing arts experiences informed by developmental theories:

- Build on children's current knowledge, skills, and development.
- Adapt visual arts experiences to be accessible for the diverse learners in your setting.
- Provide regular hands-on exploration and play with materials
- Include opportunities for large body movements to underpin fine-motor development.
- Move beyond physical development justifications for visual arts learning to plan visual arts learning experiences that build cognitive, social, cultural, emotional, and communication development.
- Holistically foster children's development across all learning domains and intelligences.
- Position children as capable regardless of their age or "developmental stage."

Conclusion

Engaging with theory to explore alternate perspectives and challenge assumptions about childhood, teaching, and learning empowers educators to make critically informed choices about visual arts education. By reflecting on sociocultural, critical, developmental, and other theoretical perspectives, educators gain the tools to critically evaluate and intentionally design visual arts experiences that respect and extend children's capabilities.

Engaging with these perspectives equips you, as an educator, to advocate for the profound ways that visual arts experiences support children's cognitive, emotional, and social development. Your willingness to question assumptions and embrace diverse theoretical approaches enriches your pedagogy and practice. By integrating insights from theory into your daily work, you can create environments and opportunities where children thrive as curious, capable, and creative learners.

References

Adolph, K. E., & Kretch, K. S. (2015). Gibson's theory of perceptual learning. In *International encyclopedia of the social and behavioral sciences* (2nd ed., pp. 127–134). Elsevier. https://doi.org/10.1016/B978-0-08-097086-8.23096-1

Barad, K. (2003). Posthumanist performativity: Toward an understanding of how matter comes to matter. *Signs: Journal of Women in Culture and Society, 28*(3), 801–831. https://doi.org/10.1086/345321

Bennett, J. (2004). The force of things: Steps toward an ecology of matter. *Political Theory, 32*(3), 347–372. https://www.jstor.org/stable/4148158
Braidotti, R. (2006). Posthuman, all too human towards a new process ontology. *Theory, Culture and Society, 23*(7–8), 197–208. https://doi.org/10.1177/0263276406069232
Bronfenbrenner, U. (1979). *The ecology of human development*. Harvard University Press.
Bronfenbrenner, U. (1994). Ecological modes of human development. In M. Gauvain & M. Cole, (Eds.), *Readings on the development of children* (2nd ed., pp. 37–43). Freeman.
Bronfenbrenner, U., & Ceci, S. J. (1994). Nature-nuture reconceptualised in developmental perspective: A bioecological model. *Psychological Review, 101*(4), 568–586.
Bronfenbrenner, U., & Morris, P. A. (2006). The bioecological model of human development. In W. Damo, & R. M. Lerner (Eds.), *Handbook of child psychology, vol. 1: Theoretical models of human development* (6th ed., pp. 793–828). Wiley.
Brooks, M. (2022a). *Drawing to learn*. Pademelon Press.
Brooks, M. (2022b). *Authentic art with children*. Pademelon Press.
Carter, C. (2018). *Theorists and theoretical perspectives*. In E. Irving, & C. Carter (Eds.), *The child in focus: Learning and teaching in early childhood education*. Oxford University Press.
Deleuze, G., & Guattari, F. (1987). *A thousand plateaus: capitalism and schizophrenia*. University of Minnesota Press.
Dewey, J. (1915). *The school and society* (2nd ed.). The University of Chicago Press.
Dewey, J. (1934). *Art as experience*. Penguin Group (USA) Inc.
Dewey, J. (1938). *Experience and education*. Kappa Delta Pi.
Edwards, C., Gandini, L., & Forman, G. (Eds.). (2012). *The hundred languages of children: The Reggio Emilia experience in transformation* (3rd ed.). Praeger.
Eisner, E. (2002). *The arts and the creation of mind*. Yale University Press.
Gardner, H. (1983). *Frames of mind*. Basic Books.
Irving, E., & Carter, C. (2018). *The child in focus: Learning and teaching in early childhood education*. Oxford University Press.
Kemmis, S. (2023). *The theory of practice architectures. Current work: The theory of practice architectures*. https://stephenkemmis.com/the-theory-of-practice-architectures/
Kind, S. (2010). Art encounters: Movements in the visual arts and early childhood education. In V. Pacini-Ketchabaw (Ed.), *Flows, rhythms and intensities* (pp. 113–131). Peter Lang.
Lindsay, G. (2015). Reflections in the mirror of Reggio Emilia's soul: John Dewey's foundational influence on pedagogy in the Italian educational project. *Early Childhood Education Journal, 43*(6), 447–457. https://link.springer.com/article/10.1007/s10643-015-0692-7
Lindsay, G. (2016). John Dewey and Reggio Emilia: Worlds apart - one vision. *Australian Art Education, 37*(1), 21–37. https://search.informit.org/doi/epdf/10.3316/aeipt.214909

Longhofer, W., & Winchester, D. (Eds.). (2023). *Social theory re-wired: New connections to classical and contemporary perspectives* (3rd ed.). Routledge. https://doi.org/10.4324/9781003320609

Malaguzzi, L. (1993). For an education based on relationships. *Young Children, 49*(1), 9–12.

Moestrup, J., & Eskesen, K. (2004). *Conversations with Loris Malaguzzi*. The Danish Reggio Emilia Network.

Penfold, L. (2019). Material matters in Children's creative learning. *Journal of Design and Science*. Retrieved from https://jods.mitpress.mit.edu/pub/bwp6cysy

Piaget, J. (1973). *To understand is to invent: The future of education*. Grossman Publishers.

Rönnerman, K., Grootenboer, P., & Edwards-Groves, C. (2017). The practice architectures of middle leading in early childhood education. *International Journal of Child Care and Education Policy, 11*(8), 1–20. https://doi.org/10.1186/s40723-017-0032-z

Schugurensky, D. (1998). The legacy of Paulo Freire: A critical review of his contributions. *Convergence, 31*(1), 17–29.

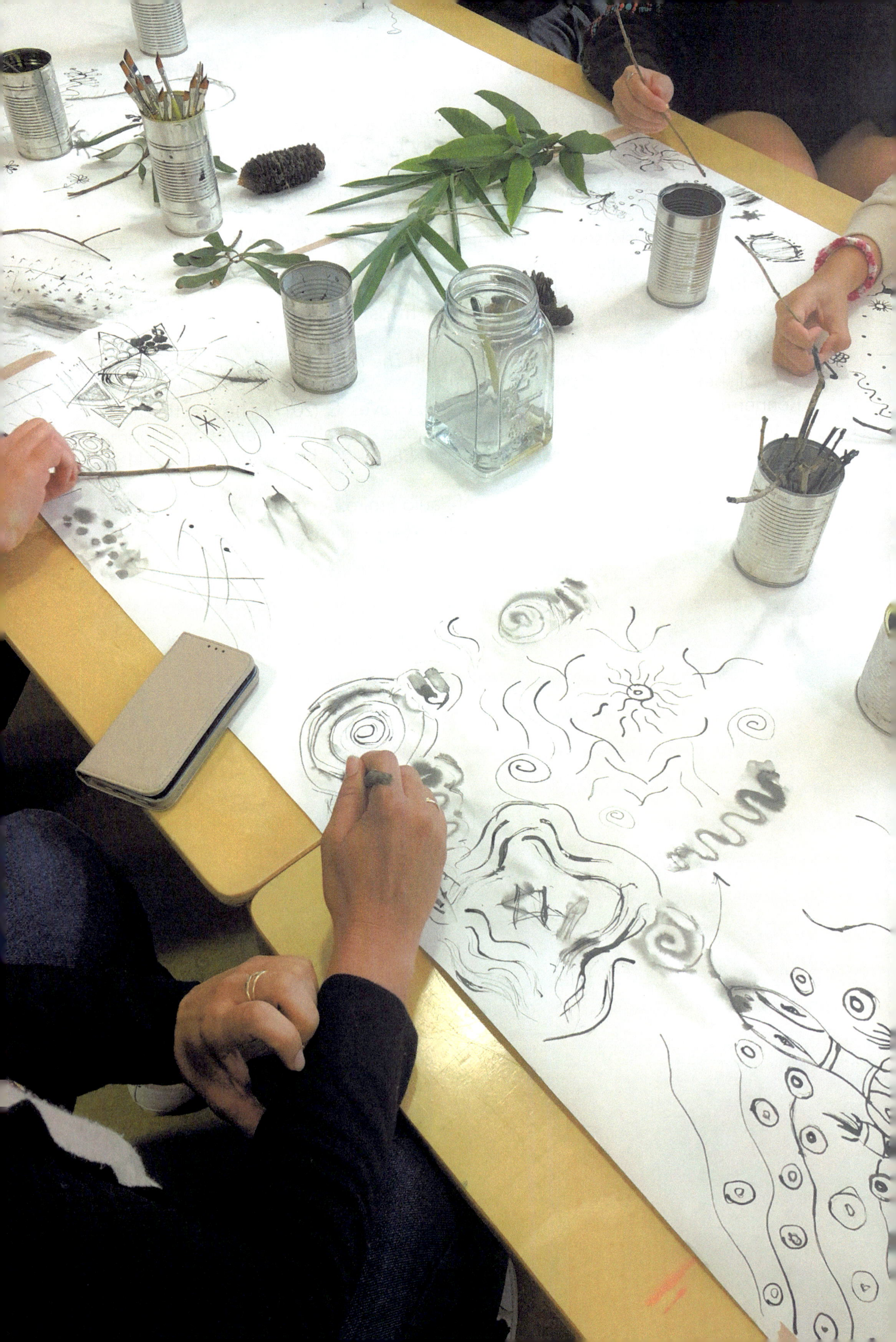

4 Examining and building a personal visual arts identity

An educator's identity and beliefs have a significant impact on the ways they interact with children. Many adults lack confidence in their creative abilities. This often comes from past experiences that valued conformity and rules over imagination, taking risks, and exploring creativity. In many education systems, the arts are marginalised in favour of subjects such as literacy, numeracy, and the sciences, reflecting a systemic and societal undervaluing of creativity. This imbalance in value for subjects can reduce opportunities to learn about the visual arts, making many people believe they are not creative or artistic, despite the critical role these skills play in fostering innovation and self-expression (Robinson, 2001). If educators lack personal visual arts confidence and knowledge, it is more likely they will be unsure about what visual arts experiences to offer and how to implement such experiences with children. Such feelings may fuel a tendency to only use familiar arts materials and processes, or to refer all visual arts planning to other colleagues. Even those who are more confident with visual arts materials and processes may feel unsure about how to support colleagues and children to develop visual arts skills and confidence.

Regardless of whether you consider yourself artistic or not, we absolutely believe it is possible to transform existing visual arts self-efficacy beliefs, attitudes, and knowledge in positive ways by reflecting on several belief-oriented theories and by embracing your inner artist to engage in practical art-making experiences. In this chapter, we encourage you to reflect on how your prior experiences have shaped your visual arts identity and offer strategies to develop your confidence to create and appreciate art works; and to be an educator who can nurture this capacity in others.

Self-efficacy beliefs

Self-efficacy describes a person's belief about their ability to apply knowledge and perform certain tasks (Bandura, 2012). Measured as high or low, self-efficacy impacts how people think, feel, and behave in certain areas of

Figure 4.1 A reflection meeting with a team of Aboriginal educators offered collaborative ink and stick mark making to combine art workshop, relaxed conversation and professional dialogue [Image: Gai Lindsay, University of Wollongong].

DOI: 10.4324/9781003561835-5

practice. Self-efficacy in the visual arts is shaped by a complex interplay of past experiences, social influences, and personal beliefs about artistic ability. For many teachers, low self-efficacy in the visual arts stems from formative experiences such as critical feedback from teachers and limited exposure to creative opportunities during their own education, or the perception that artistic talent is an innate gift rather than a skill that can be developed (Denee, 2024; Probine, 2024). Such experiences often lead to a deeply ingrained fear of failure or embarrassment, discouraging individuals from engaging with the arts altogether.

Diminished visual arts confidence and knowledge can perpetuate a cycle of avoidance. Teacher identity beliefs impact how the children they teach will come to perceive their own abilities (McArdle, 2012). On the other hand, a person with high visual arts self-efficacy will feel more confident and capable to engage with art materials, and to support others to learn about visual arts processes (Garvis & Pendergast, 2011). Understanding the origins of self-efficacy, whether high or low, is therefore crucial for empowering teachers to reframe their beliefs and build the skills necessary to confidently teach the visual arts.

Bandura's (1997) social cognitive theory, and the related notion of self-efficacy beliefs, help us to understand why some adults are more active and comfortable with visual arts education than others. Bandura suggests positive self-efficacy can be developed through:

- observing competent others who share knowledge and teach effective skills and strategies
- successful mastery experiences
- perseverance and sustained effort
- verbal encouragement and a positive, accepting, and stress-free environment

Conversely, our research shows that many adults vividly recall negative or discouraging childhood experiences that undermined their visual arts self-efficacy, such as receiving critical feedback about their artwork from a peer or teacher (Denee, 2023; Denee, 2024; Denee et al., 2024; Lindsay, 2017; 2021; Probine, 2020; 2023). Even though most educators believe the visual arts are important for children, a range of factors may impact their confidence to embrace new approaches to visual arts education with children. Being aware of these influences can be the first step to making a choice to reframe and rebuild personal visual arts self-efficacy.

Embrace your inner artist

A crucial step in rebuilding self-efficacy in the visual arts is to actively challenge the belief that you are not artistic. Every human being has the potential and right to engage in artistic and creative expression, play, and exploration. To encourage meaningful engagement with the visual arts for yourself and the children you work with, focus on exploring, enjoying, and simply playing with visual arts materials, rather than striving to create "great art." Unless you plan to become

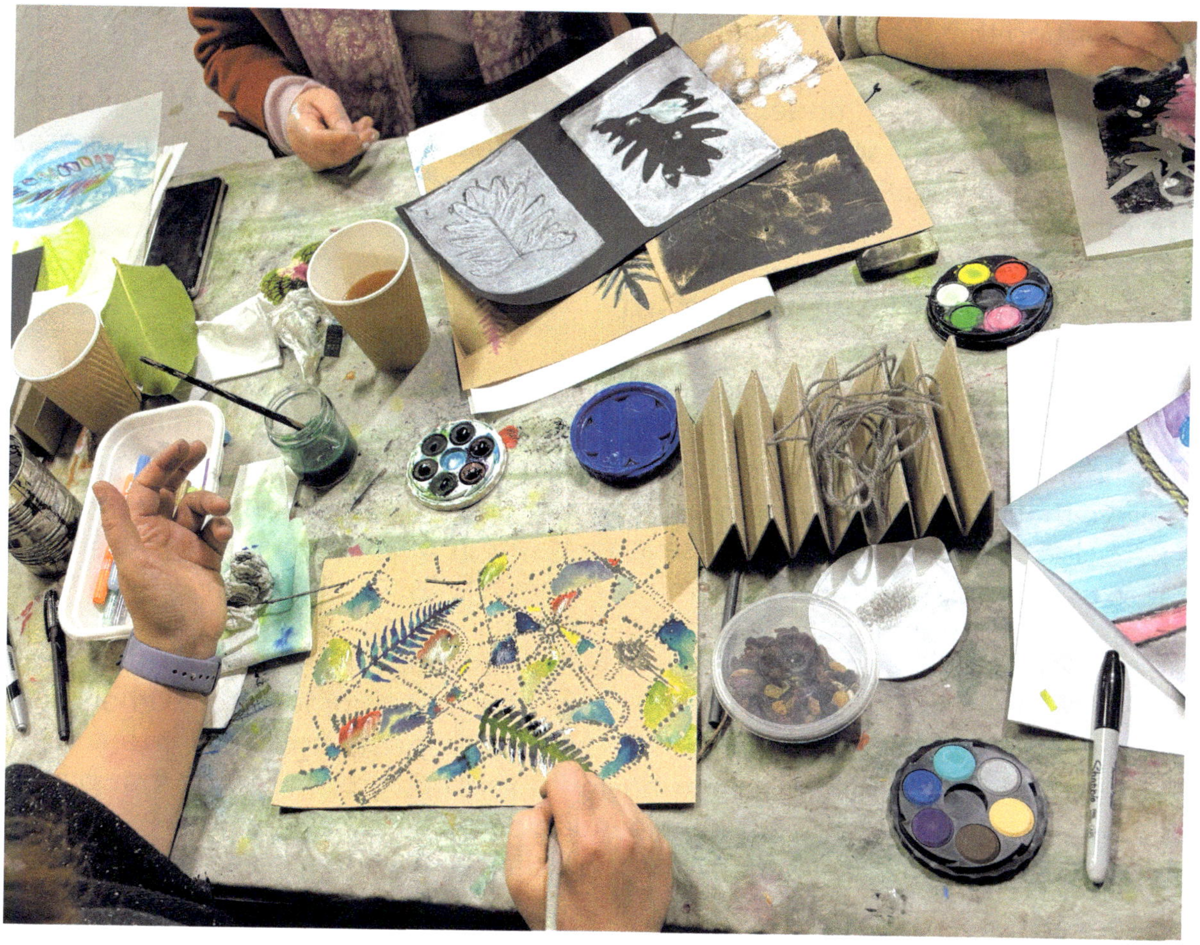

Figure 4.2 Educators build visual arts self-efficacy by making time to play with a variety of art materials and processes [Image: Gai Lindsay].

a professional "BIG A" artist and exhibit your art in a gallery, it is important to put aside expectations that your own artmaking must be perfect to be able to support children's learning. Many people decide they are not artistic after just one or two attempts with an art material or technique, or when results do not match expectations. The truth is that learning any new skill requires time, effort, and practice. For instance, we don't expect children to learn to write their names in a single sitting, so why assume that visual arts skills develop effortlessly, as if by magic? That would be as unrealistic as thinking it possible to become fluent in a foreign language after just one lesson.

You do not have to be a "Big A" artist to play with and delight in visual arts languages. Instead, embrace the joy of being a "little a" artist; someone who is open to new learning, creative experimentation, practice, and inquiry. As someone supporting children to engage with visual arts languages, the most powerful act you can make as a teacher is to embrace your own role as a learner and build your own visual arts skills and knowledge.

Self-efficacy can be shifted by making a decision to focus on:

- Building personal visual arts self-efficacy.
- Increasing visual arts knowledge.
- Embracing constructivist theories and social learning approaches.

- Accepting that art is a language which can be learned and that everyone has creative potential.
- Becoming willing to model visual arts methods and techniques with children.
- Advocating for the visual arts to be valued as highly as other curriculum areas.
- Engaging in visual arts professional development.

Developing a growth mindset

One very important factor in overcoming low visual arts self-efficacy is a person's mindset. Dweck (2007) explains that we can either apply a growth mindset or a fixed mindset to any new learning opportunity. People with a growth mindset believe that intelligence can be developed through effort and practice. A person exercising a growth mindset perseveres through difficulty and considers mistakes to be an opportunity for learning. Alternatively, those with a fixed mindset believe their current intelligence or skills are unlikely to improve greatly through effort or experience. People with a fixed mindset tend to avoid risk-taking or stepping out of their comfort zone because they fear judgment from others and would rather avoid challenges than risk feeling or appearing incompetent.

Of course, we are all capable of having a fixed or growth mindset at different times in our lives and in different learning domains. Everyone has a mixture of fixed and growth mindset beliefs, and the balance is ever-changing and evolving

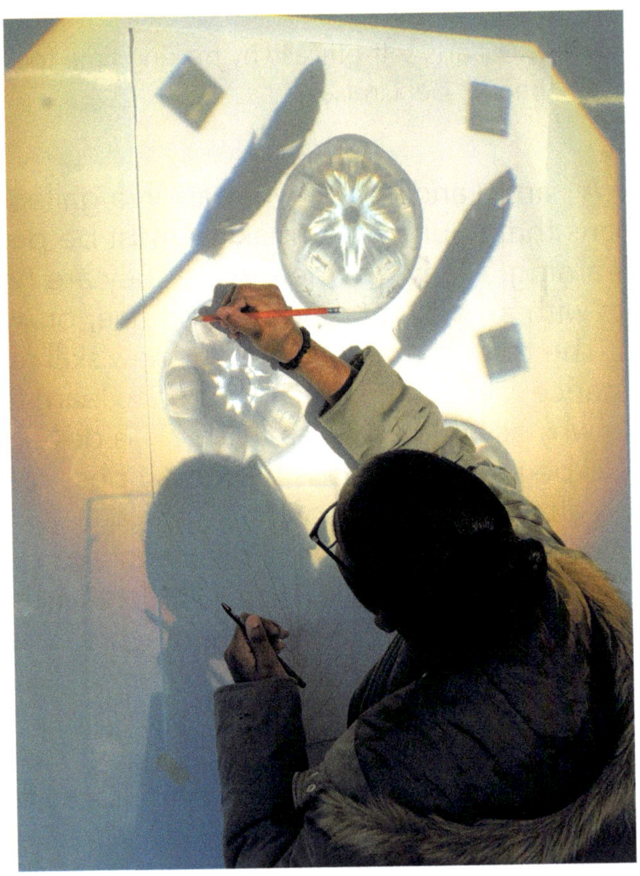

Figure 4.3 If drawing seems intimidating, educators can begin by playing with other aspects of art and mark-making. Here, an educator traces projected objects, exploring light, shadow, shape and line [Image: Gai Lindsay].

as a result of different experiences. However, it is possible to shift fixed beliefs and exercise and maintain a growth mindset for both our own benefit and to support others to develop growth mindset thinking (Dweck, 2007).

Educators play a crucial role in shaping children's attitudes toward learning, making it essential to reflect on our own mindset and self-efficacy in relation to our own ability to understand, create, and discuss visual arts. By reflecting on your underlying visual arts mindset, you can actively shift your attitude towards growth mindset thinking and allow yourself to relax into being a visual arts learner – willing to practice and make mistakes – and to learn through trial and error. This is equally important for those who already enjoy art-making and other creative activities. For example, someone who is confident to draw may have a fixed mindset about their ability with other art materials and techniques. By challenging our own fixed mindset regarding the visual arts, we are less likely to unintentionally trigger a fixed mindset in others.

Strategies to overcome low visual arts self-efficacy

Fortunately, both self-efficacy and mindset are constantly evolving, and there are a range of strategies you can explore to build greater confidence in your ability to engage with and teach the visual arts. These strategies can help both individuals and teaching teams to examine their beliefs about the visual arts and develop confidence to use visual arts materials and to make art.

Reflection exercise 1: Individual journaling

Examining and reflecting upon our personal experiences can help to identify factors that may have shaped our underlying beliefs about visual arts, as well as our perceptions of our potential in this domain (Garvis & Pendergast, 2011). This is helpful because when we disrupt self-limiting beliefs, we can develop confidence and embrace new approaches.

For this exercise, choose some paper and a writing tool that feels pleasing to use – something responsive and tactile such as a fine-line ink pen or a thick, soft pencil. Consider the questions below and remember that there are no right or wrong answers! This is an open-ended exploration. You may choose to set aside some time to work through all of these questions in one session, or perhaps spend time every few days reflecting and writing your responses. Consider doodling and drawing as well as writing, because drawing activates thinking and supports information processing (Fan et al., 2023).

- Write about the experiences and memories that have shaped your visual arts identity.
  - Describe any memories of a time when praise about your visual arts efforts made a positive impact on you.
  - Can you describe a time when critique of your visual arts efforts crushed your self-belief?
  - How have these experiences impacted your current confidence with art making?

- Think and write about the various ways you have enjoyed art and aesthetics in your life.
  - Alongside traditional arts, how have colour, architecture, crafting, food, nature, or film moved you?
- List the kinds of art you are exposed to through family, culture, traditions, and the cultural and community context you live in.
  - Are there art forms you have barely noticed because they are so familiar?
  - Are there art forms you treasure and why?
- How do you like to be creative?
  - In which domains do you feel most confident in your ability to be creative, and what factors helped you to develop confidence?
- As you reflect on your responses, how do you think these experiences have shaped the ways you currently teach the visual arts?
- Spend a few minutes writing a vision for the kind of teacher of the arts you aspire to be with children.

Reflection exercise 2: Developing shared understanding

Environments for teaching visual arts with young children often require collaboration with other adults. Many people reading this book will be working alongside other educators in schools and early education settings. While developing a positive self-identity as a visual arts educator is important, classroom pedagogy and practice are strongly influenced by the visual arts beliefs and identities of colleagues in the teaching team. Your individual identity development can be limited or expanded by your team's visual arts education understandings and practices. In a team-teaching environment, it is beneficial to establish a shared strategy and mutual understanding regarding your approach to visual arts pedagogy. When shared dialogue leads to shared understandings, teams will articulate and enact shared visual arts education methods; and children will benefit from consistent and strong visual arts education.

Three key elements support teams to develop a shared approach to visual arts pedagogy:

1. **Leadership**: Those in leadership positions have a powerful influence over the ways teams develop shared vision and understanding for visual arts (Denee, 2023; Lindsay, 2017). Leaders can support the development of shared visual arts pedagogy by mentoring, coaching, providing resources, structuring time, and sharing responsibility. In consultation with the team, leaders can ensure the visual arts are explicitly highlighted in policy documents, philosophy statements, and programme planning (Chapter 5 discusses philosophy statements and programme planning in greater detail).

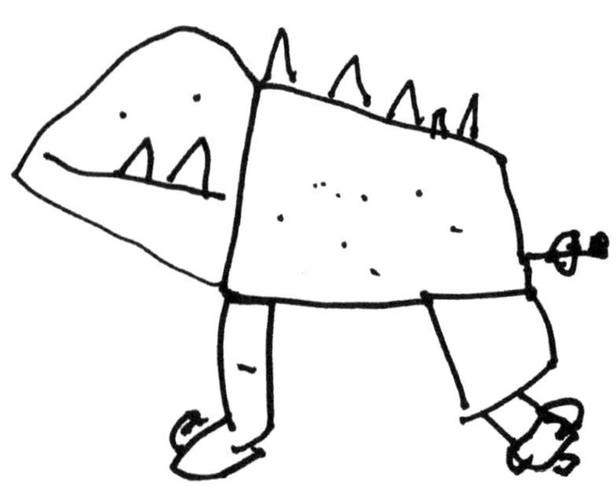

2. **Professional dialogue**: Professional dialogue, both formal and informal, is essential for developing shared understandings (Denee, 2024). Teams can schedule meetings to discuss a reading (such as a page or chapter from this book!) or to explore a current challenge or opportunity in the learning program. Informal opportunities arise daily, and casual conversations can be powerful for understanding each other's approaches, sharing different perspectives, encouraging one another, and expressing enthusiasm and joy about children's visual arts learning.
3. **Professional development**: Professional learning often occurs through everyday dialogue about pedagogy and practice, such as reflecting in teams about a reading or a specific situation. Both teachers and leaders have the ability to plan and facilitate relevant, contextual in-service professional learning for their teams. Outside experts and off-site courses offer further enrichment, new ideas, and expanded perspectives.

The following reflection questions are offered to spark professional dialogue amongst teaching teams regarding visual arts pedagogy and practice:

- What learning benefits for young children result from visual arts experiences?
- Which visual arts materials and processes do we each enjoy using the most and feel confident about when facilitating children's visual arts learning?
- What visual arts skills could we teach each other?
- What aspects of the visual arts space make you feel stressed or uncertain, and what teaching practices would you like more support in developing?
- Can you think of someone whose visual arts teaching practice you have admired and learned from in the past? What was inspiring and effective about their approach?
- If our visual arts program was outstanding, what would we observe and what would be happening?

Practical exercises for developing visual arts knowledge

The following exercises are designed to help you build confidence and skills with arts materials while deepening your understanding of their potential. By engaging with these materials as an adult, you begin to explore their possibilities and challenges, fostering a personal connection that will enrich your teaching practice. Such firsthand experiences support you to have meaningful and authentic conversations with children about their artmaking, as you are able to draw from your own play, exploration, and discoveries. As your familiarity with materials and processes grows, so too will your ability to approach art activities with greater preparation, confidence, and comfort.

These exercises are flexible and can all be completed either in one session or in a series of sessions. To get the most out of the process, set up a relaxed, distraction-free environment and allow plenty of time to fully engage. Whether you choose to work individually, as part of an educational team or with a group of friends, these activities offer a valuable opportunity to rediscover the joy of artmaking while building capacity to support children's creative learning.

Exercise 1:

Go for a walk outdoors and gather a small collection of leaves, shells or other natural treasures that inspire you. Sit quietly and closely observe and notice the patterns, lines, textures, and colours of the collected objects. Consider the range of materials and mark-making styles you could use to draw in response to these items. Play around with arranging the collected objects in ways that are visually pleasing to you. Arranging patterns of collected objects, known as ephemeral art, does not need to be representational, freeing you up to simply notice and enjoy the beauty of the items and the designs you create.

Exercise 2:

Choose a lovely thick piece of quality art paper, from your resource cupboard or an art supply shop. Gather three different mark-making tools such as a drawing pencil, charcoal, ink pen, or oil pastel. Experiment with the drawing materials. What do they feel like in your hand? What different kinds of marks can you make on the paper? Refrain from attempting to draw a particular representational image. Slow down and immerse yourself in the process, with no completed artwork in mind. This process is just about exploring the materials and making marks. Simply become absorbed in research, experimentation, non-representational mark making, and pattern making with this combination of materials over a sustained period of time.

Exercise 3:

Combine exercises one and two and explore your collection of natural materials using the paper and drawing tools. Experiment with tracing around leaves and your collected items. Focus on replicating the fine lines and shading you might not ordinarily notice. Draw without any intention to show your drawing to others. Remember that early explorations with materials are rarely an artists' final product and getting caught up with the idea of exhibition or performance can create fixed mindset barriers to growth and learning. Learn about art, by making "unfinished" art – and lots of it! (Bayles & Orland, 2023). Spend time playing with multiple ways to represent the collected items on the paper. If you feel unsure about starting to draw, loosen up, and reject the goal of perfection, by drawing without looking at the page (known as blind contour drawing), or try drawing in a continuous line without taking the drawing tool off the paper.

Sustained visual arts practice

Building confidence in the visual arts is a gradual process that thrives on regular practice, curiosity, and a willingness to experiment. Starting a sketchbook is an excellent way to explore materials, experiment with patterns, and sketch everyday scenes or items (natural or manufactured) in a low-pressure, enjoyable way. By thinking of your sketchbook as a space for fun and experimentation, rather

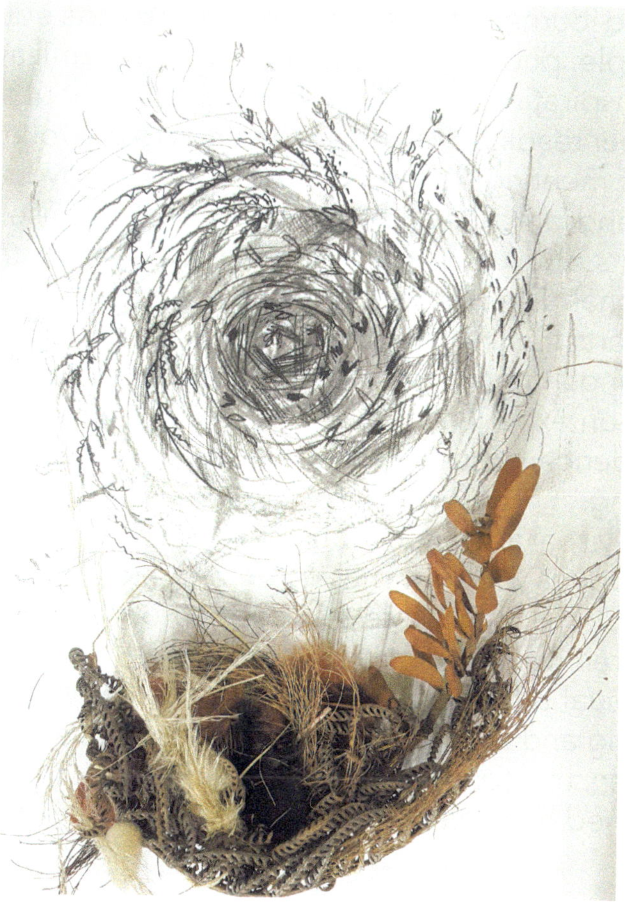

Figure 4.4 Drawing can be loose and fun, and does not need to look like a photograph. This sketch of dried leaves playfully uses varying mark weights to depict leaves, lines, movement, and shadows [Image: Rachel Denee].

than a place to create "great art," you can let go of perfectionism and focus on creative play. Simple challenges, like making a small drawing each day or creating visual diaries to capture key moments of the week, can help to establish a consistent and enjoyable habit of arts practice. Additionally, collecting inspiring images and visiting art galleries can broaden your perspective and deepen your understanding of what art can be, offering fresh ideas and sources of motivation. This approach not only builds your confidence over time but also nurtures a lifelong appreciation for the visual arts.

Supporting team professional development

To support educators to develop and enhance their visual arts pedagogy and practice, it is important to create a strong foundation of shared knowledge and resources. Consider the following strategies to support teams of educators to build a visual arts centred curriculum:

- Develop an induction pack for new staff which contains helpful readings, the service philosophy, and policy documents that articulate the importance of visual arts pedagogies.

- Collect books and journal articles focused on visual arts education for the staff library. For example, publications about the Reggio Emilia Approach provide a rich source of inspiration. The reference lists throughout this book offer suggestions for further reading. Use these readings to provoke conversations and reflection at staff meetings. Share key quotes and provocations about visual arts pedagogy and practice with educators and to raise parent awareness about the benefits of visual arts learning experiences for their children.
- Shared professional development opportunities, where a team of educators engage in visual arts training together, will align everyone's understanding and approach, fostering a cohesive and collaborative culture of visual arts learning. In-house, hands-on experiences with art materials and tools will further build the team's confidence, ensuring they are well-equipped to support children's visual arts learning.
- Invite artists and visual arts education consultants to model and demonstrate visual arts techniques, both with children and staff in the classroom and in staff training sessions. Being able to observe how to implement arts experiences with children builds educators' confidence and willingness to engage themselves in visual arts experiences with children. When adults engage in visual arts learning and artmaking as co-partners, co-learners, and facilitators alongside children, this communicates to children that the arts matter and that they can be learned and celebrated.

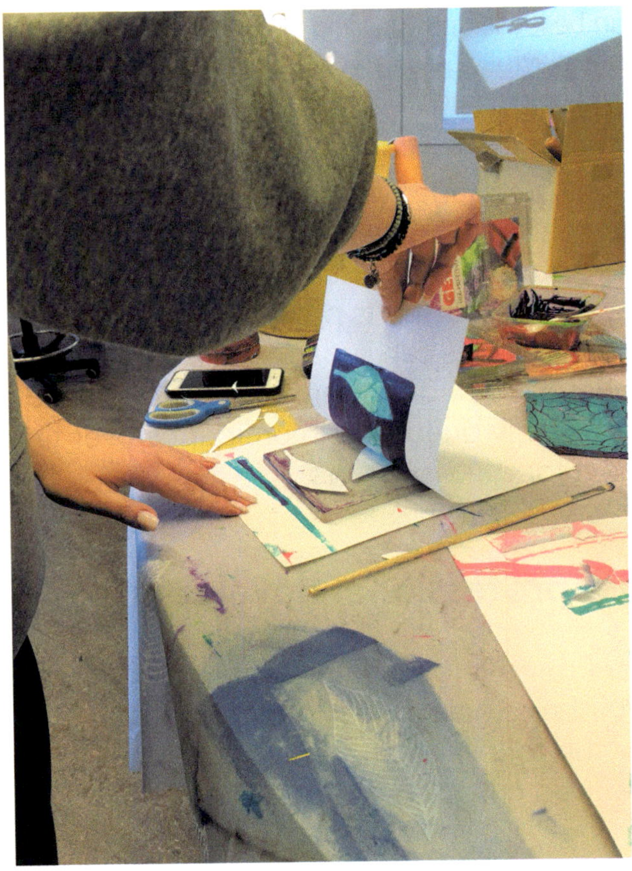

Figure 4.5 A printmaking workshop provides educators with new skills and inspiration for extending children's art learning [Image: Gai Lindsay].

- Some educational settings employ visual arts practitioners. However, these experts often only interact with groups of children for short periods of time while teachers perform other duties. We urge educators in settings with this wonderful resource to collaborate with and learn from the visual arts expert. As well as children going to the studio, bring the artist educator into the classroom so that both children and the adults who work with them can learn together about the art of teaching art. Children learn by doing and observing, and so do educators!
- Prioritise attendance at conferences and professional learning opportunities that present the latest research and practice for quality visual arts. Seek out training opportunities that provide practical, hands-on experience with materials and visual arts processes.
- Regular team meetings should include time dedicated to discussing visual arts pedagogy and practice, creating opportunities for educators to share their successes, thinking, and documentation. This not only celebrates their work but also supports cross-pollination of ideas, sparking new approaches throughout the setting.

Developing a professional learning community

Creating a professional learning community (PLC) focused on visual arts pedagogy offers a powerful avenue for collaborative growth and development. Such a community might consist of a single educational team within a single classroom, a group of educators located across a broader setting, or even educators from multiple services or schools within a community. The key is to foster an environment where current visual arts practices are actively interrogated through reflection, discussion, and hands-on opportunities for material play and exploration, skills-building, and artmaking. A well-coordinated PLC is ideally led by someone with visual arts expertise or a team member who can connect with artists, researchers, and other experts in your community to provide a range of provocative and inspiring learning experiences. One of the greatest strengths of a PLC is its sustained nature, allowing educators to collectively reflect, discuss, and learn about visual arts materials and techniques; and allowing time to experiment with these concepts in their work with children before returning to share and reflect again together (Denee, 2024). This cyclical process supports deeper learning and professional growth over time, while cultivating a collegial and supportive atmosphere where creativity and innovation can thrive.

Conclusion

When educators intentionally practice skills and seek new knowledge, they develop the confidence needed to thrive in the visual arts. This journey is not just about acquiring technical abilities – it's about grounding your identity as someone who can inspire and guide others to explore and learn through the visual arts. This book aims to support you in building that confidence by providing a foundation of knowledge, practical strategies, and a toolkit of skills.

We encourage you to embrace the joy of experimenting with various arts languages, not to become a professional artist (unless that's your goal!), but to become a confident, enthusiastic, and informed visual arts educator. As you explore these ideas and practices, reflect on how you can inspire creativity and curiosity in the children you teach. Remember, your willingness to play, learn, and grow alongside children will create the most meaningful and rewarding experiences – for them and for you. Now, take the first step, pick up a material that intrigues you, and let the adventure begin!

References

Bandura, A. (1997). *Self-efficacy: The exercise of control.* W.H. Freeman and Company.

Bandura, A. (2012). On the functional properties of perceived self-efficacy revisited. *Journal of Management, 38*(1), 9–44. https://doi.org/10.1177/0149206311410606

Bayles, D., & Orland, T. (2023). *Art and fear: Observations on the perils (and rewards) of artmaking.* Souvenir Press.

Denee, R. (2023). Distributed leadership across a network professional learning community. *Journal of Educational Leadership, Policy and Practice, 37*(1), 76–92. https://doi.org/10.2478/jelpp-2023-0005

Denee, R. (2024). The network professional learning community approach: An effective model for individual And group learning. *Teacher Development, 28*(3), 1–17. https://doi.org/10.1080/13664530.2024.2307588

Denee, R., Lindsay, G., & Probine, S. (2024). Visual arts self-efficacy: Impacts and supports for early childhood teachers. *Early Childhood Education Journal, 52*(6), 1035–1045. https://doi.org/10.1007/s10643-023-01489-5

Dweck, C. (2007). The perils and promises of praise. *Educational Leadership, 65*(2), 34–39. https://maryschmidt.pbworks.com/f/Perils+of+Praise-Dweck.pdf

Fan, J. E., Bainbridge, W. A., Chamberlain, R., & Wammes, J. D. (2023). Drawing as a versatile cognitive tool. *Nature Reviews Psychology, 2*(9), 556–568. https://doi.org/10.1038/s44159-023-00212-w

Garvis, S., & Pendergast, D. (2011). An investigation of early childhood teacher self-efficacy beliefs in the teaching of arts education. *International Journal of Education and the Arts, 12*(9), 1–15.

Lindsay, G. (2017). *Art is experience: An exploration of the visual arts beliefs and pedagogy of Australian early childhood educators* [Doctoral dissertation, University of Wollongong] https://ro.uow.edu.au/theses1/170

Lindsay, G. (2021). Visual arts pedagogy in early childhood contexts: The baggage of self-efficacy beliefs, pedagogical knowledge and limited pre-service training. *Australasian Journal of Early Childhood, 41*(6), 80–92. https://doi.org/10.1177/1836939120979061.

McArdle, F. (2012). The visual arts: Ways of seeing. In S. Wright (Ed.), *Children, meaning-making and the arts* (2nd ed., pp. 30–56. Pearson Australia.

Probine, S. (2020). Examining the in-between: Contextual factors on how young children learn through the visual arts [Doctoral dissertation, University of Auckland]. http://hdl.handle.net/2292/52825

Probine, S. (2023). Becoming an artist/teacher: Supporting pre-service teachers to develop their confidence and pedagogical knowledge to effectively and actively teach the arts in early childhood. *Journal of Early Childhood Teacher Education*, *44*(1), 1–21. https://doi.org/10.1080/10901027.2021.1963890

Probine, S. (2024). Colouring outside the lines: Re-exploring the teacher's role in visual arts learning in early childhood. *NZ International Research in Early Childhood Education Journal*, *26*(1), 14–29. https://oece.nz/members/research/2024-nzirece-journal/teacher-role-visual-arts/

Robinson, K. (2001). Mind the gap: The creative conundrum. *Critical Quarterly*, *43*, 41–45. https://doi.org/10.1111/1467-8705.00335

Part 2

WHAT to do and think about when developing a visual arts curriculum

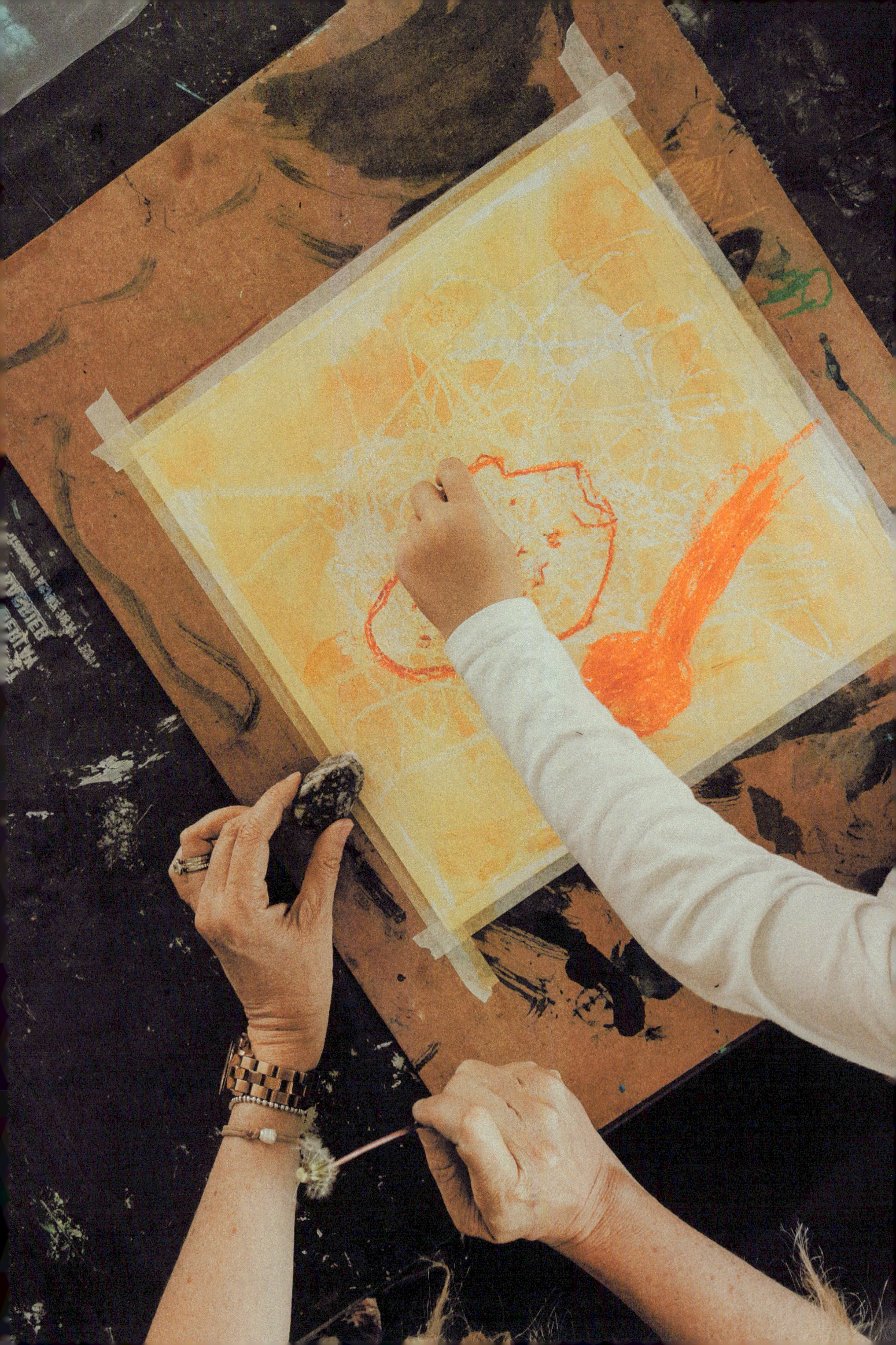

5 Artful Pedagogy

The role of the educator

To intentionally support children's visual arts play and inquiry requires a knowledgeable partner who plans for meaningful visual arts learning experiences, and evaluates the impact on children's learning and development. Postwar approaches to art education, developed for children's art therapy contexts, suggested that adults should avoid intervening in children's creative processes. However, while there are times when it may be preferable to foster children's free play and exploration with arts materials, an educator's responsibility is also to be an active co-learner and co-researcher with children. Observation, documentation, and reflection about children's learning experiences fosters deeper understanding about children's progress and informs planning for future learning experiences that support each child's unique potential.

Creating rich contexts for learning in and through the arts is a professional duty which demands active and informed intentional teaching. This chapter explores the role of the educator in developing inspiring and authentic visual arts learning experiences with children. It outlines the reflective thinking and practical steps educators can take to become confident and knowledgeable facilitators, designers, and co-constructors of children's artistic learning.

A choice to make

Conflicting messages about what is considered to be appropriate practice significantly influences how educators approach teaching visual arts with children. For example, some educators firmly believe it is not appropriate to teach visual arts techniques or to offer suggestions to children as they create. Others think it is not appropriate to "intervene" in children's creative processes in any way. On the other hand, educators who embrace constructivist approaches actively participate alongside children in visual arts experiences; choosing to model, demonstrate, and make suggestions to support children's engagement. Some quote the often-heard phrase, "it's the process, not the product," while others value both process and product. Some refuse to allow structured activities, while others justify them for a range of reasons. It's no wonder that many educators feel unsure about what is okay and what isn't when it comes to visual arts

---

Figure 5.1 Meaningful visual arts experiences thrive when educators actively engage as co-learners and co-researchers [Image: Bomaderry Community Preschool].

DOI: 10.4324/9781003561835-7

planning and practice (Richards & Terreni, 2022). So, is there a "right way" or a "wrong way" to implement visual arts experiences with children? The answer is not straightforward or simple! Like most things, thinking about meaningful visual arts learning and teaching requires deep critical reflection. What works or makes sense in one setting or culture may differ in other contexts.

When educators actively role model the dispositions of artists, and position themselves as researchers of young children's learning, they are well-placed to partner with children in meaningful and joyful visual arts learning experiences (Kind, 2018; Probine, 2022). McArdle (2012) emphasises the need to intervene, model, and demonstrate skills in order to effectively scaffold children's understanding and support their development. This aligns with Tarini and White's (1998, p. 379) reminder that:

> Reggio educators would say that it is not always sufficient to put materials, even provocative ones, on a table and expect that children are going to make cognitive leaps on their own. Surely this does occur at times, and free exploration is an integral part of any program (as is the case in the Reggio classrooms) but constructed situations are also important.

This truth, that educator's intentional teaching and curriculum design are central to the provision of meaningful and rich learning experiences, highlights the need to revisit the philosophies and beliefs that drive intentional teaching in and with the visual arts.

Developing a visual arts philosophy

In Chapter 4, we discussed strategies for exploring and shifting personally held beliefs and attitudes about the visual arts as a domain of practice. Developing new approaches to visual arts pedagogy begins with reflecting on both personal and organisational philosophies about teaching, about children and how they learn, and about the role of the educator. A philosophy statement communicates the core values, beliefs, and approaches that guide educators' work with children. It provides a foundation for decision-making, shaping how educators plan and implement learning experiences, interact with children and families, and create inclusive and meaningful environments. A well-articulated philosophy inspires reflective practice, ensures consistency across teaching practices, and helps educators align their work with broader educational goals and principles. It also serves as a tool for communicating the unique vision and priorities of an educational setting to families and the community. Decisions about supporting children's learning in the visual arts are shaped, consciously or unconsciously, by the beliefs, training, theoretical perspectives, philosophical views, and past visual arts experiences of the adults who work with children. For example, participants in Lindsay's (2017) research recalled the negative self-efficacy impacts of hearing well-meaning, but critical comments made by teachers during art education lessons, while others recalled how engaging in well-supported visual arts learning experiences built their positive attitude toward artmaking. As you consider inclusions for a visual arts philosophy of practice, it can be helpful to reflect on the teachers who best supported or challenged your learning, and nurtured your potential. Drawing upon a range of theoretical perspectives can also guide philosophical choices. Such reflection offers valuable insights for evaluating current educational practices and pedagogical choices.

At the core of a philosophy of teaching are educator beliefs about children and how they learn. An understanding of children as competent, capable, and active learners forms the foundation for teaching and learning approaches in any domain. Malaguzzi (1993, p. 10) reminds us that all children are "rich in potential, strong, powerful, competent, and, most of all, connected to adults and other children." He noted educators have the responsibility to maintain an image of the "strong and beautiful" child (Malaguzzi, 1994, p. 5). Similarly, Esteban-Guitart and Moll (2014) note that all children have the right to be valued for their unique identities, ideas, and funds of knowledge. Rather than positioning artmaking as a skill only accessible to those deemed to be talented, the visual arts empower joyful and meaningful learning for all children, allowing everyone to develop creative and expressive abilities.

Developing a clear philosophy about the value of visual arts languages will ground a culture of rich visual arts learning and foster a shared approach to embedding the visual arts across the curriculum. To develop a philosophy that articulates visual arts play and inquiry consider the following suggestions:

- **Review the service or school philosophy and policy documents**: Begin by evaluating whether these documents include a clear focus on visual arts pedagogy, practice, and the role of educators in supporting children's visual arts play and inquiry.
- **Explore educational philosophies and theories**: Investigate a range of educational philosophies and theories, such as the Reggio Emilia approach, inquiry-based learning, and constructivism, to reflect on values and practices that support children's visual arts learning. Such research can clarify educators' beliefs and intentions.
- **Engage in reflection**: Take time to support educators to reflect on their value for, and approach to visual arts education. Consider how personal beliefs and attitudes align with, or contradict, educational theories and current practices in the service.
- **Facilitate group discussions**: Transition from individual reflection to team dialogue. Share ideas with colleagues to build a more cohesive approach, discussing common values, challenges, and goals for visual arts education.

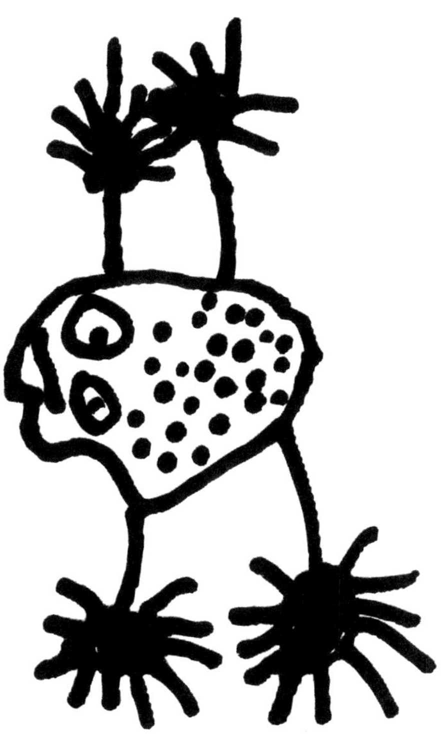

- **Create a collective vision**: Use these discussions to form a collective vision for how visual arts will be positioned and practised in your setting. Ensure that the resulting philosophy reflects the diverse perspectives and expertise of the team.
- **Refine and implement the philosophy**: Once a shared vision has been defined, refine it into a practical, actionable philosophy that guides a child-centred, holistic approach to visual arts teaching, ensuring it is flexible and evolves as it is implemented and evaluated.

Intentional teaching

The concept of intentional teaching underscores the informed and proactive responsibility of the educator (Epstein, 2007). The term "intention" emphasises the need to draw upon experience, knowledge about children's learning, pedagogical and learning domain knowledge, and knowledge of families and communities to plan for children's learning. Having a strong foundation of visual arts content knowledge, and a belief in the importance of the arts, empowers educators to intentionally create meaningful learning environments for young children, select appropriate art materials and processes, and in a nutshell, know what to teach and how to teach it (Probine, 2024). Table 5.1 summarises how beliefs and knowledge guide intentional teaching responses.

The most important way to extend intentional visual arts practice is to proactively build educator's visual arts content knowledge and practical skills. While it is not necessary for educators to become visual arts experts or professional artists,

Table 5.1 Pedagogical knowledge and beliefs inform intentional teaching

Beliefs and knowledge	Intentional teaching response
Children learn through active, hands-on experience.	Plan opportunities for exploring and playing with visual arts materials and tools.
Children are capable and agentic learners.	Facilitate opportunities for children to make their own choices and express their own ideas using visual arts materials. Empower children to initiate, plan, evaluate, and revisit their visual arts learning.
Children learn through cognitive conflict and problem-solving.	Create opportunities for children to experience trial and error experimentation as they explore working theories and work to solve their own problems.
Children learn through social collaboration and co-construction of knowledge.	Design visual arts experiences where children, educators, and even families can work together to explore concepts, share skills and knowledge, and embrace different perspectives.
Children learn through interaction with the educational environment.	Design the environment as an invitation and a provocation for rich visual arts learning and opportunities to play with, explore, and actively engage with a wide range of quality visual arts materials and tools.

their knowledge, enthusiasm, and willingness to explore and learn alongside children directly influence how children experience visual arts in the curriculum (Lindsay, 2023). When you intentionally role model open and playful approaches to visual arts engagement and share your appreciation for the arts, you can powerfully inspire children's interest, curiosity, and engagement with visual arts languages. Chapter 4 provides further strategies to develop your visual arts confidence and content knowledge.

Planning a visual arts curriculum

Planning meaningful and relevant visual arts experiences for children requires educators who observe, listen, and actively partner with children to support them to inquire about and make sense of their world, and communicate their ideas visually (Brooks, 2022a). Planned and spontaneous experiences should relate to and extend on children's interests, foster children's development, capabilities, and dispositions, and be aligned with the overarching educational goals of your setting and curriculum. Clark's (2023) advocacy for slow pedagogy, which emphasises the need to value unhurried time for learning, offers a reminder to allow time for meaningful, exploratory, and authentic visual arts experiences.

To plan meaningful visual arts experiences, it is helpful to consider your current context, the children's existing strengths, interests, and inquiries, along with your pedagogical intentions. What will a project of inquiry focus on? How might potential topics of inquiry emerge? Research local artists, community artworks and sites that could inspire children's inquiry and resulting artmaking. To extend children's visual arts learning through connections with artists, educators can explore the questions and working theories that emerge from the children's material and process explorations. Creating opportunities for children to share their thoughts and make their learning visible to one another fosters collaboration and deeper understanding (Probine, 2020; 2024). By selecting materials and processes that encourage meaningful engagement and aesthetic exploration, educators can design experiences that build on children's prior knowledge and experiences, inspiring further exploration, inquiry, and expression.

Careful preparation is key to implementing successful and enjoyable arts experiences for both children and educators. To achieve the learning goals of a planned experience, decide on the group size that will best support children's effective participation. Smaller groups usually allow for more meaningful adult interactions and reduce time and space management demands. However, it is good to remember that there may be times when you want to involve more children to inspire collaborative work and foster group energy and dynamics. Regardless of group size, make staffing decisions that enable an educator to remain present and supportive throughout the experience. Consider the quantity of materials required for the number of children and adults involved. Minimise waste and encourage respect for the materials offered. Set up the experience to support children to actively participate in cleaning up responsibilities. You can read more about practical planning strategies in Part 3 of this book.

Organising the environment

The physical and social environments designed by educators, and the choices made in those spaces, all communicate their value for teaching and learning with young children. The way spaces are designed can invite calm, creative, and engaged learning and play. When educators in Reggio Emilia call the learning environment the third teacher, they are acknowledging the constructivist notion that children learn through relationships with people, places, and materials (Edwards et al., 2012). The selection and arrangement of materials and the creation of contexts for visual arts learning convey important messages about the value placed on the visual arts and strongly influences what happens in practice (Richards & Terreni, 2022). Planning for meaningful visual arts learning requires attention to light, aesthetic choices, furniture, work surfaces, material selection and display, experience location, and practical cleaning and safety considerations.

Invitations for learning

Provocations offer invitations to explore, play, think, and learn through inquiry-based responses to questions, suggestions, problems, and challenges. A provocation differs from an activity that has a predetermined outcome because it invites childrens' participation, but does not dictate how children should use materials or engage in the experience (Stacey, 2019). A provocation should be designed to foster inquiry,

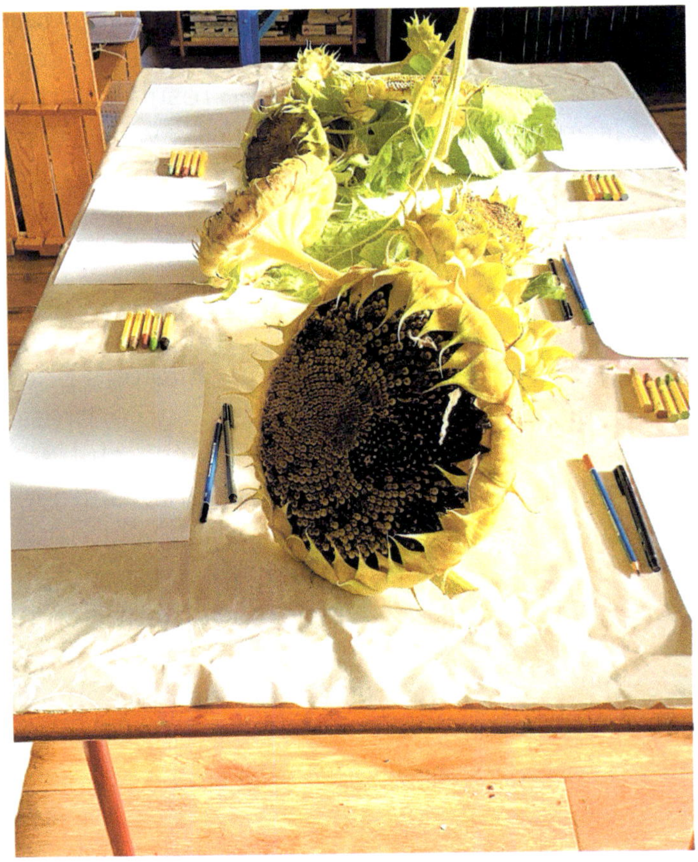

Figure 5.2 Thoughtfully arranged materials act as provocations—inviting children to explore, wonder, and express their ideas creatively [Image: Adrienne Wilkins, Sophia Preschool].

exploration, and wonder. In response to children's interests or inquiries, provocations can be offered spontaneously or thoughtfully pre-planned. For example, if children discover a caterpillar in the garden, you could gather magnifying glasses to look closely, support children to take close-up photos, and research caterpillars in books and online. Following this, as an invitation to explore and communicate their knowledge and ideas about caterpillars, printed caterpillar images could be presented along with paper, pens, and watercolour paints.

Children's choice and agency

Every child has unique preferences, dispositions, and developmental capacities, and just like adults, some children are drawn to sensory and tactile experiences or mess-making, while others may avoid them. When designing visual arts learning experiences, it is essential to consider each child's development and preferences, adapting activities to promote inclusion and encourage engagement. Rather than forcing participation, educators can create gentle invitations for children to explore by consistently offering the same materials over time to build familiarity and confidence. For example, a child who initially hesitates might eventually feel comfortable enough to join a charcoal drawing experience after observing it over several weeks. Educators must remain open to children's individual ways of interacting and communicating. Even with a planned activity in mind, such as exploring colour mixing on a light box with translucent papers and watercolour, an educator may observe a child who is more focused on layering papers and paint, demonstrating their curiosity about how the paper changes form. Rather than forcing a set outcome, it is crucial to be flexible enough to expand upon children's natural curiosity and sense of agency to drive responsive and meaningful exploration of materials.

Being present and active

As outlined in Chapter 3, socio-cultural theories highlight the important role of relationships in learning. Brooks (2022a) reminds us that socio-cultural theories provoke us to remain pedagogically active as children explore visual arts materials. Both educators and children bring existing funds of identity and knowledge (i.e. the historical, cultural, and social experiences that form a person's self-awareness and self-expression) to every learning experience (Esteban-Guitart & Moll, 2014). Therefore, in a community of learners, it is important to value the unique knowledge, skills, and life experiences educators and children can share as they learn to express their ideas in multiple ways. The challenge is to ensure a balance between child-led experiences and purposeful adult guidance. Too much adult direction can lead to children becoming overly reliant on others for instruction and losing confidence in their own capabilities and skills. On the other hand, offering no guidance at all limits children's opportunities for meaningful learning and skills development. When adults facilitate open-ended experiences and offer sensitive guidance, children develop agency and the confidence to express themselves using visual arts materials and processes. Embrace the role of a co-learner and co-researcher by expressing genuine curiosity and wonder alongside children

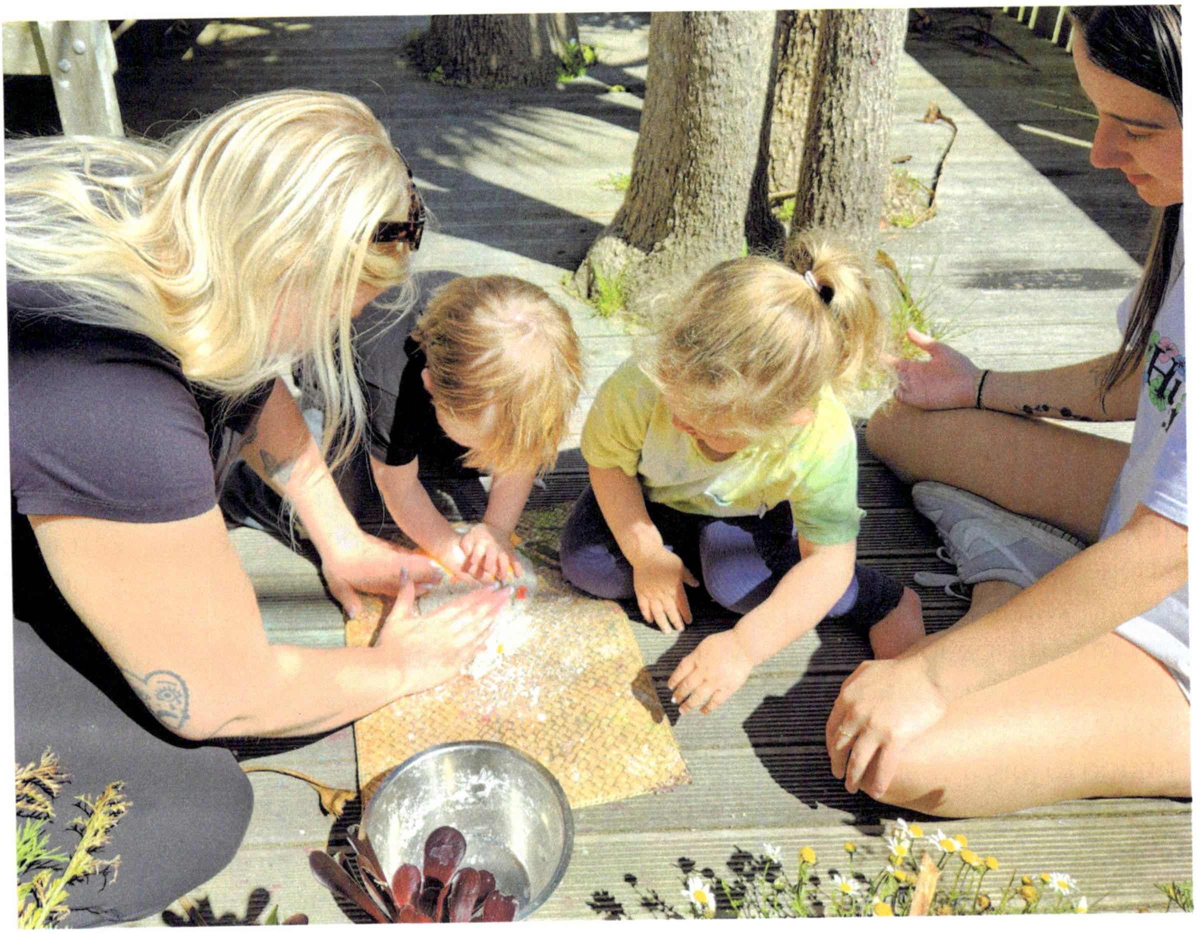

Figure 5.3 When educators join children in exploring materials, they model curiosity and creativity, encouraging children to take risks, explore ideas, and build confidence in their own capabilities [Image: Daisies Early Education & Care Centre].

(Kind, 2018). This approach fosters an environment where children feel supported to explore their ideas, take risks, and view mistakes as valuable steps in the learning journey. Intentionally choosing to be present with children during artmaking experiences provides important opportunities for educators to:

- Observe, listen, and interact with children
- Actively engage with materials as co-players and explorers
- Model the language and vocabulary of arts tools and techniques
- Give feedback and encouragement
- Teach techniques in context
- Extend children's ideas and thinking
- Provide inspiration for further exploration of ideas and art-making processes

Talking to children about their artmaking

Talking to children about their artmaking presents rich opportunities for learning, problem-solving, and appreciation for children's thinking. There are times when it is best to sit quietly alongside children who are absorbed in their work. Equally important, educators must act on opportunities to talk with children about both their artwork and thinking (Brooks, 2022b). Deciding when to speak and how much to say is a delicate pedagogical balance, requiring thoughtful judgement about when to engage, question, and guide, and when to step back and let children lead their own learning and exploration. Constant talk and comments can risk dominating the process and interrupting children's flow. Instead, it is essential to slow down, observe, and make space for children's thinking. Allow your curiosity about children's knowledge, engagement, and development, along with your learning goals, guide you in deciding when to offer support or suggestions and when to encourage children to solve problems independently.

Engaging with art materials alongside children creates wonderful opportunities to talk about your own artmaking actions, processes, and challenges as a way to spark conversation (Knight, 2008). To build children's confidence and engagement, pose open-ended questions. Questions that start with "I wonder" are particularly effective because they allow space to hear children's unique ideas, without making assumptions about their actions or aims. Create a community of collaboration and shared inquiry by providing opportunities for children to share their thoughts with both peers and educators when working in groups. For example, when a child demonstrates a particular technique, invite them to share their new skill or discovery with their peers and offer specific comments about children's efforts.

When commenting on children's artwork, rather than offering praise about beautiful or creative products, affirm children's efforts, discoveries, and dispositions

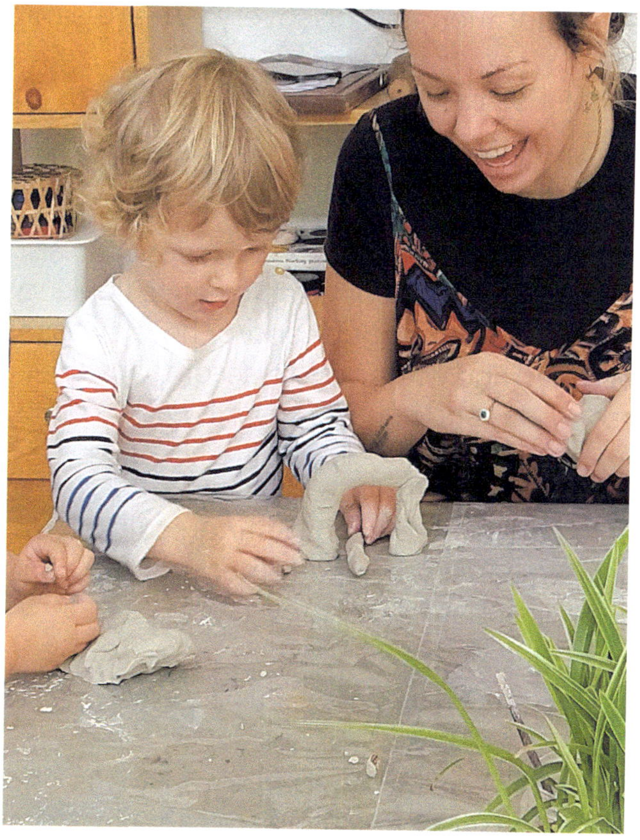

Figure 5.4 An educator's thoughtful engagement during artmaking fosters creativity and problem-solving. Open-ended questions and affirmations of children's effort encourage children to reflect on their choices, build confidence, and develop a deeper connection to their work [Image: Denise Savins, Saigon Kids Early Learning Centre].

for learning, such as problem-solving and persistence. Dweck (2007) notes that praising children for their intelligence (or an abstract notion like creativity) reduces motivation and resilience, and fosters fixed mindset vulnerabilities. If you want to comment on the product of children's work, focus on the art elements (such as colour, shape, line, texture, and pattern) the children have utilised and draw attention to their actions or choices. For example, rather than saying, "Oh, you are so creative!" (which gives children no specific information about what you actually value about their work), you could say things such as: "I'm so impressed with the way you worked hard to cover that big piece of paper with charcoal!"; "That shade of black is the darkest I have ever seen."; or, "I wonder how you made it so dark?" This kind of comment pays attention to children's efforts, ideas, and persistence and encourages learning dispositions that support creative thinking and learning. You can also express your own observations and wonderings about children's work, drawing attention to the elements of art and the principles of design that you notice. For example:

- I notice you're carefully pasting those shapes on top of each other
- I notice you've spent a long time working out how to join those pieces of clay together
- How did you make that line/shape/effect?
- I wonder if that shade of blue will fill up the whole area?
- When I use charcoal like this, I wonder what will happen. (Role-model the same types of free exploration and discovery you are aiming to encourage in the children).
- Let's look again, what else can you see?....Which shape do you want to make on the paper first?
- I wonder how we could make that join stronger?

Thoughtful "What if?" and "How might we?" questions can also be used to support children to brainstorm their ideas and develop creative thinking skills, and when finished their work, invite them to talk about it and/or how it was made. If children offer a story, this can be recorded and written up to accompany their artworks. Educators can encourage diverse stories and conversations by asking questions such as:

- I wonder if these marks tell a story?
- Would you like to tell me about your painting/sculpture?
- How did you feel when you worked with these materials?
- If your marks could talk, what would they say?

Being a reflective practitioner

The role of the educator in visual arts pedagogy involves ongoing critical reflection to ensure that planning and teaching are meaningful and child-centered. Being a responsive and reflective educator aligns with action research processes (Moss, 2018). By observing, documenting, discussing, and analysing children's play, learning, and development, educators engage in a reflective planning cycle that positions children's ideas and voices at the forefront and informs a responsive curriculum aligned with children's inquiry processes (Probine, 2024). It is essential to evaluate whether the visual arts experiences offered to children are meaningful and open-ended. For example, educators may reflect on:

- How children engaged with the experience, the environment, and the materials
- Whether the experience was manageable
- What might work better next time
- How children's ideas could be extended further with an art medium

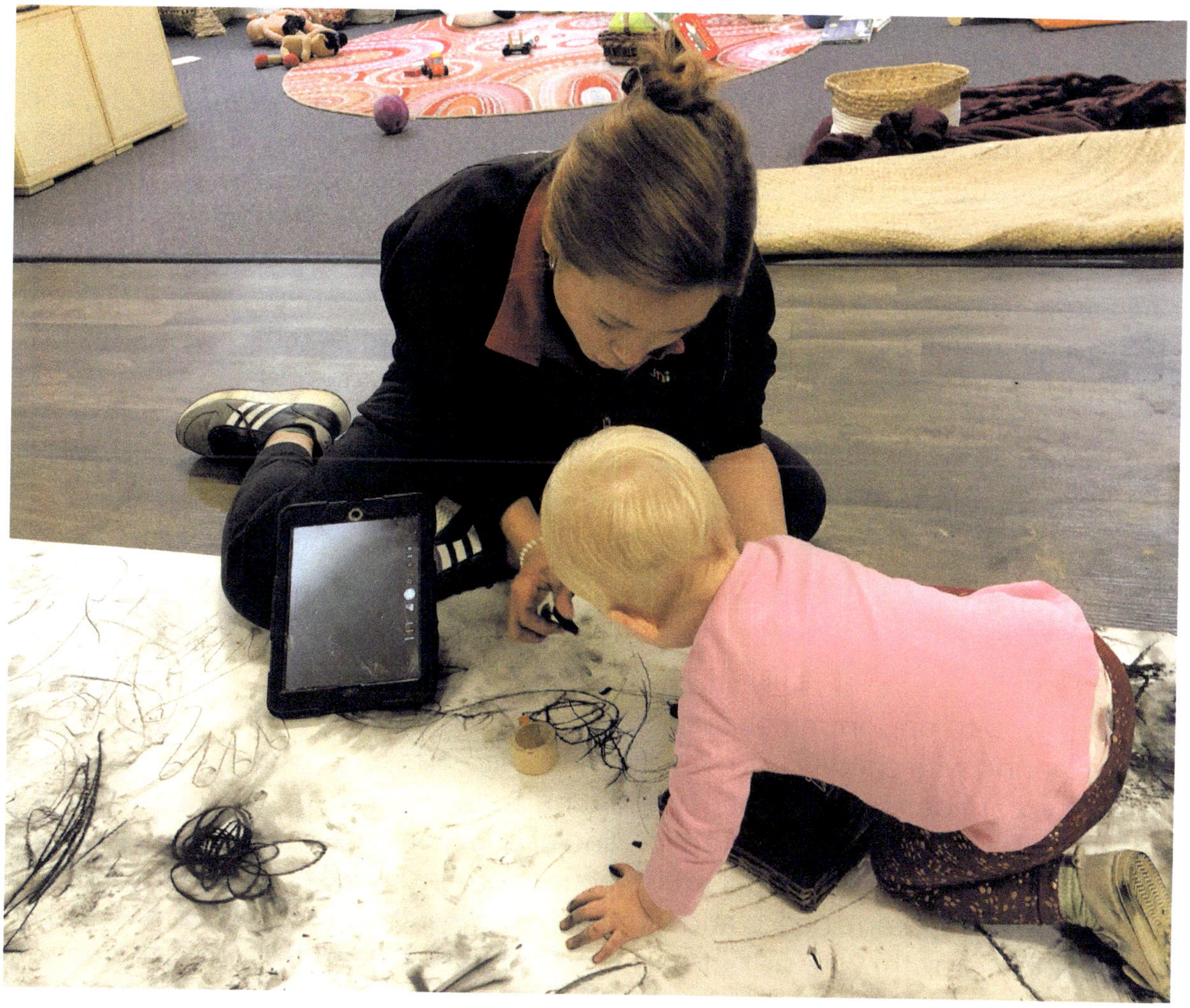

Figure 5.5 Reflective practice transforms visual arts pedagogy into a dynamic process of learning and growth. By documenting and analysing children's engagement, educators align teaching with children's interests and inquiries, fostering meaningful, open-ended exploration [Image: Gai Lindsay at UOW Kids Uni Pulse].

Evaluation and documentation

While children are engaged in play, educators should actively observe and assess their engagement and possible learning, noting that it is not possible to capture all of the learning that is occurring in a moment. One of the most important factors to evaluate is the effectiveness of the teaching methods employed, the alignment of programs with learning goals, and the organisation of activities to consider whether they aligned with children's interests and development. Such reflective practice and self-evaluation, as McArdle (2012) highlights, are essential for adapting teaching strategies and creating meaningful learning opportunities that promote holistic development.

Collecting, documenting, and evaluating information about children's interests and participation in visual arts inquiry is an act of pedagogical reflection and research in practice (Moss, 2018). These processes, often called pedagogical documentation, support educators to analyse and reflect on children's learning (Buldu, 2010; Moss, 2018). Documentation invites children and families to learn about and appreciate children's play, learning, and development. It also supports children to revisit their artwork, reminds them of their prior thinking and prompts them to continue their investigations around a particular project of inquiry. Educators play a critical role in supporting such processes when they carefully collect, curate, and document children's artwork and plan opportunities for small groups of children to talk about their art and revisit their learning. Other ways you can support children to revisit their prior thinking is to document their art-making processes using photography or video, and record their conversations through written observations. Recording and including children's dialogue enables later reflection about children's thinking. Displaying such documentation can foster children's conversations about their artwork and the ideas they have been exploring. Documentation can also remind children about learning strategies they previously used to solve problems and apply these strategies again in new contexts. (Chapter 7 provides additional reading about the use of documentation in projects of inquiry.)

Conclusion

When educators intentionally and reflectively plan for children's visual arts learning, they create opportunities for authentic, meaningful, and rich engagement. By partnering with children as co-learners and co-artists, you can empower their creativity, confidence, and agency while nurturing your own growth and joy in teaching. Through ongoing reflection and alignment with your service's philosophy, you can ensure that visual arts practices are intentional, open-ended, and responsive to children's needs and interests. By staying curious and committed to professional growth, you will not only enrich children's learning but also deepen your own practice. As you explore new ways to inspire and engage, remember that your role is pivotal in creating environments where children feel confident to express themselves and discover the endless possibilities of the visual arts.

References

Brooks, M. (2022a). *Drawing to learn*. Pademelon Press.

Brooks, M. (2022b). *Authentic art with children*. Pademelon Press.

Buldu, M. (2010). Making learning visible in kindergarten classrooms: Pedagogical documentation as a formative assessment technique. *Teaching and Teacher Education, 26*(7), 1439–1449. https://doi.org/10.1016/j.tate.2010.05.003

Clark, A. (2023). *Slow knowledge and the unhurried child: Time for slow pedagogies in early childhood education*. Routledge.

Dweck, C. (2007). The perils and promises of praise. *Educational Leadership, 65*(2), 34–39. https://maryschmidt.pbworks.com/f/Perils+of+Praise-Dweck.pdf

Edwards, C., Gandini, L., & Forman, G. Eds. 2012. *The hundred languages of children: The Reggio Emilia experience in transformation*. Praeger.
Epstein, A. S. (2007). *The intentional teacher*. National Association for the Education of Young Children.
Esteban-Guitart, M., & Moll, L. C. (2014). Funds of identity: A new concept based on the funds of knowledge approach. *Culture & Psychology, 20*(1), 31–48. https://doi.org/10.1177/1354067X13515934
Kind, S. (2018). Collective improvisations: The emergence of the early childhood studio as an eventful place. In C.M. Schulte & C.M. Thompson (Eds.), *Communities of practice: Art, play and aesthetics in early childhood* (pp. 5–22). Springer.
Knight, L. (2008). Communication and transformation through collaboration: Rethinking drawing activities in early childhood. *Contemporary Issues in Early Childhood, 9*(4), 306–316. https://doi.org/10.2304/ciec.2008.9.4.306
Lindsay, G. (2017). *Art is experience: An exploration of the visual arts beliefs and pedagogy of Australian early childhood educators* [Doctoral dissertation, University of Wollongong] https://ro.uow.edu.au/theses1/170
Lindsay, G. (2023). *Visual arts in early childhood settings. Everyday Learning Series. 21*(1). Early Childhood Australia.
Malaguzzi, L. (1993). For an education based on relationships. *Young Children, 49*(1), 9–12.
Malaguzzi, L. (1994). Your image of the child: Where teaching begins. *Child Care Information Exchange, 3*(1), 52–61.
McArdle, F. (2012). The visual arts: Ways of seeing. In S. Wright (Ed.), *Children, meaning-making and the arts* (2nd ed., pp. 30–56). Pearson Australia.
Moss, P. (2018). What might Loris Malaguzzi have to say? *European Journal of Education, 53*(1), 82–85. https://doi.org/10.1111/ejed.12256
Probine, S. (2020). Examining the in-between: Contextual factors on how young children learn through the visual arts [Doctoral dissertation, University of Auckland]. http://hdl.handle.net/2292/52825
Probine, S. (2022). How young children come to value and engage in the visual arts: Examining the impact of bi-directional interactions on children as imaginative visual researchers. *Early Childhood Education Journal, 50*(5), 795–809. https://doi.org/10.1007/s10643-021-01204-2
Probine, S. (2024). Colouring outside the lines: Re-exploring the teacher's role in visual arts learning in early childhood. *NZ International Research in Early Childhood Education Journal, 26*(1), 14–29. https://oece.nz/members/research/2024-nzirece-journal/teacher-role-visual-arts/
Richards, R. D., & Terreni, L. (2022). Intentionally supporting and extending young children's learning about and through the visual arts: Suggestions and strategies for early childhood education teachers. *Curriculum Matters, 18*(1), 88–106. https://doi.org/10.18296/cm.0061
Stacey, S. (2019). *Inquiry-based early learning environments: Creating, supporting, and collaborating*. Redleaf Press.
Tarini, E., & White, L., (1998). Looking in the mirror: A reflection of Reggio Emilia practice in Winnetka. In C. Edwards, L. Gandini & G. Forman (Eds.), *The Reggio Emilia approach - advanced reflections* (2nd ed., pp. 375–403). Ablex Publishing Corporation.

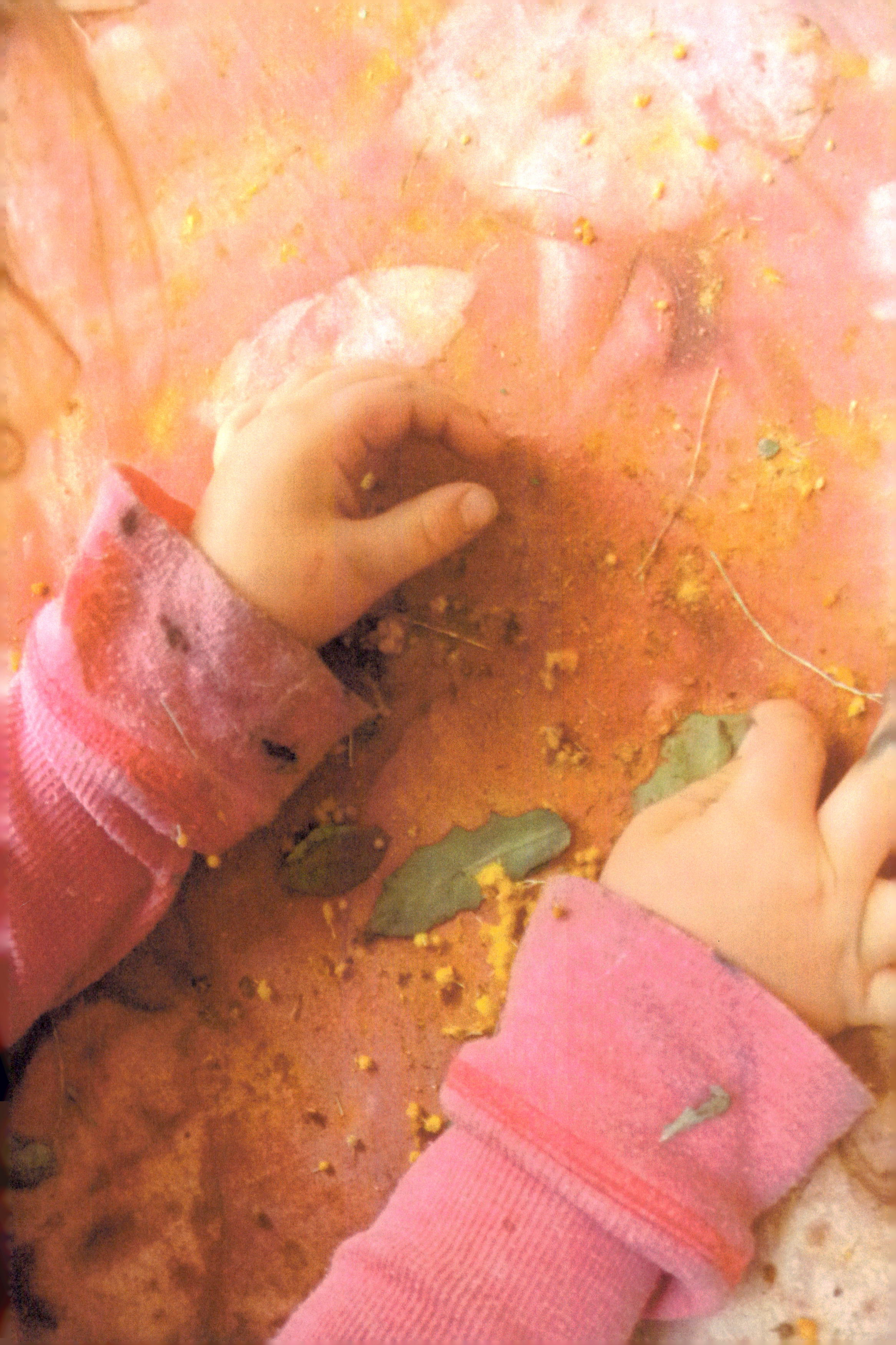

6 Aesthetic encounters and material research

From the moment they are born, children are driven by an innate curiosity to explore and make sense of the world around them. In the visual arts domain, this means that from infancy, children have the ability to investigate and explore materials using all of their senses. Open-ended and playful encounters with art materials support children to develop their creative preferences and strengthen their skills as researchers and thinkers. To support children to experience the rich potential of sensory and open-ended learning, educators can plan hands-on encounters with beautiful and interesting materials and encourage children's engagement in aesthetic experience. Through such explorations, important cognitive and social-emotional learning occurs as connections are developed between children, adults, materials, and the environment. Dewey (1915) emphasised the value of practical, hands-on, and playful learning, noting that children are naturally drawn to concrete experiences and real-world interactions. Aesthetic pedagogies also enrich educator's work, bringing joy and wonder into the environment and the curriculum. In this chapter, we explore the role of aesthetics, beauty, and rich sensory experiences in children's visual arts learning and consider what this means for educators' practice.

Developing aesthetic awareness

Aesthetic awareness is an important element of human experience and intelligence. Deeply embedded in art practice and art appreciation, aesthetic awareness also plays a significant role in our everyday experiences and encounters with the world. Beautiful materials, objects, and environments all have the potential to fascinate and enchant (Ferrari & Giacopini, 2005). When children and adults are drawn to a work of art, nature, an image, or the beautiful design of an object, they experience diverse sensory, emotional,

Figure 6.1 Invitations to notice, experience, and appreciate the beauty of everyday things inspire curiosity and nurtures the development of aesthetic awareness [Image: Bomaderry Community Preschool].

DOI: 10.4324/9781003561835-8

and intellectual responses to aesthetic qualities. Light, texture, pattern, colour, interesting objects, and beautiful things can arouse curiosity, heighten the senses, and inspire a sense of awe and wonder (Kind, 2014). Cultivating the skills to engage with, interpret, and appreciate diverse forms of art and beauty fosters aesthetic awareness and the development of artistic sensibilities.

> **"Unhurried and unstructured time to perceive things - through all the senses - is vital if we are to find magic and mystery in things with children" (Kolbe, 2007, p. 11).**

Adults play an important role in supporting the development of children's aesthetic awareness. A sensory-rich environment, and the careful arrangement of interesting materials, invites curiosity and draws attention to the importance of aesthetic encounters in children's lives and learning. With time and opportunities to connect and engage with the beauty of everyday things, children learn to slow down, be present in the moment, and engage deeply. Supported to observe and describe colours, textures, images, and forms, children develop aesthetic sensibilities and build the vocabularies to describe their aesthetic experiences (a'Beckett, 1991). Such aesthetic experiences engage the senses and elicit emotional and cognitive responses, bringing hands, hearts, and minds together to notice, respond to, and develop deeper understandings of the world.

Key aspects of aesthetic awareness and aesthetic appreciation include:

- **Sensory Perception:** Enjoyment of how something looks, sounds, feels, or engages the senses.
- **Emotional Response:** Feelings such as awe, joy, or calmness brought about by the object or experience.
- **Cognitive Engagement:** Thinking about the meaning, purpose, or technique of an artwork.
- **Cultural and Personal Context:** Personal tastes, preferences, and cultural influences shape how we see, interpret, and value art and beauty.

Aesthetic encounters

Although the study of aesthetics is generally associated with the domains of art and philosophy, in the schools of Reggio Emilia in Italy, beauty and aesthetics are positioned as powerful contributors to knowledge-building across all learning domains (Ferrari & Giacopini, 2005). Vea Vecchi (2010, p. 5), a Reggio Emilia atelierista (visual arts specialist teacher) describes the value of aesthetic encounters for making meaning and developing aesthetic appreciation:

> Perhaps first and foremost it is a process of empathy relating the self to things and things to each other. It is like a slim thread or aspiration to quality that makes us choose one word over another, the same for a colour or shade, a certain piece of music, a mathematical formula or the taste of a

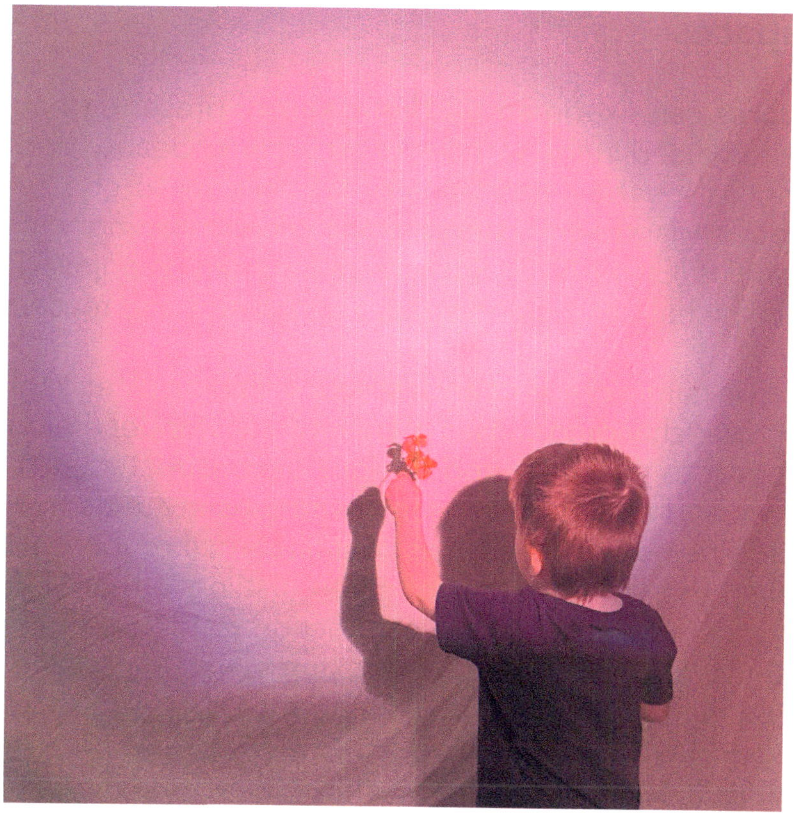

Figure 6.2 The practice of close observation and slow looking helps children to notice details that support discoveries and the development of knowledge [Image: Daisies Early Education & Care Centre].

> food. It is an attitude of care and attention for the things we do, a desire for meaning; it is curiosity and wonder; it is the opposite of indifference and carelessness, of conformity, of absence of participation and feeling.

The ability to perceive and appreciate the beauty in everyday objects and environments is an important life skill, with benefits extending beyond visual artmaking. Everyday experiences can be expanded and enriched when children are encouraged to develop their capacity for careful observation. For example, collecting wildflowers for the dining table or arranging shells on a windowsill invites close observation, attention to detail, and slowing down to appreciate life's simple pleasures.

Reflection: If you have ever drawn a deep breath as you delighted in the colour of a sunset, or been immersed in the velvety green texture of a new leaf, then you have appreciated beauty and have experienced an artistic way of looking at the world. The world is made up of colours, lines, forms, and textures. If your eye can take that in, if your hands can feel, if your spirit delights, and if your mind can wonder, then you can develop an artistic and aesthetic way of looking and support children to do the same.

Aesthetic spaces

Places and spaces can exude an aesthetic sense, presenting an invitation to pause and be immersed in the wonder of art, nature, beauty, and design. Slow pedagogy emphasises the importance of taking time to observe and notice, fostering deeper engagement, curiosity, and more meaningful connections to the world around us (Clark, 2023). Such invitations can be enjoyed in the natural environment, in the halls and grand spaces of galleries and museums, and even in classrooms.

Spending time in nature presents an aesthetic invitation by engaging the senses and offering an ever-changing canvas of beauty and wonder (Pelo, 2013). Nature provides a contrast to the structured designs of constructed spaces, offering a sense of renewal and awe. Multisensory invitations invite us to pause, notice, and appreciate intricate details, such as light filtering through leaves, the gentle curve of a river, or the varied shades of green rustling in the wind. Moments of aesthetic recognition awaken a deep connection to the environment, drawing us into its rhythms, colours, shapes, and textures. Keyte-Hartland and Lowings (2025) remind us that building rich, sensory, intra-active pedagogies in relation with nature supports relational knowing, wondering, and thinking in and with the world. By encouraging mindfulness and engagement, nature becomes not just a backdrop but an active participant in fostering children's sense of wonder and well-being.

Spending time in a gallery or museum provides another unique opportunity to slow down, be immersed in deep observation, reflect, and connect with the ideas and experiences of artists. Carefully curated spaces, with harmonious lighting, thoughtfully arranged exhibits, and reverent atmosphere, invite us to breathe more deeply, both physically and mentally. Such environments foster a sense of presence, where distractions fade, focus sharpens, and full engagement with artworks, artefacts, and their stories becomes possible. This immersion also aligns with the principles of slow pedagogy, fostering mindful observation and an unhurried appreciation of detail and meaning (Clark, 2023). In such spaces, we often find ourselves "in the zone," where time feels suspended, and we relate to the works on display. Experiencing connection with cultural and artistic life within communities, societies, and histories offers an aesthetic and contemplative experience that can nourish well-being and curiosity and uphold a human right educators are responsible to share with children (Lindsay, 2023). The rich potential of connecting with art in community and public spaces is further explored in Chapters 8 and 9.

Resources and time for aesthetic and material exploration

Spaces may be interpreted in a multitude of ways. Spaces may include the physical environment, the surfaces we paint or draw on, and the social environment. Consider the various contexts and spaces in which children explore art materials and how these may impact children's exploration and experience (Richards & Terreni, 2022). For example, what does it feel like to draw with a tiny pencil on a small square of paper, compared to using a large brush and wet paint on an expansive piece of calico? What happens if painting is done with broomsticks on a painting drop sheet instead of using paintbrushes on paper? Offer children varied spaces, resources, and contexts, so that they can explore materials and engage in aesthetic research. It is also important to slow down and allow plenty of time for children to engage deeply and repeatedly with materials; giving them time to closely observe and get to know the finer details of particular materials (Pacini-Ketchabaw et al., 2024).

Ideas for varied spaces and contexts:

- Offer children opportunities to draw on a variety of sizes and shapes, for example very large paper, small pieces of paper, circular paper, and long strips of paper, on tables, standing at easels, or sitting on the floor.
- Be mindful of the creative appeal for some children in using tiny materials and small paper.
- Create opportunities to work both individually and in large and small groups.
- Intentionally design experiences considering how younger and older children may physically explore the materials in different ways.
- Facilitate large movements and big open spaces for visual arts exploration.
- Create art opportunities for material exploration outdoors, in nature, on excursions, and in public places.

Material research

Sensory and tactile explorations are central to children's learning and form the foundation of their role as researchers and creators. Such explorations are integral to the creative processes of art-making, inviting children to engage deeply with materials through hands-on action research. As they investigate the properties of materials, children discover the inherent beauty of colour, explore the expressive potential of marks, and revel in the textures, shapes, and forms they bring to life. Through repeated encounters, children deepen their understanding about the ways materials can be manipulated and transformed; cultivating an aesthetic sensibility and a rich appreciation for the creative possibilities inherent in each medium.

Children explore and experiment with materials, not only when invited to engage in carefully planned provocations, but in a naturally curious form of aesthetic research (Kind, 2014). For example, consider the times you may have observed children making patterns in a foggy window with their fingers, feeling the texture of a surface, or arranging food into lines or patterns as they eat. Children are driven to collect, sort, and arrange found treasures and collections into patterns and designs. In a similar way, artists sort and arrange materials according to their intentions, the medium, or the desired outcome of their work. Sorting, organising and manipulating materials often starts with exploration of the material properties, such as texture, colour, and form, which consequently influences how they are used. Whether sorted by colour, texture, function, size, or conceptual grouping, the arrangement helps shape the visual and tactile experience of the artist's work.

Children also require space and time for sustained interactions with materials (Kind, 2014; Kolbe, 2007; 2014). Experimental and playful material encounters are foundational to children's later artistic and creative expression (Lewin-Benham, 2023). Becoming familiar with a material or medium can't be rushed, and children benefit from unlimited, open-ended time to play with, and "get to know," art materials and tools. Each art material and tool offers unique characteristics and affords children unique sensory experiences and challenges to overcome. Instead of offering one-time activities with novel or gimmicky materials, plan to offer children regular and repeated invitations to use quality materials and tools (Lindsay, 2023). Give children ample time to build relationships with materials and art tools, supporting them to explore the unique possibilities and interesting limitations of each medium and tool (Pacini-Ketchabaw et al., 2024).

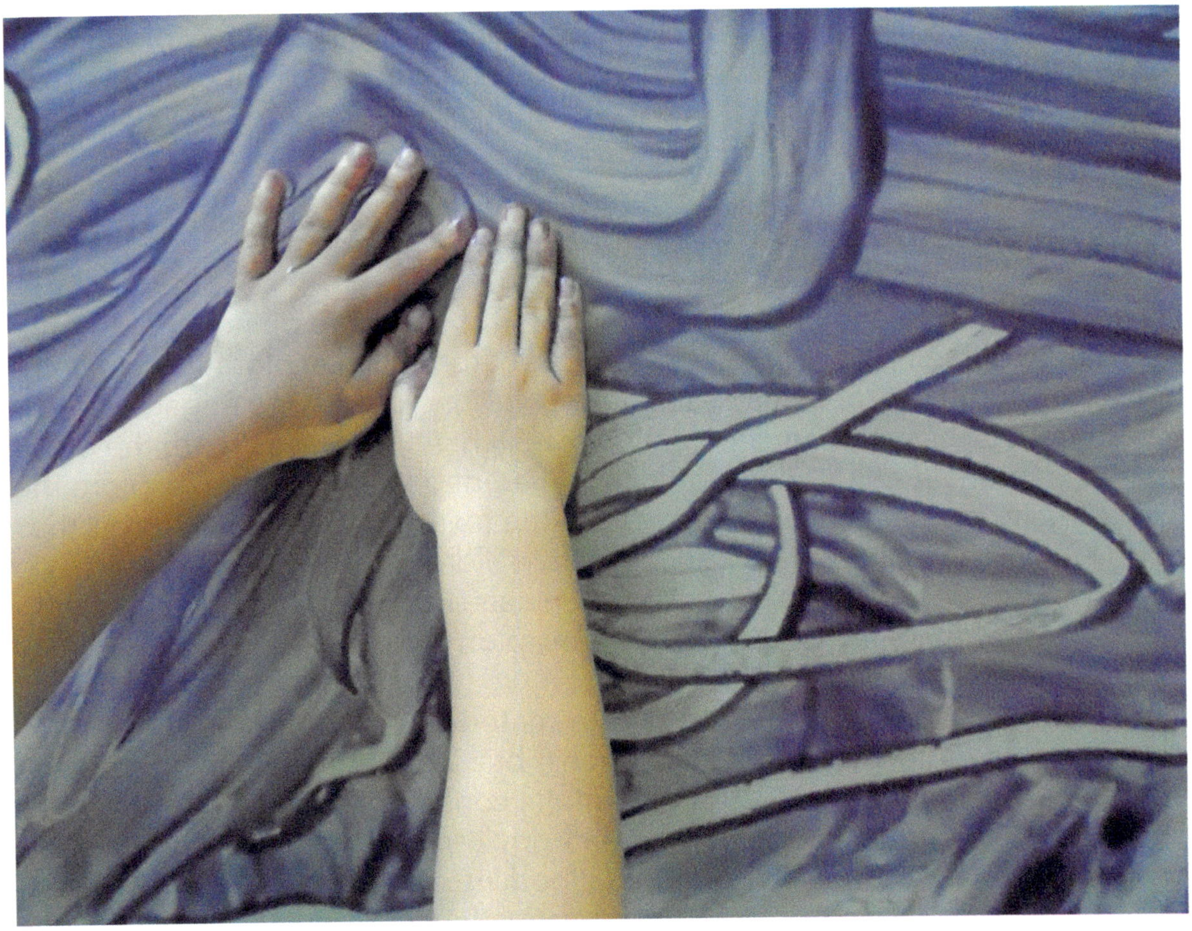

Figure 6.3 Smooth and fluid finger paint provides a rich sensory experience for engaging with paint, colour, and mark making. Providing paint directly onto a table surface offers children space for big movements [Image: Denise Savins. Saigon Kids Early Learning Centre].

Open-ended exploration is important because each visual arts material has different properties as well as techniques for their application. For example, making marks with dark charcoal provides a different visual and sensory experience for children than working with felt pens, hard wax crayons, or soft oil pastels. Similarly, working with liquid water paints and inks will require children to master different techniques and will result in different outcomes than painting with thick acrylic paints. It is valuable to give children experiences with a variety of media, and it is important to provide generous amounts of time and repeated experiences to fully allow the process of research and exploration to unfold.

Introducing children to visual arts materials and tools for the first time

Regardless of age, development, or ability, introducing children to new materials requires intentional planning and thoughtful implementation. These initial "meetings with materials" form the foundation for children's visual arts learning and help cultivate dispositions for creative exploration. Early interactions with materials invite children to engage in hands-on research, where they explore sensory and aesthetic properties that can shift and evolve during play. These transformations open up new possibilities for experimentation, enabling children to deepen their learning and add complexity over time.

Material exploration plays a crucial role in early childhood development by engaging the senses. Interactions with materials, such as feeling textures, manipulating shapes, and experimenting with colours, activate multiple areas of the brain, fostering cognitive, sensory, and motor development (Dehaene, 2020). As Lewin-Benham (2023, p. 13) explains:

> Materials stimulate the senses, which respond by developing networks in the brain. In time, networks enable us to use high-level brain functions and to build relationships among complex ideas. Materials educate the hand, which drives language, movement, attention, planning, and scores of other essential brain functions. The combination of hand and materials is essential to virtually any endeavor.

Hands-on experiences are essential for brain development and foster curiosity, problem-solving, and creativity – skills crucial for lifelong learning. Introducing children to a variety of materials, techniques, and tools supports them to explore shapes, colours, textures, and forms. Such playful, exploratory activities ignite curiosity, encourage experimentation, and build a foundation for material knowledge, aesthetic understanding, technical skills, and creative confidence. Through grasping, stacking, shaping, and arranging objects, children develop fine and gross motor control, enhancing spatial awareness, emotional regulation, and cognitive flexibility.

This is particularly important for infants and toddlers who have a natural capacity for open-ended aesthetic exploration and discovery. Before children become interested in representational drawing, they will engage deeply in the sensory aspects of art materials, exploring textures, colours, and the ways materials move and transform. Sensory exploration and experimentation help young learners to become familiar with visual arts materials, testing how they interact with surfaces and discovering the possibilities of mark-making (Lewin-Benham, 2023; Visser, 2013). These early experiences provide a powerful foundation for visual arts learning, helping infants and toddlers build confidence and skills to express their artistic ideas more intentionally as they develop (Denee, 2024). Whether discovering the translucence of watercolour paints, the vibrancy of oil pastels, or the malleability of clay, children begin to develop a language of materials that supports them to visually communicate their ideas and actions. As children revisit materials, they develop mastery and aesthetic awareness, while strengthening their creative confidence.

Equally important, exploring materials allows children to understand how different tools and techniques work. For example, experimenting with brushes, sponges, or fingers to apply paint introduces children to the possibilities of mark-making, while manipulating clay helps them understand form, structure, and three-dimensional space. Through tactile interactions, children build a range of vocabularies for visual arts making, eventually developing understanding about how materials and tools work together to achieve specific results. During early

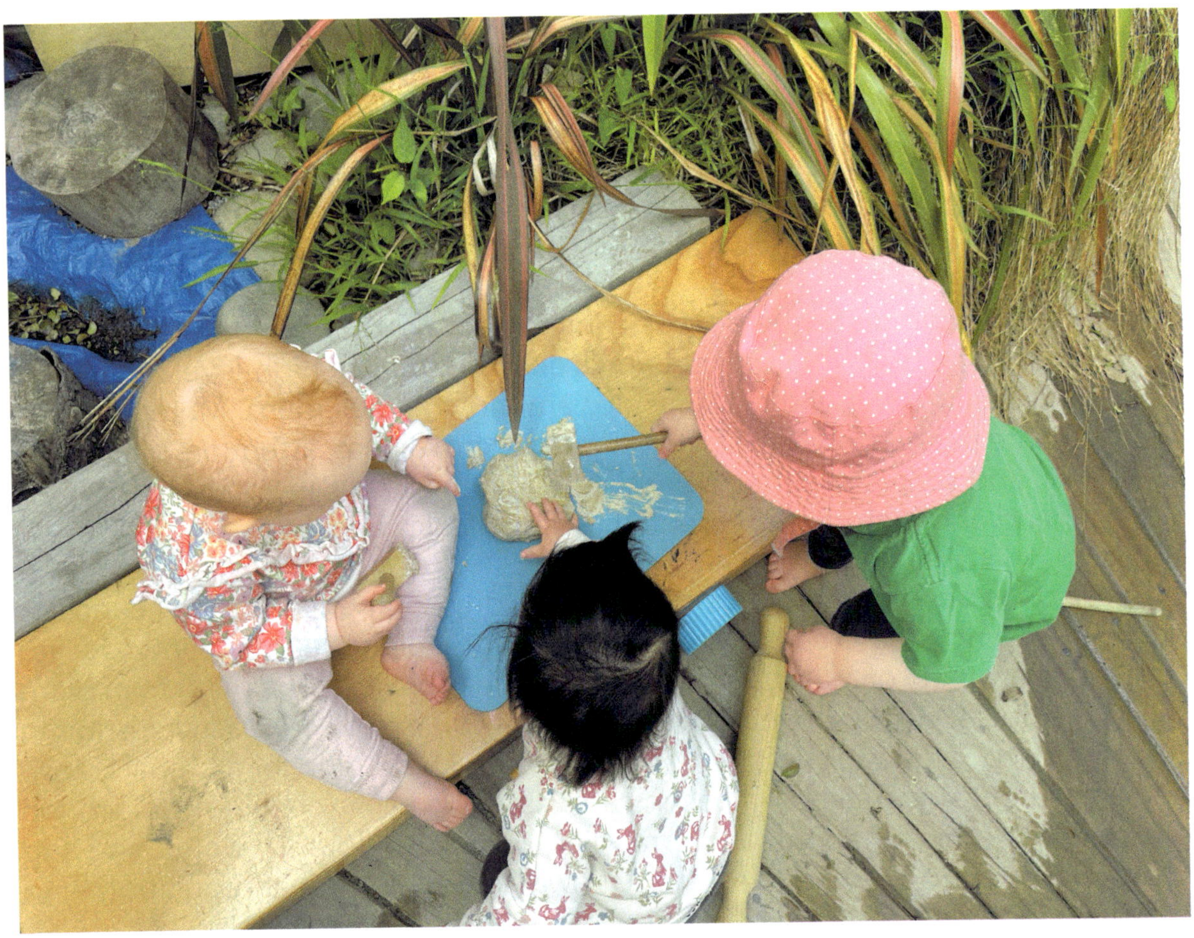

Figure 6.4 Early arts encounters that focus on the sensory, aesthetic and transformative properties of art mediums support knowledge building and deeper relationships with art materials [Image credit: Daisies Early Education & Care Centre].

arts encounters, it is most important to value children's hands, eyes, and brains as the primary tools for art exploration, rather than focusing on specific activity outcomes. This helps children to form close relationships with materials, emphasising the sensory, aesthetic, and transformative possibilities of a single medium. It also lays the groundwork for deeper explorations and deconstructed material encounters, where the simplicity of working with one material or one aspect of a visual arts process invites children to expand their creative understanding through focused discovery.

Deconstructed material encounters

When designing experiences for children who are encountering art materials or processes for the first time, it is helpful to focus on the basic elements. It can be tempting for adults to rush children toward the completion of a finished product, which very unrealistically demands knowledge and mastery of a range of visual arts materials and tools. Instead, children's first visual arts learning experiences should focus on basic elements and materials and always remain open-ended, with enough flexibility to enable children to make decisions about how they explore (Richards & Terreni, 2022; Visser, 2013). By deconstructing an arts experience into singular introductions to materials, tools, and techniques, children can gradually build their understanding of each component of an arts experience. Such focused explorations support children to develop foundational knowledge through multi-material experiences. Breaking traditional art and craft experiences into elemental meetings with materials, tools, and techniques offers rich ways to plan for a visual arts curriculum which is grounded in aesthetic encounters. For example:

- Rather than expecting young children to draw something (before they have had the chance to experience a range of drawing tools and surfaces), focus instead on the action of stroking a charcoal stick onto a large piece of sturdy paper to make rich, dark marks.
- Rather than expecting children to navigate a painting experience using multiple colours and painting tools, focus instead on the technique of dipping one brush into a container of paint or water. Teach the skill of wiping the brush on the side of the container and applying the loaded brush onto a surface.
- Rather than always working on a small scale, think about the ways young children use their whole bodies to learn, and offer opportunities for large mark-making movements. Consider setting up gross-motor mark-making experiences in the outdoors, across a floor, or covering a whole wall.

When planning children's aesthetic encounters with visual arts materials and processes, consider all of the skills or techniques that would usually work in combination to create an artwork. Like choosing one word from a sentence or one block from a tower, select one material, one process or one tool from what would usually be a complex combination of processes, skills, and techniques.

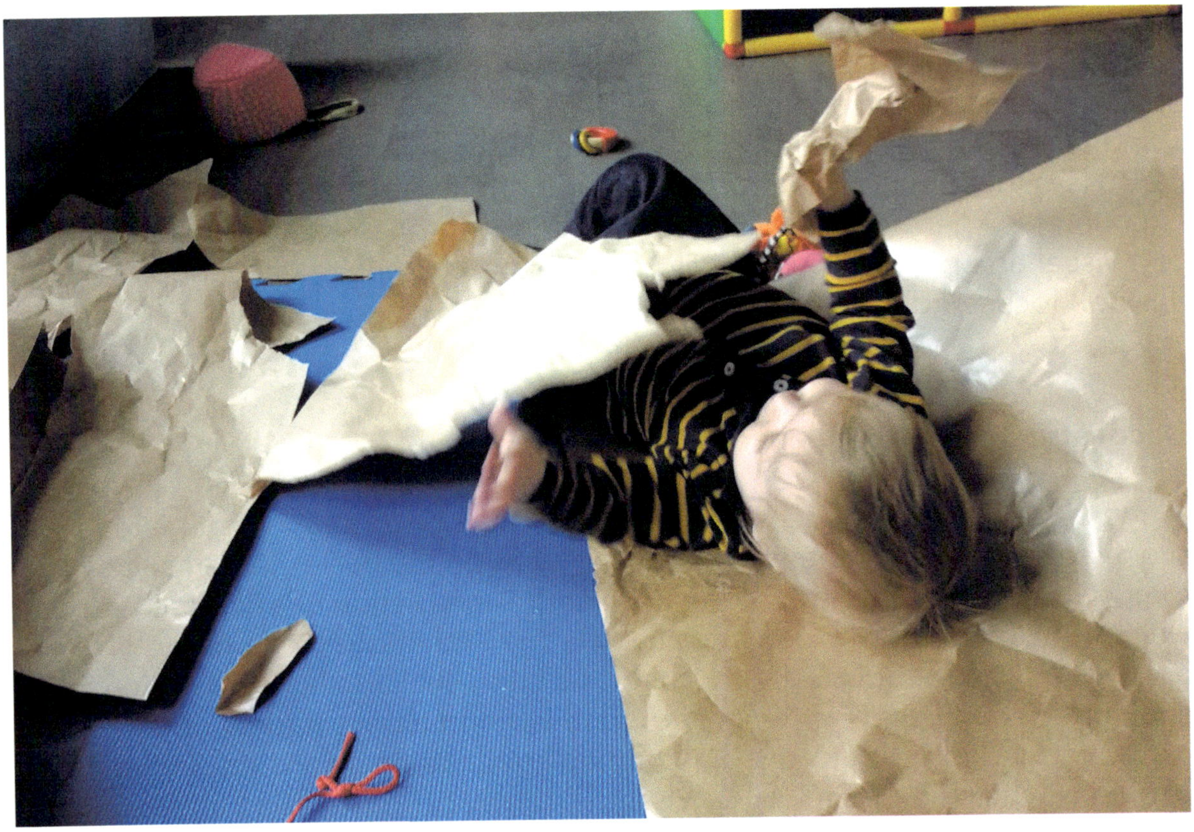

Figure 6.5 Deconstructed material encounters, like this exploration of brown paper, focus on singular materials or processes, encouraging open-ended, sensory-rich experiences [Image Joke den Haese].

Plan for children to encounter and experience the deconstructed elements of an arts experience many times. Consider children's current development and prior experience with materials and visual arts processes to determine adjustments that will enable their inclusion and engagement. For example:

- When offering clay to babies (or children of any age if it is a first encounter), simply provide the clay on a large piece of sheeting on the floor enabling them to physically touch and poke the clay with their fingers to delight in its cool, sensory and tactile qualities.
- Children who experience sensory reluctance can be supported to meet colour mixing through the provision of translucent materials on a lightbox.
- Children unable to grasp a paintbrush can apply paint using a sponge, paint roller or brayer, or simply their fingers and hands.

Design each component of the learning experience to serve as the foundation for an elemental encounter with aesthetics and materials. By scaffolding and repeating these experiences over time, children can engage in aesthetic and material research that progressively builds their skills, knowledge, and development. The following examples illustrate how more complex arts education experiences can be deconstructed into singular encounters with materials and processes, fostering children's understanding of materials, aesthetics, and artistic techniques.

Example 1: Painting encounters

- Paint with water
- Feel the texture of paintbrushes
- Paint with hands and fingers
- Scaffold techniques such as dip, wipe, and rinse in between mixing colours
- Explore painting and colour mixing with multiple types of paint and painting surfaces

Example 2: Collage encounters

- Rip, scrunch and tear paper
- Explore multiple paper types and textures
- Stick collage materials onto contact/adhesive plastic
- Snip firm cardstock with scissors
- Sort collected materials into groups
- Make patterns with loose parts
- Introduce a range of glue types

Example 3: Clay encounters

- Unwrap clay from its plastic wrapping
- Regular opportunities to poke, prod, and roll clay with hands
- Make marks and draw onto clay slabs
- Poke natural materials into clay
- Add water to clay
- Learn how to cut the slab with wire and how to store and care for clay

Example 4: Fabric weaving encounters

- Offer baskets of fabric to explore, feel, and sort
- Explore fabric textures and colours
- Play over and under games
- Play poking and posting games
- Cut or rip strips of paper
- Collage with fabric
- Weave along fences

Collecting and recycling materials for artmaking

Collecting and sorting beautiful materials for artmaking with children is a joyful and inspiring process that inspires and enriches material encounters (Weissman Topal & Gandini, 1999). Whether gathering natural treasures such as leaves, shells, and stones, or assembling an array of vibrant fabrics, ribbons, and recycled objects, the act of collecting sparks curiosity and imagination. Sorting materials with children transforms the process into a shared exploration of texture, colour, shape, and pattern, encouraging them to appreciate the beauty and potential of everyday items. Curated material collections not only inspire artistic expression

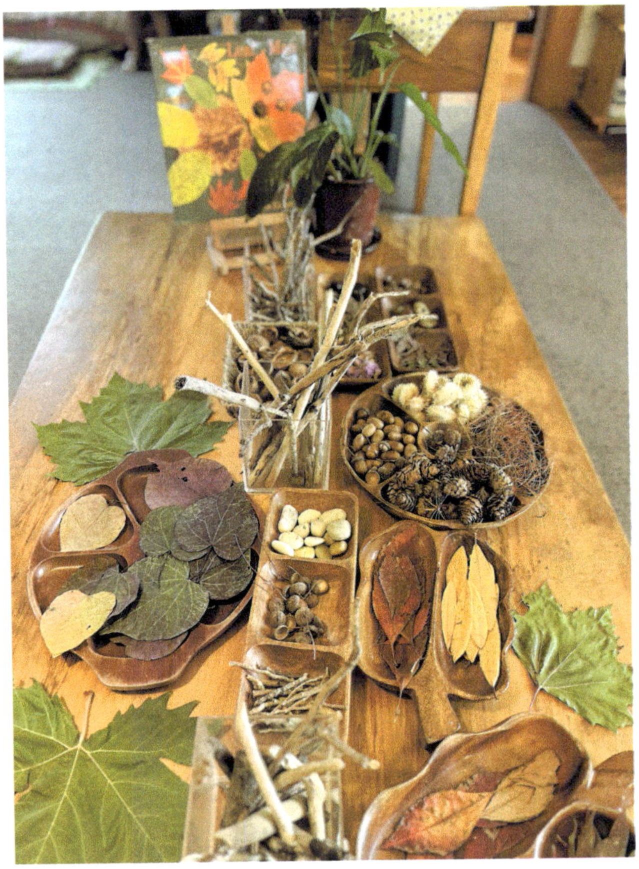

Figure 6.6 The thoughtful selection and presentation of materials engages the senses, invites participation, and fosters aesthetic appreciation [Image: Adrienne Wilkins, Sophia Preschool].

but offer children the opportunity to develop relationships with and value for diverse materials, fostering a sense of wonder, inquiry, and resourcefulness. Through collaborative collection and material encounters, children build relationships with materials as active entities (Penfold, 2019). Aesthetic encounters with materials invite children to actively engage in playful research and inquiry, transforming simple objects into meaningful, expressive partners in their creative exploration of their world.

Collaborative art experiences

The social context has a powerful effect on children's art play and inquiry and their exploration of materials. Children and adults are influenced by the knowledge and skills of the people around them and by the social-emotional context they are interacting in. When we facilitate collaborative exploratory experiences, we provide rich opportunities to learn about visual arts materials and processes from others; and importantly, how to work together in a group (Richards & Terreni, 2022). One of the joys of researching art materials is that they can be mysterious, tricky and pose many problems. This tension creates fertile ground for investigation, perseverance, curiosity, and creativity (Kind, 2014). When children grapple with such encounters together, they practice communicating, sharing, and negotiating roles and theories. Creating and exploring in a group provides children with a powerful opportunity to collaborate meaningfully, express ideas, and build connections, both with the materials they explore and with one another (Pacini-Ketchabaw et al., 2024).

Educators as co-researchers

Educators play a vital role as co-researchers during children's aesthetic encounters. By modelling curiosity, asking open-ended questions, and encouraging experimentation, educators collaborate with children to explore the creative potential and aesthetic properties of materials. These initial interactions with materials are more than an introduction to materials and processes. Rather, thoughtful and intentional material introductions are invitations to imagine, investigate, wonder, and create. Through shared exploration, children develop skills, confidence, and a deep appreciation for art as a powerful tool for communication, inquiry, and self-expression.

An educator's active pedagogy and interactions brings children's aesthetic research into focus, inviting children to examine arts materials and processes from new perspectives, to pay attention to details, and to examine closely using all of their senses. When we learn to slow down alongside children, we can help them to notice, experience, feel, interpret, and connect closely with their surroundings, and to be attentive and careful observers (Clark, 2023). By adopting this way of being in the world, educators can, in partnership with children, learn to appreciate the beauty of everyday materials.

Preparing arts experiences with intention and care is essential for fostering children's positive engagement and attention to aesthetic qualities. Thoughtfully curated materials, such as intentional selection and grouping of colours, shapes, textures, or patterns, can further inspire children's curiosity and aesthetic appreciation, enriching their engagement with art. Ensuring all materials are prepared and that the space is set up for both the activity and clean-up helps create a manageable, stress-free experience. A powerful planning strategy is to engage with visual arts materials and processes yourself prior to offering them to children (Denee et al., 2024). Play with and explore the materials and experiment with the possibilities and challenges they present. Such prior experience will enhance your interactions with children by allowing you to draw on your familiarity with the materials, thereby helping children engage more successfully in the learning process. Collaborate with colleagues to ensure the visual arts experience is well supported in terms of staffing. For example, arrange for a colleague to take responsibility for observing and supporting children who are not engaged in visual arts experience, or ask them to take photographs of

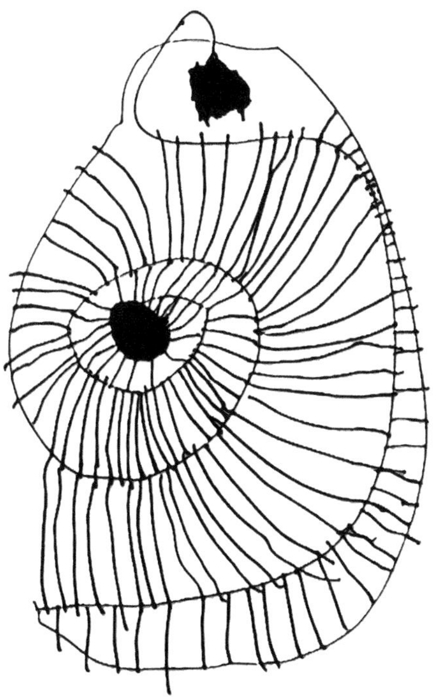

the experience so you can give the children your full attention. Intentionally planning for effective documentation approaches enables the learning experience to be further evaluated and refined.

For very young children, or those who have not previously used particular materials, the presence of a supportive adult is vital. Educators can scaffold children's exploration and learning by narrating the experience, describing the colours, textures, actions, sounds, and patterns as the exploration unfolds. At times, staying quiet and engaging through non-verbal communication may be more appropriate, allowing children to lead their own discovery. Offering children regular opportunities for aesthetic and material research provides a foundation for a lifetime of appreciating and participating in the visual arts. Such experiences support children to develop rich relationships with materials and develop the skills that will allow them to express their thinking, ideas, creativity, and stories in the future. While young children are naturally drawn to material inquiry and research, these early explorations hold immense potential to inspire an energised and aesthetically rich journey of lifelong engagement with the visual arts.

Conclusion

Aesthetic encounters and material research form a vital foundation for children's exploration of the visual arts, fostering sensory, cognitive, and emotional development. By engaging with the beauty and potential of materials, children build meaningful connections with their environment, their peers, and their own creative processes. Through intentional planning, thoughtful curation, and a pedagogy of listening, educators act as co-researchers and partners with children. They encourage children to slow down, observe closely, and experiment with materials; fostering both artistic confidence and aesthetic awareness. These early experiences not only enhance children's ability to express themselves but also lay the groundwork for a lifelong appreciation of the arts and the beauty in the world around them.

References

a'Beckett, C. (1991). Promoting aesthetic appreciation in young children. In S. Wright (Ed.), *The arts in early childhood* (pp. 35–52). Prentice Hall.

Clark, A. (2023). *Slow knowledge and the unhurried child: Time for slow pedagogies in early childhood education*. Routledge.

Dehaene, S. (2020). *How we learn: Why brains learn better than any machine… for now*. Viking.

Denee, R. (2024). Visual arts with infants and toddlers: Developing respectful and intentional pedagogy. *The First Years Ngā Tau Tuatahi: New Zealand Journal of Infant and Toddler Education*, *26*(1), 5–10.

Denee, R., Lindsay, G., & Probine, S. (2024). Visual arts self-efficacy: Impacts and supports for early childhood teachers. *Early Childhood Education Journal*, 52(6), 1035–1045. https://doi.org/10.1007/s10643-023-01489-5

Dewey, J. (1915). *The school and society* (2nd ed.). The University of Chicago Press.
Ferrari, A., & Giacopini, E. (Eds.). (2005). *REMIDA day* (L. Morrow, Trans.). Reggio Children.
Keyte-Hartland, D., & Lowings, L. (2025). Learning to live well together: Art and ecological research with young children. In Z. Moula & N. Walshe (Eds.), *Art in nature with children and young people: A guide towards health equality, wellbeing and sustainability* (pp. 98–107). Routledge. DOI: 10.4324/9781003357308-9
Kind, S. (2014). Material encounters. *International Journal of Child, Youth and Family Studies, 5*(4.2), 865–877.
Kolbe, U. (2007). *Rapunzel's supermarket. All about young children and their art* (2nd ed.). Peppinot Press.
Kolbe, U. (2014). *Children's imagination: Creativity under our noses*. Peppinot Press.
Lewin-Benham, A. (2023). *Infants and toddlers at work: Using Reggio-inspired materials to support brain development* (2nd ed.). Teachers College Press.
Lindsay, G. (2023). *Visual arts in early childhood settings. Everyday Learning Series. 21*(1). Early Childhood Australia.
Pacini-Ketchabaw, V., Kind, S., & Kocher, L. M. (2024). *Encounters with materials in early childhood education* (2nd ed.). Routledge.
Pelo, A. (2013). *The goodness of rain: Developing an ecological identity in young children*. Exchange Press.
Penfold, L. (2019). Material matters in children's creative learning. *Journal of Design and Science*. https://jods.mitpress.mit.edu/pub/bwp6cysy
Richards, R. D., & Terreni, L. (2022). Intentionally supporting and extending young children's learning about and through the visual arts: Suggestions and strategies for early childhood education teachers. *Curriculum Matters, 18*(1), 88–106. https://doi.org/10.18296/cm.0061
Vecchi, V. (2010). *Art and creativity in Reggio Emilia: Exploring the role and potential of ateliers in early childhood education*. Routledge.
Vecchi, V., & Giudici, C. (Eds.) (2004). *Children, art, artists: The expressive languages of children, the artistic language of Alberto Burri*. Reggio Children.
Visser, J. (2013). Changing times and changing contexts: Examining visual arts provision for infants and toddlers. In B. Clark, A. Grey, & L. Terreni (Eds.), *Arts in early childhood education: Kia tipu te wairua toi: Fostering the creative spirit* (pp. 52–65). Pearson.
Weissman Topal, C., & Gandini, L. (1999). *Beautiful stuff!: Learning with found materials*. Davis Publications Inc.

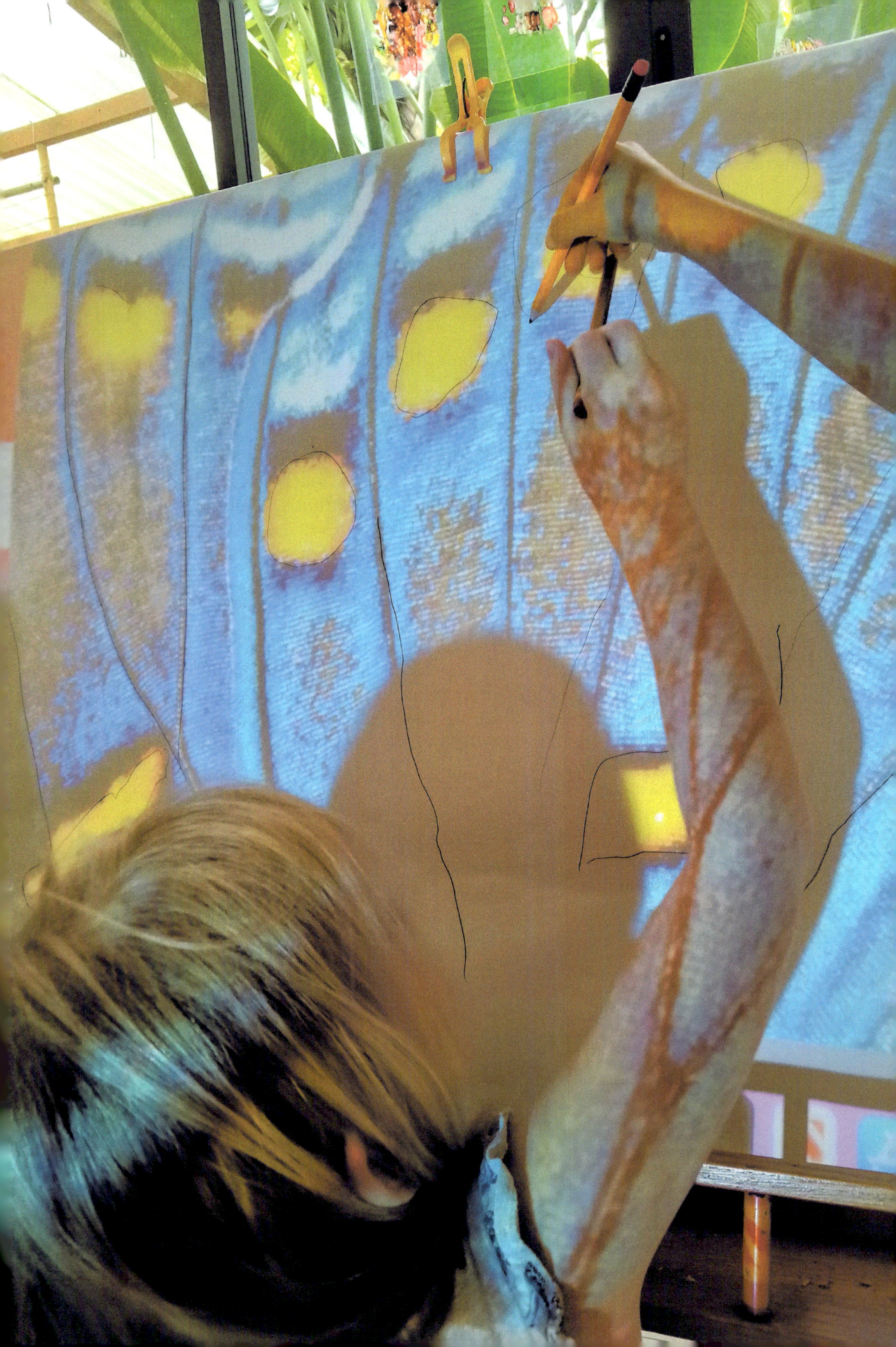

7 The visual arts in children's projects of inquiry

The visual arts powerfully support children's engagement in robust investigative experiences. Inquiry-based learning has become an increasingly popular approach due to its capacity to engage children's curiosity and interest in their learning, while valuing the active role that educators play in this process. When learning is based on children's questions and interests, they are encouraged to collaborate as they explore and inquire, fostering connections and active participation as citizens in both their local and broader communities. This chapter builds upon Chapter 5 which explored the role of the educator in developing and facilitating rich, contextualised visual arts experiences. In this chapter, we expand on these ideas with a focus on children's inquiries. We explain the value of inquiry-based projects and the role the visual arts can play in this approach. We examine the role of the educator in developing their own unique inquiry approaches as they utilise visual arts materials within children's inquiry projects.

What is an inquiry-based project?

Inquiry-based projects are also known as "project-work," "the project approach," "investigations," or "children's inquiry." In the infant and toddler and early childhood centres of Reggio Emilia, Italy (world renowned for their long-term collaborative projects with children), such projects are known as "progettazione," which can be translated as "flexible planning" (Gardner & Jones, 2016). All these approaches share the common idea that children and educators collaborate as active participants in the learning process, engaging over time to explore an interest, question, concept, or working theory. It is a co-constructivist approach meaning that both parties (children and educators) play equally important roles (Stacey, 2019). Educators focus intently on children's theories, ideas, and learning. They do this by observing and documenting children's play, questions, engagement, and conversations as a way to understand their developing thinking.

Figure 7.1 Inquiry-based learning comes alive when visual arts are integrated into children's explorations. By respecting children's ideas and fostering curiosity, educators support meaningful investigations that empower young learners as active participants in their world [Image: Carolyn Prawius, Saigon Kids Early Learning Centre].

DOI: 10.4324/9781003561835-9

When children collaborate to find answers and solve problems, they build the skills and attitudes required to become enthusiastic, resilient lifelong learners. Respecting children's decisions and conclusions fosters their sense of agency and confidence, empowering them to conduct their own research and solve problems independently.

For this reason, it is less important that children discover scientifically accurate answers than it is for them to value their own and other's ideas, theories, and capabilities (Edwards, 2012). At the same time, educators have a critical role in progressing the inquiry and making decisions that enrich and extend children's thinking and learning. Educators who are attuned to children's learning can provide materials, provoke and facilitate new experiences without overpowering children's interests and agency in the process.

Why are the visual arts so important in supporting children's inquiries?

The arts, and particularly the visual arts, play a critical role in supporting a project of inquiry as it progresses. Children have numerous ways to express, explore, and represent their thoughts and ideas. The visual arts provide young children with a vital mode of communication to enrich each stage of an inquiry as it progresses. Through visual art-making processes, children can explore their ideas, further develop their thinking, adapt their ideas as they create, and use their art to share their thinking with peers, educators, and families (Brooks, 2022a). Communication

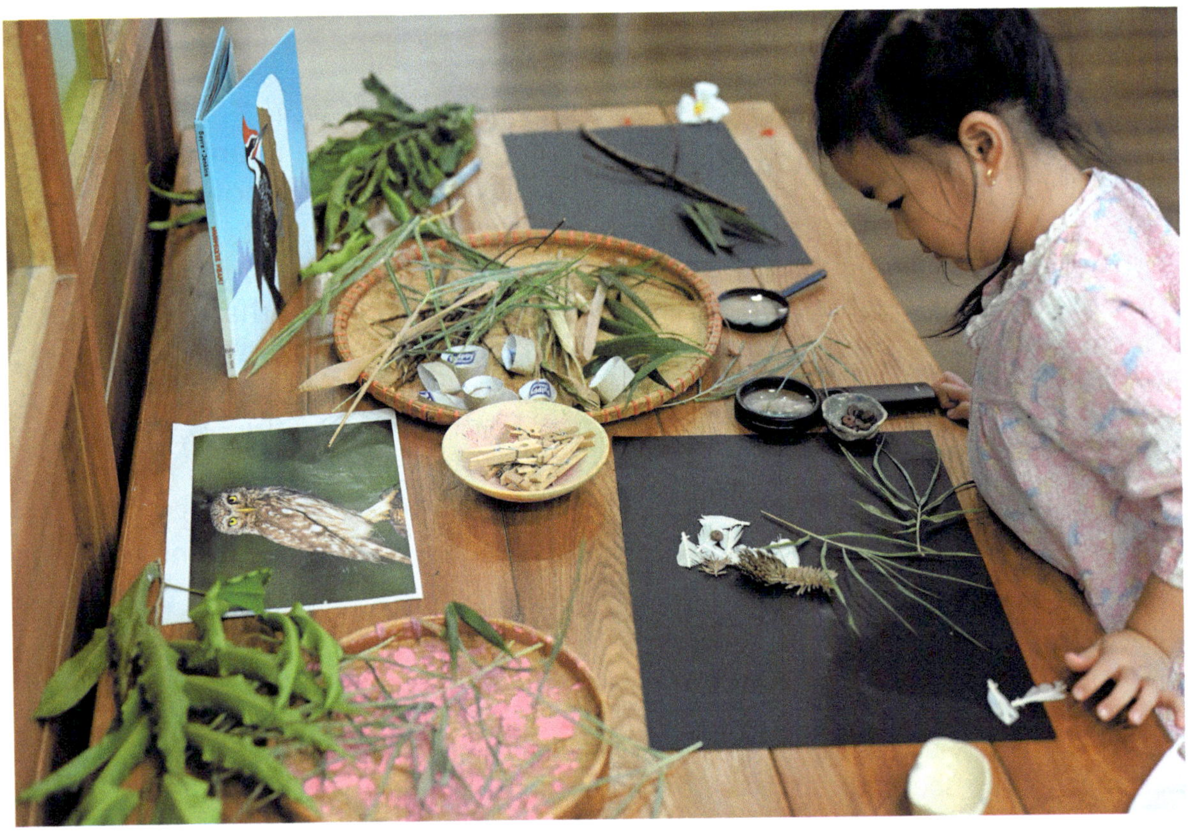

Figure 7.2 Visual arts enrich inquiry-based learning by giving children tools to explore, express, and evolve their ideas [Image: Aurora International School of the Arts].

through the visual arts also supports children to revisit their previous understandings before taking the next step in an inquiry. For instance, during an inquiry project exploring how a caterpillar transforms into a butterfly, educators might encourage children to draw their initial thoughts about how they believe the process happens. Having drawn their ideas, children can refer to their artwork to explain their thinking to others. Their artwork may be revisited multiple times as children engage in discussions and debates about their understanding, perhaps agreeing or challenging each other's ideas. As the inquiry progresses, children may have opportunities to observe caterpillars, chrysalises, and butterflies; again being invited to record their thoughts using a range of visual arts materials. On subsequent days, educators can use children's visual artworks (and documentation photos) as a prompt to return to the inquiry and continue the exploration. As discussed in Chapter 5, recording their ideas and theories through drawing helps children internalise new information and potentially adjust their thinking as they draw and express their ideas and theories (Brooks, 2022a).

Another important contribution the visual arts can offer at the end of an investigation is when children are supported to reinforce their learning by creating an artwork that celebrates their inquiry journey (Chard et al., 2017). For example, in a project focused on caterpillars and butterflies, a final collaborative project could involve children working together to design a mural, create a mosaic for a butterfly garden, or design and build a chrysalis with a viewable interior. Creating a final collaborative piece offers children a valuable opportunity to experience a sense of accomplishment and closure regarding the inquiry (Stacey, 2019). However, the true value of a project of inquiry is in the processes of theory building, collaborative inquiry, problem-solving, and shared wondering. It is during an inquiry that children learn to communicate their thinking, collaborate and negotiate with others, persist and work through challenges, and learn the value of asking for help as part of the learning process.

The foundations of an inquiry project

Any inquiry-based approach is underpinned by several key theoretical concepts. It is helpful to begin by reflecting on how these aspects of early childhood education are valued by individual educators and educational teams. Inquiry-based learning is strongly informed by socio-cultural and constructivist theories. These theories suggest that knowledge is not universal, but varies for each individual and is valued differently in each unique place and community. Knowledge is understood to be constructed between people, places, and things, which means educators acknowledge and prioritise the collaborative co-construction of knowledge with children. This

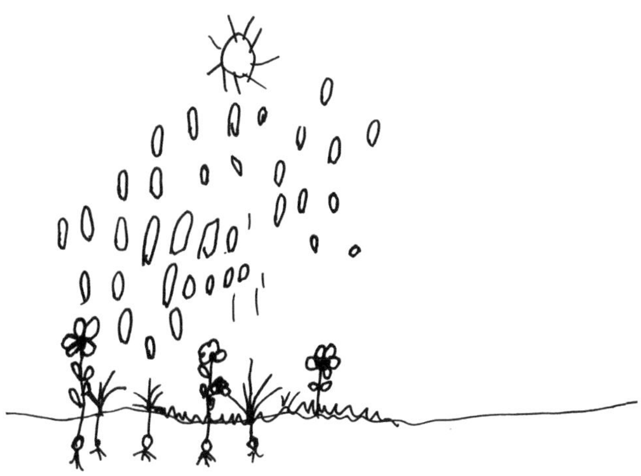

perspective, grounded in constructivist notions about how children learn, emphasises that children are powerful learners from the moment they are born. Children enter early education settings already filled with experiences, knowledge, and perceptions about their world (Hedges, 2022). All of this is shaped by their cultures, families, and their beliefs and values. Educators or teaching communities aiming to adopt inquiry-based project learning can begin by reflecting on their values and perspectives in relation to the following foundational concepts:

Conceptions of childhood:

The ways children are valued, in their homes, classrooms, communities, and cultures impact the choices and actions made both with and for them. Children deserve respect and support to engage as equal protagonists in their own education. In an inquiry-based learning approach, children are positioned as active participants in their education, capable of constructing their own understandings and meanings.

Conceptions of learning:

A helpful way to reflect on how learning happens for children is to consider our personal learning preferences. Perhaps you value being shown how to do something by an expert? Maybe you appreciate having time to experiment with materials and ideas with no fixed purpose or instruction. Some people find talking about their ideas with others helpful, while others find recording their thoughts using notes and sketches is an effective way to process their thinking. It's possible that several of these approaches may resonate to some extent, however one or two strategies are likely to stand out as particularly beneficial depending on individual preferences. Learning is a complex and unique process for everyone, regardless of age. Children, therefore, require knowledgeable and sensitive educators who are able to pick up on their cues and support their learning journey in ways that both empower and challenge them.

Conceptions of teaching and learning

Inquiry-based learning projects are co-constructed, meaning that children and adults build meaning together, each contributing in valuable ways. As a result, educators work in partnership with children, observing, discussing, questioning, and planning encounters with materials. Through this lens, effective learning experiences are those where children are supported to collaborate, revisit previous ideas and theories, and deepen and extend their thinking as they investigate and explore.

Fostering a culture of experimentation and collaboration

After your learning community has explored these foundational ideas and determined their core values, a classroom learning culture can be established. Inquiry-based project work is based on the belief that children are naturally curious, with significant capacity to make sense of their experiences. However, the classroom culture can either enable or restrict this from happening. Children must be supported to understand that it's okay to experiment, make mistakes, and appreciate that satisfying results sometimes take time. In fact, challenges should be valued as an integral part of the learning process. Continuous access to a wide range of open-ended materials is one way to invite creativity, exploration, and problem-solving. Throughout an inquiry project, it is also important to create opportunities for children to come together, reflect on their past work, share ideas, and make new plans for learning. In creating this kind of learning culture, children come to understand that their ideas are respected, and that curiosity and exploration are valued attributes. Such an atmosphere supports children to become enthusiastic, empowered, and resilient learners who understand that acquiring knowledge and learning new skills takes time and effort.

Beginning an inquiry project

An inquiry-based learning project is very different from the traditional, and often structured, topic-based projects many remember from their school days. Many will recall creating a "solar system" or making pre-designed products by copying a teacher's example. In contrast, an inquiry project often, though not always, begins with children's ideas, questions, and interests (Chard et al., 2017). A project of inquiry may begin with one child or with a group who share an emergent interest. The first important step for educators is to be attentive to children's play and conversations and to facilitate opportunities for children to exchange their ideas.

Once we determine the questions, interests, or curiosities that become evident through children's play and conversations it is helpful to exchange ideas amongst the teaching team. Each educator can share their ideas about what they think might be happening, drawing upon their own observations, notes, and other documentation such as photographs and videos. Ideas about how the inquiry could potentially evolve should be recorded. The teaching team can then do some reading and research about the potential focus of inquiry in order to be equipped to support meaningful conversations about the particular interest or inquiry.

Following this initial reflection, the next steps will depend on the age group of the children involved. If working with infants and toddlers, the next step could be to offer a provocation or invitation to learn more. However, if working with children who are able to verbally contribute their own perspectives to the planning process, they can be involved in the early planning stage. This supports educators to seek clarification about children's questions and evolving working theories. Alternatively, educators can also choose to present a provocation to older children to further refine the focus of their interest, or to reignite or reintroduce a previously identified inquiry focus. How you approach the early stage of an inquiry will very much depend on the unique learning community, the children involved, and the concepts being explored. There is no "one way" to begin or progress an inquiry-based project.

Provocations and encounters with materials

A provocation is an invitation for learning. It is an act of intentional teaching where educators propose an idea or a question or arrange the classroom environment and materials in a specific way to invite exploration and engagement from the children (Kaynak-Ekici et al., 2021; Stacey, 2019). Provocations are essential to inquiry-based learning, offering valuable opportunities to incorporate visual arts materials and experiences into the inquiry process. A central requirement for any provocation is to ensure children have the freedom to engage with and interpret it in their own way, rather than being forced to follow educator expectations. Even though it can be initially disappointing when children engage with a provocation in a completely different way than you intended, these moments can reveal children's true intentions and interests more clearly. In this way provocations are an important way of avoiding exploring broad topics or only exploring interests at a superficial level. For example, educators having observed an interest in painting, may hypothesise that there is an emergent interest in colour mixing. Through offering the provocation of paint on a lightbox, children may instead become absorbed in pattern making, revealing more about their interest and suggesting it might be more about exploring different ways of making marks.

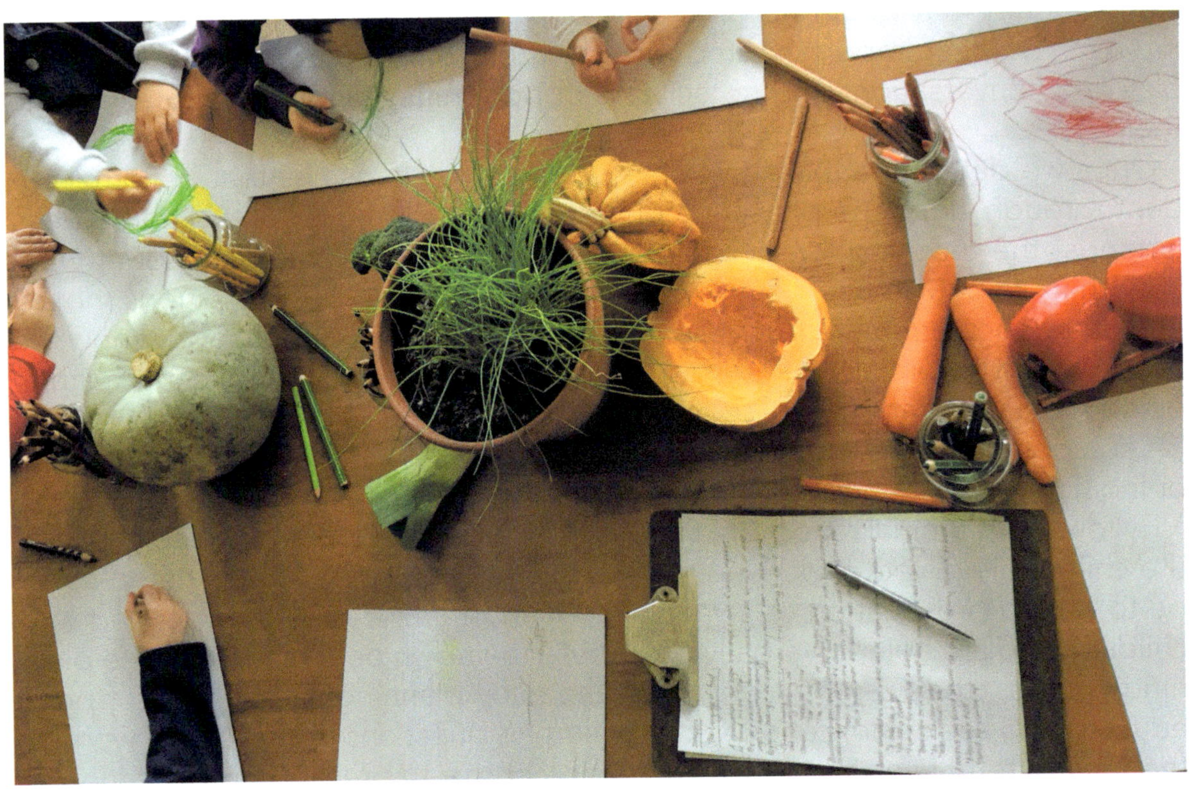

Figure 7.3 Provocations invite children to engage deeply with materials and ideas, fostering curiosity and exploration. Through observation, reflection, and collaboration, educators can co-construct meaningful inquiries that honour children's questions, theories, and creativity [Image: Adrienne Wilkins, Sophia Preschool].

Questions for educators to keep asking throughout an inquiry are:

- What are the questions and working theories the children are exploring?
- What challenges are children encountering?
- What experiences and materials may deepen children's thinking further?
- Who is leading the inquiry? Do children have the autonomy to explore and interpret materials in their own way, and are their ideas and interpretations honoured and respected?

When applied in this research-focused way, provocations are an effective way to investigate children's curiosities, wonderings, and intentions, and better understand their strategies for learning.

However, it is important that educators do not passively observe children engaging with a provocation. As discussed in Chapter 3, socio-cultural and constructivist theories remind us about the need to be pedagogically active and to partner with children as they engage with and explore materials. If children are unfamiliar with certain materials, it can be helpful for an educator to intentionally provide strategies and model skills to help children use the materials effectively and discover the affordances of the materials (Lewin-Benham, 2023). Inviting a group of children to engage with a material provocation offers a powerful opportunity to spark curiosity, interest, and excitement, while also communicating boundaries and expectations. Once children have started working together, adult partners can actively ask questions, make suggestions, navigate tensions, and mediate conversations between children. Educators play an important role in helping children to work in groups to co-construct ideas and solutions together (Edwards, 2012). In such collaborative learning contexts, draw children's attention to each other's strategies for exploring and learning. If one child appears to be struggling, suggest they ask for help from another child who has developed a successful strategy. Instead of immediately offering solutions and fixing problems for children, ask carefully crafted questions such as, "I wonder how we could solve that problem?" Educators can also role model their own strategies for using materials and overcoming challenges. For example, with a child who is struggling, the educator may say, "When I'm feeling really frustrated, I find that taking a short break can help." In these ways, educators engage in genuine conversations to learn about and support children's learning, also highlighting that adults are also learners (Probine, 2020).

Careful choice of materials

Materials play an important role in any inquiry. They need to be chosen with intention and care based on the children's questions and the potential of each material to support and expand children's explorations. It is important to select materials that are open-ended to offer unlimited possibilities. Engaging with high-quality materials doesn't need to be expensive. As discussed in Chapters 8 and 10, and in Part 3 of this book, some of the most open-ended materials are respectfully collected natural materials, leaves, pinecones, shells, or recycled materials. Collected and displayed in aesthetically pleasing ways, such materials invite children in to explore, play, and inquire.

Drawing is an immediate, easy, and effective way for children to record their ideas and mediate their thinking (Brooks, 2022a). It is therefore helpful to provide ready access to drawing materials, not just in designated artmaking spaces. Drawing can be undertaken in the sandpit, the construction area, or wherever an inquiry is taking place. Developing a culture where children and adults regularly draw their ideas and plans can support children to see themselves as powerful communicators. This practice also demonstrates to children that drawing is a valuable tool for expression in a wide variety of situations and contexts. Clipboards provide a hard, smooth surface for drawing anywhere and help keep artwork from blowing away in the wind.

Learning about a new material is like learning a new language. When learning a new language, it is helpful to have plenty of practice, along with guidance from someone who is already fluent in the language. Similarly, when new materials are offered to children, it's crucial they have many opportunities to repeatedly use materials and become familiar with them. No new learning experience should be a "one-off, succeed -or-fail exercise" (McArdle, 2012, p. 48). With repeated experiences and support from peers and educators, children will quickly develop strategies for working with new materials. Once confident in using a material, children can use it as a tool for expressing their inquiry and making meaning (Lewin-Benham, 2023).

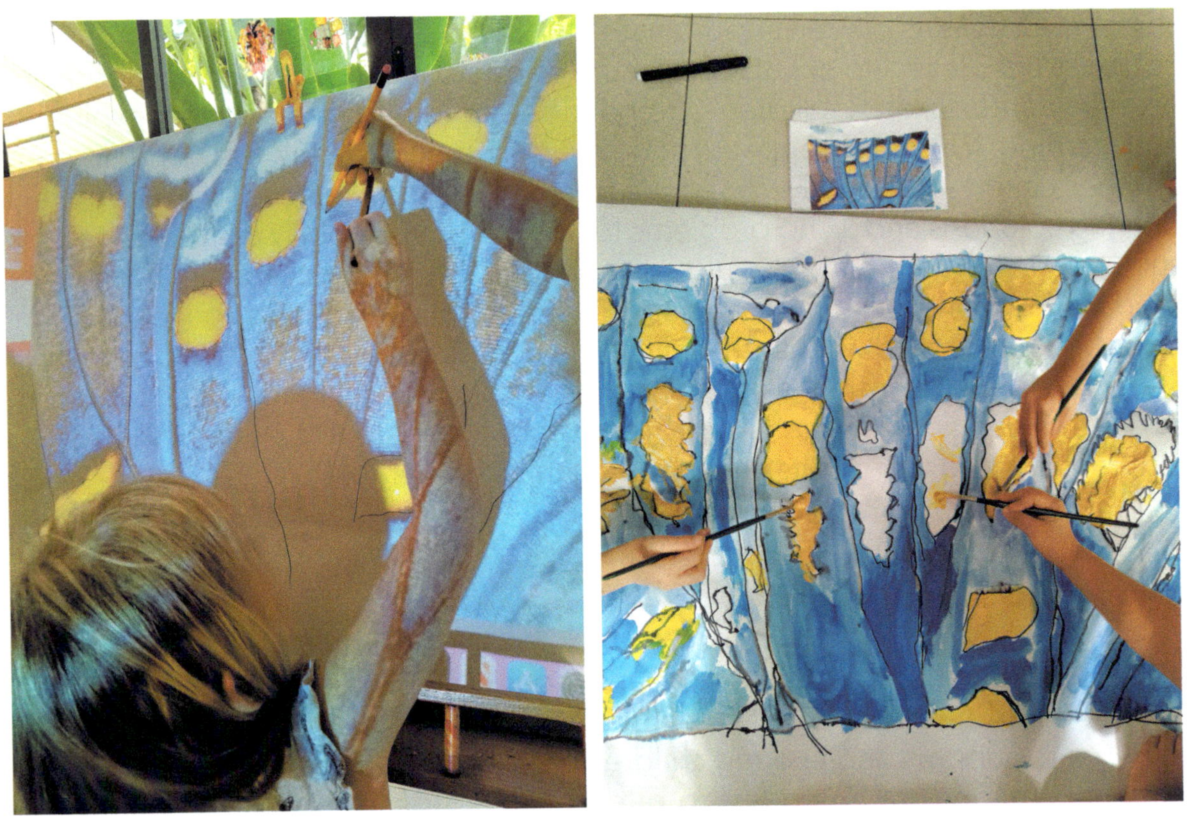

Figure 7.4(a,b) Carefully chosen materials provide endless opportunities for children to explore, create, and express their ideas. Repeated experiences with diverse media allow children to deepen their thinking, refine their skills, and uncover new questions and thinking [Images: Carolyn Prawius, Saigon Kids Early Learning Centre].

Although children need many encounters with each material or medium in order for it to become a tool for inquiry, it does not mean that they only need one medium. As children develop and refine their thinking within inquiry progresses, it is important that they have opportunities to represent their thinking through a range of media. This is because each new medium provokes different types of questions. For example, drawing and clay can be applied to extend and provoke children's inquiry and learning. Children can explore a particular focus of inquiry using drawing for a number of weeks; developing their thinking using two-dimensional artmaking. Later in the project, they can be invited to work in three-dimensions using clay, extending on their prior learning, while encountering new challenges and new questions related to their inquiry.

Progressing an inquiry – The role of documentation

An inquiry-based project develops in a cyclical way. Educators identify and respond to children's emergent interests. Children then engage in designed provocations and learning experiences. Educators carefully document children's engagement, responses, and conversations (if they are verbal). Documentation then informs teaching team analysis and discussions about what has occurred prior to making further plans to progress and deepen children's inquiry and learning experiences. Such inquiry project planning ideally happens in collaboration with children. Children's visual art and educators' documentation provide important tools to remind children, educators, and families about children's prior knowledge and thinking before taking next steps in a project of inquiry (Dahlberg, 2012; Stacey, 2019).

Documentation is often positioned as a way to share the results of an inquiry at the end of a project, rather than as a tool for progressively understanding the learning as the project unfolds. However, documentation can do both of these things and more. The act of documenting children's engagement in an inquiry is critical. Documentation supports educators to:

- Learn about children's learning strategies
- Analyse how children interact with each other and with materials
- Develop understanding about children's developing working theories
- Collaboratively analyse and make sense of children's learning
- Enrich the progress of an inquiry project through a range of perspectives
- Share children's learning with them to remind them of their previous thinking and learning strategies
- Maintain children's engagement in the learning project
- Help families to access and engage with the inquiry, and their children's learning
- Empower families to make meaningful contributions to the project
- Share more formal documentation created at the conclusion of a project to make children's learning, and educators' work visible.

The methods of documentation used by educators will vary depending on the inquiry. For example, a teaching team might use video to document infants exploring clay; allowing them to carefully analyse each infant's engagement with

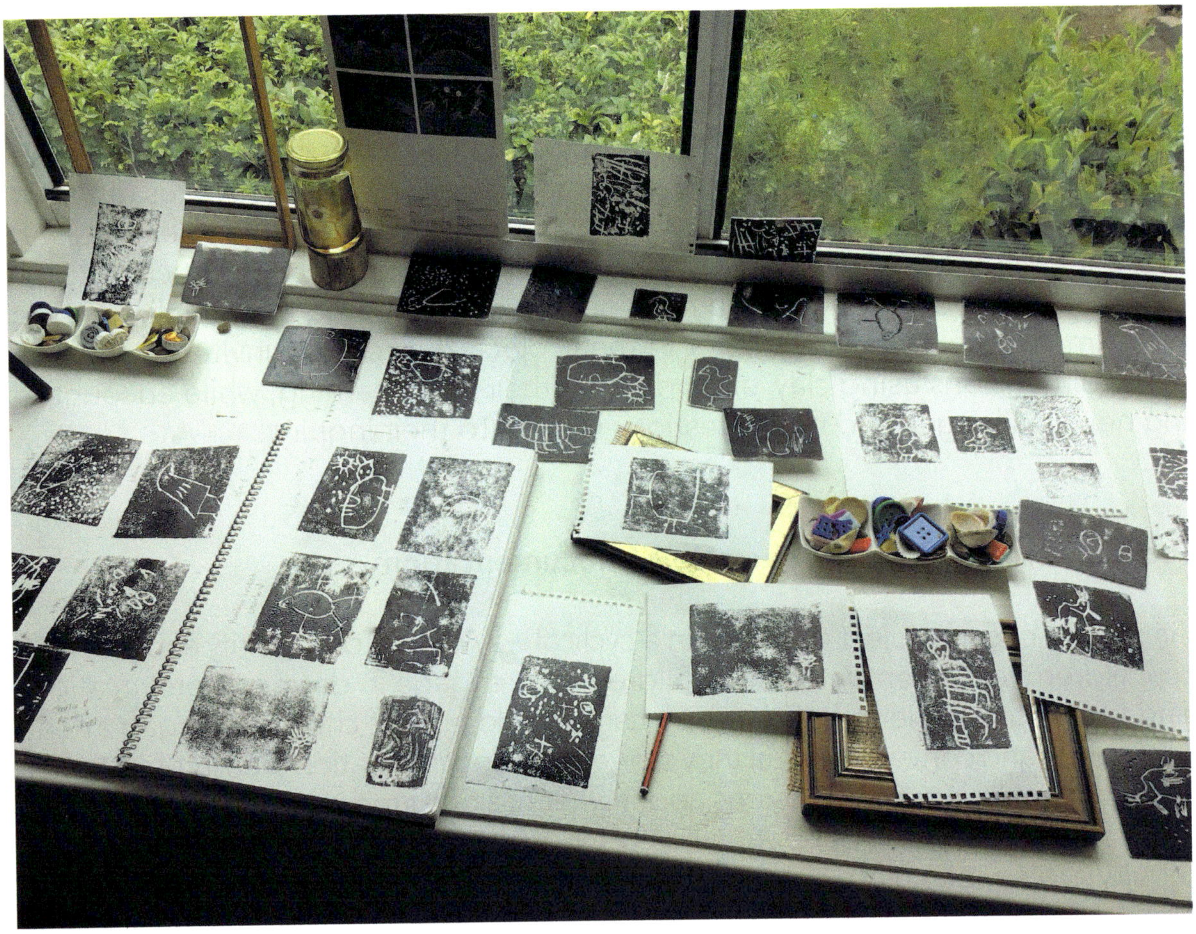

Figure 7.5 Documentation is a powerful tool in inquiry-based learning, capturing children's engagement, strategies, and evolving ideas. By reflecting on this evidence, educators can deepen the inquiry, evaluate learning, and revisit learning with children, families and the community [Image: Bomaderry Preschool].

the new material, while keeping their hands free to support and guide the experience. The same teaching team could then choose to document the project as a whole in a booklet format, knowing that each family will treasure a keepsake of their child's first encounters with clay. Visual artworks are themselves a form of documentation. Children's artworks can be included in wall displays, in paper-based and digital documentation for added interest. The regular inclusion of visual arts experiences in inquiry-based projects produces visible records of children's work that can support and enhance the engagement of the whole learning community.

Inquiry with infants and toddlers

A common misconception is that inquiry-based projects can only be conducted with older children. This belief potentially exists because many of the inquiry-based projects documented in books and resources feature older children with much attention given to children's conversations. However, infants and toddlers are serious researchers of materials, textures, senses, and movement

(Lewin-Benham, 2023); making projects of inquiry ideal for younger children. Effective infant and toddler inquiries require educators to closely observe and interpret the interests or questions that younger children may be expressing non-verbally as they engage with materials. By offering provocations, trialling different materials, and making adjustments throughout an experience, educators can begin to uncover the youngest children's motivations, questions and developing working theories. Following the children's cues and their progression of thinking and learning, educators can plan rich and meaningful experiences that connect and develop over time. Inquiry project plans should include regular and repeated opportunities for infants and toddlers to engage with visual arts materials and processes. In such material encounters, infants, toddlers, and educators become co-researchers, each with different research aims and questions.

Inquiry and inclusion

In more traditional classroom settings, it is the adults who mostly make decisions about what children will create, often resulting in everyone making the same thing. When this occurs, a classroom culture of comparison and competition can develop, leading to inequities and reducing children's confidence to explore, be creative, and feel fully included. In contrast, inquiry-based projects within play-based, child-honouring contexts provide authentic opportunities for everyone to contribute and be included. Educators play a crucial role in fostering inclusion as they adapt their levels of support to enable children to engage and contribute to an inquiry in ways that are meaningful and motivating for them. This requires that educators know each child in their setting very well, enabling them to be flexible and adaptive across the group. The imperative to be intentionally inclusive applies equally to inquiry projects and to visual arts learning experiences. Educators can invite combinations of children to work together in an inquiry project learning experience, knowing that one child might be an excellent leader, while another might be particularly empathetic and supportive of their peers.

Children with additional support needs, whether physical or cognitive, have the right to be included meaningfully in group projects of inquiry. This requires a focus on what children can do and contribute rather than on what they cannot (Rinaldi, 2001). The visual arts offer so many opportunities for genuine inclusion! For example, a child with delayed language development may take a lead role in drawing their ideas or in creating a collage of images related to the inquiry topic. Materials such as clay invite many different modes of engagement. While one child may immerse themselves in the sensory delights of clay, another may be working alongside them using clay to communicate an idea or theory. All children have the right to be actively included as active protagonists within inquiry-based learning experiences. Depending on the inquiry focus, it can also be valuable to invite a child who challenges others' thinking and asks divergent questions. You may also consider inviting children who are new to the inquiry process to work with other more experienced child-researchers so that they can be supportively initiated into this way of working.

The collaborative nature of inquiry-based project work means that every child can play an important role (Probine et al., 2023). As children learn to work together to explore ideas and questions, they learn to listen to each other and learn from each other through observation and co-participation with more capable peers. When children work and play in such dynamic partnerships something very special and very important occurs. Together, and through trial and error, children learn that there is not one correct answer, nor one correct perspective, on a topic. Instead, children can learn to appreciate that each human being is diverse and unique. On a wider political, ethical, and social level, this is one of the core purposes of education; to learn how to belong and operate in a community. The democratic nature of inquiry-based learning offers its deepest value. Within collaborative projects of inquiry, the visual arts offer a rich means by which children can think, inquire, adapt ideas, and communicate their ideas to others as they explore and learn about their worlds together.

Conclusion

Inquiry-based learning, enriched by the visual arts, fosters children's natural curiosity, empowering them as active participants in their education. By engaging collaboratively in investigations, children develop critical skills such as problem-solving, communication, and resilience, while learning to value diverse perspectives and processes over predefined outcomes. The visual arts offer a powerful medium for children to express, refine, and revisit their ideas throughout an inquiry, supporting them to communicate and deepen their understanding in meaningful ways.

As an educator, you play a vital role in shaping inclusive and democratic inquiry-based projects, serving as co-researchers who observe, document, and guide children's explorations with intention and care. By creating a culture that values experimentation, collaboration, and reflection, educators can foster an environment where children's voices, creativity, and agency are celebrated. Ultimately, inquiry-based projects, supported by the visual arts, inspire children to think critically, explore collaboratively, and engage deeply with their worlds.

Reference list

Brooks, M. (2022a). *Drawing to learn*. Pademelon Press.

Chard, S., Kogan, Y., & Castillo, C. (2017). *Picturing the project approach: Creative explorations in early learning*. Gryphon House.

Dahlberg, G. (2012). Pedagogical documentation: A practice for negotiation and democracy. In C. Edwards, L. Gandini, & G. Forman (Eds.), *The hundred languages of children: The Reggio Emilia experience in transformation* (3rd ed., pp. 225–231). Praeger.

Edwards, C. P. (2012). Teacher and learner, partner and guide: The role of the teacher. In C. Edwards, L. Gandini, & G. Forman (Eds.), *The hundred languages of children: The Reggio Emilia experience in transformation* (3rd ed., pp. 147–172). Praeger.

Gardner, A. F., & Jones, B. D. (2016). Examining the Reggio Emilia approach: Keys to understanding why it motivates students. *Electronic Journal of Research in Educational Psychology, 14*(3), 602–625.

Hedges, H. (2022). *Children's interests, inquiries and identities: Curriculum, pedagogy, learning and outcomes in the early years*. Routledge.

Kaynak-Ekici, K. B., İmir, H. M., & Temel, Z. F. (2021). Learning invitations in Reggio Emilia approach: A case study. *Education 3-13, 49*(6), 703–715. https://doi.org/10.1080/03004279.2020.1775272

Lewin-Benham, A. (2023). *Infants and toddlers at work: Using Reggio-inspired materials to support brain development* (2nd ed.). Teachers College Press.

McArdle, F. (2012). The visual arts: Ways of seeing. In S. Wright (Ed.), *Children, meaning-making and the arts* (2nd ed., pp. 30–56). Pearson Australia.

Probine, S. (2020). Examining the in-between: Contextual factors on how young children learn through the visual arts [Doctoral dissertation, University of Auckland]. http://hdl.handle.net/2292/52825

Probine, S., Perry, J., Burke, R., Alderson, J., & McAlevey, F. (2023). An examination of inquiry-based project learning in early childhood settings in Aotearoa/New Zealand. *Early Childhood Education Journal, 52*(6), 1083–1093. https://doi.org/10.1007/s10643-023-01495-7

Rinaldi, C. (2001). Reggio Emilia: The image of the child and the child's environment as a fundamental principle. In L. Gandini & C. Edwards (Eds.), *Bambini: The Italian approach to infant/toddler care* (pp. 49–54). Teachers College Press.

Stacey, S. (2019). *Inquiry-based early learning environments: Creating, supporting, and collaborating*. Redleaf Press.

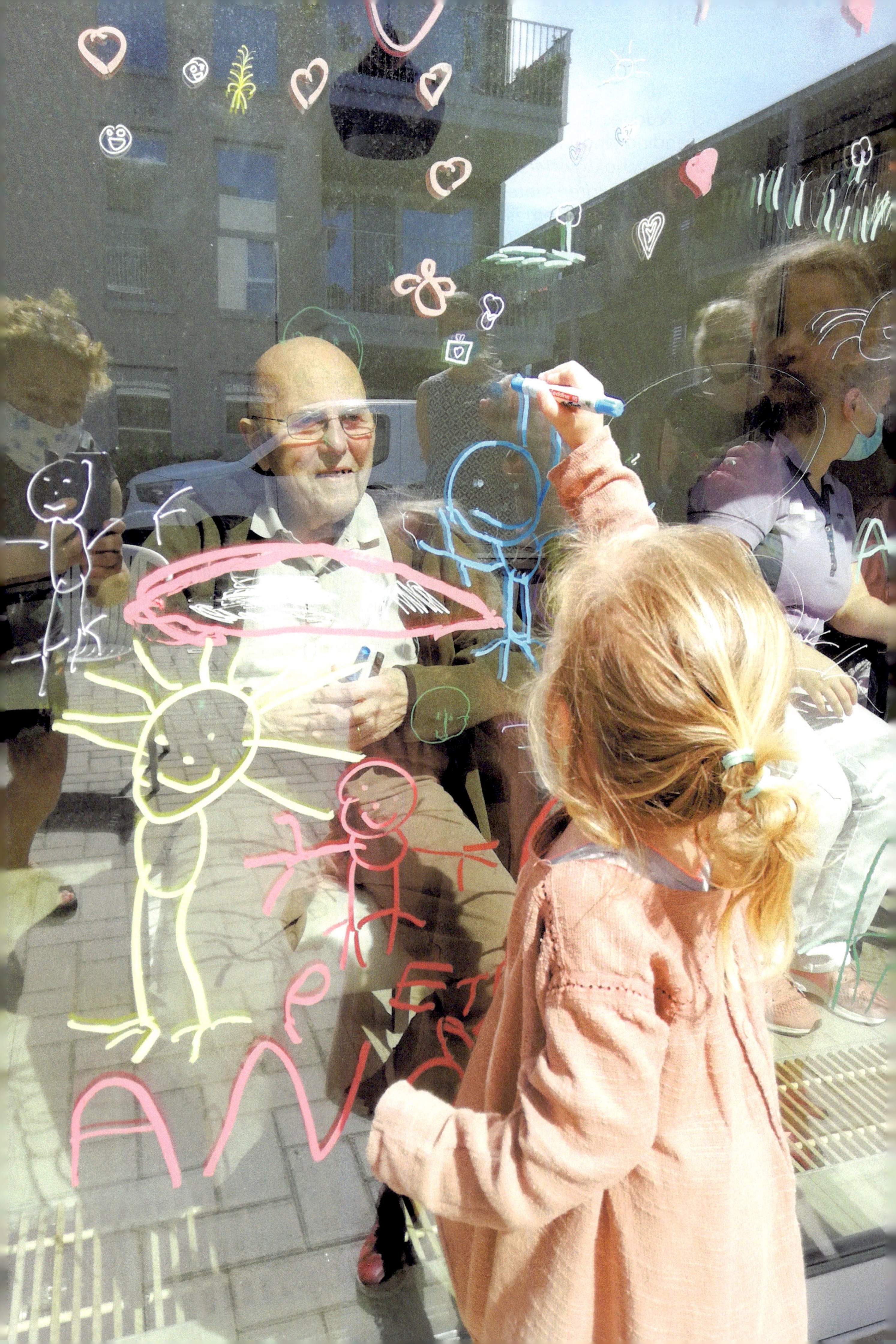

8 Art in and with the community

The visual arts offer powerful ways to foster children's connection to the places they live, including the broader community, natural environments, and cultural traditions. As children engage in everyday experiences with people, places, and materials in their local communities, they become active participants in learning that is relevant to their personal context (Fuemana-Foa'i et al., 2009). When we invite children to explore and engage in their communities, we make them visible in that space, and open up opportunities for them to contribute to that place and to be valued as citizens in their communities. Engaging children as citizens of their communities "transforms the places of the town" as a "form of democratic participation" (Piccinini, in Turner & Wilson, 2009, p. 10). The visual arts provide valuable opportunities for children to share their responses to community, engage in collaborative interactions within it, and communicate their unique perspectives. Connecting children with people and places in the local community through visual arts encounters supports children to care about their local place, and to develop their own sense of identity and belonging within their communities (Probine et al., 2024).

In this chapter, we explore a range of possibilities for community-related visual arts education. Visual arts experiences can support children to connect with and make sense of the communities and cultures that surround them, and foster learning about the cultures, histories, traditions, and stories of their place (Fuemana-Foa'i et al., 2009). We emphasise the significant role traditional crafting and artisan techniques play in culture and society and advocate for their inclusion in the repertoire of arts experiences offered to children. Visual arts and crafts experiences can nurture children's connection with natural environments and promote sustainable thinking (Lindsay, 2024). Social and community arts events offer rich potential to not only connect children with others in their community, but also to elevate children's presence and rights as citizens within their communities. Finally, we suggest ways to engage with both artworks and artists in your local area to provoke creative exploration, discussion, and social connections.

Figure 8.1 During the Covid-19 pandemic, Erasmus Brussels University early childhood students used drawing to connect children with aged care residents living at WZC OASE in Wolvertem, Belgium. The joy of intergenerational dialogue through art is clear on Mr André De Boodt's face [Image: Joke den Haese].

DOI: 10.4324/9781003561835-10

Exploring community

Visual arts materials and processes are a perfect way to support children to explore and make sense of their ideas about the places, spaces, and people of the communities in which they live. Local histories, cultural and environmental knowledge may feel somewhat abstract, however the visual arts provide children with concrete ways to discover and express ideas. Educators can purposefully create art-based opportunities for children to engage with the local environments and communities that they live in. Additionally, making art with other people in the community environment creates a context for building relationships and fostering a sense of belonging.

A great way to start is to undertake regular local community walks with no particular agenda in mind (see The Point Preschool case study). Educators and children can relax and take time to talk about the surroundings; inviting children to notice what is around them and closely explore things that interest them. Cameras and tablets present a very effective invitation for children to focus on objects and record what interests them with photographs or video. Opportunities to draw in the environment or community invites children to slow down, notice, and record the natural and built environments around them. This offers valuable insights into how children view their world, what they notice and find important or interesting, and supports consideration about the questions and curiosities that drive their learning (White, 2015). Such discoveries offer meaningful starting points for curriculum development and inquiry-based learning projects. The images children capture or create also present great potential once back in the classroom. For example, photographs can be printed and used to support children to revisit and talk about their experiences with others. Drawings and images can also be utilised as provocations for further learning and reflection; inviting children to remember, reflect and communicate their experience in the community through artmaking.

Case study – The point preschool

The children and educators of The Point Preschool in Oyster Bay, Australia, walk on Dharawal Country, exploring the bushland, creek, and river in their local neighbourhood. Guided by Ann Pelo's belief that time is intimacy (2013), we connect with nature's subtle, unfolding changes. Weekly walks, grounded in returning and revisiting, offer opportunities to slow down, see with fresh eyes, and notice the delicate transformations of the landscape across days, months, and seasons. Each visit invites a deeper appreciation of nature's beauty. As we walk on Country (Yanma Nura), the land speaks to us in quiet ways. It's here, among the trees and grass, that Georgia found a sense of connection. "I love it when I see trees and the grass when I walk on Yanma Nura," she shared. The children are inspired by what they see. They notice the bumpy sandstone track, the bird's overhead, the ripples of the creek's incoming tide, and the changing light across the landscape. Noticing textures others may overlook, Hazel used a camera to focus closely on the path, announcing, "I'm taking a photo of the bumpy sandstone track." Fin also noticed the lines of the track and drew the earth from an aerial perspective, "like you are looking from the sky in an aeroplane." Colours selected by some children responded to the vibrant rainbow

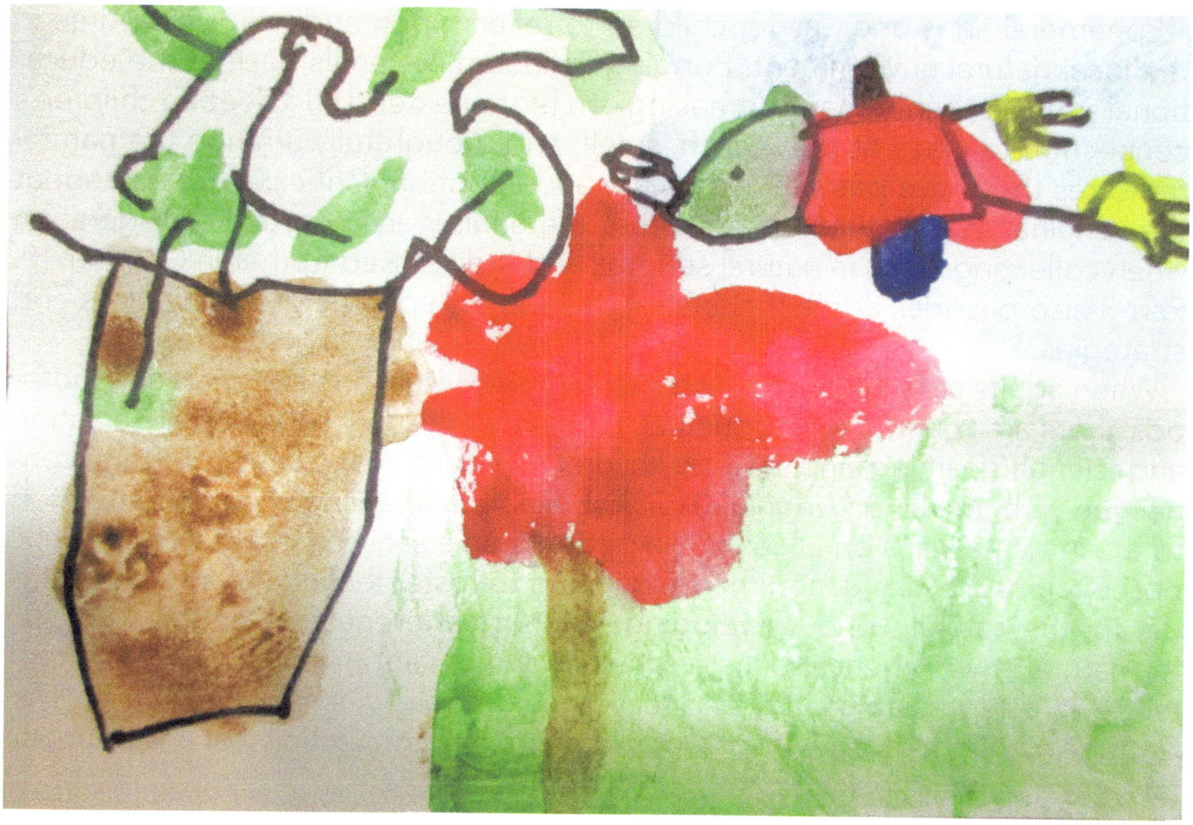

Figure 8.2 Vanessa responded to the vibrant colours of the rainbow lorikeet observed during a walk on Country [Image: The Point Preschool].

lorikeets observed during their walk: "For the rainbow lorikeet - I need all the colours!" said Vanessa as she recorded her rich observations using paints. The children's art (drawings, photographs, collage, clay works) are a testament to the connection they feel with the earth beneath their feet. Through this connection, art not only enriches the children's learning, but reminds the wider community of the importance of noticing, slowing down, and developing a lasting appreciation for the land.

Environmental education

The natural environment has inspired artists around the world since prehistoric times, and Indigenous art forms feature strong connections to the natural world (Heta-Lensen & Wrightson, 2019). Plants, animals, landforms, and bodies of water inspire the use of visual arts materials to express ideas and responses to environmental provocations. In recent years, the visual arts have become a means for environmental artists to explore and highlight environmental issues and human factors impacting the earth; issues that impact all citizens, whether child or adult. Educators have a responsibility to introduce environmental concepts to children, and to reflect on their role in promoting sustainable practices and environmental advocacy (Alcock & Ritchie, 2018). At the same time, rather than learning about nature, children can learn in nature, developing empathy and expressing their ideas and connections through art and inquiry (Keyte-Hartland & Lowings, 2025). Children cannot be expected to care for the earth without first having opportunities to develop awareness and appreciation for it.

Ephemeral art is one way for children to reflect upon and revisit their time in the local natural environment. Bringing collected materials back to the educational setting for ephemeral artmaking can further extend and deepen children's connection to place as they touch, smell, and thoughtfully arrange the natural treasures they have gathered with care and intention. Critical reflection about the sustainable and ethical use of natural materials is an important consideration when collecting items in natural settings and is discussed further in Chapter 10. Part 3 also provides additional information about ephemeral art practices and strategies.

When adults and children explore nature using visual arts materials and methods, there are countless opportunities to enhance children's focused observation and scientific learning, and to foster children's sense of responsibility for, and connection with, the land (Wright, 2015). For example, drawing children's attention to the intricate veins on a leaf or the patterns on a seashell integrates scientific observation, artmaking, and theory-building to foster feelings of awe and wonder for the natural world. Developing children's awareness of, and passion for, the natural environment also fosters their awareness about issues of environmental stewardship, sustainability, and recycling. The following case study from The Cottage highlights the power of regular community connections for environmental learning and artmaking.

Case study: Community classrooms – Blue Gum Community School

"*Community Classrooms*" is a unique early childhood program at Blue Gum Community School, located in Canberra, Australia. This program positions wider community settings as classrooms and enacts a vision to support our youngest students (3–5-year-olds) to be valued as active citizens in their community. By fostering genuine connections with spaces and places over an extended time period, deep relationships are formed. Children's curiosity and exploration leads to questions and inquiry. In a recent community classroom project, the preschool class visited the Australian National Botanic Gardens (ANBG) fourteen times across several months. From the first visit, the children were enraptured by the myriad of colours, shapes and forms in the ANGB. Informed by a pedagogy of listening (Rinaldi, 2013), we moved slowly and stopped often, allowing sparks of curiosity to be stoked. As one student noted: *"When we look closely, we can see the pattern in things." This* observation became a focus for inquiry for about seven months.

After just a few visits, the children quickly learned to spot recurring textures and colours in both natural and human-made garden elements. However, their joy was disrupted by frequent reminders not to remove items from the gardens. Many discussions followed about the ANBG being a sanctuary for plants, with reminders that as visitors we could still observe and connect with nature's wonders. The children debated how to capture the intriguing patterns they found, while respecting the environment's right to be safe from plunder. Educators also faced the challenge to satisfy students' curiosity, while teaching respectful interactions with nature.

Visual arts provocations offered children many opportunities to observe, notice, collect textures, and capture their observations in rich and meaningful ways. Equipped with art journals, children initially completed observational drawings using the familiar languages of pencil and paper. Graphite rubbings of textured surfaces and foliage complimented our collection of textures. Back at school, these sketches and rubbings inspired watercolour painting, where the various shades of colour added a different form of communication and connection with the children's experiences: *"I painted some blue there. I mixed it all together to make a cloud, because it was going to rain. My body felt grey, like the fog is grey."* Feeling that we had not yet captured nature's essence, we turned to clay, another familiar art language. The extra dimension offered by this medium was the missing piece. The children delighted in taking texture impressions and creating small-scale sculptures. At last, they had found satisfying, respectful ways to capture their beloved textures and shapes. Back at school, their research into patterns also continued via letter and number patterns, geometric designs, indigenous and abstract art analysis, and music.

Immersion in this intense cycle of observation, reflection, and re-creation, enabled the children to gradually make sense of their experiences through connection with familiar art materials. As their final act in this inquiry-based learning journey, the children were keen to create a thankyou gift after having

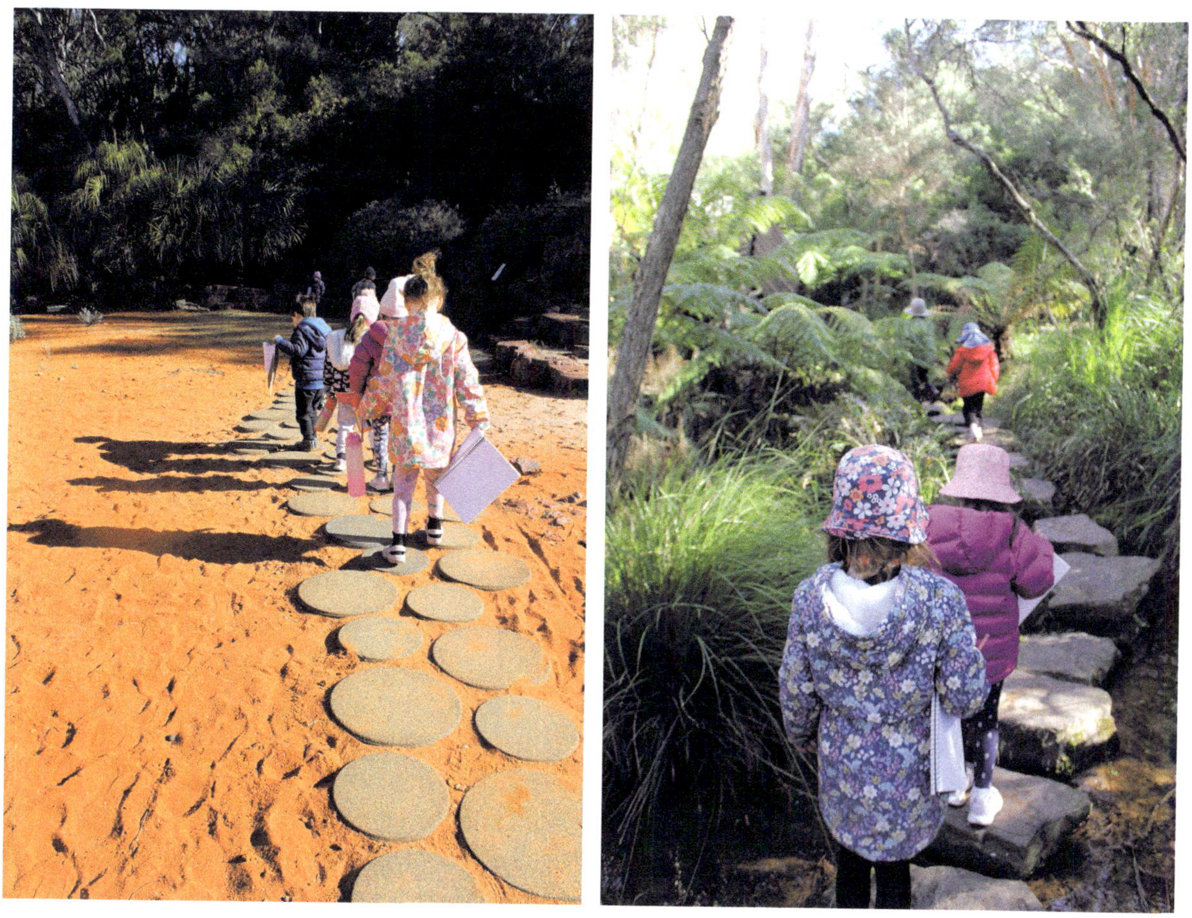

Figure 8.3(a,b) Children explored and documented their observations and inquiries through art during regular community classroom excursions to the Australian National Botanic Gardens [Image: Blue Gum Community School].

gained so much themselves. What better way to capture the colour patterns they loved, than by creating a clay and fibre art sculpture they called "The Pattern Rainbow." Gifted to the ANGB staff, the sculpture was both a powerful act of gratitude and a reminder from children to "look closely" at the amazing natural world around them.

Exploring art in the community

Looking for artworks in the local community can reveal a surprising abundance of artistic works to explore with children. Besides local art galleries (which we discuss in the following chapter), many communities are filled with wall murals, street art, sculptures, art installations and even garden art crafted by homeowners, showcasing rich local artistic culture. Experiencing such diverse forms of art conveys the important message that art is for everyone. A wonderful benefit of community art is that it is easily accessible which means that children can enjoy repeated experiences with it, supporting them to make connections, ask questions, and explore related ideas or techniques. If you find an artwork in your community, investigate the following:

- Who is the artist? Can you make contact or find out more about them?
- What is the intention, the story, or the meanings explored in the artwork?
- Are there important themes or lessons to be explored through the artwork?
- What kinds of visual arts materials and processes could you explore with children?
- What are the children's interpretations and ideas about the work? Invite children to think about what the artist was trying to communicate, what they like or do not like about the work, and why the artwork is placed in the space.

Just as local communities are filled with art in surprising places, it is likely there are artists working in your local community. Connecting with local artists offers wonderful benefits for children, teachers, and the artists themselves (Shulsky & Kirkwood, 2015). Research local artists by visiting local galleries and keeping an eye out for public events and exhibitions. Learning about public artworks in the local community can lead to discovering local artists you could connect with. To ensure respectful and positive interactions, carefully recruit artists who appreciate young children as capable citizens. Acknowledge the professionalism and time of local artists by offering them payment, rather than assuming voluntary involvement in any collaboration projects.

There are many ways that artists can become involved with educational communities. It can be as simple as extending an invitation for them to visit the setting with some examples of their work, or as complex as employing them to create a collaborative artwork in partnership with children (Fuemana-Foa'i et al., 2009). As the relationship develops, explore opportunities to organise an excursion to their studio or workshop. Partnerships with local artists are of great value to children and educators. Such artist connections provide first-hand exposure to the many methods, techniques, and approaches that artists use; broadening awareness about what art is and how to make it. Opportunities to connect with practising artists also support children to make connections between the person, their processes, and the artwork itself. Partnerships between artists and children offer immense value for artists too, exposing them to children's wonder and joy as they experience new things for the first time. Observing children's interpretations and listening to their ideas offers practising artists fresh perspectives about their own practice.

Community connections through art

Community excursions, public events, and exhibitions of children's work make children and their learning visible, highlighting their rights as community members who deserve equal access to shared spaces and opportunities to influence their world (Edwards et al., 2012). Not only is this beneficial for children, it is also valuable for community members to see children being active participants in society and share in their wonder and delight. Providing an inspiring act of political advocacy for children to be seen and heard in their communities, Loris Malaguzzi took children into the community and implemented preschool activities in the piazzas and porticos of Reggio Emilia, Italy, to raise community appreciation for children's rights and capabilities (Edwards et al., 2012). In contemporary Reggio Emilia, the belief that children are citizens with the right to actively engage and contribute to the life of the community is considered as a form of transformational democratic participation (Rinaldi interview, in Turner & Wilson, 2009). Similarly, an intergenerational arts project in Brussels, utilises arts experiences to connect children and older community members, enriching the lives of all involved.

Case study – Intergenerational arts project

BrOLL (Brussels Open Living Lab) is a vibrant intergenerational project initiated in the Bachelor of Early Childhood Education and Care (BECEC) program at Erasmus Brussels University of Applied Sciences and Arts. BrOLL brings together children and older adults from diverse cultural and socioeconomic backgrounds in shared creative spaces, where they connect, collaborate, and co-create using discarded materials from local organisations. Located in the heart of Brussels, BrOLL transforms these "loose parts" – objects often seen as clutter or waste – into tools for expression, dialogue, and learning. Embracing the "100 languages" concept from the Reggio Emilia approach, participants are encouraged to communicate in various creative forms, bridging generational gaps and inspiring each other's perspectives. Inspired by Hannah Arendt's view of intergenerational education, the project supports children to explore visual expression through play with materials. At the same time, the elderly participants rediscover play through their partnerships with children, gaining insight into what children value, worry about, and envision for the future. Through collaborative art and conversation, BrOLL nurtures empathy, cultural awareness, identity-building, and a shared community vision,

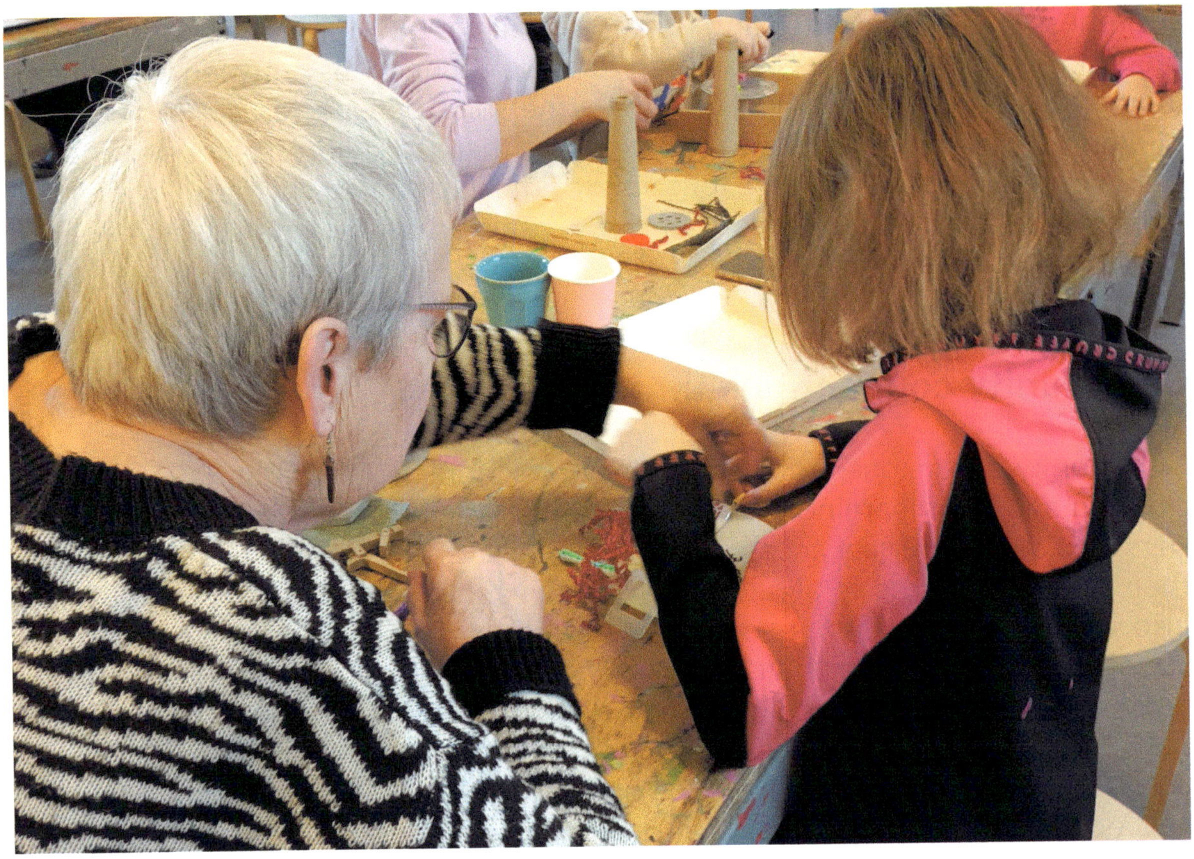

Figure 8.4 Children, elderly people, and university students collaborate, co-create, and build relationships through art in the Brussels Open Living Lab intergenerational project [Image: Joke den Haese].

empowering the BECEC student coaches to become reflective educators who value the potential of every individual. Through art, play, and dialogue, BrOLL builds a shared community vision and promotes identity, tolerance, and respect for diverse experiences, empowering all participants to see themselves and each other in new ways (Den Haese, 2019; Verhaeghe & Den Haese, 2020).

Exhibitions of children's work

Much of the early intent underpinning the work of the atelier and the exhibition of children's projects in Reggio Emilia, Italy, revolved around a desire to visually communicate with the public (Vecchi, 2010), and particularly with children's parents, to elevate awareness about children's intelligence, ideas and capabilities (Malaguzzi, 1994). Vecchi (2010, p. 72) explains that the products of children's work give parents a "new image of their own children and children in general." Drawing on such ideas, educators can use visual arts projects and pedagogical documentation to amplify children's voices beyond the classroom; making children more visible and valued in their communities. By thoughtfully and respectfully displaying children's work and visual arts explorations and products, educators foster meaningful connections between children, families, and the wider community, reinforcing children's role as co-constructors of culture, and participants in democratic social change (Turner & Wilson, 2009).

Connections with culture, history, and artistic traditions

The community places, spaces, and people surrounding education settings are rich in culture, history, and artistic traditions. The children, families, and staff in educational settings embody culture, histories, and stories which offer many opportunities to make and build connections. Understanding the cultures and traditional practices embedded in the communities where people live, work, and play helps educators and adults in children's lives to appreciate the diverse cultural representation in the community and in the classroom. It is so important to ensure that the curriculum experiences offered to children reflect the communities they live in. Connecting visual arts learning experiences with cultural events and festivals, and the cultural and artisan traditions associated with them, opens up dialogue, awareness, and opportunities to maintain cultural traditions and collective memories. Consider which cultural festivals are relevant to the local community and the lives of the children in your classroom. Invite community members to share culturally relevant artisan skills and traditions. Display images of local and traditional architecture, craft and artisan materials, and artwork. When introducing children to the work of artists, seek out artists in your own community to expand children's connections and awareness of the diverse cultures, people groups, and artistic traditions. Investigating personal and family histories can affirm both individual and collective cultural identities.

Culture, history, and stories of people and their lands

The visual arts provide meaningful ways for educators to balance age-appropriate teaching, while supporting young children to develop new understandings about reconciliation, cultural knowledge, and social justice. By exploring the stories, values, and beliefs of local Indigenous cultures, children cultivate critical thinking, empathy, and respect for diverse perspectives. Engaging with Indigenous art practices and visual storytelling offers a rich way to understand a culture's beliefs, values, history, and connections to place (Heta-Lensen & Wrightson, 2019). Visual arts experiences support children to retell and reflect on these stories, deepening their connection to their environment and heritage (Heta-Lensen & Wrightson, 2019). Educators play a crucial role in guiding children to encounter the lessons, and themes within stories and artwork, while carefully and honestly navigating cultural and historical complexities.

Regardless of location or prior knowledge about local cultures, educators are encouraged to research, learn, and experience local art forms with children. When planning to share cultural knowledge, educators must first develop their own understanding of the significance of cultural art practices, ensuring they approach traditions, values, and protocols with respect. Building personal knowledge of cultural art forms is essential to avoid tokenism and

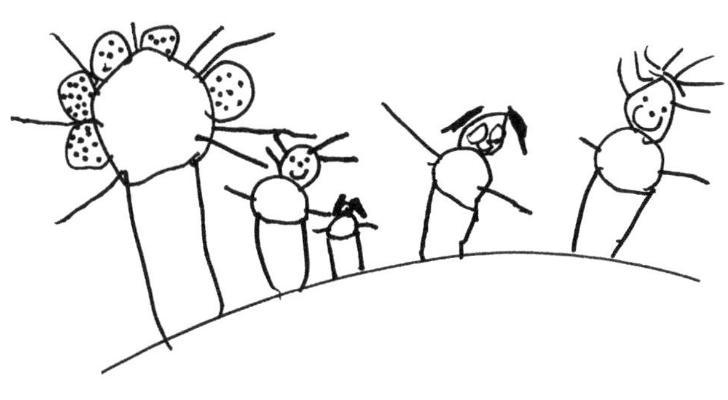

create meaningful, authentic learning experiences that honour the traditions and practices of Indigenous communities. When planning to incorporate local Indigenous and Aboriginal art practices into the curriculum, consider the following strategies:

- Have a conversation with fellow educators and families who may have cultural knowledge, insights, and lived experience they could share.
- Conduct research, utilising the local library and online resources and connecting with local groups and respected local elders.
- Extend personal understanding about cultural art practices by attending a course, or learning from community experts who are willing to share their knowledge.
- Collect children's books that include authentically produced Indigenous art and illustrations.
- Include local and culturally endorsed resources and images in the learning environment.
- Arrange excursions within the local community, galleries, and museums to view examples of Indigenous art.
- Invite young children to be curious about the deeper meanings, lessons, and metaphors that are embedded in cultural and Indigenous stories and art. This is supported by raising open-ended "wondering" questions which have no specific response in mind.
- Welcome children's questions, interpretations, and ideas about cultural artefacts and Indigenous artworks.

Embedding Indigenous knowledge and art forms into the visual arts curriculum requires intentionality and reflection. Educators should actively incorporate Aboriginal and Indigenous perspectives within the curriculum, ensuring that visual arts offerings reflect the cultural diversity and the unique spaces and environments of the local community. Regular evaluation of these practices helps to create a meaningful and inclusive curriculum that respects and celebrates Indigenous cultures and fosters deeper connections and understanding amongst children and their communities.

Arts and traditional crafts

Another rich way to engage in cultural histories and traditional cultural practices is by introducing traditional crafts and artisan processes. Introducing children to the skills, methods, and materials used for sewing (threading/stitching), fibre explorations (fabric arts, clothing design), weaving, woodwork, paper crafts (quilling, origami, paper-making), and cultural traditions such as making kites, traditional lanterns, and baskets are a rich way of maintaining and engaging with cultural heritage and traditions. These experiences offer rich potential to foster community connections and maintain cultural traditions. Age-old methods can be maintained and celebrated when artisans and family members are welcomed into early education settings to demonstrate and share their skills and expertise.

In our experience, there is an immersive joy when a small group of children are supported to master crafting processes and methods. Like quilting circles, sharing these skills and methods with children creates a context for conversation, focus, problem-solving, and mastery.

Such skills and techniques used to be commonplace in early education settings. However, Lindsay's research (2016; 2017) identified that such learning experiences have largely disappeared from early education classrooms. This loss of important skills and processes may be attributed to a range of factors. Some educators perhaps avoid the inclusion of activities that appear too instructional; believing that all step-by-step activities with an outcome or end-product goal should be discouraged and rejected as being too teacher-led. Additionally, some educators mistakenly believe the complex skills involved in artisan methods and techniques are beyond young children's capabilities. Some adults perhaps consider tools such as scissors, needles, sewing machines or hammers too risky for children. Others may believe the processes required for artisan work are too labour-intensive in a busy classroom. And, sadly, such skills and knowledge may already be disappearing from the repertoire of educators, parents, and teachers, to the point that they are not even considered as options.

We therefore advocate for the inclusion of crafts and artisan methods, not only for all of the reasons outlined, but because we know children are capable. With support, children will embrace complex processes and the challenge of mastering the use of artisan and crafting tools. Even the youngest children can be introduced to the materials, tools, and underlying skills associated with artisan and crafting methods. [See Part 3 for practical ideas.] When educators are confident to deconstruct the processes and materials utilised in craft and artisan techniques, children of any age or stage of development can be supported to engage, learn and enjoy their right to be immersed in cultural and artistic life (UNCRC, article 31).

Fostering curiosity and inquiry

Inquiry-based learning, which was explored in Chapter 7, can be a powerful way to develop children's connections to the places they live and play (Probine et al., 2024). Children may express an interest in a natural feature, such as a mountain or body of water, a building, a person, or a story from their community. This can provide an exciting starting point for an inquiry project through which educators can also broaden children's worldviews by intentionally introducing new ideas and concepts. For example, following play and exploration about bridge constructions and design, children's explorations could be extended by sharing many images of bridges from around the world. Children could be prompted to consider the engineering required to design and build bridges and provided with drawing materials and tools to design bridges. Educators could also set up a construction station with loose parts such as wood offcuts, heavy cardboard strips, papers, fabric, and glue. Educators might encourage children to experiment with building their own bridges for toy vehicles or animals, asking open-ended questions and challenges such as, "How can we make this bridge

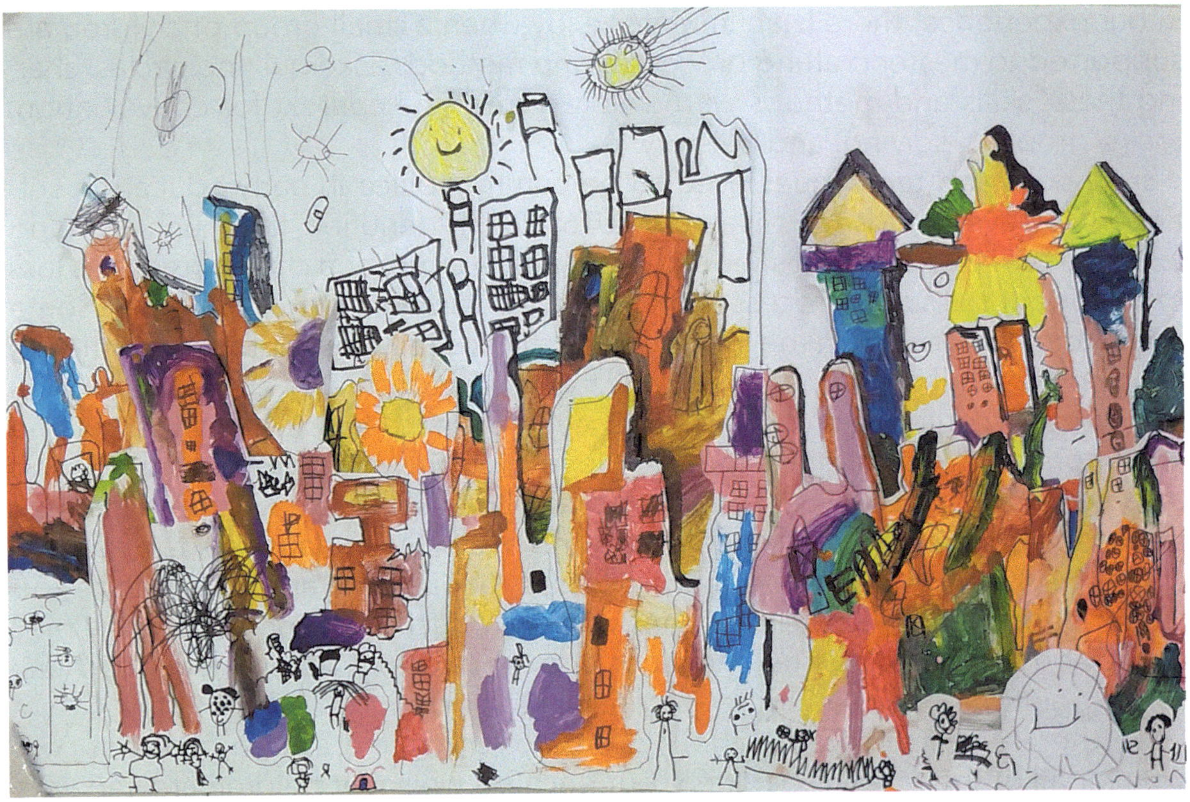

Figure 8.5 Children share their knowledge and perceptions of Ho Chi Minh City in a collective mural artwork [Image: Carolyn Prawius, Saigon Kids Early Learning Centre].

strong enough to hold your truck?" or "What happens if we make the bridge longer?" Such hands-on exploration and creative problem-solving help children to develop skills and test theories while making connections to their local environment.

When exploring local spaces and places, creating a collaborative giant map or mural of the streets, buildings, and landmarks within the community can support children to develop spatial awareness. Images of local people, natural features, local plants, and animals can be added to the map to expand children's sense of belonging and extend the connections they make between places, people, and things located in their community and their world. Children's learning and experience can be further expanded and consolidated by collaborating with them to write and illustrate a book about their focus of inquiry within their community.

Once an interest or question is identified about the community and environment, educators can utilise visual arts methods to enhance children's inquiry. For example, if a specific location has sparked the children's curiosity:

- Plan to spend extended periods of time exploring and engaging in the space.
- Support careful observation of the surrounding environment, and help children to pinpoint the view they would like to focus on, by providing a cardboard frame with a hole to look through.

- Provide small clipboards as a very useful steady surface for drawing while out on excursions.
- Offer small watercolour palettes or coloured pencils for children to add colour to their representations. This can be a way to slow the process down and encourage children to look more closely.

Observational drawing invites children to connect with the world around them and to observe more closely. The provision of magnifying glasses, paper, and drawing materials invites children to recognise and translate the shapes, patterns, and colours they observe into a visual representation of their discoveries. Educators can guide children's observational drawing by creating opportunities for deep engagement and reflection. The following strategies enhance children's drawing skills while extending their capacity to observe, analyse, and creatively interpret the world around them:

- **Explore objects together**: Begin by examining the object or focus of drawing collaboratively, discussing shapes, textures, colours, and even scents. This shared discovery helps children build a detailed understanding of the object or place being drawn.
- **Encourage representation**: Support children as they translate their observations into drawings, helping them focus on specific details or elements they find interesting.
- **Model the process**: Drawing alongside children provides a valuable opportunity to model techniques, share challenges, and demonstrate problem-solving strategies. This collaborative approach demystifies the process and encourages perseverance.
- **Foster dialogue**: Engage children in conversations about their drawings, encouraging them to articulate their observations and the decisions they make during the process. Listen carefully to find out more about what the children are curious about, their theories, and narratives, as drawing together can foster dialogue and shared learning.

Conclusion

Local communities and their diverse environments provide a rich canvas for visual arts education, enabling children to develop meaningful connections with the people, places, and stories that shape their world. Through creative engagement, children not only explore their surroundings but also become active participants in their communities, contributing their unique perspectives and voices. Visual arts experiences offer powerful tools for children to express their identity, reflect on their place within the community, and deepen their sense of belonging.

By fostering these connections, in your role as an educator, you can empower children to care for their environment and develop a sense of social responsibility. Further, through making children's participation and their art visible educators can amplify children's voices and ideas within their communities. Such experiences build bridges across generations, cultures, and histories, through encouraging dialogue, collaboration, and respect for diverse perspectives. Visual arts education rooted in community engagement enables children to see themselves as contributors to the cultural and environmental fabric of their world, fostering curiosity, empathy, and a lifelong appreciation for the interconnectedness of people, places, and the arts.

References

Alcock, S., & Ritchie, J. (2018). Early childhood education in the outdoors in Aotearoa New Zealand. *Journal of Outdoor and Environmental Education, 21*(1), 77–88. https://doi.org/10.1007/s42322-017-0009-y

Den Haese, J. (2019). The role of the pedagogical coach in the encounter between older adults and children in Belgium. In M. Kernan, & G. Cortellesi (Eds.), *Intergenerational learning in practice* (pp. 189–204). Routledge. https://doi.org/10.4324/9780429431616

Edwards, C., Gandini, L., & Forman, G. (Eds.) ((2012). *The hundred languages of children: The Reggio Emilia experience in transformation* (3rd ed.). Praeger.

Fuemana-Foa'i, L., Pohio, L., & Terreni, L. (2009). Narratives from Aotearoa New Zealand: Building communities in early childhood through the visual arts. *Teaching Artist Journal, 7*(1), 23–33. https://doi.org/10.1080/15411790802344371

Heta-Lensen, Y., & Wrightson, H. (2019). Toi tū te whenua: A study of māori visual arts as dialogue with papatūānuku. *International Art in Early Childhood Research Journal, 1*(1), 1–21. https://artinearlychildhood.org/journal/2019-research-journal-1

Keyte-Hartland, D., & Lowings, L. (2025). Learning to live well together: Art and ecological research with young children. In Z. Moula, & N. Walshe (Eds.), *Art in nature with children and young people: A guide towards health equality, well-being and sustainability* (pp. 98–107). Routledge. doi:10.4324/9781003357308-9

Lindsay, G. (2016). Do visual art experiences in early childhood settings foster educative growth or stagnation? *International Art in Early Childhood Research Journal*, 5(1), 1–14. http://artinearlychildhood.org/2016-research-journal-1/

Lindsay, G. (2017). *Art is experience: An exploration of the visual arts beliefs and pedagogy of Australian early childhood educators* [Doctoral dissertation, University of Wollongong] https://ro.uow.edu.au/theses1/170

Lindsay, G. (2024). Visual arts learning: Beyond the easel and beyond the gate. Play *Outdoors Magazine. Winter*, *4*(4), 28–30.

Malaguzzi, L. (1994). Your image of the child: Where teaching begins. *Child Care Information Exchange*, *3*(1), 52–61.

Pelo, A. (2013). *The goodness of rain: Developing an ecological identity in young children*. Exchange Press.

Probine, S., Perry, J., Alderson, J. M., Heta-Lensen, Y., Burke, R., & McAlevey, F. L. (2024). Inquiry-based project learning as an approach to foster wellbeing, sustained focus, and bi-cultural practice in early childhood education. *Australasian Journal of Early Childhood, 49*(1), 49–62. https://doi.org/10.1177/18369391231212685

Rinaldi, C. (2013). *Re-imagining childhood: The inspiration of Reggio Emilia education principles in South Australia*. Government of South Australia.

Shulsky, D., & Kirkwood, D. (2015). Beyond tempera paint: Authentically exploring visual art in early childhood. *Childhood Education*, *91*(5), 363–369. https://doi.org/10.1080/00094056.2015.1090851

Turner, T., & Wilson, D. G. (2009). Reflections on documentation: A discussion with thought leaders from Reggio Emilia. *Theory Into Practice*, *49*(1), 5–13. https://doi.org/10.1080/00405840903435493

UNICEF. (n.d.). United Nations Convention on the Rights of the Child (UNCRC). https://www.unicef.org/child-rights-convention/convention-text

Vecchi, V. (2010). *Art and creativity in Reggio Emilia: Exploring the role and potential of ateliers in early childhood education*. Routledge.

Verhaeghe, K., & Den Haese, J. (2020). Narratives, identity and cultural awareness. In M. Gasper, & R. Walker. (Eds.), *Mentoring and coaching in early childhood education* (pp. 163–179). Bloomsbury.

White, E. J. (2015). Seeing is believing? Insights from young children in nature. *International Journal of Early Childhood*, *47*, 171–188. https://doi.org/10.1007/s13158-014-0118-5

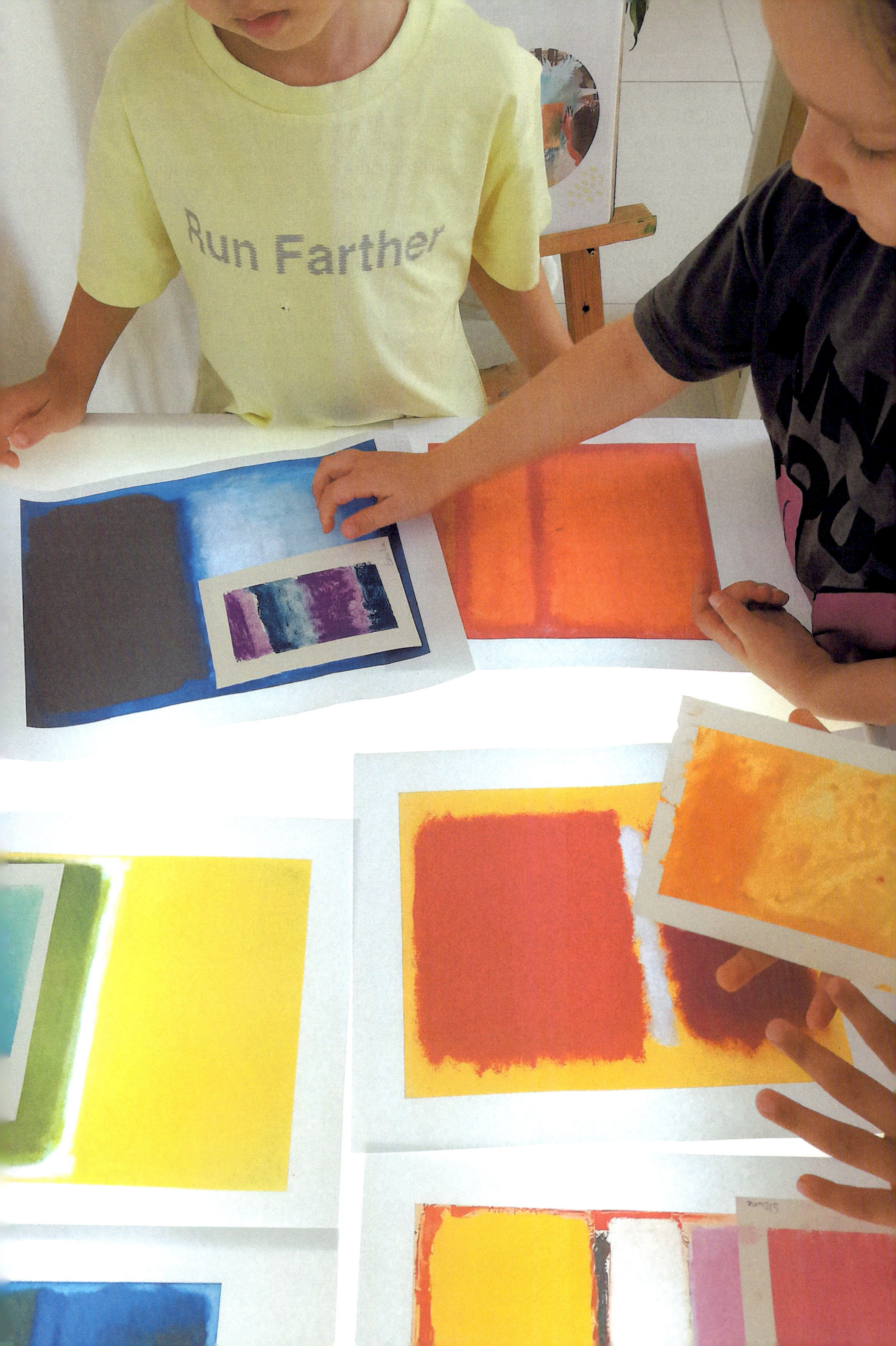
Run Farther

9 Engaging with the world of art, artists, and galleries

Engaging with and appreciating the work of visual artists is a wonderful way to inspire and expand children's visual arts learning. By observing and discussing the artwork of others, both children and adults enhance their visual arts literacy, broadening the possibilities for visual arts curriculum planning. Whether engaging with original works of art in a gallery space, or discussing book illustrations and art reproductions, art appreciation experiences provide a range of avenues for enhancing children's knowledge of art and enriching their art making experiences. In this chapter, we explore the benefits of integrating art appreciation experiences both within and outside of education settings. A range of approaches to art appreciation offer strategies to explore, perceive, interpret, and appreciate the visual world with young children.

Art appreciation: A world of learning

Viewing and talking about art with young children is an exciting way to bring depth and vitality to visual arts learning experiences. Engaging with art provokes sensory engagement, curiosity, and can elicit a range of feelings and physical responses in young children (Piscitelli et al., 2003). Infants and toddlers benefit significantly from observing and engaging with art. From a very early age, they develop preferences for specific artworks and are capable of communicating these preferences to others (Danko-McGhee, 2023). Through art appreciation experiences, children are connected to art, community, and culture and can be inspired in their own artistic practice (Mai, 2013). Research has also identified that by engaging in processes of observing, thinking about, and discussing art, children develop a range of skills and dispositions including aesthetic perception, imagination, critical thinking, creativity, and visual literacy skills. (Housen, 2007; Kim et al., 2018; Pavlou, 2015; Terreni, 2015). These skills and dispositions help children connect with and interpret the visual worlds and support their evolving identities as confident and informed art makers.

Figure 9.1 Children engage in art appreciation by viewing, discussing, and comparing images of Mark Rothko's colour field paintings with their own (oil pastel) explorations [Image: Carolyn Prawius, Saigon Kids Early Learning Centre].

DOI: 10.4324/9781003561835-11

Such positive outcomes for children are enhanced in supportive learning environments that value the arts and the learning potential of art appreciation experiences (Eckhoff, 2008; Pavlou, 2015). Creating opportunities for children to meaningfully engage in art making and art appreciation nurtures their ability to look closely, reflect on their observations, and join in discussions about art. Educators can support such processes by modelling curiosity, asking questions, and exploring artworks with children (Piscitelli et al., 2003).

Embracing the world of art

An exciting way to learn more about the world of art, and engage in art appreciation is to visit art galleries and museums. These wonderful places are full of opportunities for learning. The experience of being immersed in the architecture and lighting of curated spaces and looking at artworks and cultural objects can invite wonder, provoke thinking, and inspire rich conversations (Piscitelli et al., 2003). Such formative experiences foster profound aesthetic encounters for children, allowing them to interact with light, colour, movement, and sound in ways that deeply engage their senses (Britt, 2018). Immersive encounters like these can leave lasting impressions on young children, fostering a love of art and a lifelong interest in experiencing and appreciating it (Bell, 2011; Probine, 2020).

Some might assume children are too young to appreciate the art and objects displayed in galleries and museum spaces. Others might think children don't know how to behave in such spaces, worrying they might be too noisy or disrupt the experience for other (usually adult) visitors. However, those who exercise an image of young children as capable, agentic learners will embrace the opportunity to afford children (who are also citizens!) the right to visit public spaces. It is also important for the broader community to observe and delight in childrens' engagement with art. Bringing children into museum and gallery spaces enables others to witness how infants, toddlers, and young children respond to art with wonder and delight. Additionally, such experiences honour the United Nations Convention on the Rights of the Child [UNCRC] Article 31 goal for children to be connected to, and participate in, artistic and cultural life within their communities (Britt, 2018; Mai, 2013). It is encouraging that many galleries and museums are increasingly recognising this right. Child-centred programs, including exhibition tours, artist talks, and interactive exhibitions specifically designed for children ensure that audiences of all ages have opportunities to engage with art (Piscitelli & Penfold, 2015; Terreni, 2015).

Connections with local galleries

When educators plan gallery visits for young children, their experience will depend on each specific gallery's philosophy and offerings. Some galleries are designed primarily for adult audiences, with exhibitions curated at heights and in formats less accessible to children. However, others, recognising the importance

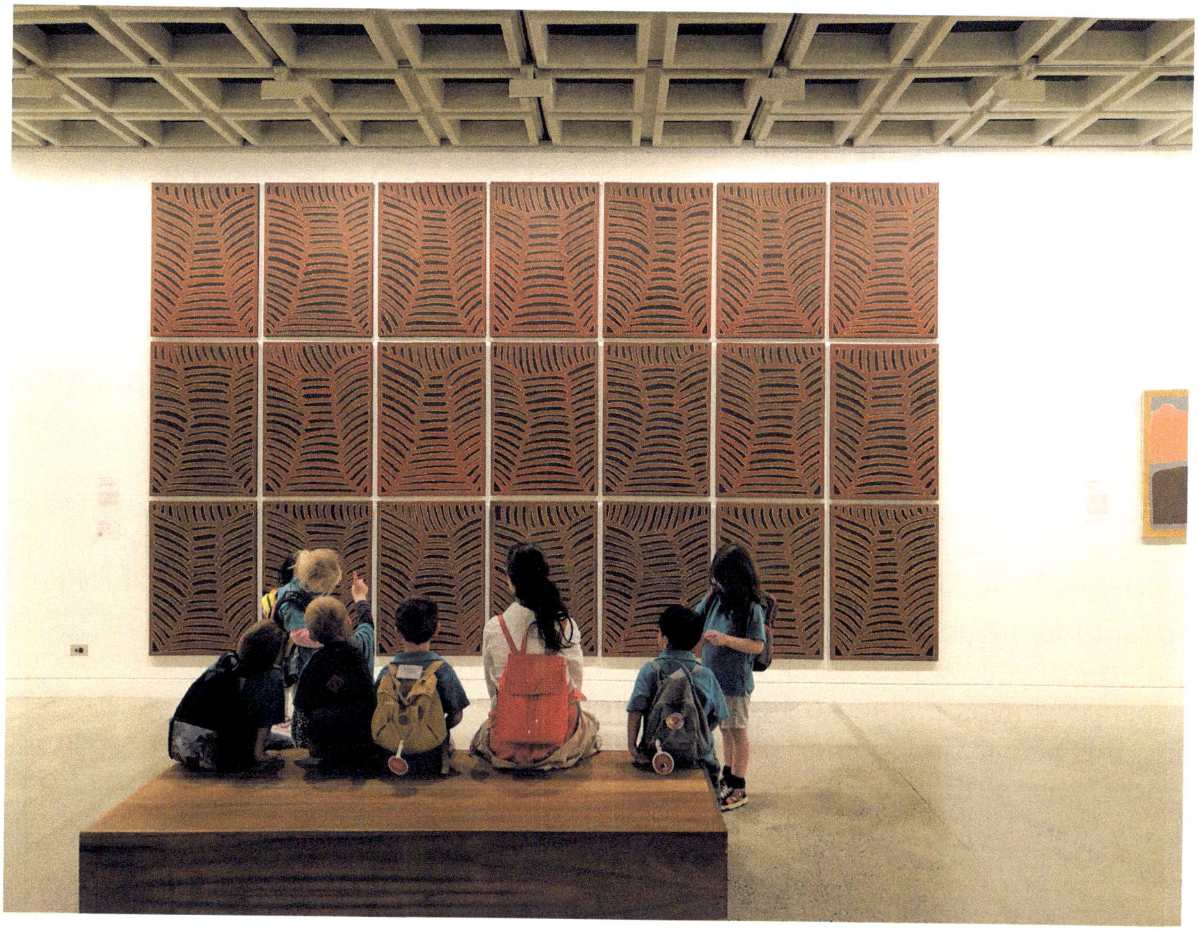

Figure 9.2 An educator and small group of children engage with the artwork of Gloria Tamerre Petyarre at the Art Gallery of NSW as participatory citizens in their community [Image: Gai Lindsay, Explore and Develop, Castlereagh St Early Learning Centre].

of engaging young audiences, curate exhibitions specifically for children, often including tactile, sensory experiences where children can touch and interact with materials (Terreni, 2015). Many galleries also provide the support of gallery educators who facilitate child-centred learning through strategies such as storytelling, questioning, and exploration (Anderson et al., 2002; Eckhoff, 2008). Additionally, some galleries support young visitors to explore art materials, techniques, or concepts connected to the work of a particular artist. The Bundanon case study below beautifully exemplifies this approach. These spaces, particularly when paired with opportunities for art-making activities, can foster meaningful connections between viewing and creating, enhancing children's engagement and understanding (Clarkin-Phillips et al., 2012; Eckhoff, 2008; Terreni, 2017).

Case study – A story of LOOKING from Bundanon

Bundanon, a wildlife refuge, art museum, and a provider of cultural and educational programs located on the Shoalhaven River in New South Wales, Australia, is a unique cultural and environmental destination. The Bundanon Learning

Team has, historically, designed and delivered learning programs primarily for high school students. In recent years, the learning program has expanded to include learners of all ages in high-quality creative workshops inspired by art, artists, place, and Country. (In Aboriginal culture, "Country" refers to the deep spiritual, cultural, and physical connection between the land and its people, encompassing identity, law, and reciprocal care.)

An important part of Bundanon's remit is to create connections and access for the wider community. Learning program workshops are delivered at low or no cost to the public in a range of formats, including Bundanon Minis (for parents/carers with under 5s), Bundanon Inspire (school holiday program for 12–18-year-olds), and Family Fun Day (school holiday intergenerational day visit, 5–12-year-olds).

Bundanon delivered a creative *LOOKING* workshop inspired by Bundanon's 2024 summer exhibition *Bagan Bariwariganyan: Echoes of Country.* The workshop design process included consultation with two artists featured in the exhibition, local Elders Aunty Julie Freeman and Aunty Cheryl Davison. Davison's limited palette of yellow, red, black, and white directly informed explorations of colour mixing. Leaves collected from the ground were the subject matter, anchoring this activity in Country and place. In addition to consultation with Freeman and Davison, the Bundanon Learning team collaborated with educators from Early Start, University of Wollongong to adapt the *LOOKING* creative workshop

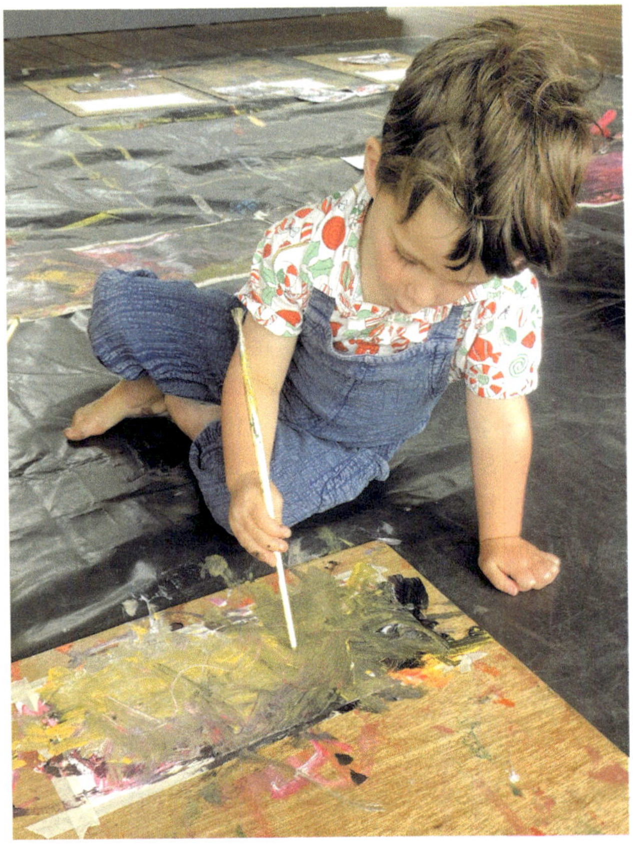

Figure 9.3 Young learners engaged in a wide range of artistic practices and deepened their knowledge of art, artists, place, and Country through the Bundanon art workshop 'Looking' [Image: Bundanon].

experience for younger learners, in line with best practice for this cohort within Museum settings. Using the leaf provocation suggested by Aunty Cheryl we asked, "are all leaves green?" To explore this question, children were encouraged to engage in close looking, examining leaves with eyes, hands and magnifying glasses. The children were invited to notice the leaf shapes, and the many colours and marks on the leaves. Following these rich discussions and discoveries, the use of printing brayers (rubber rollers) was introduced to experiment with blending red, yellow, black, and white acrylic paints on a shared, long piece of quality paper. The whole arm movement of the brayers and the joy of discovering the many resulting colours and shades was highly motivating. The children were also offered tools to scratch lines and marks into the paint, again being prompted to recall their close LOOKING at the collected leaves. Children then took "prints" on small squares of paper from their collaborative colour-mixing work. When the prints dried, children added a drawing of the outline and defining features of their leaves using black marker pens. This resulted in a large format colour mixing work for their classroom and smaller individual works for each child to keep. The interactive dialogue between children and educators was busy, joyful, and curious, demonstrating the rich potential in being guided and inspired by art, artists, place, and Country.

Fostering belonging in galleries and museums

Visits to a local gallery or museum enrich the experience and learning of children, educators, and museum staff. Regular visits to gallery spaces foster familiarity and a sense of belonging, helping children and educators build positive relationships with the environment, the art, and museum staff, while also enhancing educators' confidence and ability to discuss art with children (Britt, 2018; Terreni, 2017). For example, by observing and listening as gallery educators engage children with strategies such as gameplay, storytelling, and a range of questioning techniques (Eckhoff, 2008; Piscitelli et al., 2003), educators can enhance their skills for viewing and discussing art with children in their own practice. For museum educators, regular interactions with a specific group of children enables them to tailor learning experiences to the group's interests and development; creating more meaningful and engaging programmes.

Some educators may feel apprehensive about visiting galleries, especially if these spaces have not been part of their previous educational or personal experiences (Terreni, 2014). Galleries can sometimes feel intimidating, causing educators to question their place in these spaces or their ability to engage knowledgeably with artworks. Feelings of hesitation are often amplified by limited training or professional development in the visual arts, causing educators to feel underprepared to facilitate such experiences for children (Bowell, 2011; Eckhoff, 2008). Reflecting on such feelings and visiting a gallery prior to visiting with children can build confidence and comfort within the space, without the added pressure of guiding a group. Such visits allow educators to explore the space, engage with the art on their own terms, and begin to feel a sense of belonging in such cultural settings, paving the way for more meaningful experiences with children. Parents and caregivers may have similar pre-conceptions and hesitations about entering gallery spaces. Inviting families to support gallery visits can be an effective way to help them feel more comfortable in such spaces, which can lead to increased engagement and inspire art-making experiences at home (Piscitelli & Penfold, 2015).

For infants and toddlers visiting gallery spaces, it is essential to let the child take the lead in selecting artworks to respond to, as they often express preferences through gestures such as pointing, smiling, or gazing intently (Danko-McGhee, 2023). Once a child shows interest, educators can describe elements of the artwork, using expressive and descriptive language, such as naming colours or textures, to enrich the experience. For example, introducing terms like "turquoise" or "bumpy" stimulates curiosity and supports language development (Danko-McGhee, 2023). While tactile exploration can deepen engagement, even simple conversations about the artwork's features create meaningful connections and foster early aesthetic awareness.

Terreni (2017) proposes the concept of a "third space" as a potential framework for collaboration between early childhood educators and gallery staff. This approach seeks to blend the child-led, interest-driven pedagogy of early childhood education with the sometimes more structured, outcomes-focused practices

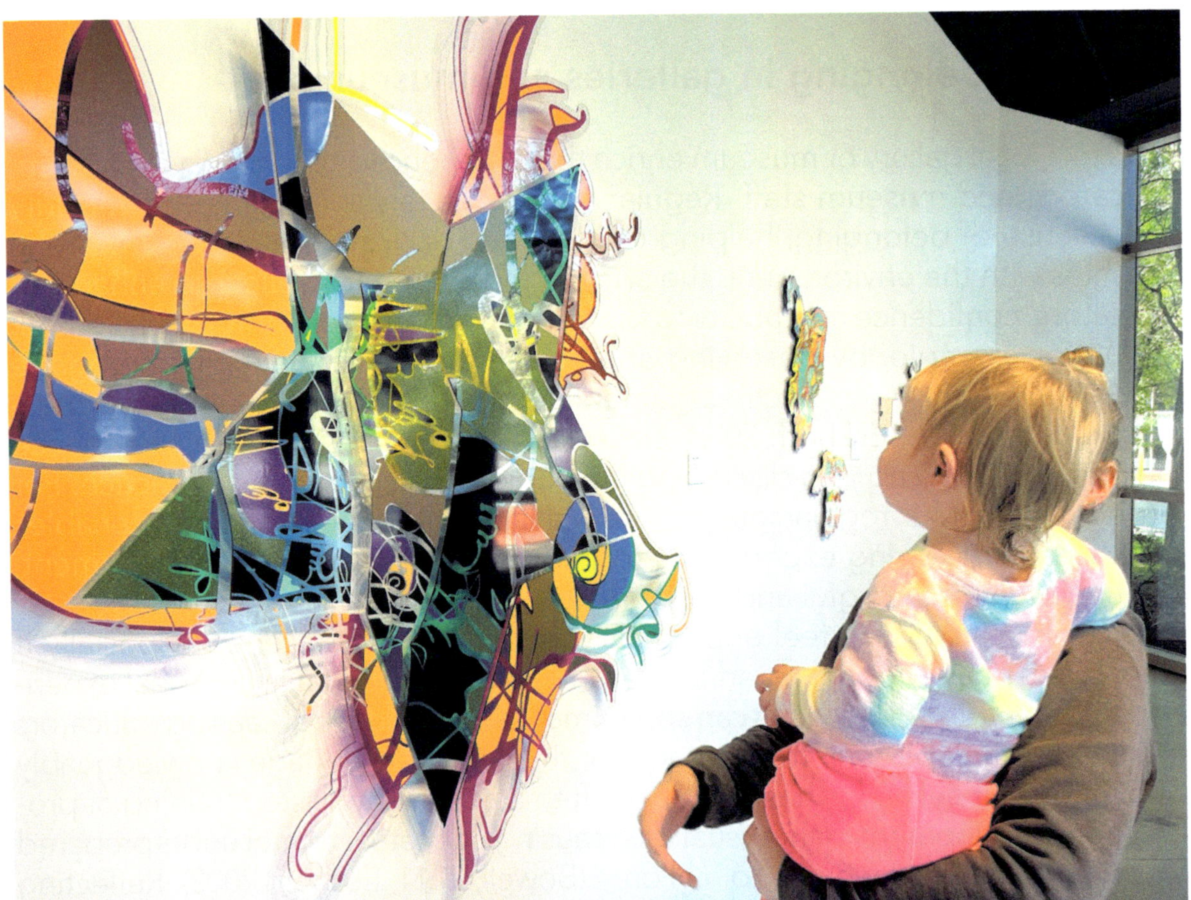

Figure 9.4 Educators can enrich art viewing experiences with infants and toddlers by talking about the features that engage their interest. Even simple conversations about colours, lines and textures can foster early aesthetic awareness [Image: Kathy Danko McGee, Art work by Sherry Polley, Art Link Gallery, Fort Wayne, USA].

used in gallery settings. By fostering communication, collaboration, and flexibility, Terreni's framework aims to establish a new territory for shared learning where the strengths of both pedagogical frameworks can coexist. Within this proposed space, educators and gallery staff could co-design learning experiences that reflect the needs and interests of the children, while respecting the educational goals of both contexts. A collaborative approach will strengthen professional relationships between educators and gallery staff to design inclusive, meaningful, and dynamic learning experiences, while deepening children's engagement and understanding.

Extending learning after a gallery visit

Following a gallery visit, educators play an important role in making connections between children's gallery experience and ongoing learning in their educational setting. Carr et al. (2012) suggest the use of "boundary objects" (i.e. artefacts or images that link different settings or contexts) to create ongoing connections and learning extensions. Photographs of the exhibition and educators' pedagogical documentation about the gallery visit support children to reconnect with the ideas generated in the gallery, potentially informing ongoing responsive art-making experiences (Terreni, 2015). By introducing art and art appreciation experiences into the curriculum, whether inspired by a gallery visit or not, educators can ensure children have access to art in their everyday lives and experience the wonder and well-being that comes from viewing, thinking about, and appreciating art.

Art can be viewed and appreciated in early childhood settings when original artworks, artefacts, art reproductions, textiles, and quality art books are incorporated into the environment. Thoughtfully displayed artworks bring a joyful, aesthetic quality to learning spaces and can be used to engage children in planned or spontaneous art conversations. When curating a collection of art examples and artefacts, it is essential to reflect the cultural backgrounds of the children in the setting and to represent a broad spectrum of artistic traditions. Seeing their own cultural heritage represented helps children connect with art more deeply and fosters a sense of belonging (Terreni, 2015). Expanding beyond the dominance of Western art also broadens children's perspectives and emphasises the diverse values within the art world.

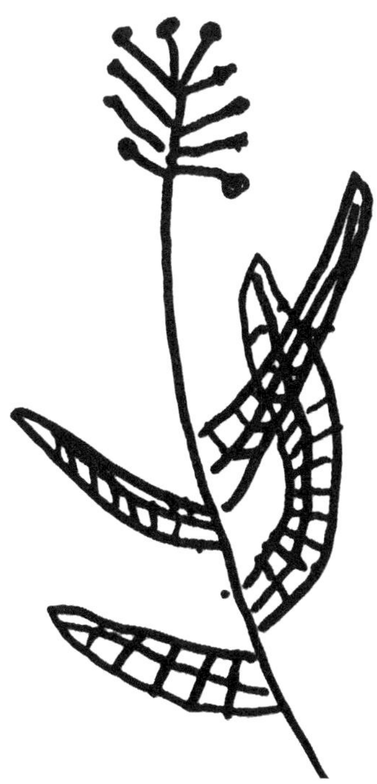

To build a diverse collection of art appreciation resources, visit second-hand stores, community markets, and garage sales to find interesting fabrics, art books, gallery catalogues, prints, and art reproductions. Calendars and greeting cards that feature artists' work are also an inexpensive way to collect good-quality art reproductions. Art images can also be collated from copyright-free websites. However, where possible, we recommend using resources that ensure artists receive recognition or compensation for their work. The local library also offers a rich collection of books and videos to explore. Children's books are an excellent resource for quality art images and can be used to engage children in conversations about art and art-making methods. Taking the time to look closely and talk about how illustrations represent aspects of a story fosters children's interest in art and enhances their visual literacy skills (Mai, 2013).

Learning to read the visual world

Art appreciation offers many opportunities for developing communication and visual literacy skills (Housen, 2007; Kim et al., 2018). Visual literacy is the ability to read and use visual images, and is grounded in an awareness that images, symbols, and artistic elements can be used in different ways to convey meaning. Diagrams, book illustrations, road signs, logos, maps, and graphs are everyday examples of how information can be communicated visually. From a young age children can develop visual literacy skills to understand these kinds of visual communication. In an increasingly visual world, developing visual literacy skills is essential. From their earliest interactions, children engage with visual and multimodal texts that convey meaning through diverse semiotic systems (Crafton et al., 2009). As Berger (2008) notes, "seeing comes before words" (p. 7), highlighting the importance of visual experiences in early literacy development. It is important to understand that visual texts are created with specific meanings, especially as increasing access to digital technologies expose children to a wide variety of images (Crafton et al., 2009; Hestholm, 2023). Visual literacy not only enhances children's ability to decode and interpret visual messages, but also empowers them to critically engage with their environment, fostering awareness and self-expression.

Expanding personal art knowledge and developing visual literacy skills supports educator confidence to plan for, and engage in, art appreciation experiences with children. While reading and interpreting an artwork can be a complex process, by looking closely, thinking about, and reflecting on what they see, educators can strengthen their visual literacy skills. To support this process, it can be helpful to revisit the concept of art as a language and consider the many ways that visual images can express ideas, emotions, and concepts. To do this, educators can:

- Reflect on their current knowledge of art, revisiting artists and artworks they are already familiar with.
- Engage the senses and evoke feelings and memories by considering why an artwork is liked or disliked.
- Think about the stories, ideas, or feelings an artist was exploring and trying to convey through their artwork.
- Think about how the artist used elements like light, line, colour, or texture to convey meaning.

There are many ways to approach and engage with artworks, and no right or wrong way to interpret them. Like all pedagogical practices, the skills to read and talk about art can be developed over time through repeated experience and by reflecting on ways to expand current thinking and practice.

Approaches to viewing and discussing art

Art as inspiration

Art appreciation experiences can inspire children's curiosity to engage with art and enhance their art-making experiences (Eckhoff, 2008). Taking the time to think about the how, what, why, and when to engage children with artworks will support children's engagement and enhance learning outcomes. For example, art appreciation experiences can be planned to instigate an art project or to inspire and expand an existing project of inquiry. They can be an opportunity to introduce children to new techniques and materials, and diverse artistic practices. Conversations about art can also support children's understanding of artmaking as a powerful language for telling stories, expressing ideas, or sharing cultural knowledge.

Choosing artworks that are familiar or potentially meaningful to children will enhance their interest in viewing and talking about art. For example, if children are exploring an art medium or material (such as cardboard, charcoal, or plastic), try researching, looking at, and discussing artists that use a particular material. Similarly, if children are exploring an element of art (such as texture, colour, or

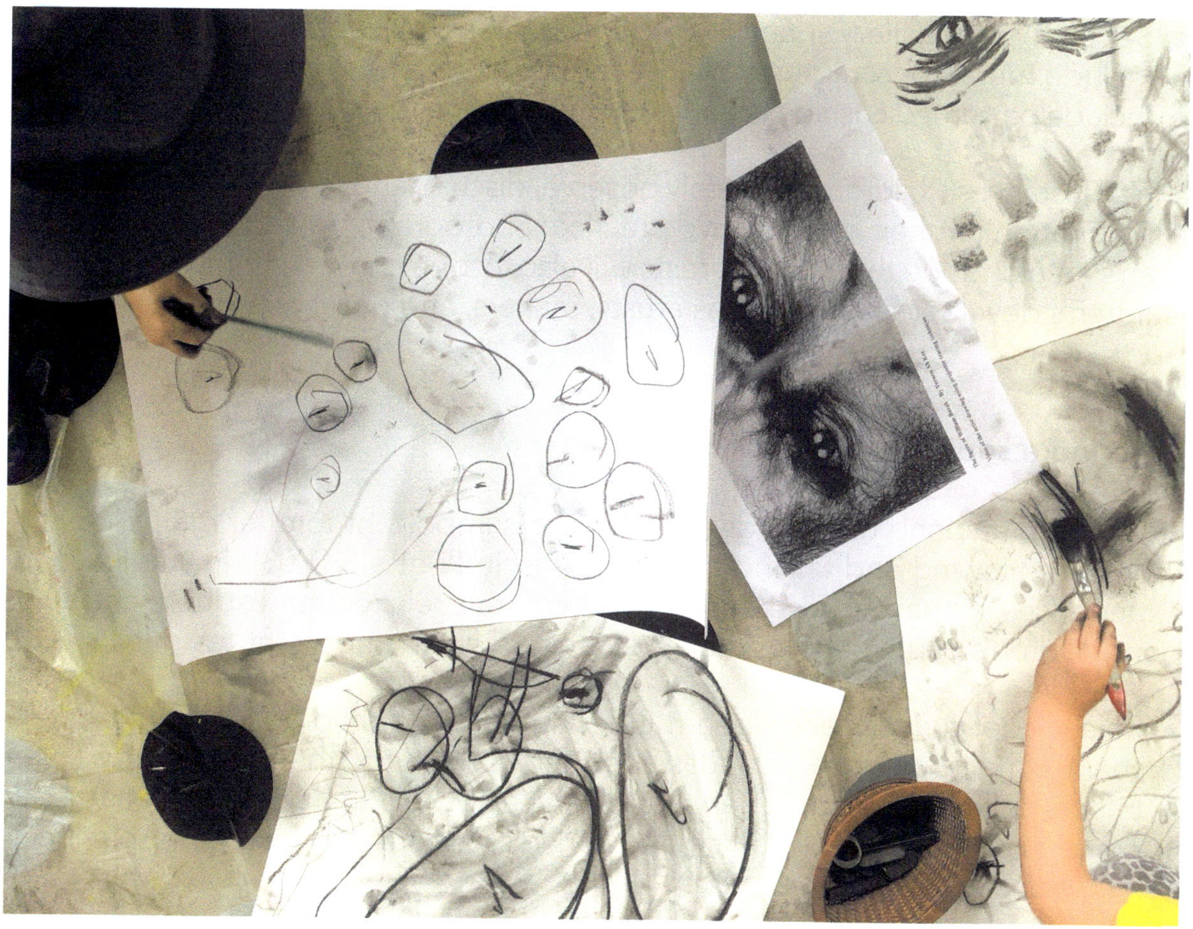

Figure 9.5 Introducing children to Vernon Ah Kee's work for charcoal explorations inspires new artistic possibilities through viewing and discussing artists' techniques [Image: Gai Lindsay, at UOW Pulse Kids Uni].

line), or have an interest in a particular subject matter (such as horses, pets, or flowers), a collection of artworks can be viewed to explore the diverse ways artists have represented these interests in their work.

By introducing children to artworks that are connected to their interests and projects of inquiry, educators will facilitate meaningful contexts for children to engage in art appreciation, as well as providing inspiration for their art-making (Eckhoff, 2008). The intention here is not to copy or replicate an artwork, but to view and talk about an artist and their work as a provocation to expand children's thinking and inspire them to explore new ways of engaging with art materials.

Displaying images, reproductions, or original artworks in an environment where they can be easily viewed by children is another way to inspire discussions about art. This can happen in a range of spaces and curriculum areas. For example:

- Display images of bridges or castles in the block area if children are exploring these types of constructions in their play.
- Introduce children to images created by nature-based artists to inform and provoke design and ephemeral art with natural materials.
- Have a collection of hand-woven baskets or mats for children to observe and explore as inspiration for weaving experiences
- Set up a collection of ceramic art and pottery for observation and discussion as children explore clay work.
- Set up a quiet gallery space to display, view, and talk about art together.
- Include murals or sculptures by local artists in the outdoor environment.
- Include patterned cushions, fabrics, and wall hangings in children's play spaces.

In all instances, children can closely observe, discuss, and use artworks or images as inspiration for their own creative practice. Photographing and displaying children's art alongside the work of artists will also inspire conversations and support children's developing identities as artists, makers, and designers.

Creating a supportive environment

As children respond to art in diverse ways, it is important to offer multiple entry points for viewing and talking about art (Piscitelli et al., 2003). In small group experiences, casual conversations help to create a relaxed atmosphere and support children's participation. As an educator, it is also important to:

- Role model curiosity and open-mindedness so that children feel comfortable sharing their thoughts and ideas about artworks with others.
- Ensure children are comfortable and can easily view the artwork or image.
- Pre-plan a focus or entry point for artwork discussions using a few pre-planned, intentional questions.

Over time, plan art viewing experiences to introduce children to diverse art-making practices including drawings, paintings, sculptures, printmaking, weaving and textiles, video art, installations, and photography. Explore a range of male and female artists from diverse countries and cultural backgrounds, as well as a range of realistic and abstract art, and examples of both contemporary and historical artmaking practices.

Intentional teaching strategies

The following strategies for engaging children with artworks can be used independently or in combination to extend art discussions. Remember, there are multiple possibilities and no right or wrong way to view or respond to art. The overarching aims of art viewing experiences are to help children make thoughtful connections with artwork and participate in arts-based conversations. Your conversations may diverge in many directions, and that's okay! The most important thing is to provide a supportive environment, invite curiosity, and welcome diverse responses from children.

Games to encourage observing and responding

Looking and finding games are a fun way to help children focus their attention and engage with a work of art. This approach involves factual rather than interpretive inquiry, using questions that are easy to answer because they are observable in the artwork. This approach encourages children to look with curiosity and openness to what they can find, and supports them to describe what they see without judgement (Pavlou, 2015). For younger children or those new to art appreciation, realistic paintings and illustrations that have familiar content can be used to ask factual questions such as, "how many birds can we find in this picture?" Similarly, a game such as "I-Spy" can inspire children to seek out items located in the artwork. For example, "In this painting, I can see a white dog, can anyone else find a white dog?" When the object has been found, each child can take a turn to look for and describe something they see in the artwork that others can search for.

Observation games are particularly useful when selecting abstract artworks to view with children. Questions can focus on looking for familiar elements in the artwork such as lines, colours, shapes, textures, and patterns. Example questions for this type of observation include: What shapes can you see?; What colours has the artist used?; What is the smallest/biggest thing you can see in this painting?; and, How many white squares can you find? Creating opportunities for children to describe the observable elements of art adds complexity and supports children's art vocabulary development. This focused approach helps children to develop sensitivity to variances within art elements and explore aspects of composition. For example, conversations can draw children's attention to straight, curved, fuzzy, thin, thick, wiggly, or smudgy lines; light and dark colours; smooth and bumpy textures; big and small shapes; or empty and full spaces.

Simple observation games help children to develop the skills to look closely, notice the finer details of an artwork, and engage in simple art-based dialogue.

These basic skills can also be used as a springboard for wondering about the artwork more holistically (What time of day do you think it is in this painting?); or thinking about how it was made (Is this a painting, drawing, or collage?). Such open-ended questions will engage children in more challenging conversations and extend their ability to interpret visual information. Looking for and describing aspects of an artwork in this way is often referred to as the "aesthetic approach" to art appreciation (Piscitelli et al., 2003).

Story telling

Creating a story around an artwork is another helpful way to start art appreciation experiences with young children. This approach focuses on narrative inquiry and invites children to engage with art through the medium of story (Piscitelli et al., 2003). For example, historical artworks can tell a story about another place or time (Eckhoff, 2008). Children can also be invited to make up their own stories about what is happening in an artwork. This approach encourages children to engage in imaginative thinking and inspires them to offer personal responses to an artwork. A story can also be a way to introduce children to an artwork or artist. The story about the artwork can include the name of the work, who it was made by, and a little information about the artist. It can include historical, technical, and cultural information that extends children's knowledge about art, art-making processes, and artmaking motivations.

For example, to discuss artworks by the artist Sol LeWitt, an educator could explain,

> *These paintings were made a long time ago by an artist called Sol LeWitt. Sol LeWitt was an American artist who liked to draw and paint lines. He often painted huge artworks onto the walls of art galleries. He also drew and painted smaller artworks on paper and canvas.*

Likewise, to introduce children to the artworks of Yayoi Kusama, an educator could gather a collection of Yayoi's work and explain,

> *I have some pictures of artworks made by Yayoi Kusama. Yayoi Kusama is a Japanese artist who likes to create paintings of flowers and pumpkins. She often uses very bright colours and likes to cover everything with polka dots. Yayoi also creates sculptures and installations, and has made whole rooms filled with dots that you can walk inside.*

Such stories about art and artists can inspire questions and support ongoing conversations. Using a collection of artwork images by a chosen artist, children can be engaged in conversations that "compare and contrast" different aspects of the artist's work (e.g. big and small, black and white or colour, apart and overlapping). Children can also be asked questions like, "What is your favourite part of this painting?" Or "Do you have a favourite artwork by this artist?"

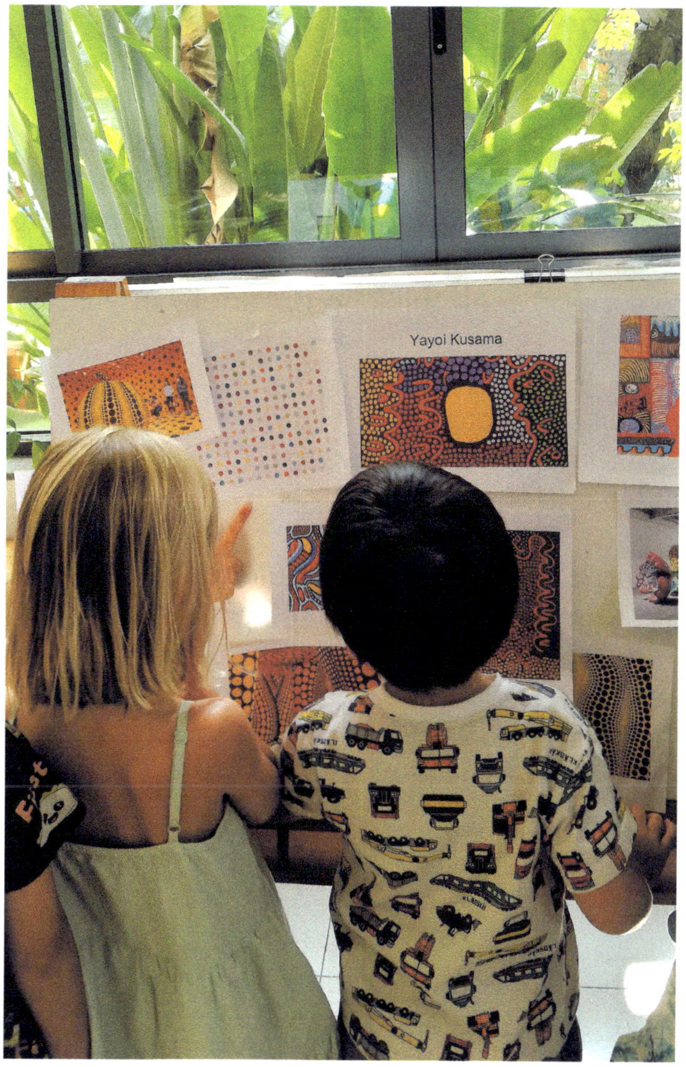

Figure 9.6 Children explore and discuss images of Yayoi Kusama's brightly coloured paintings and sculptures as part of their investigation of artists who paint with dots [Image: Carolyn Prawius. Saigon Kids Early Learning Centre].

Technical inquiry

Technical inquiry, which can be integrated into other approaches or lines of inquiry, involves thinking about and discussing how an artwork was made (Eckhoff, 2008). It is particularly useful when looking at sculptures, artefacts, textiles, and three-dimensional artworks. Questions can focus on thinking about which materials may have been used by the artist (wood, metal, plastic, glass, or fibre), as well as which art techniques and tools may have been used to create the artwork. Conversations can focus on whether the artwork was made from a solid mass, whether individual pieces were joined together, and how they might have been joined. Conversations about sculptures can also include wondering how they are balanced and what supports the artist may have used to help them do so. If able to access original artefacts, textile works, and sculptures, invite children to hold and handle them, or collect samples of the materials for them to touch and feel.

Questions to encourage thinking and interpretation

As children develop their confidence to engage with and talk about artworks, including more open-ended questions can encourage deeper thinking and interpretation. Using the Visual Thinking Strategies (VTS) framework supports this approach to art appreciation (Housen, 2002). A sequence of three simple questions encourages close observation and open discussion to encourage children to find evidence to support their thinking (Connolly et al., 2019). The questions used in VTS are:

1. *"What is going on in this picture?"*
2. *"What do you see that makes you say that?"*
3. *"What more can we find?"*

The value of applying VTS is that it is an inquiry-based approach where children are encouraged to "look" and "look again," providing ongoing opportunities to construct meaning and build on their skills to observe and evaluate visual information (Housen, 2007). When using VTS strategies, multiple responses are encouraged so that children can share their ideas and perspectives and discover that there are many ways to think about and interpret the world of art.

Tactile explorations

Providing opportunities for young children to explore materials, techniques, concepts, or ideas related to a specific artwork or exhibition is an essential component of art appreciation experiences. Such activities can take place within the gallery, facilitated by skilled gallery educators, or in an education setting or home. These art appreciation experiences can occur before, during, or after a gallery visit. The use of boundary objects act as a bridge between the gallery and the education or home environment, helping children recall and extend their experiences (Carr et al., 2012; Terreni, 2015). It is crucial, however, that these activities emphasise exploration and personal interpretation rather than replication of an artwork. This approach respects children's agency, allowing them to respond to, and engage with, the ideas in the artwork in ways that are meaningful and appropriate for them (Danko-McGhee, 2016; Piscitelli & Penfold, 2015).

Inspired by encounters with an artwork or exhibition, tactile activities that involve manipulating materials can support children to deepen their understanding of concepts such as texture, light, or movement (Britt, 2018; Terreni, 2015). Embodied experiences are crucial for young children's learning because kinesthetic engagement supports sensory exploration and helps connect physical experiences with cognitive and emotional responses (Britt, 2018; Piscitelli et al., 2003). By experimenting with materials in creative, open-ended ways, children are encouraged to collaborate, discover, and play. This enables children to form stronger connections to the art they encounter, building an intrinsic appreciation for creativity while supporting skills such as problem-solving and critical thinking.

Tactile explorations with infants and toddlers

As highlighted earlier in this chapter, there are rich and important benefits when infants and toddlers have opportunities to interact with visual art in gallery spaces. Danko-McGhee's (2010; 2023) research shows that art-viewing experiences support infants' brain development by engaging their rapidly growing neural networks through rich sensory stimulation and interaction. During the first two years of life, the brain develops at an extraordinary rate, forming millions of new connections between brain cells. These connections are strengthened by repeated stimulation, helping the brain process information more efficiently. Visual experiences play a vital role in developing the brain's visual system (Danko-McGhee, 2023). Art viewing and responding to art, provides infants with complex visual stimuli as they experience colours, patterns, and textures. When paired with interactive "serve and return" exchanges with educators and caregivers, art viewing also supports early language development and social bonding. Together, these experiences create a multi-sensory environment that nurtures infants' overall brain development.

Tactile experiences are especially vital for infants and toddlers because they enable children to connect with artworks on a sensory level. Danko-McGhee (2023) emphasises that aesthetic experiences for very young children involve sensation and emotion, forming a foundation for cognitive development. When children physically explore elements related to artworks, such as textures, colours, or shapes, their aesthetic responses are heightened, fostering a deeper understanding and appreciation of art. Experiences that enable infants and toddlers to touch materials and manipulate objects, such as patterned scarves, weaving, and art reproductions, can provide meaningful, multi-sensory engagement, supporting both perceptual and emotional development (Danko-McGhee, 2023). Such interactions not only encourage creativity and curiosity but also nurture early visual literacy by helping children make sense of the world through art.

Conclusion

When educators combine and connect art making with opportunities for looking at art and responding to the visual world, they are providing diverse contexts for visual arts learning, and delivering a comprehensive visual arts program. All art is linked to histories, traditions, and cultural practices, and as such offers rich opportunities for inquiry, discussion, and artistic knowledge building. Different approaches and entry points can inspire diverse ways to engage with and discuss art, and lead to the development of new perspectives and technical knowledge. Engaging with art using open-ended inquiry processes will inspire children to ask questions of their own; and such questions can be the inspiration for new lines of artistic inquiry. While spontaneous conversations about art are valuable, intentionally planning for and implementing regular opportunities to view and discuss art with children enables art appreciation to become an exciting, dynamic, and inspirational component of your visual arts program.

References

Anderson, D., Piscitelli, B., Weier, K., Everett, M., & Tayler, C. (2002). Children's museum experiences: Identifying powerful mediators of learning. *Curator: The Museum Journal*, *45*(3), 213–231. https://doi.org/10.1111/j.2151-6952.2002.tb00057.x

Bell, D. (2011). Seven ways to talk about art: One conversation and seven questions for talking about art in early childhood settings. *International Journal of Education Through Art*, *7*(1), 41–53. https://doi.org/10.1386/eta.7.1.41_1

Berger, J. (2008). *Ways of seeing*. Penguin.

Bowell, I. (2011). Supporting visual art teaching in primary schools. *Australian Art Education*, *34*(2), 98–118.

Britt, C. (2018). Dancing with Pipilotti: Young children's encounters with contemporary art. *Pedagogy Magazine*, *4*(1), 26–29. dancing-with-pipilotti.pdf

Carr, M., Clarkin-Phillips, J., Beer, A., Thomas, R., & Waitai, M. (2012). Young children developing meaning-making practices in a museum: The role of boundary objects. *Museum Management and Curatorship*, *27*(1), 53–66. https://doi.org/10.1080/09647775.2012.644696

Clarkin-Phillips, J., Carr, M., & Paki, V. (2012). *Our place: Being curious at Te Papa*. Teaching & Learning Research Initiative Nāu i Whatu Te Kākahu, He Tāniko Taku. 9265-Summaryreport.pdf

Connolly, T., Skinner, R., & Harlow, D. (2019). Sparking discussion visual thinking. *Science and Children*, *57*(4), 44–49. https://www.jstor.org/stable/10.2307/26901563

Crafton, L., Silvers, P., & Brennan, M. (2009). Creating a critical multiliteracies curriculum: Repositioning art in the early childhood classroom. In M. Narey (Ed.), *Making meaning: Constructing multimodal perspectives of language, literacy, and learning through arts-based early childhood education* (pp. 31–51). Springer.

Danko-McGhee, K. (2010). The aesthetic preferences of infants: Pictures of faces that captivate their interest. *Contemporary Issues in Early Childhood*, *11*(4), 365–387. http://dx.doi.org/10.2304/ciec.2010.11.4.365

Danko-McGhee, K. (2016). First encounters: Early art experiences and literacy development for infants. *International Art in Early Childhood Research Journal*, *5*(1), 1–12. https://artinearlychildhood.org/journal/2016-research-journal-1

Danko-McGhee, K. (2023). *Viewing art with babies: First encounters*. Routledge.

Eckhoff, A. (2008). The importance of art viewing experiences in early childhood visual arts: The exploration of a master art teacher's strategies for meaningful early arts experiences. *Early Childhood Education Journal*, *35*, 463–472. https://doi.org/10.1007/s10643-007-0216-1

Hestholm, G. N. (2023). Competence and mastery in practice: On participation, responsibility and believing in your own abilities. *Video Journal of Education and Pedagogy*, *8*(1), 1–16.Video Journal of Education and Pedagogy Volume 8 Issue 1 (2023) (brill.com)

Housen, A. (2007). Art viewing and aesthetic development: Designing for the viewer. In P. Villeneuve (Ed.), *From periphery to center: Art museum education in the 21st century* (pp. 172–179). National Art Education Association

Housen, A. C. (2002). Aesthetic thought, critical thinking and transfer. *Arts and Learning Research, 18*(1), 2001–2002.

Kim, K. J., Wee, S. J., Han, M. K., Sohn, J. H., & Hitchens, C. W. (2018). Enhancing children's art appreciation and critical thinking through a visual literacy-based art intervention programme. *International Journal of Education Through Art, 13*(3), 317–332.

Mai, L. (2013). Behold: Art appreciation in the early years. In R. Ewing (Ed.), *Creative arts in the lives of young children: Play, imagination and learning* (pp. 47–64). Australian Council for Educational Research (ACER) Press.

Pavlou, V. (2015). Understanding art: Preparing generalist school teachers to teach art with artworks. *International Journal of Art & Design Education, 34*(2), 192–205. https://doi.org/10.1111/jade.12020

Piscitelli, B., & Penfold, L. (2015). Child-centered practice in museums: Experiential learning through creative play at the Ipswich art gallery. *Curator: The Museum Journal, 58*(3), 263–280. https://doi.org/10.1111/cura.12113

Piscitelli, B., Weier, K., & Everett, M., (2003). Museums and young children: Partners in learning about the world. In S. Wright (Ed.), *Children, meaning making and the arts* (pp. 167–192). Pearson Education Australia.

Probine, S. (2020). Examining the in-between: Contextual factors on how young children learn through the visual arts [Doctoral dissertation, University of Auckland]. http://hdl.handle.net/2292/52825

Terreni, L. (2014). It's a matter of distinction: Bourdieu, art museums, and young children attending early childhood services in New Zealand. *International Art in Early Childhood Research Journal, 4*(1), 1–10. https://artinearlychildhood.org/journal/2014-research-journal-1

Terreni, L. (2015). Young children's learning in art museums: A review of New Zealand and international literature. *European Early Childhood Education Research Journal, 23*(5), 720–742. https://doi.org/10.1080/1350293X.2015.1104049

Terreni, L. (2017). "I know what that is! It's modern art!" Early childhood access to and use of art museums and galleries in Aotearoa New Zealand. [Doctoral dissertation, University of Wellington] https://doi.org/10.26686/wgtn.17064842.v1

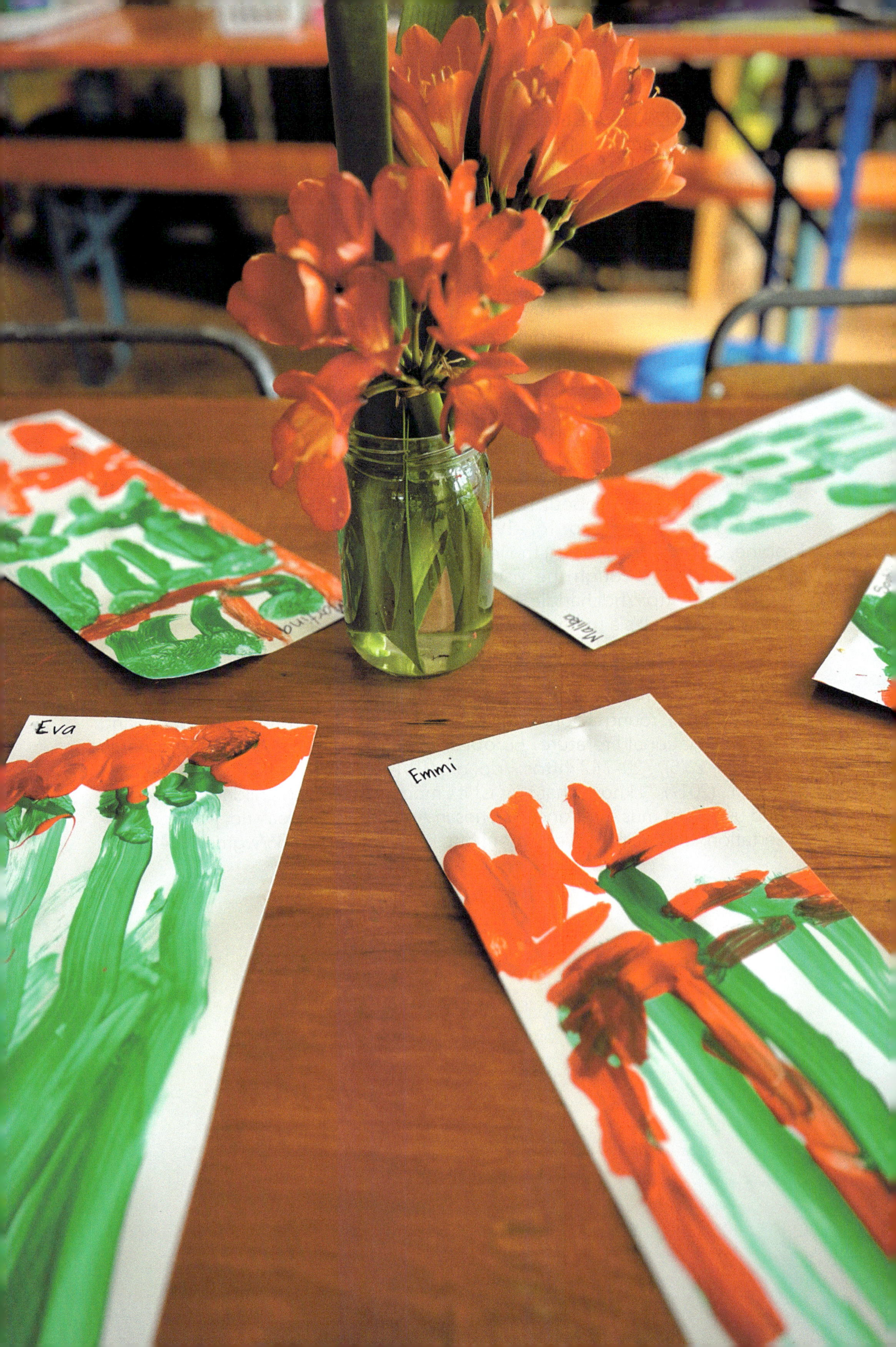
Eva
Emmi
Malika

10 Creating inspiring visual arts spaces

The physical environment, and the materials in it, powerfully influence children's experiences and learning. In this chapter, we explore how a carefully planned and well-resourced environment can support both the work of educators and enhance children's learning in and through the visual arts. Whether designing a new art studio or thinking about existing learning areas, we offer guidance and inspiration for the creation and maintenance of art spaces that function well and support effective visual arts practice with children. We discuss the role of aesthetics and beauty within the environment and consider the intentional organisation of space, materials, furniture, and resources. We look at ways to create inviting, inclusive, and inspiring spaces where children feel comfortable to create, explore, play, and learn with others.

Spaces and invitations

Visual arts experiences can occur in a variety of places and spaces; however, there is significant value in creating special areas dedicated to the visual arts. Such spaces create rich contexts for creative encounters and support both children and educators to engage in deeper learning about visual arts and visual arts making processes. More than a physical location, designated spaces for creating art embody a way of working, inquiring, and engaging with materials. Pacini-Ketchabaw et al. (2024) explain that such spaces invite the intersection where body, materials, surfaces, and spaces converge, enabling a dynamic interplay of exploration and creation. An art studio space, regardless of its physical location, is an invitation to slow down, to attune to visual and sensory perceptions, and to engage in emergent, collective experimentation.

Young children benefit from the predictability of a familiar space, which they can frequently return to easily find and work with consistently available materials. A space that is separate from the noise, foot traffic and distractions of a busy classroom invites focused attention and supports children to immerse themselves in work for extended periods of time. An organised space enables educators to work alongside children to support engagement in the visual arts.

Figure 10.1 Clivia flowers in a jar provide a beautiful focus for painting, with selected colours related to the subject [Image: Adrienne Wilkins, Sophia Preschool].

DOI: 10.4324/9781003561835-12

The skills and knowledge children develop within a studio space are transferable to all other areas of their play, learning, and inquiry.

Establishing a visual arts studio space

Developing an inspiring and functional visual arts space takes time, commitment, and attention to detail. It also requires a passionate belief that the arts deserve a valued and important place in our lives and learning environments. In Chapters 4 and 5, we explored the value of developing a shared philosophy for the visual arts to support the development of a rich culture of visual arts learning. When reviewing an existing environment or designing a new space to inspire visual arts learning, it is crucial to first revisit the philosophy and values important to the setting (Curtis & Carter, 2014). When educators develop a clear vision about the types of learning they want children to experience, they are well equipped to design spaces and select materials and tools that will facilitate rich learning opportunities that realise this vision. For example, if a teaching philosophy strongly emphasises collaborative play, visual arts spaces should be designed with room for multiple children to inspire and encourage group collaboration.

Before purchasing furniture for an art studio space, think about the size of the space and how many children will be using it. If there is adequate space, purchase a large table that will accommodate a small group of children and an adult with room to spread out, and a smaller table for individual and paired work.

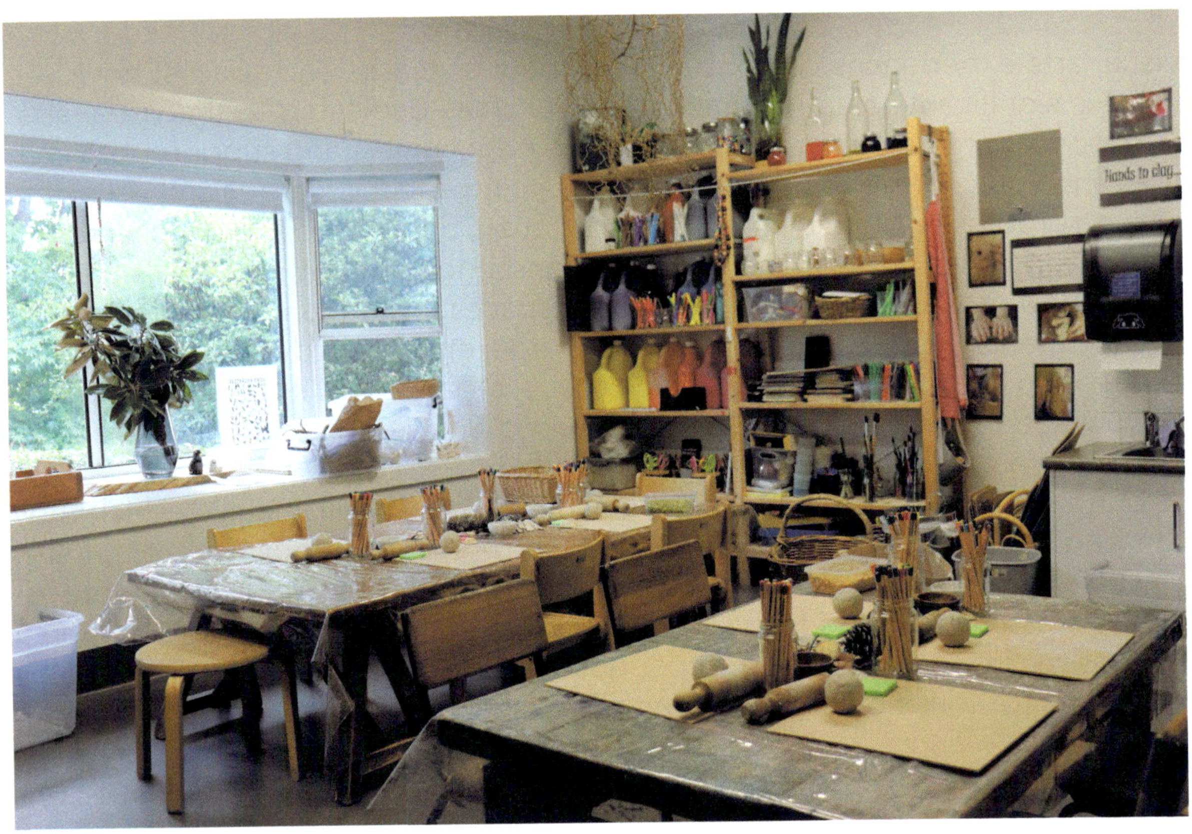

Figure 10.2 An art studio set up for children with well-organised storage, natural light, washing area and attractive work spaces [Image: Bomaderry Community Preschool].

Adjustable easels offer an alternative work surface. Consider sourcing second-hand furniture as a sustainable and affordable option that can also add to the character of your studio area.

Whether setting up a permanent studio space or a temporary location for art making, always keep the purpose of the space in mind to ensure that time and energy are not wasted on the act of "beautifying" a cramped or poorly organised environment. When reviewing or setting up a new studio space, start by considering practicalities. Ideally, a studio space will:

- Support children's focus and attention by being located away from high-traffic areas and noisy play areas.
- Have enough space for at least four children and an educator to comfortably explore art-making together.
- Support messy encounters, with easily cleaned surfaces and floors.
- Have well-lit workspaces with natural, flexible, and adjustable lighting.
- Have access to electricity for using lightboxes, projectors, or glue guns.
- Incorporate open storage spaces and shelves to allow children to see, select, and easily access materials and tools, as well as store their unfinished work to return and rework at a later time.
- Have easy access to recycling bins, brooms, dustpans, cloths, a water source, and cleaning resources.

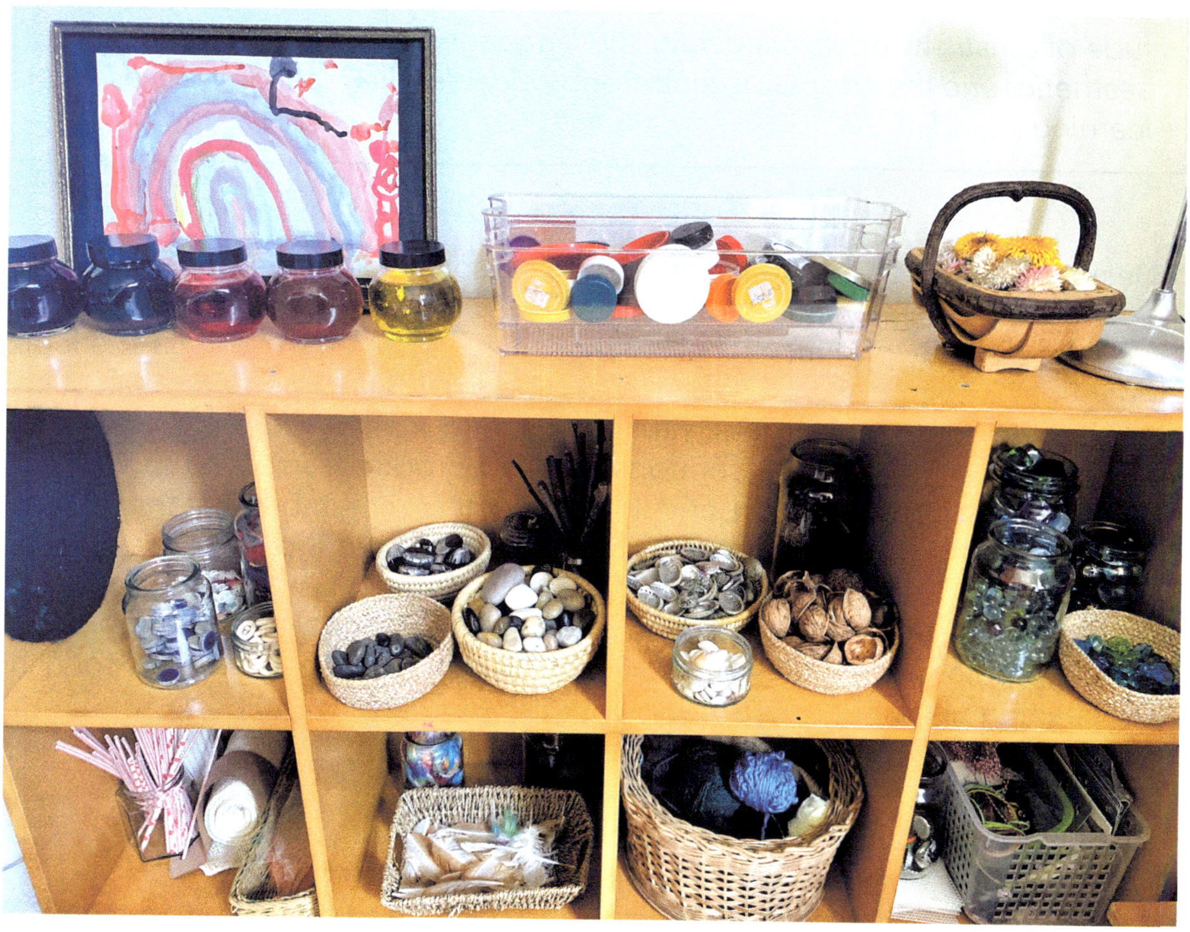

Figure 10.3 Materials are attractively displayed using interesting baskets, boxes, and jars. Low, open shelving empowers children to make creative choices [Image: Adrienne Wilkins, Sophia Preschool].

Other considerations relate to staffing and how the adults in the setting should intentionally guide, support, and facilitate intentional and engaged arts encounters for and with children. Several points to consider in this regard include:

- Locate arts learning experiences in a variety of settings to stimulate interest. For example, use fences, climbing frames or set up drawing materials in the garden or block corner.
- Organise a team of educators to ensure active participation and engagement with children in the arts space and to ensure care and maintenance of both materials and the learning experience.

Engaging with the Reggio Emilia approach highlights the importance of viewing the physical environment and its materials as active contributors to the quality of children's experiences, rather than as a passive backdrop to their learning (Schwall, 2005). Supporting every child's right to explore and express their creativity, each Municipal school in Reggio Emilia incorporates large and small Ateliers (studios) that serve as fundamental spaces for learning and participation within the larger school environment. The beauty of each atelier is unique and inspirational; however, they are much more than physically beautiful, inviting, and inspiring spaces. As places for research, communication, and inquiry, the ateliers of Reggio Emilia embody an attitude of artistic wonder, respect for the languages of art, and the belief that aesthetics and the arts play a central and valuable role in children's lives and learning (Gandini, 2005).

Designing and setting up an art studio or space dedicated to visual arts learning can present unique challenges specific to each learning environment. Given the diversity of educational settings, it is important to address the individual needs and obstacles that may arise. However, with careful selection and arrangement of resources, furnishings, and staffing most areas can be transformed into functional, comfortable, and productive spaces to work in. Developing a vision takes time, and it's important to remember that the ateliers of Reggio Emilia have evolved through experimentation, experience, reflection, and years of ongoing research. Be inspired by other spaces and places, while valuing your unique design and aesthetic choices. This will enable the resulting studio space to develop a unique identity, and become a hub for rich and meaningful learning.

Beauty and aesthetics

After addressing the practical aspects of a space, the next step is to create a studio space that is uncluttered while providing a warm and inviting atmosphere, making it a place where both children and educators will enjoy spending time.

In Chapter 6, we explored the value of initiating and exploring notions of beauty and aesthetics with young children. Providing a rich sensory environment supports the development of children's aesthetic awareness, while fostering their appreciation for beauty and aesthetic design. This cultivates an ongoing relationship with materials, and nurtures children's openness to the "beauty, artistry, and wonder" of the world (Pacini-Ketchabaw et al., 2024, p. 10). Therefore, create spaces filled with light, patterns, colours, textures, and interesting objects and collections. Purchase shelves and display boxes to exhibit interesting objects, documentation, and children's artworks. Such attention to detail communicates that children's work has value and should be cared for. Ensure art materials are well-organised, accessible, and attractively displayed. Regularly maintain materials to ensure they are in good working order. Rather than being limited to using child-sized furniture, consider sourcing interesting second-hand tables, chairs, and furniture to create a warm invitation to participate and engage in the space. Explaining the significant relational potential of studio spaces, Pacini-Ketchabaw et al. (2024, p. 10) described their studio as "a quiet place where children could pause with us to notice the materials movements and invitations, follow the sounds of their drawings, negotiate ideas, follow lines of thought, and be with, or dwell with, ideas, processes, and materials."

Documentation and display

The respectful display and documentation of children's visual arts experiences in the environment is an important way to celebrate and acknowledge children's work and ideas; and to share the importance of the visual arts in children's lives with others. Keep in mind that a carefully curated display will be more engaging, interesting, and effective than an overwhelming display of every child's work being featured all at once. Think about the space you have and how to use it effectively. To achieve an aesthetic display, frame children's art in simple frames that complement the colours of the artwork without overwhelming it. Trim and mount children's artworks on a background to present them with respect and to show value for their efforts. Pinning the mounted artworks to neutral-coloured pin boards also works well, as the plain background helps the art stand out, avoiding the distraction of patterned backgrounds. Sculptures, constructions, and other three-dimensional artworks can be displayed on bench tops, table-tops, shelves, or cabinets. In a similar way to gallery exhibitions, individual works can be accompanied by information labels showing the artist's name and age, the title of the artwork (if there is one), and the materials or methods used to make it. As you develop your skills in the creation of visual displays, build a story around the children's artwork. Displaying children's artwork, along with documented images and educator insights and reflections about children's learning, demonstrates deep appreciation for children's efforts and recognises value for their growth, development, and learning. As previously detailed in Chapter 5, documenting children's learning is a powerful way to advocate for the rich learning that takes place in and through the visual arts.

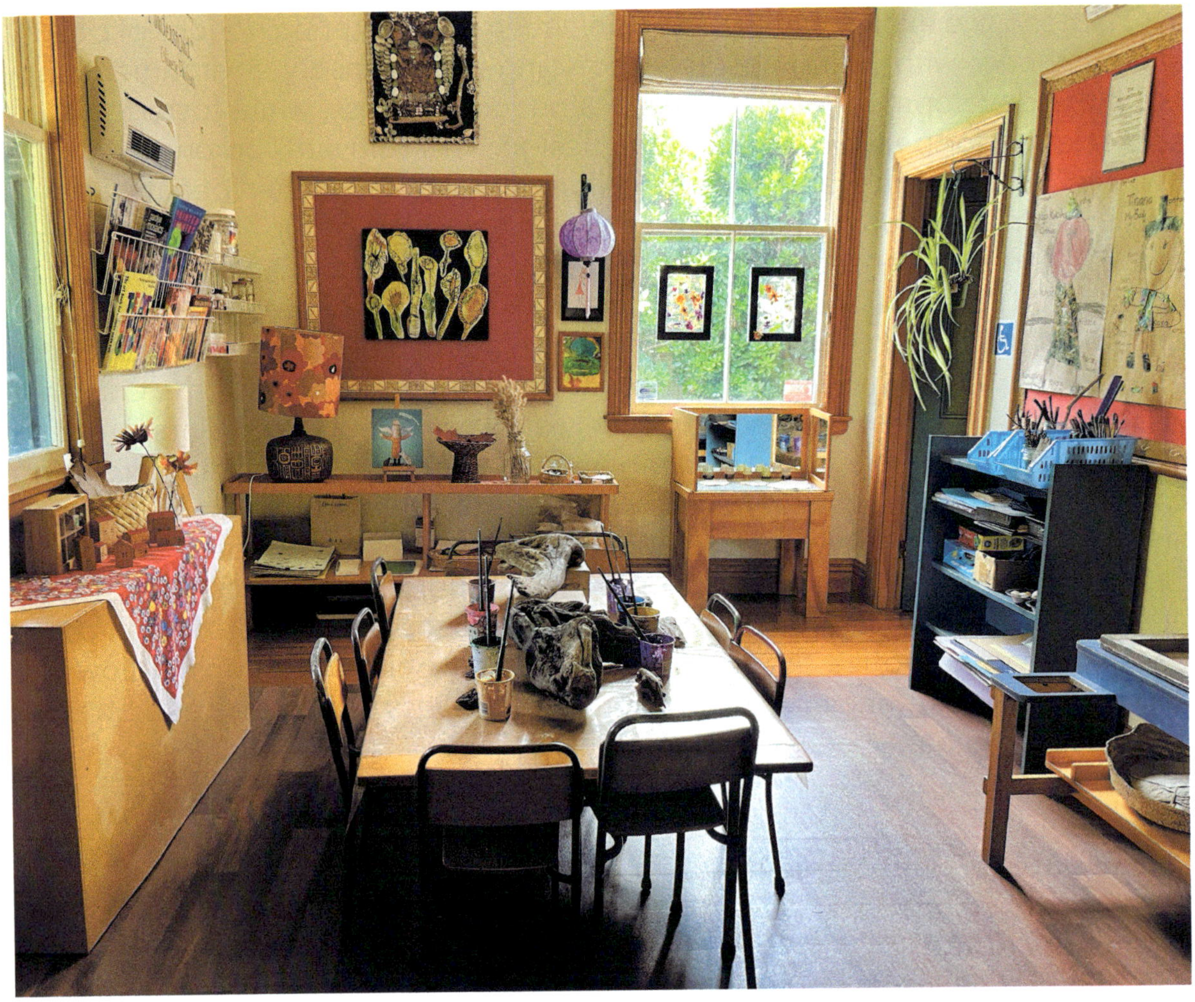

Figure 10.4 Children's art has been displayed around the art studio walls, using a variety of methods to present the work with care and appreciation [Image: Adrienne Wilkins, Sophia Preschool].

Selecting art materials and tools

Setting up an art studio space with a range of quality arts materials may seem daunting. However, careful selection and thoughtful arrangement of materials creates the conditions for open-ended, creative arts play, offering significant potential for visual arts exploration and learning. While visual arts materials, and the tools used with them, are typically physical and tangible (e.g. clay, paint, paper, ink, wool, pencils, cardboard, metal, wood, and plastic), non-physical elements like sound and light can also be used. Developing familiarity with art materials and mastering art tools takes time. It is therefore important to provide repeated opportunities for children to explore visual arts materials and processes, to build on prior learning, and develop confidence to use materials and tools effectively (Carr, 2011; Lewin-Benham, 2023; McArdle, 2012).

Although all materials have value, it is not necessary to offer every type of art material to provide engaging and effective art experiences for young children. We suggest starting with a selection of basic materials for drawing, painting, collage, clay work, and ephemeral art, with the aim to collect additional resources over time. It is also important for educators to intentionally bring their own knowledge of art materials and techniques to the art studio. Children's learning is enhanced, and their competency with visual arts mediums is expanded, when educators engage in authentic conversations about the possibilities and challenges of each material while co-exploring with the children (Brooks, 2022).

Quality matters

The quality and type of materials offered to children can impact learning and engagement (Brooks, 2022). Quality art materials offer rich visual and tactile feedback. They are a good investment because they tend to outlast and outperform cheaper materials and actively engage children's senses to support sustained interest in visual arts experiences. For example, consider the thick, flowing line a fountain pen makes compared to a standard ballpoint pen. While more expensive materials are often of a higher quality, it is possible to source less expensive materials that are both affordable and sustainable. Whenever possible, try materials out before purchasing, or seek advice from colleagues and artists. The key is to experiment with materials to determine whether they are sensory, pliable, expressive, and responsive in their application. Consider whether the materials inspire and encourage play and experimentation. Choose materials that are easily manipulated, offer scope for exploration, and support children to express their ideas in visual form. Art materials that are visually engaging and physically responsive will inspire children's imaginations, nurture their natural curiosity to explore and investigate, and will support the development of visual arts skills and knowledge.

Provide a range of two and three-dimensional art mediums

Each art medium has its own character and offers a range of sensory exploration, skill development, and visual representation possibilities. As children respond to different materials and processes, present opportunities to work with both wet and dry materials, and to work with both two and three-dimensional art media. Artworks described as two dimensional are generally flat works of art such as photography, paintings, drawings, and collage. Three-dimensional art has volume and mass and includes various forms of sculpture. Offering children opportunities to explore a particular idea or concept through both two and three-dimensional media enriches their thinking and learning (Probine, 2020). When selecting art media, consider the following (which are further detailed in Part Three):

Two-dimensional art media: To offer children varied opportunities to explore making marks, images, and patterns in two dimensions, provide good quality drawing and painting materials, and a range of brushes, glues, collage materials, and papers. As children develop familiarity and

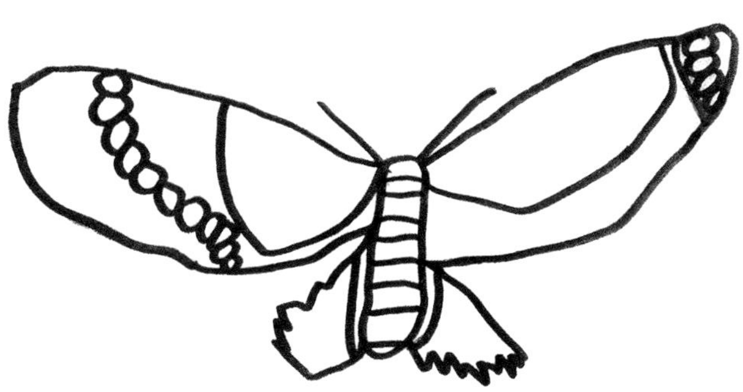

competency, inks, printmaking, and photography will present additional opportunities for self-expression and image-making in two dimensions.

Three-dimensional art media: Children who may be less inclined to engage in painting, drawing, or collage experiences will often find their passion in clay work, box construction, textile art (such as weaving), or sculpting with wire and modelling materials. By providing opportunities to work with three-dimensional art media, children can discover new ways of expressing their ideas in visual form using the elements of form, space, weight, and balance.

Integrate technology and media arts

Integrating technology into art-making processes invites children to explore tools that interest them while extending their engagement with visual arts tools and materials. This kind of integration facilitates "experimentation, discovery, problem-solving, and knowledge building" (Engelbright-Fox & Schirmacher, 2012). It inspires children who might otherwise avoid traditional arts activities and supports them to create meaningful non-print-based visual representations that transcend the limitations of written literacy (Wright, 2012). Tools such as tablets with cameras and photo editing applications, cameras, digital microscopes, photocopiers, light tables, digital projectors, and computers offer highly engaging, active, and open-ended ways to expand children's visual vocabularies. These technologies present opportunities for children to explore photography, electronic design and drawing, stop-motion and digital animation, movie and film production, as well as exploratory play with shadows, light, and projections. (See Part 3 for further detail about the rich learning potentials of digital technology and electronic media for open-ended arts exploration and expression.) Creative use of media is collaborative, interactive, and multidisciplinary, allowing children to engage in a range of visual literacy and Information and Communication Technology (ICT) practices (Wright, 2012). Through technology, children and educators can also connect virtually with museums and galleries to research diverse artworks and practices (Engelbright-Fox & Schirmacher, 2012). Technology can therefore be positioned as a tool that enhances, rather than replaces, hands-on, material art making.

The role of adults in children's media play is crucial, as their involvement directly impacts the quality of the experience. Educators must provide time, space, resources, and opportunities for media play, ensuring activities remain open-ended for creativity and collaboration. When selecting software, such as drawing applications, educators should ensure the tools are multi-sensory and interactive, and avoid restrictive, drill-based tasks which limit imagination and creativity (Engelbright-Fox & Schirmacher, 2012). It is important for teachers and learners to work together, learning about the tools and technology collaboratively (Wright, 2012). Teaching technology through the arts requires adults guide children by teaching the skills of one discipline to enhance the other, enabling meaningful connections between technology and artistic expression (Wright, 2012, p. 141). By embracing this intentional and active role, teachers nurture children's ability to connect with a world of artistry, wonder, and innovation.

Making sustainable choices

Many commercially produced materials traditionally offered in early childhood settings (e.g. glitter, pom-poms, balloons, collage materials) contain microplastics that never break down in the environment. Other materials, such as felt pens, acrylic paint and markers, are predominantly made of plastic. These commonly used materials often end up as landfill or contribute to water pollution when sent home. To reduce your environmental footprint consider using plastic materials sparingly (or not at all) and assess the value of each material for children's learning. You may also like to reflect on how materials will be used and the purpose they serve in your art program to ensure thoughtful and sustainable choices.

The inclusion of natural and recycled loose parts collections is a wonderful way to support sustainable art practices. Collections of natural (shells, pinecones, feathers, leaves) and recycled materials (bottle tops, wood offcuts, cardboard, and fabric) are not only affordable, they are often free! Such collections can be repeatedly explored for their tactile and aesthetic qualities through ephemeral artwork and pattern-making. Be sure to critically evaluate where natural materials are sourced from. It is important to question whether taking natural materials from the environment might negatively impact particular ecosystems. Additionally, when ordering materials from online catalogs, ensure their origins are known and that they have been sourced ethically.

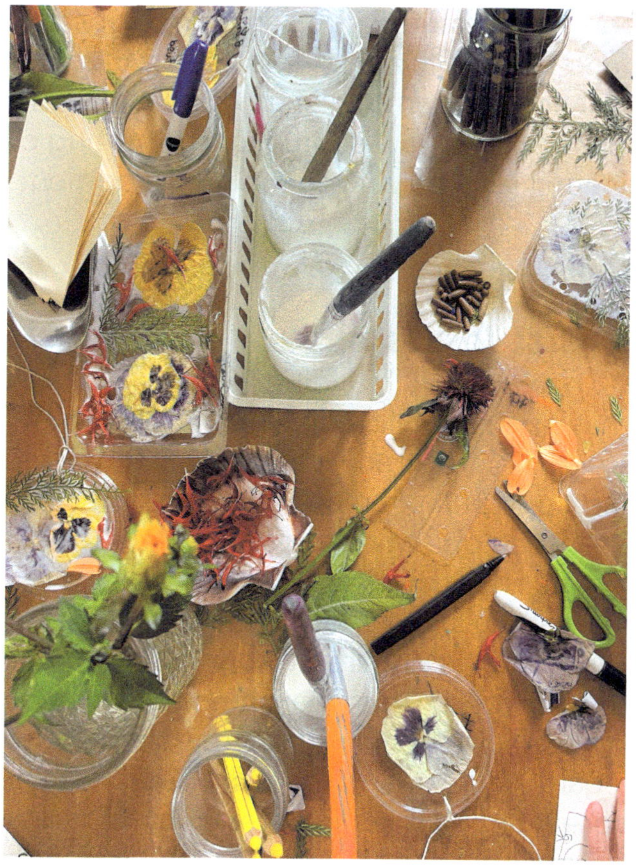

Figure 10.5 Various recycled clear plastic lids and containers were used to create translucent artworks with pressed dried flowers and leaves [Image: Adrienne Wilkins, Sophia Preschool].

Another way to encourage and implement sustainable art practices is to role model and intentionally teach children how to care for and use visual arts materials and tools respectfully. The expense of arts materials is often considered a barrier to delivering quality arts experiences. However, by teaching children to respect, value, and care for materials and tools, they are learning valuable life lessons about sustainability and respect for materials. For example, with consistent guidance and intentional support, children can learn how to clean and store paint brushes, put lids back on felt pens, and leave work surfaces clean for the next person to use the space. When educators and children engage in such practices together, materials can be maintained in good condition, reducing the need for constant replacement. Caring for materials, equipment, and spaces, and learning to respect the rights of their peers to access clean spaces and undamaged materials, is as important a learning focus as the art-making process itself.

Open-ended and flexible materials

Rather than being limited to a single purpose or predetermined use, open-ended materials can be used in a variety of ways. Their flexible nature provides a sense of freedom for children as they explore, transform, arrange, manipulate and organise them. Art materials that are open-ended (boxes, clay, paper, paint, pencils, loose part collections, and natural materials) provide children with a broad range of possibilities for exploration, creative play, and self-expression. Flexible-use and open-ended materials open up rich possibilities for children to explore their ideas, and to visually communicate in multiple ways (e.g., symbolic representation, decoration, pattern making, and storytelling). Open-ended art materials are therefore an essential resource for supporting children's autonomy, fostering their imagination, and enhancing their development as creative thinkers and designers.

A final reminder that less is more

There is no doubt that offering children choice is important. However, we note that in the visual arts domain, too many materials and choices can be overwhelming (and create a clean-up nightmare most would prefer to avoid!). The minimalist idea that "less is more" is helpful when choosing and organising materials for an arts studio space. Introducing materials slowly also allows educators to evaluate safety risks and avoid materials, tools, or processes where potential risks cannot be easily managed. Introducing children to one or two materials at a time supports them to get to know each unique art medium and develop the skills and techniques specific for their use. It is important to establish clear expectations and consistent routines regarding the use and care of visual arts materials and spaces - a task that is much more manageable when fewer materials are presented. With intentionally selected material choices, along with time and repeated practice, children become skilled, resourceful, and respectful; developing creative thinking while learning to be responsible contributors in the art space.

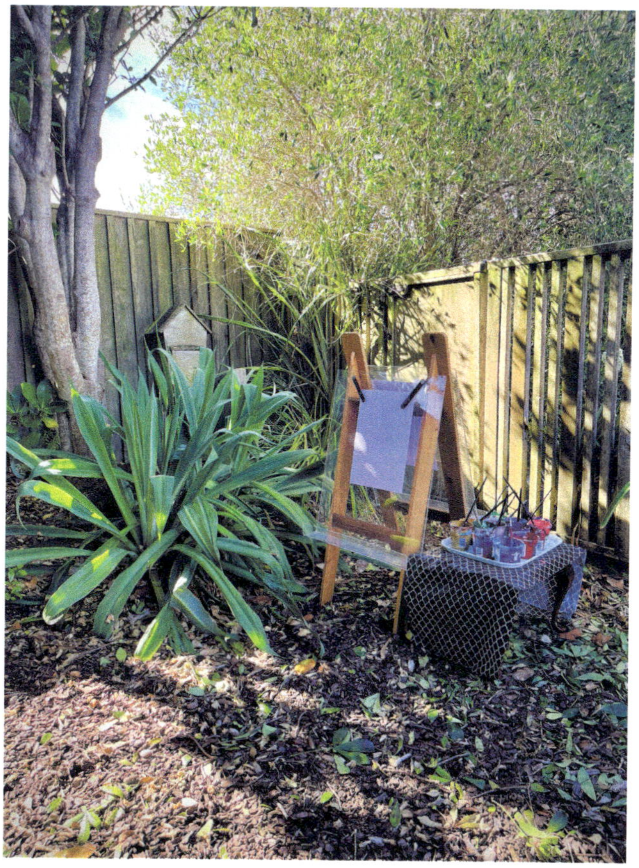

Figure 10.6 Create a peaceful context for creativity by setting up easels and paint in the garden [Image: Adrienne Wilkins, Sophia Preschool].

Conclusion

Creating an inspiring and functional visual arts space requires thoughtful planning, careful material selection, and a commitment to fostering creativity. A well-designed studio space not only supports the practicalities of art-making but also invites children into an environment that values beauty, aesthetics, and meaningful engagement. Such spaces empower children to explore materials, develop skills, and express their ideas, while also cultivating an appreciation for art and the creative process.

By integrating sustainable practices, open-ended materials, and thoughtful organisation, educators can create environments that nurture children's autonomy and encourage their imaginative potential. These spaces are more than physical locations; they are hubs of inquiry, collaboration, and self-expression. When children are immersed in well-curated, aesthetically pleasing environments, they are inspired to slow down, observe closely, and engage deeply with the materials and processes around them.

Ultimately, a thoughtfully designed visual arts space fosters a culture of respect for materials, peers, and the creative process. Such spaces affirm the importance of visual arts in early education, offering children opportunities to explore, innovate, and find joy in the transformative power of artistic expression and support you as an educator to guide, model, and co-create with children, enriching their shared experiences.

References

Brooks, M. (2022). *Authentic art with children*. Pademelon Press.

Carr, M. (2011). Young children reflecting on their learning: teachers' conversation strategies. *Early Years, 31*(3), 257–270. https://doi.org/10.1080/09575146.2011.613805

Curtis, D., & Carter, M. (2014). *Designs for living and learning: Transforming early childhood environments*. Redleaf Press.

Engelbright-Fox, J., & Schirmacher, R. (2012). *Art & creative development for young children* (7th ed.). Wadsworth Cengage Learning.

Gandini, L. (2005). The whole school as an atelier: Reflections by Carla Rinaldi. In L. Gandini, L. Hill, L. Cadwell, & C. Schwall (Eds.), *In the spirit of the studio: Learning from the atelier of Reggio Emilia* (pp. 169–174). Teachers College Press.

Lewin-Benham, A. (2023). Infants and toddlers at work: *using Reggio-inspired materials to support brain development* (2nd ed.). Teachers College Press.

McArdle, F. (2012). The visual arts: Ways of seeing. In S. Wright (Ed.), *Children, meaning-making and the arts* (2nd ed., pp. 30–56). Pearson Australia.

Pacini-Ketchabaw, V., Kind, S., & Kocher, L. M. (2024). *Encounters with materials in early childhood education* (2nd ed.). Routledge.

Probine, S. (2020). Examining the in-between: Contextual factors on how young children learn through the visual arts [Doctoral dissertation, University of Auckland]. http://hdl.handle.net/2292/52825

Schwall, C. (2005). The atelier environment and materials. In L. Gandini, L. Hill, L. Cadwell, & C. Schwall (Eds.), *In the spirit of the studio: Learning from the atelier of Reggio Emilia* (pp. 16–31). Teachers College Press.

Wright, S. (2012). *Children, meaning-making and the arts* (2nd ed.). Pearson Australia.

Part 3

THE HOW: Practical visual arts knowledge and methods

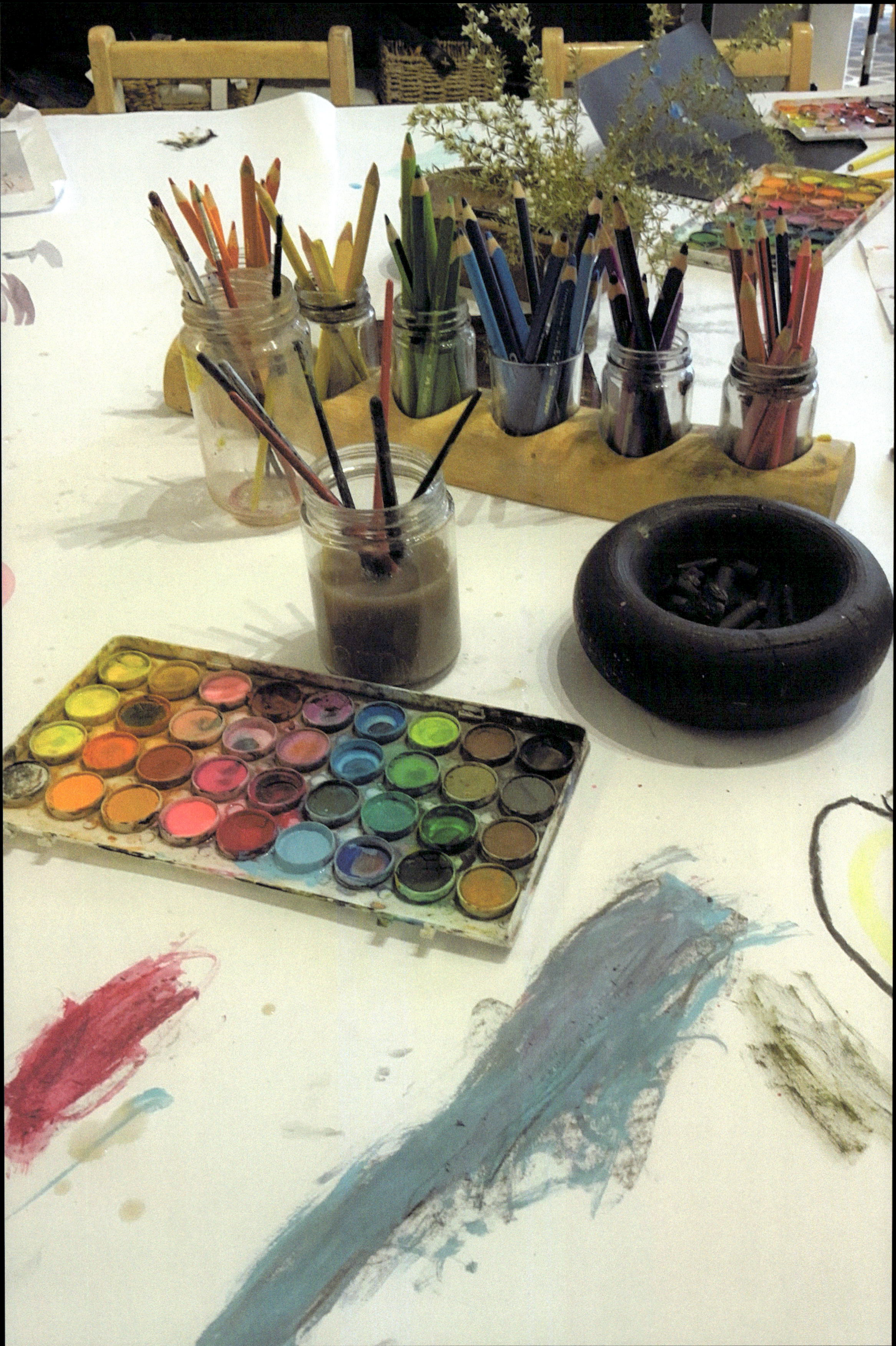

PART 3 Introduction

In parts one and two, we explored why learning through, in, and with the visual arts is important in the lives of children and offered a range of theoretical and practical suggestions to broaden children's visual arts experiences. In this section, we offer additional information to support educator's knowledge in relation to art materials and art making processes. We begin with practical guidance on selecting, presenting, and storing visual arts materials, along with ideas for sustainable practices and the maintenance of art materials and spaces. This introduction leads into a closer look at specific visual art languages, including drawing and mark making, painting, printmaking, clay play and sculpture, ephemeral art, collage and assembly, traditional crafts and artisan processes, and photography, light, and lenses. By engaging with this practical information, educators can deepen their knowledge of diverse approaches to art making, build on their confidence to explore open-ended art materials and processes, and expand their repertoire for meaningful visual arts learning with children.

Introducing materials to children

It takes many "meetings" with materials to learn what materials can do, how to use them, how to handle and care for them and to become confident with making marks to communicate ideas visually. Adults should actively model processes and techniques in a playful, discovery-led approach to learning. Partner with children to model, share, and propose techniques rather than making children follow set instructions. Listen to, and sometimes comment on, children's ideas, discoveries, and wonderings. Delight with children in the visual arts materials and processes. Developing and maintaining a mindset of open exploration and playful investigation will support children to do the same and create a positive culture of arts inquiry.

Figure P3A.1 A thoughtfully arranged art table invites children to explore and experiment with diverse materials, fostering creativity and open-ended learning [Image: East Maitland Preschool].

DOI: 10.4324/9781003561835-14

Thinking about art surfaces

It is important to provide a range of surfaces for children to paint, draw, and make art on. Select surfaces that offer a variety of textures and sizes. Be selective regarding the weight, finish, and colour of paper, cardboard, canvas, and other surfaces to ensure that art materials will apply easily and visibly. (If you have ever tried to draw on coloured paper with pale pencils you will appreciate how frustrating the lack of visible mark can be!) When an arts experience demands a sturdier multi-media paper (e.g. painting, printmaking, collage, and multi-media work), select a paper that is at least 150 gsm (grams per square metre). In education settings, cartridge paper (matt on both sides) and litho-paper (matt on one side and shiny on the other) both offer a very resilient surface for mixed-media, painting, and printmaking. Regardless of the surface you select, test it out yourself before setting up an experience to ensure you consider all of the variables and know that the results will be satisfying.

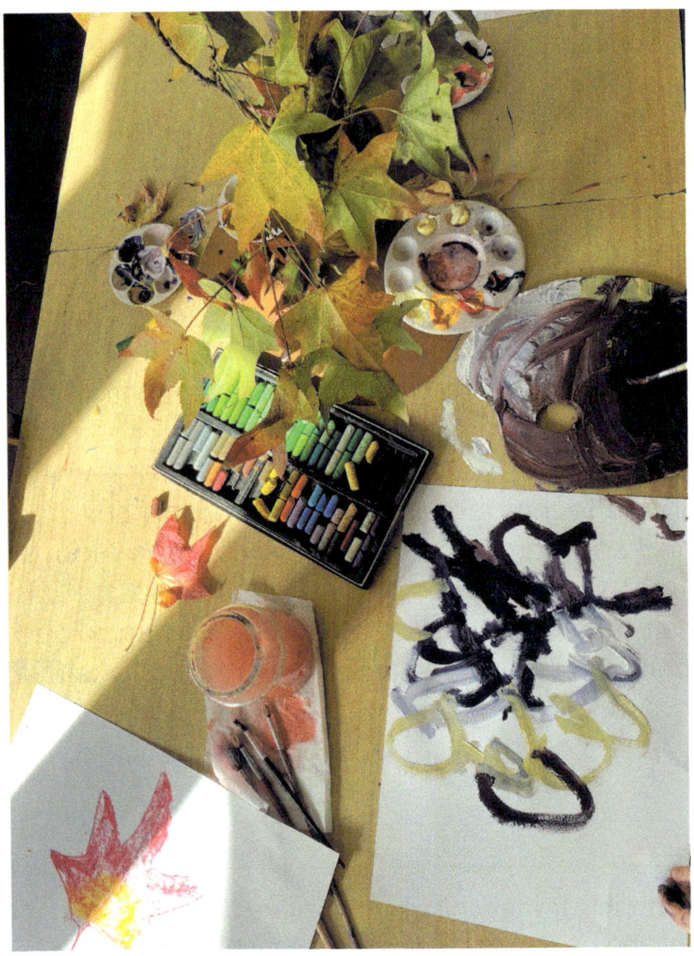

ART SURFACES: cartridge paper, watercolour paper, cardboard, recycled boxes (NOTE: turn boxes inside out to remove the advertising and provide beautiful blank surfaces), newspaper, magazine images, recycled photocopy paper, photocopied images, architect paper, paper offcuts from a printery, timber offcuts, plastics and acetate film, alfoil, recycled packaging, canvas, fabric, glass, mirrors, concrete.

Figure P3A.2 Quality surfaces for painting and mark making enhance exploration, enabling a more satisfying application of art materials [Image: East Maitland Preschool].

Sustainable choices

We encourage educators to collect and choose sustainable and ethically sourced materials. For example:

- Source recycled papers from local businesses, such as printers and architects.
- Avoid unnecessary plastics (e.g. foam shapes, balloons, glitter)
- Be aware that acrylic paint is a plastic. Use sparingly and minimise wastage. For some children, ingesting or applying acrylic paint to skin may cause allergic or sensory reactions.
- Evaluate whether commercially sold items such as feathers, shells and natural materials have been ethically and sustainably sourced. Use such items sustainably as loose parts, rather than as disposable materials that need to be replaced.
- Recruit children and families to collect recycled materials for art making and loose parts play. For example, boxes, cardboard, wrapping paper, magazines, bottle lids, sewing spools, timber offcuts, string, fabrics, and any objects with interesting shapes and textures.

Storage and care for materials

The way materials are stored and presented to children communicates how you value resources and how you expect children to care for them. Store mark-making tools, such as pencils, felt pens, and markers, in organised ways. Store felt pens tip down or horizontally so that the paint or ink in the tube does not dry out. A great idea for organising drawing implements so that they are easily accessible on a work table is to fold heavy cardboard into a zig-zag concertina and lay items in the creases.

Planning for success

Set up learning spaces to ensure a successful learning experience in terms of children's participation and engagement, and in terms of easy cleaning. You should also be prepared for and accept a certain amount of mess. When planning an experience, think about everything you will need to enable you to stay present and active during the learning experience and to support children to participate in keeping the area well organised and tidy. Think about strategies that will make cleaning up efficient and effective. Consider the following:

- Use floor and table coverings to catch spills.
- Set up near a sink or ensure access to a small bucket of warm soapy water, sponges and rags.
- Dress for mess or think about using aprons or smocks to protect children's clothing from stains.
- Avoid overcrowding and ensure that materials are within each child's easy reach.
- Define group size and supervision strategies to enable staff to work effectively with children.
- Plan where artwork will be placed to dry.

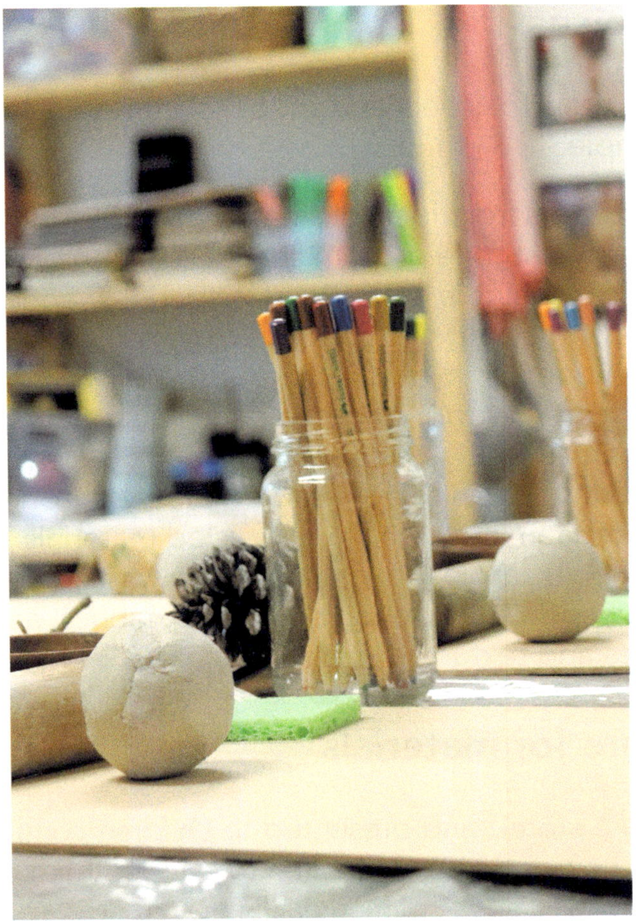

Figure P3A.3 Organising and presenting materials thoughtfully fosters respect and care while supporting engaging, and manageable learning experiences [Image: Bomaderry Community Preschool].

Another important factor in planning for success is applying consistent intentional teaching strategies and high expectations for children. As a co-learner, model, and guide, consistently teach children to tidy up the materials and spaces they have used before they move away to another play choice. This is part of learning to be a responsible member of the learning community. For example, children can be encouraged and expected to:

- Replace lids on felt pens
- Pick up dropped items and return to their storage containers
- Put paint brushes back in same colour paint pot
- Hang or lay artworks on a hanging rack or shelf
- Wipe surfaces clean
- Leave spaces clean and ready for the next child to engage

Display and respect

The ways children's work is curated and displayed communicates respect for both children and their efforts. A consistent colour scheme of mounting boards, signage, or framing presents work aesthetically and creates a collective grouping of the children's work. The suggestions below outline a range of options to care for and display children's work in ways that communicate it is valued:

- Use a guillotine or large ruler and scalpel knife to cut paper with straight lines and 90-degree angles on corners.
- Mount artworks and documentation on cardboard for display.
- Images of children in the act of creating and quotes of comments they make about their artwork can be featured in documentation to accompany artwork.
- Cover a pinboard with paper or fabric and pin-mounted artworks in a gallery display.
- Punch holes in the top and bottom of carboard frames and hang artworks on a suspected pole or hoop.
- Hang artworks and images using pegs or bulldog clips on a horizontal line, netting, bamboo frame, or trellis.
- Mount work back-to-back on a window using small squares of double-sided tape to enable viewing from either side.
- Mount work behind a large sheet of Perspex attached with screws to a wall at children's eye height. This protects the artwork and prevents ripping and removal of pins or putty.
- Create a grid of picture frames for hanging work gallery style.
- Cover large boxes with sturdy brown paper. These can be used to display artwork and documentation away from walls and can also be used as plinths for displaying three-dimensional work.

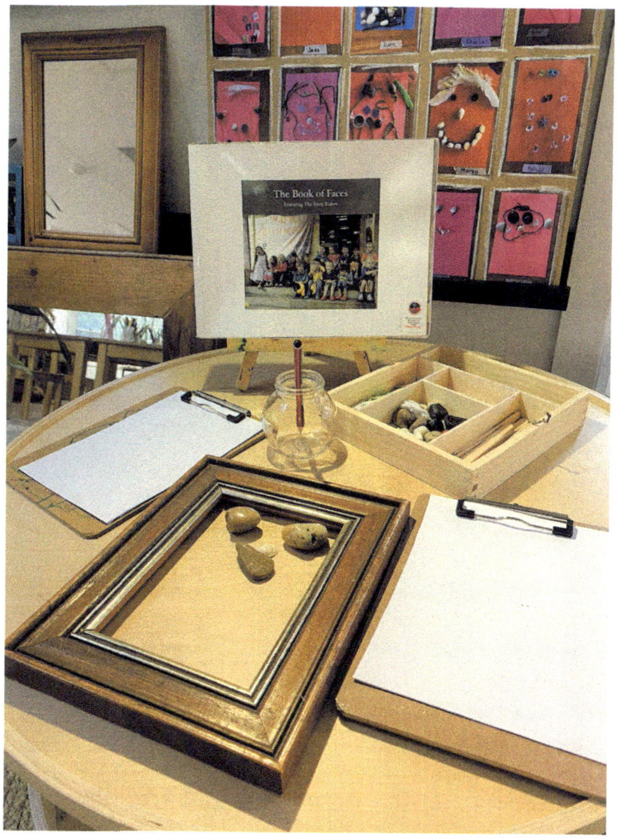

Figure P3A.4 Thoughtful and aesthetic displays of children's work communicate respect for their creativity, fostering a sense of value and pride, while inspiring new ideas through revisiting past creations [Image: Bomaderry Community Preschool].

Supporting children through relational partnerships

Most importantly, relationships must be placed at the heart of our visual arts play with children. Building our appreciation for children's play, thinking, meaning-making, problem-solving, and exploratory delight with materials underpins meaningful and purposeful visual arts play. A purposeful joy permeates the curriculum when children are supported to enter a deep "zone" of playful engagement and exploration with materials. As outlined in Part 2 of this book, that requires engaged, intentional educators who build their visual arts self-efficacy and pedagogical content knowledge.

To support your own and children's art appreciation and art making, become familiar with the elements of art and the principles of design. The elements of art include line, shape, form, colour, texture, space, and tone. Arranged, combined, and manipulated, these elements visually communicate ideas, create interest, or express an aesthetic or mood. The principles of art (also referred to as the principles of design) include balance, contrast, emphasis, movement, pattern, repetition, rhythm, unity/variety, and scale/proportion [an online search will

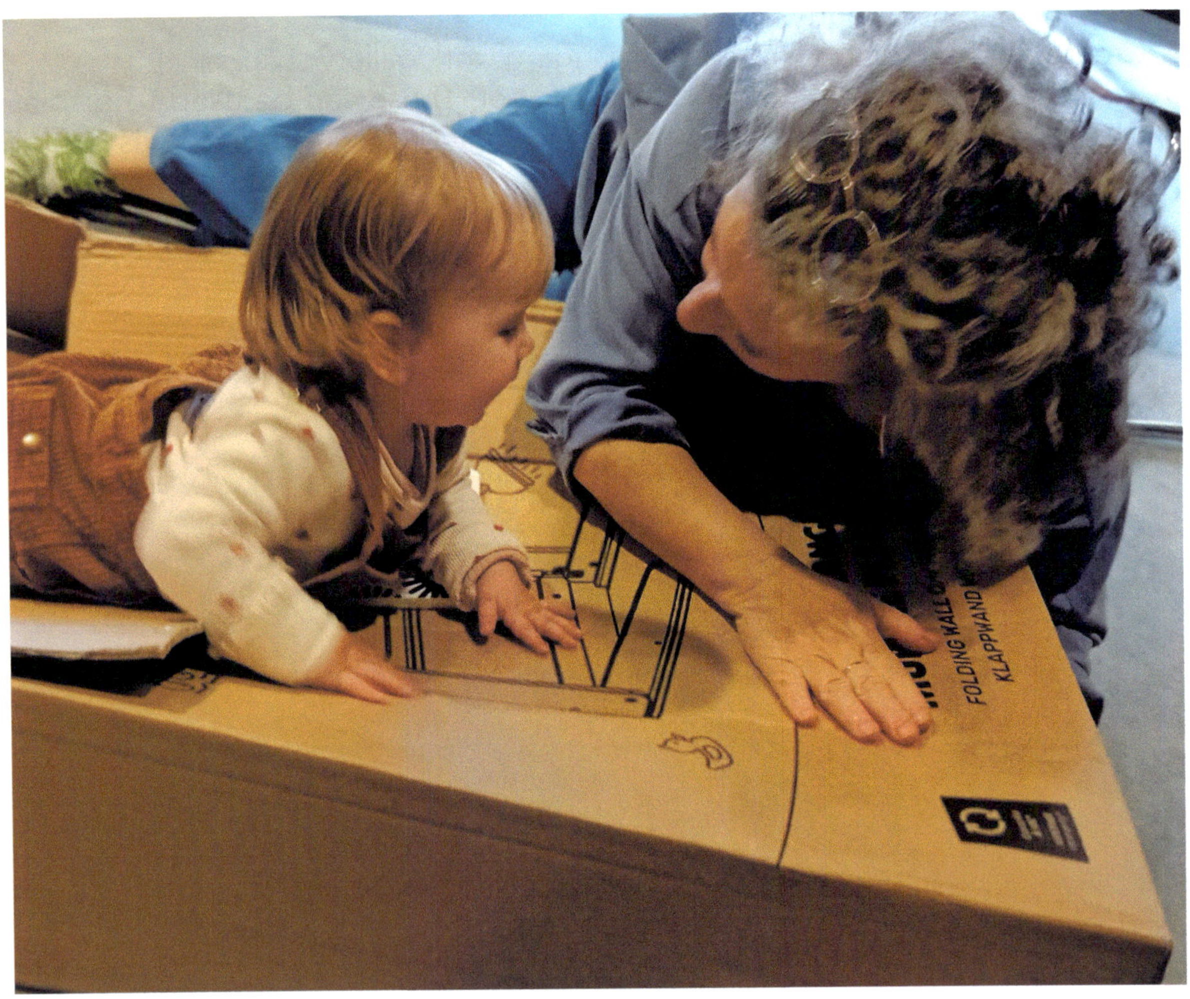

Figure P3A.5 Placing relationships at the heart of visual arts play and inquiry fosters meaningful engagement and exploration. When educators and children learn and create together, they build deep connections which provide a foundation for collaborative discovery [Image: Joke den Haese].

further provide information and examples]. Brooks (2022b) suggests it is helpful to apply the studio practices employed by contemporary artists to think about ways to visually express and communicate ideas with materials (e.g. explore metaphors and symbols, deconstruct and abstract art elements and materials, look for possibilities and solve problems). Additionally, Harvard's Project Zero (2003) developed eight "studio habits of mind," which describe how children develop creative thinking and dispositions through engaging in visual arts work. The habits include Observe, Envision, Stretch and Explore, Engage and Persist, Express, Develop Craft, Understand Art Worlds, and Reflect. Aim to always plan visual arts learning experiences that foster children's learning dispositions.

In the following pages we suggest materials, tools, and basic processes for a range of visual arts methods. Terminology and techniques are included to inspire possible applications in your own educational setting. As we have endorsed throughout this book, the way to learn and build knowledge and confidence with visual arts methods, processes, and techniques is to play with visual arts materials, tools, and processes; whether you are an adult or a child. We all learn through repeated experience and through trial and error, play, and experimentation. So, have fun and relish the process of learning and playing alongside children.

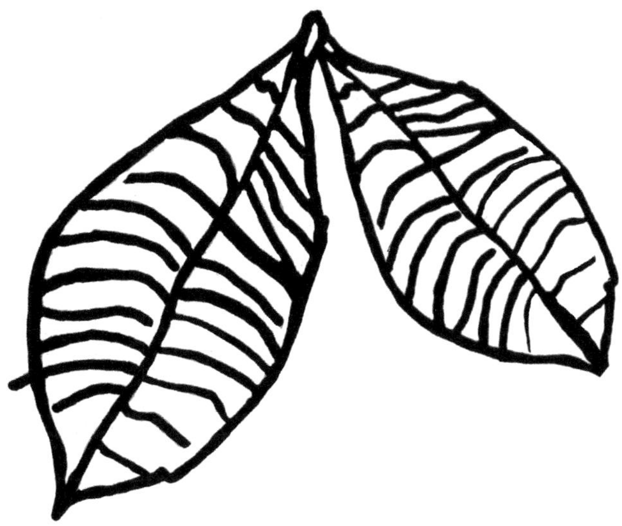

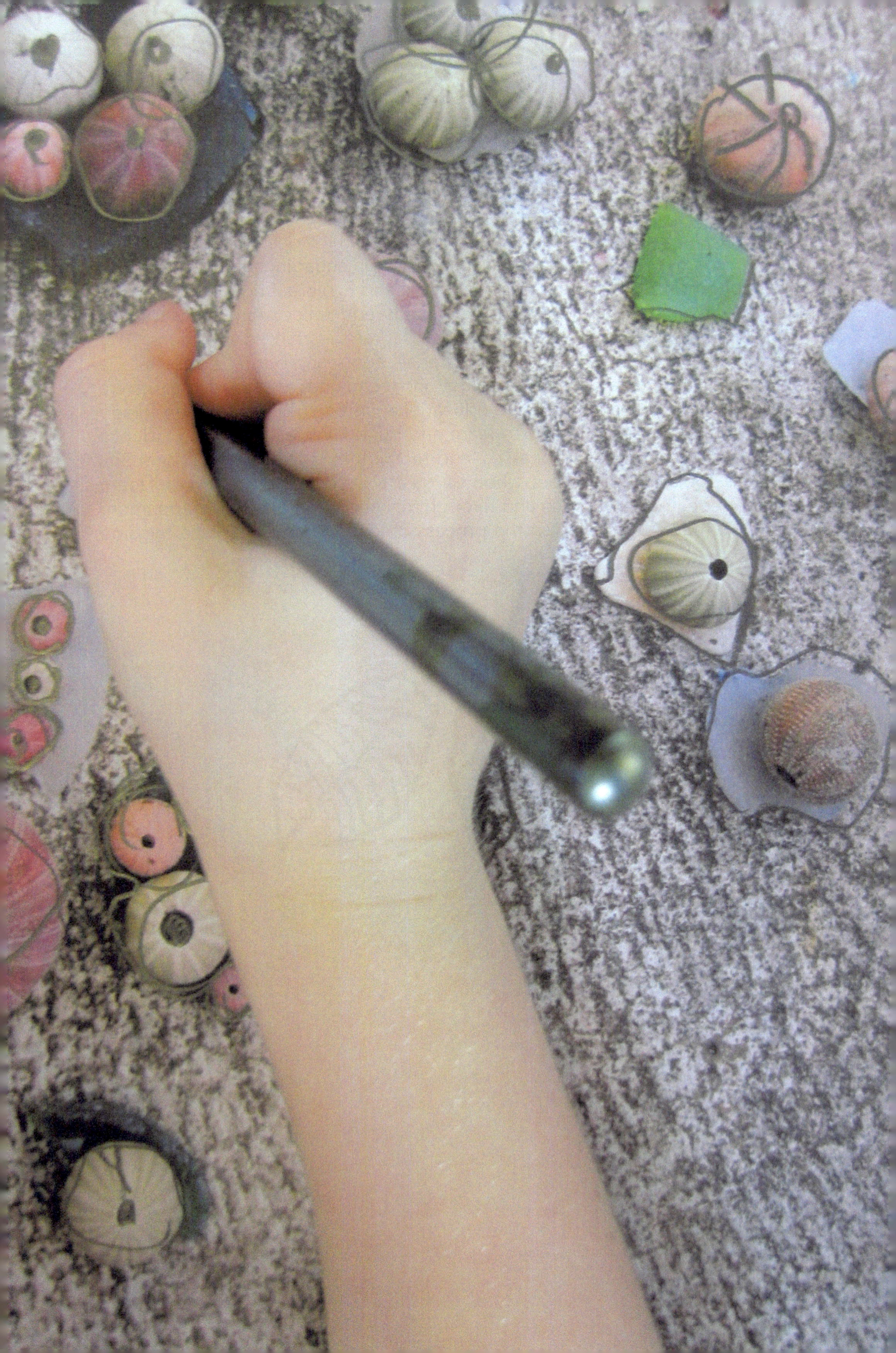

3.1 Drawing and mark making

Mark making and drawing enables children to communicate their ideas, theories, and wonderings or simply experiment with materials and the marks they make. As well as the obvious benefits related to physical skills development and hand-eye coordination, drawing, and mark-making exercise cognitive processes to foster communication, problem-solving, divergent thinking, and imagination. These processes also support us to listen to and value children's ideas and actions.

Mark-making can occur in many ways and extend beyond drawing on paper. For example, marks and drawing can happen when:

- Using sticks in the sandpit
- Tracing marks in flour or sand in clear trays on a lightbox
- Scratching marks in clay or paint with tools or sticks
- Drawing with soap on mirrors or glass

Introducing children to drawing and mark making

When introducing drawing materials to children:

- Introduce one material at a time.
- Allow time and repeated opportunities for children to experiment, play with, and become familiar with the affordances and qualities of each material.
- Support children to build knowledge and skills to use materials.
- Offer suggestions rather than instructions.
- Model techniques and draw attention to new discoveries (your own and those made by participating children).

Observational drawing

Observational drawing is a wonderful way to invite children to connect with the world around them and observe more closely. This is a useful strategy for combining scientific investigation with aesthetically pleasing creative processes. The provision of magnifying glasses, paper, and drawing materials invites children to recognise and translate the shapes, patterns, and colours

---

Figure P3B.1 Combine technology and drawing by providing children with printed images to draw on. In this case, children traced over images of their own ephemeral artworks to create mono-prints. The tracing transferred ink onto paper placed beneath the printed image [Image: Gai Lindsay, Lyrebird Preschool].

DOI: 10.4324/9781003561835-15

they observe into a visual representation of their discoveries. The following strategies enhance children's drawing skills while extending their capacity to observe, analyse, and creatively interpret the world around them:

- **Explore objects together**: Begin by examining the object or focus of drawing collaboratively, discussing shapes, textures, colours, and even scents. This shared discovery helps children build a detailed understanding of the object or place being drawn.
- **Encourage representation**: Support children as they translate their observations into drawings, helping them focus on specific details or elements they find interesting.
- **Model the process**: Drawing alongside children provides a valuable opportunity to model techniques, share challenges, and demonstrate problem-solving strategies. This collaborative approach demystifies the process and encourages perseverance.
- **Notice and discuss details**: Highlight the intricate details observed in the object or place and invite children to share their interpretations and methods for representing what they observe.
- **Extend children's learning and engagement**: Encourage children to translate their drawings into three-dimensional constructions or use two-dimensional drawings to inform three-dimensional constructions or sculptures.

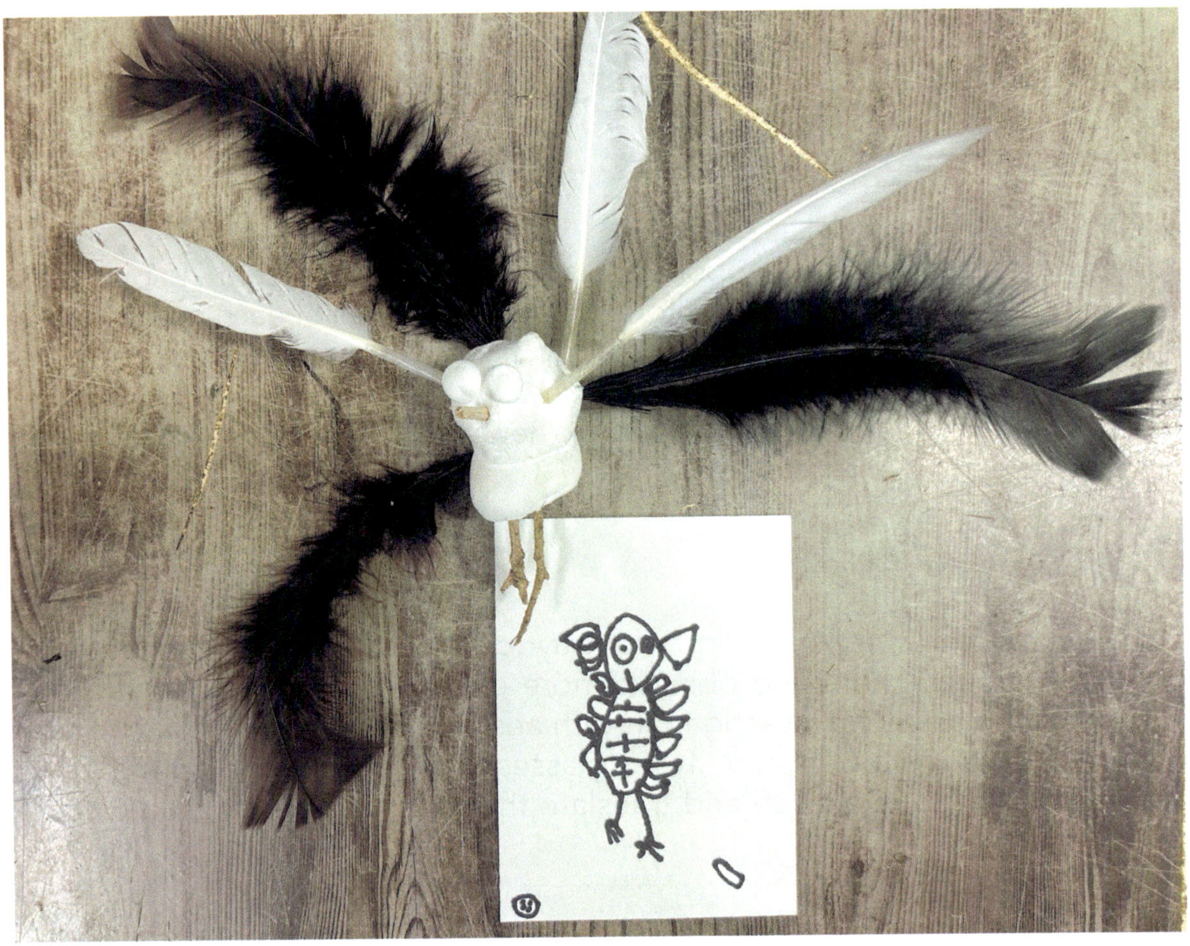

Figure P3B.2 Extend children's arts focus by encouraging them to draw their constructions or sculptures, such as this bird made of feathers, sticks and white clay; or alternatively prompt them to turn drawings into three-dimensional creations [Image: Denise Savins, The Friends Long Day Childcare Centre].

- **Foster dialogue**: Engage children in conversations about their drawings, encouraging them to articulate their observations and the decisions they make during the process.

Planning for mark-making and drawing

The potential of drawing and mark-making is unlimited. When planning a drawing experience, choose a drawing material that will suit the intended purpose of the experience. For example, for clear and detailed drawings, choose a material that will not smudge. If you plan to use watercolour paints to embellish a drawing, choose a waterproof drawing implement such as wax crayons or waterfast pens.

Drawing materials and tools

Charcoal

Charcoal is made of wood that has been burnt in a low-oxygen environment. Willow or vine charcoal is made of sticks and is very soft and responsive, while compressed charcoal is more resilient. Compressed charcoal is made from powdered charcoal that is held together with a binder and pressed into tubes or rectangular sticks. Charcoal pencils also come in a range of colours and shades.

The responsive blackness of charcoal is why it is such a wonderful material to use with children of all ages. With little strength required, even the youngest children can experience the impact of their mark-making. When using charcoal, model the

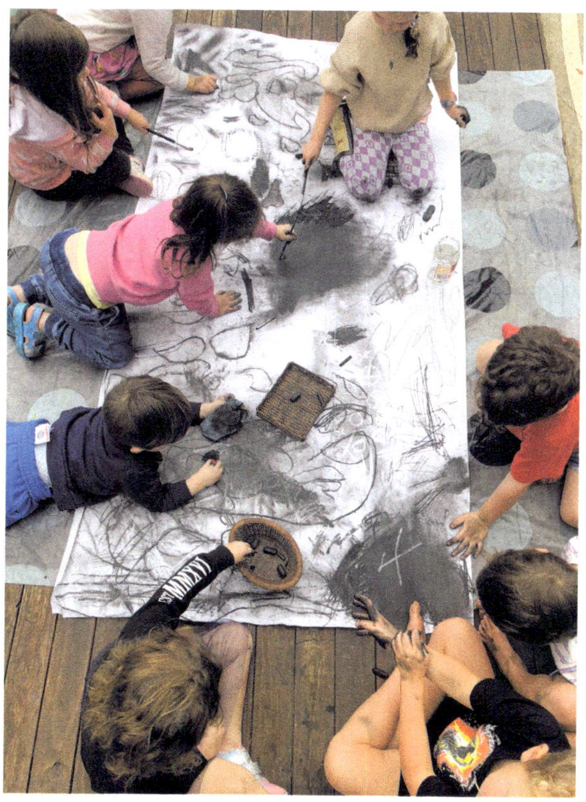

Figure P3B.3 Experiencing charcoal for the first time in a collaborative group setting supports children to joyfully explore, experiment, and share ideas without worrying about the charcoal's 'messiness' or what to draw [Image: Gai Lindsay, taken at UOW Pulse Kids Uni].

joy in learning about what charcoal is, what it can do, and how it can be used. If you express concerns about "mess" making, children will pick up on your anxiety, whereas if you embrace the material for its rich, responsive marks, children will be empowered to explore and make wonderful marks. Because charcoal transfers easily to faces and other surfaces, set up hand washing or wiping materials nearby to prevent charcoal fingerprints throughout the play area.

Experiment with various types of charcoal to learn about the marks they make and how they feel to work with. For example:

- Rub charcoal marks with fingers to create smudged lines and areas of shading.
- Use erasers to remove charcoal to create white lines and spaces.
- Stick paper tape onto the drawing surface prior to applying charcoal. Then encourage children to peel away the strips of paper tape to reveal the stark white shapes and patterns below.
- A light spray of fixative or hairspray prevents charcoal from smudging.

Chalk and chalk pastels

Chalk is made from compressed limestone or gypsum powder, while chalk pastels are made from compressed mineral pigments. Both make delightful, coloured marks on concrete, blackboards, fences, and bricks and can be wiped away with a duster, wet rag, or sponge. Another option is to draw onto wet (sturdy) paper to create a brighter and slightly blurred line. Like charcoal, fixative or hairspray prevents further smudging.

Crayons and oil pastels

Crayons, whether wax or oil-based, are familiar drawing materials. Modern wax crayons are generally made of coloured synthetic wax-like materials, while oil pastels combine pigment with an oil or wax binder. It is important to try out different brands and types of crayons to select those that smoothly apply rich creamy colour and make expressive marks. There is nothing more frustrating than hard, insipidly coloured crayons that barely show on the page. Due to their water-resistant nature, brightly coloured crayons (as well as candles and even the "too hard" pale crayons) are wonderful to use in combination with a water paint wash over the top of the crayon marks to create colour resist patterns and colour contrasts that are very pleasing to the eye. When crayon stains tables or other surfaces, it can be removed with a mild abrasive cleaner.

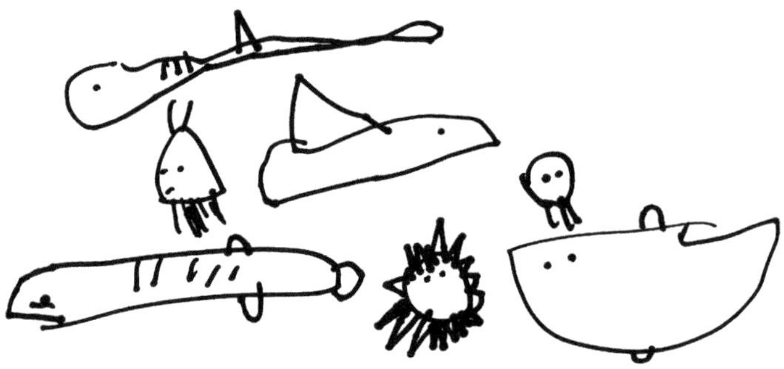

Graphite and coloured pencils

Pencils come in countless ranges of colour and levels of density and quality. Whether choosing coloured or graphite pencils, select pencils that are soft and responsive so that the

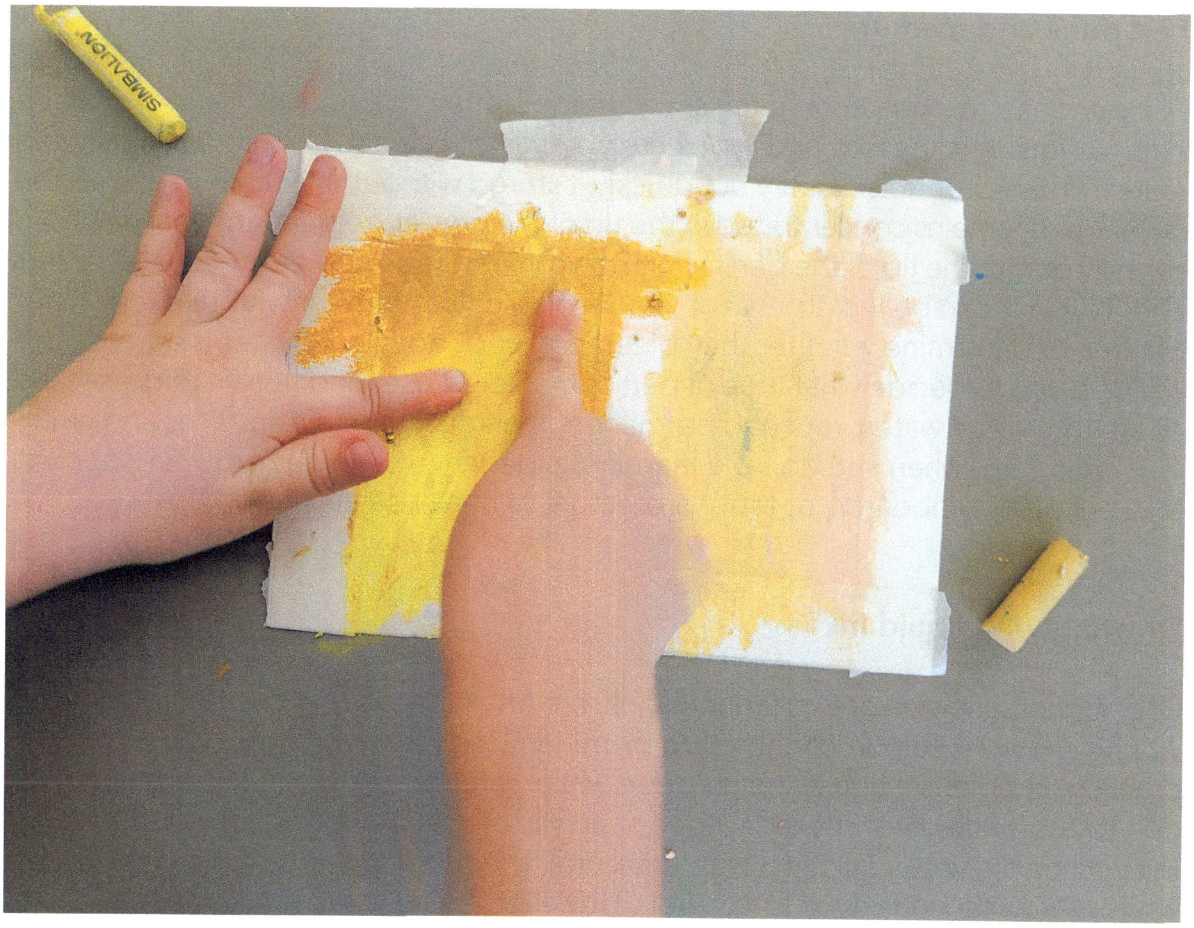

Figure P3B.4 Drawing and mark making isn't limited to creating recognisable images. Ensure children have repeated opportunities to experiment and delight in the colours and qualities of each material, such as these luscious rich creamy oil pastels [Image: Carolyn Prawius, Saigon Kids Early Learning Centre].

mark they make is rich and "creamy." Wherever possible, try before you buy to ensure pencils are responsive and enjoyable to draw with. The great thing about pencils is that they are easy to set up and clean up. Keep pencils sharp, a task children will be very happy to assist you with! (In fact, old and non-responsive pencils can be used simply for sharpening – a learning experience in and of itself!

Graphite pencils are graded according to their softness or hardness. Hard pencils have a letter H for "hard" in the label. The higher the number (2H, 4H, etc.), the harder the graphite core and the lighter the line it creates. Similarly, softer pencils have a B for "black" in the label (2B, 4B, 6B, etc.), ranging from soft to very soft. The higher the number, the softer and darker the line will be. That is why regular standard pencils are labelled HB in the middle of the range of hardness and blackness. Pencils that are hard and lack colour density quickly lose their attraction for children because the mark they make is very thin and light. With such pencils, children tend to press harder, trying to produce more colour or darkness. Rather than achieving better colour application, this strategy mostly results in frustration and broken pencils.

Watercolour pencils extend drawing into a painting experience. They are water-soluble meaning that when water is added the colour bleeds to create a wash of colour. Children can either draw on wet paper or paint water onto a drawing to achieve delightful dense watercolour effects.

Felt pens and markers

Felt pens and markers enable the smooth application of liquid ink via the tip of the pen. Various thicknesses and types create satisfying black or coloured lines and marks. These products can dry out quickly if stored without their lids. To ensure the ink or paint remains concentrated in the tip of the pen, store pens and markers horizontally or with the tip of the pen facing down in a storage cup or container. Markers and felt pens can be waterproof or water-soluble. Experiment with different types of pens to determine whether they bleed colour or not when water is added. This will help you to decide what type of pen or marker to use for different purposes. Be aware that some waterproof and permanent markers may stain surfaces and clothing. Therefore, when setting up a learning experience consider providing aprons, thicker paper, clipboards, or table protectors to minimise clean-up.

Drawing with liquid ink

Drawing inks (sometimes called India ink) are an ancient water-based drawing and writing material coloured with plant or mineral pigments or dyes. Water soluble drawing inks bleed when water is added while waterproof inks are more permanent due to the addition of shellac binder or acrylic emulsion. For drawing and writing, ink was traditionally applied with a natural, metal, or glass quill; and these are options you can introduce to children. However, we suggest a more cost effective and technique-free option is to apply ink with sticks and small twigs. A very small amount of ink goes a very long way. Drop approximately half a teaspoon into a jar or sturdy container and dip sticks into the ink. Drawing with an inky stick creates delightful fluid lines and marks. Do avoid applying ink with paint brushes as not only will it absorb too much ink and be too thick on the page, but it will waste ink unnecessarily.

Inks come in black and a wide array of colours. The density and fluidity of black inks are a delight to explore and experiment with. A small jar of clear water and a paintbrush can extend the ink drawing experiment process. Either wet the drawing surface before adding dots or lines of ink or wet the ink lines afterwards to spread and blur the ink before it dries.

Inks can stain clothing, so old clothes or an apron, as well as an absorbent table covering can minimise the likelihood that ink will splash and stain. A soak in warm soapy water effectively removes most ink from skin. Any unused ink can be poured into an airtight container for reuse at another time.

Mark-making experiences and extension ideas

Ideas and extensions for drawing and mark-making are literally endless. Here are just a few ideas to get you started:

- As well as individual experiences, plan for group explorations with materials. Drawing together creates opportunities for shared dialogue. For example, set up a large roll of heavy paper or a cardboard box for group mark-making.

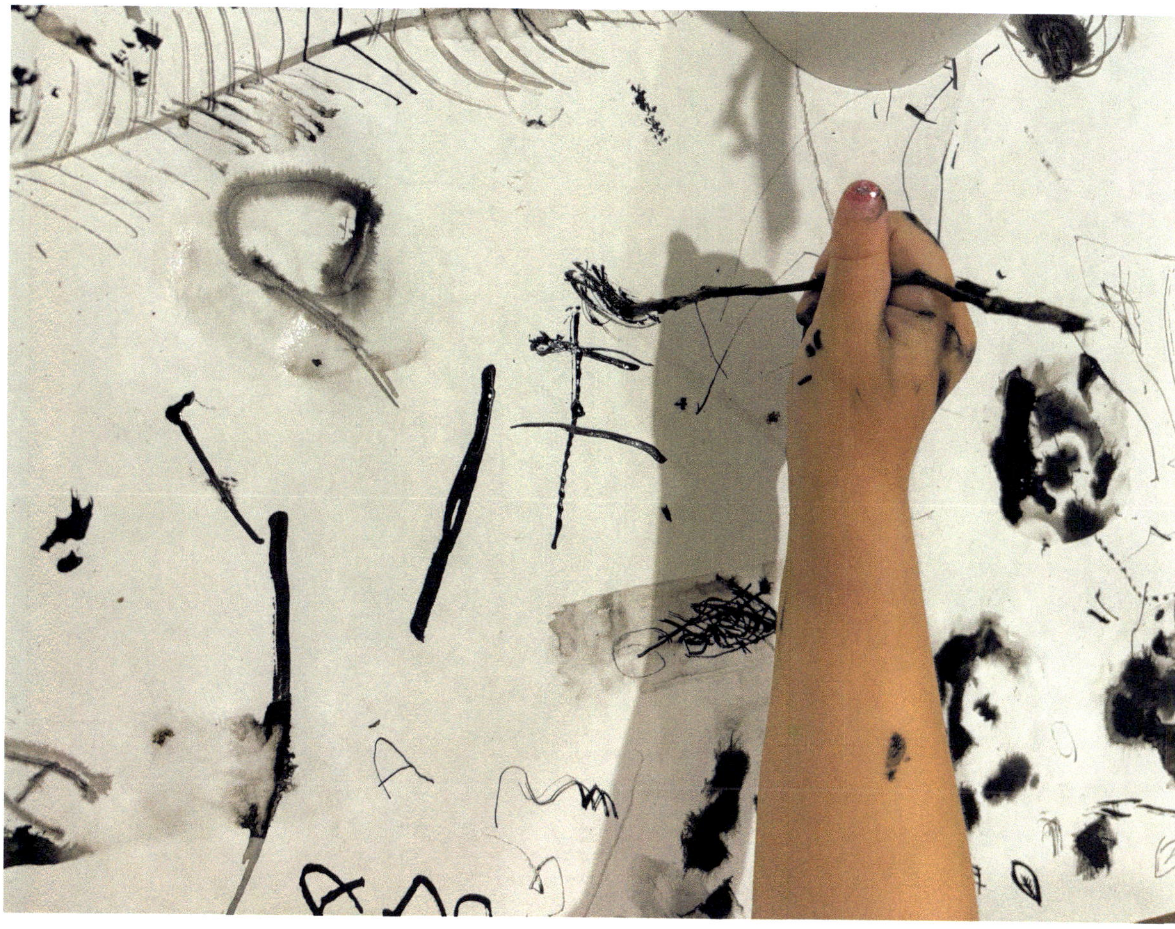

Figure P3B.5 Applying ink with a stick rather than a brush creates a fluid and responsive line that fascinates children, especially when applied to dampened paper [Image: Gai Lindsay, taken at Dripstone Children's Centre].

- Drawing on circular paper or paper of different sizes and shapes can inspire innovative drawing experiences. The lack of an obvious baseline provokes problem-solving and new perspectives.
- Trace and draw shadow lines (see photography, light, and lenses).
- Wrap boxes in plain paper to create three-dimensional objects to draw on. Who knows, they may end up as a city in the block or construction area; or as vehicles, masks, or something you never even imagined!
- Explore texture rubbings using crayons and pastels.
- Explore observational drawing using blackline markers. Drawings can be left plain or embellished and coloured with pencils, crayons, watercolours, or paints.
- Photocopy children's blackline drawings and use multiple copies to explore embellishment with a range of materials. (This is much more child-centred than offering commercial colouring-in sheets that have been drawn/created by adults!)
- Use photography to inspire drawing. For example, printed black-and-white images can be drawn, painted, or coloured.
- Bring engineering and design into the arts space by making drawing robots (search for "Draw bots" online for lots of instructional videos).

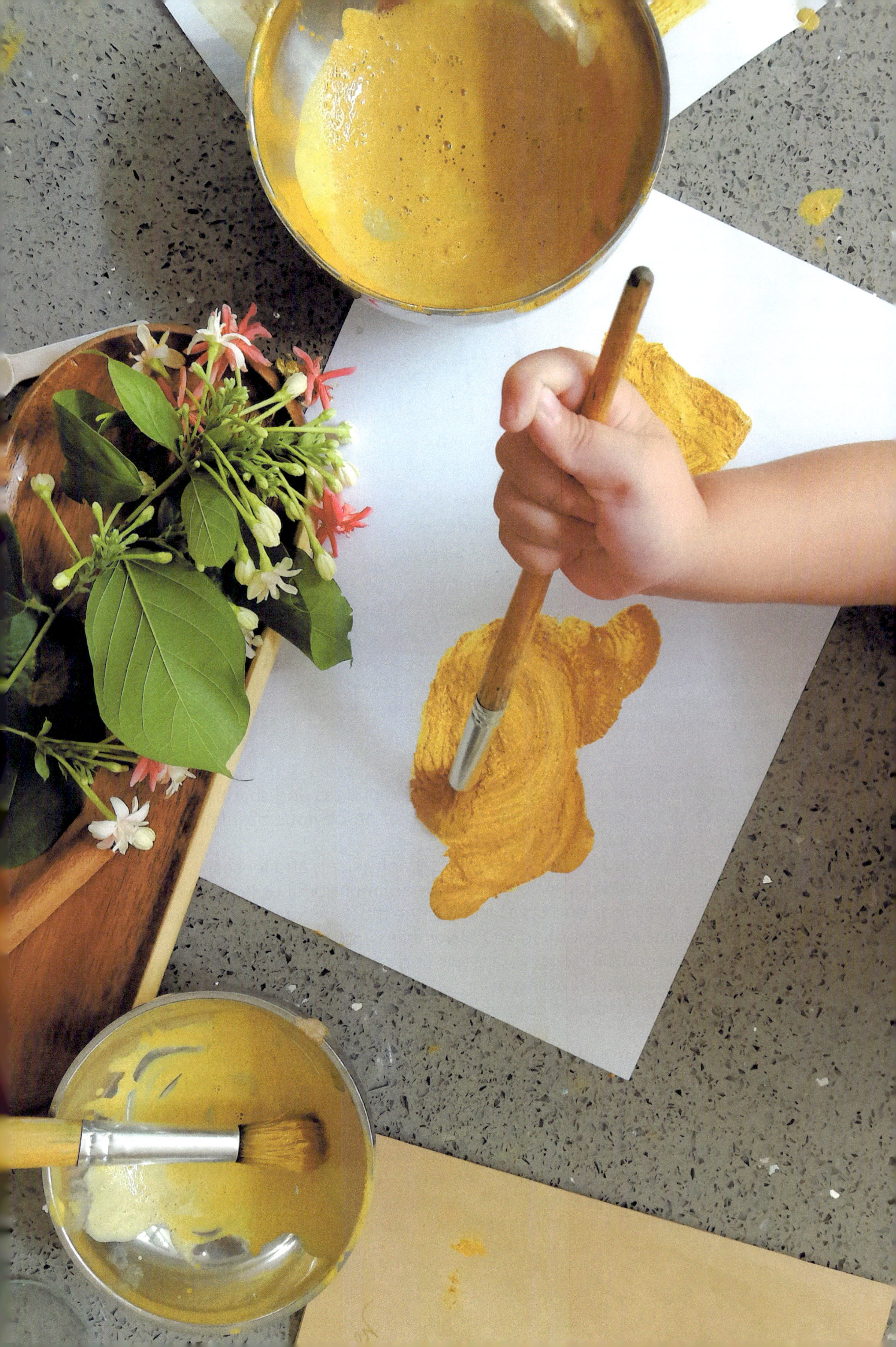

3.2 Painting

Painting in all its forms provides rich contexts for children's artistic growth and learning. From thick poster paints to fluid watercolour paints, the characteristics of different painting mediums present children with diverse sensory experiences, a range of challenges, and specific skills to master. Like drawing, painting is full of potential for imaginative thinking, problem-solving, and the development of art concepts. Painting also offers additional and unique possibilities for mark-making, aesthetic exploration, and visual communication.

Young children and painting

Before children use paint as a medium for image making and storytelling, they need ample time to experiment, play, and discover the joy of paint. The simple act of applying paint to a surface is a valuable learning experience and an important skill to master for young children and painting beginners. Initially, the focus will be on the paint itself; exploring how it moves, what it feels like, and how it can be manipulated. Through repeated encounters, children develop personal understandings about paint and what it can do; learning to control brushes, and develop a range of mark-making techniques. Such foundational painting skills are vital to support future skills development.

Arranging and organising, patterns and symbols

As children gain experience with paint and develop brush control skills, they can explore mark-making in new ways. With ongoing opportunities for open-ended exploration, children may create patterns through the repetition of lines and dots, fill a page with meandering lines, create and colour in shapes, or simply enjoy covering an entire page with colour. Through such playful explorations, children discover the potential of paint for representation and picture-making. Through a range of paint explorations, children discover a range of ways to use painting to communicate ideas and create visual images.

Figure P3C.1 Learning how to paint takes time, but discovering how paint moves and exploring brush techniques provides a strong foundation for ongoing skill development [Image: Carolyn Prawius, Saigon Kids Early Learning Centre].

DOI: 10.4324/9781003561835-16

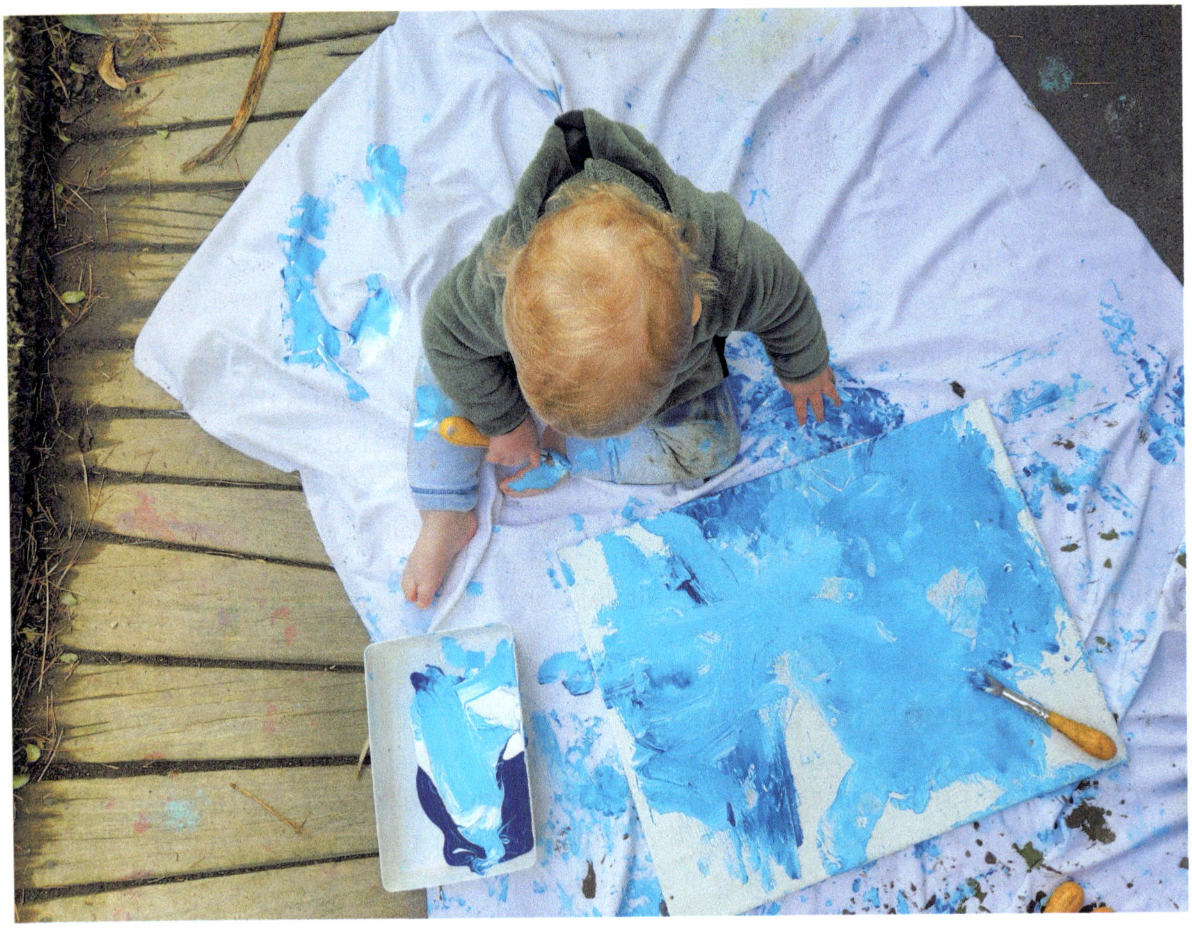

Figure P3C.2 Exploring a simple combination of colours with rollers and brushes is a rich sensory experience for young learners, supporting the development of diverse skills and painting knowledge [Image: Daisies Early Childhood Education & Care Centre].

Planning encounters with paint

Educators can nurture children's ability to use painting as a language for self-expression by creating supportive environments that respect each child's individual learning style and unique approach to painting. Whether introducing new painting mediums, modelling positive attitudes toward painting, or demonstrating how to care for brushes, your presence and interest will play an important role in supporting children's development and learning. The following strategies will support you to nurture confident painters and inquiry-based painting practices:

- Respect children's innate curiosity to experiment with materials while teaching sustainable painting practices. Painting is a very sensory and sometimes messy experience, however, as an art resource, we encourage developing a culture where paint is used with care and respect and waste is minimised.
- Plan repeated experiences with the same materials to build knowledge and skills.
- Novelty and challenge can be provided by offering different sized, textured, and shaped surfaces to paint on and varying the paint types and painting tools offered.
- Encourage children to share ideas and experiences by creating opportunities for children to paint side by side.

- Offer contextual variety by painting at easels, on table surfaces, or on the floor. Each context will provide different physical experience and perspectives for children to explore painting surfaces.
- Encourage independence by making materials readily accessible and demonstrate how children can attach paper to an easel, place their work on a drying rack or hanger, and clean their brushes.

Painting materials and tools

Paint

A variety of non-toxic, good-quality painting mediums will provide children with engaging and varied painting experiences. Water-based paints such as tempera, acrylic, vegetable dye, and ink are ideal for early childhood settings, providing different textures and consistencies for children to explore. All water-based paints can be diluted or thinned with water. However,

> All paints are made from pigment powders and binding substances, which also work like a glue to help paint stick to surfaces. Cheaper paints generally contain less pigment and more binder, making the colours less vibrant. Quality paints have a higher concentration of pigment, producing rich colours and more pleasing results.

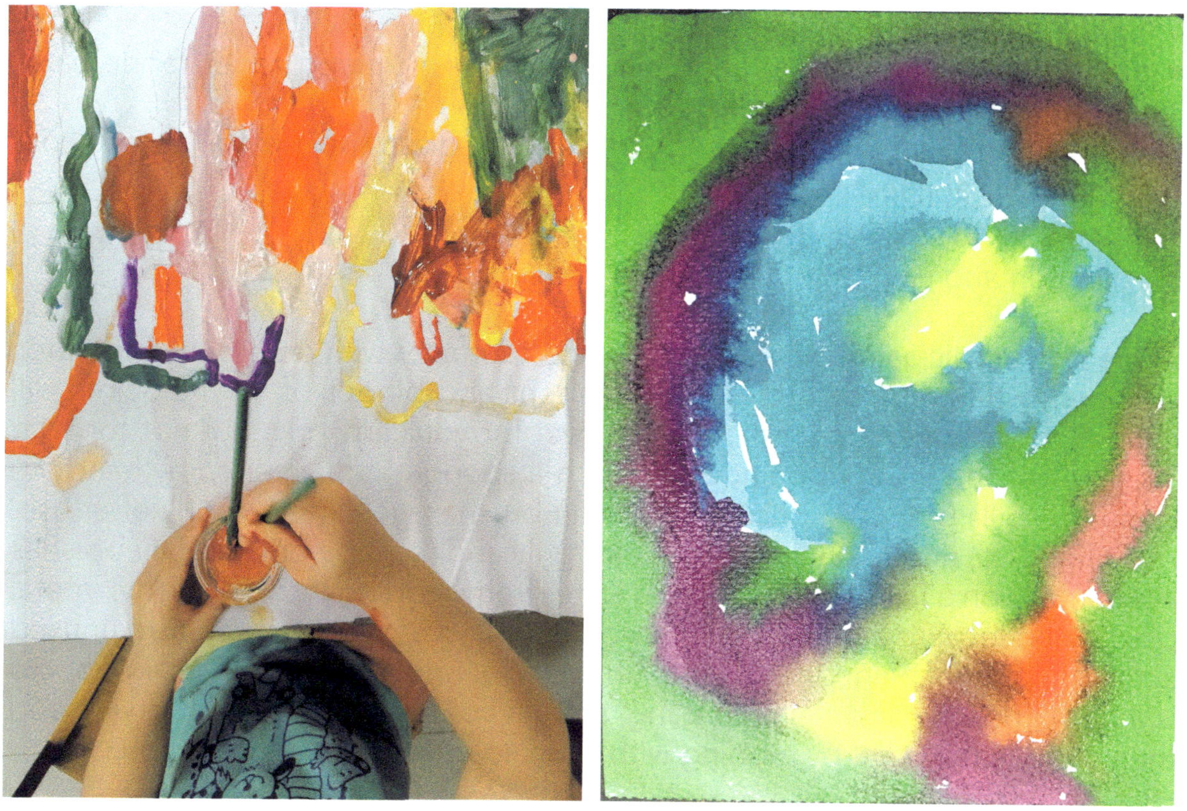

Figure P3C.3(a,b) Engaging with the varying characteristics of painting mediums offers children a range of sensory experiences and outcomes, helping them discover more possibilities for creating images [Image P3C.3a: Carolyn Prawius, Saigon Kids Early Learning Centre. Image P3C.3b: Denise Savins, The Friends Long Day Childcare Centre].

each type of paint has unique characteristics and will produce varying results, depending on their quality and the surface you choose to paint on.

To ensure the best results for your painting projects, choose a painting medium that suits the surface you are painting on. For example, most paints will adhere to porous surfaces such as paper, fabric, cardboard, stone, and wood. If you want to paint on non-porous surfaces such as glass, metal, or plastic, specialist paints are usually required. The following information provides more detailed information about the unique makeup and characteristics of a range of painting mediums, as well as some ideas for their use with young children.

Acrylic paints

Acrylic paints are made with finely ground pigments and an acrylic resin that binds everything together. Natural and synthetic pigments are used in acrylic paints to create a wide range of colours including metallic, fluorescent, and iridescent options. You can also choose between thin or thick acrylic paints, however purchasing a thick, creamy version is a cost-effective option as they can be diluted with water, or homemade corn flour paste if a thinner paint is required. If painting on glass, a few drops of liquid detergent mixed into the paint will make washing the windows easier when you are ready to change the display.

Qualities and characteristics:

- Dries to a smooth, permanent finish
- Can be used on a wide range of porous surfaces including paper, fabric, cardboard, canvas, foam, wood, concrete, and stone.
- Will adhere to some non-porous surfaces (e.g. glass and metal) if a base coat of primer is applied.

Preparation and use

While wet, acrylic paints are easily cleaned off surfaces with detergent and water. However, when exposed to air, the pigment and binder of acrylic paints will harden to a permanent finish. This is great for your artworks but not for your brushes, mixing trays, or paint pots. Keep a sponge and water spray handy to clean up spills promptly. Ensure you clean brushes well immediately after use. After washing, rinse paint brushes thoroughly and reshape bristles. Dry brushes horizontally on a flat towel to prevent water from seeping into the ferrule (metal part) which loosens the glue and causes shedding of the bristles. Store unused acrylics in airtight paint pots or jars with lids. Wearing aprons or painting smocks is a good idea. If paint stains clothing, soak in cold water to prevent drying and then remove the paint by rubbing with plain soap or washing detergent.

Tempera paint

Also known as poster paint, tempera paint is made from pigments held together with starch, glue, or cellulose. Traditionally, this kind of paint was made by mixing coloured pigments with egg yolk; however, it is now commercially produced. Tempera paint can be purchased as a thick liquid or as powder, or hard discs that look similar to large watercolour pans. It comes in a variety of bright colours that are non-toxic. Because some tempera colours don't blend well, it is helpful to purchase secondary colours (purple, orange, and green), white, brown, and black, along with the primary colours of blue, red, and yellow.

Qualities and characteristics:

- Fast drying and odourless
- Dries to a matt, sometimes chalky finish
- Less likely to stain than acrylic paints but is less durable and may flake, crack or fade.
- Best used on paper or cardboard
- Safe to use but should not be ingested or used as face or body paint

Preparation and use:

Liquid tempera paint: Pour directly out of the bottle into a jar or paint pot. As a water-based paint, you can mix it with a little water to make a thinner paint if desired.

Powdered tempera: Using about one part water to two parts powder, add a little water to the powder to make a paste, then gradually stir in water until you have a smooth consistency. For thicker paint, add this mixture to prepared cornflour paste. Making cornflour paste is like cooking a white sauce. Blend 8 tablespoons of cornflour/cornstarch mixed with a little water to make a paste. Boil 2 litres of water and whisk quickly into the paste to make a transparent, thick substance. Add edicol or tempera to colour. Cool before use (although warm cornflour paint is a delight to finger paint with on a cold day!)

Tempera palettes: Rather than the two-step process of paint pot to paper, compressed tempera discs require the addition of water to activate and liquify the paint. They are easy to clean and store, and create less waste than the liquid tempera. The following steps introduce children to the wonder of tempera palettes:

- Show how a dry brush on a dry paint disc won't produce a result
- Introduce jars or cups of water and dampen a disc with a wet brush
- Gently "mix" the water and paint together to load the brush with paint
- Apply the paint to paper, encouraging gentle brush use rather than scrubbing movements.
- Demonstrate how to wash the brush well before choosing a new colour. (This will keep the colours bright.)
- Once discs are well dampened, reminders to wipe wet brushes will help keep the paints from becoming oversaturated
- As children explore this material, prompt them with the three-step mantra: "first water, then paint, then paper." With practice, these steps will become familiar, however at first children may take the brush straight from water pot to paper

Water colour paints

Watercolour paints are made by combining finely ground colour pigments with water-soluble adhesive to produce a semi-transparent paint ideal for painting on paper. Professional watercolour artists add water to thick liquid watercolour paints sold in small tubes. However, for educational settings we recommend watercolour palettes which contain dried blocks or discs of watercolour paint.

Qualities and characteristics:

- Fast drying and odourless
- non-toxic
- vibrant and semi-translucent
- easy to use and clean up
- Ideal for painting on paper

Preparation and use

The use of watercolour paints follows the same process as for tempera palettes described above. Because watercolour paints are finer and more transparent (translucent) than tempera paint, experiment with layering colours to achieve

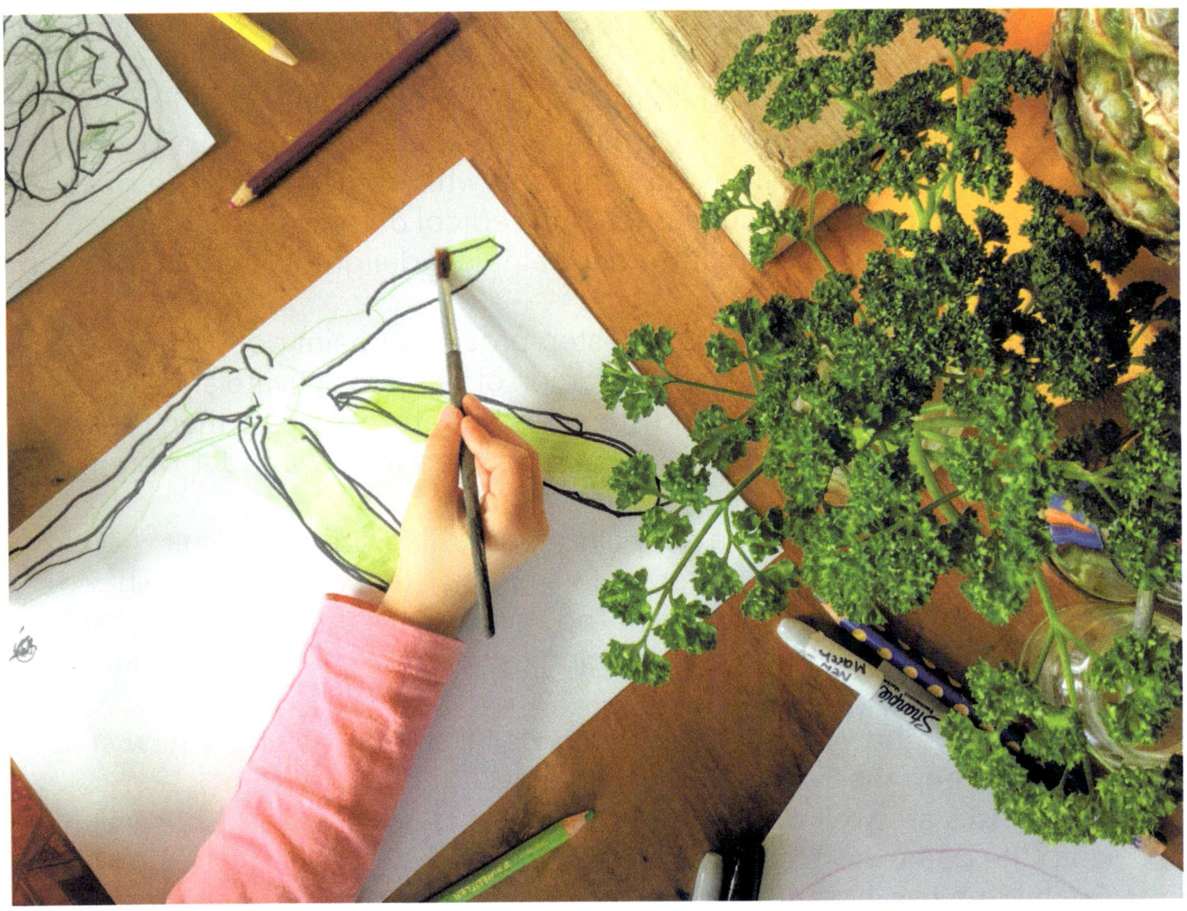

Figure P3.C.4 The transparency of liquid watercolours makes them perfect for painting over drawings created with oil pastels, wax crayons, or permanent markers [Image: Adrienne Wilkins, Sophia Preschool].

interesting results. As well as painting a new colour over dry paint (wet-on-dry), try wetting the paper prior to applying colour (wet-on-wet) to obtain different effects. When setting up the learning space, provide children with heavy-based water containers for rinsing brushes. A collection of smaller paint brushes with soft, responsive bristles will offer children a range of mark-making potentials. Additionally, some absorbent paper or rags for wiping brushes in between colour applications keeps colours vibrant and "clean."

Vegetable dyes and inks

Powdered vegetable dyes (also called edicol dyes) are non-toxic and make brilliantly coloured water paints when diluted with water. While dyes in powder form can be expensive, when stored properly they have a long shelf life, and their intensity means very small amounts are required to create vibrant paints. For convenience and reduced preparation time, you can purchase vegetable dyes pre-mixed with water that are ready to use straight from the bottle. These are sometimes referred to as liquid water colours and their intensity and vibrancy will vary between brands. Quality vegetable dyes can be purchased from art and craft suppliers and from kitchen suppliers as they are also used as food colouring. Vegetable dyes are also available in Supermarkets however these are generally too diluted to use effectively for painting. Powdered and pre-mixed vegetable dyes can also be used for colouring playdough and dyeing fabric, wood, wool, and raffia. To explore inks and natural dyes further search online for videos and resources that demonstrate show you how to make your own dyes or inks for painting with.

Qualities and characteristics

- Produce vibrant, translucent colours.
- Primary colours can be mixed to create secondary colours, however you can purchase dyes in a variety of bright colours.
- Most colours will stain clothes, floors, and tabletops, therefore aprons, table and floor covers are recommended.
- Some colours will stain hands, but fade from the skin after washing a few times with soap and water. Wear gloves when preparing undiluted powder dyes to prevent staining.
- In powder form, dyes will harden over time, so keep free of moisture and close container lids tightly.

Preparation and use

Easel and table use: Mix powdered vegetable dye with a small amount of water, then add to a starch-based paste (such as corn flour paste) to create a thick, translucent paint. This can be thinned with water to ensure the paint is smooth and flows across paper easily. Offering liquid paints in small jars on a table surface is a good way to introduce children to liquid water paints. To support skill development, demonstrate how to reduce drips by wiping brushes on the side of the paint pot before applying the paint to paper. To prevent colours from becoming muddy, offer each child a set of colours with a brush in each colour. Older children can be shown how to wash and dry their brush between colour applications. Provide paper towels or clean washcloths for dabbing and drying brushes to remove any remaining colour. Be aware that painting at an easel with liquid watercolours can be frustrating due to their "drippiness."

Paper choice: Use liquid paints on a strong paper that is textured (rather than smooth and glossy) as it will be more absorbent and produce better results. Thin paper such as newspaper print should be avoided as it will tear easily. For special projects, use heavier watercolour paper, however, be aware that even thick papers can buckle and distort if too much water or paint is applied. Keep paper towels or clean cloths handy to soak up excess water and spills.

Extension ideas

Mixed media: Because of their transparency, liquid watercolours are perfect for painting over the top of drawings created with oil pastels, wax crayons, and permanent markers. Offer children flat, thick brushes to cover large spaces with colour and finer round brushes for painting in small shapes and figures.

Cotton bud painting: The fine dots and lines created by cotton buds encourage children to explore more detailed mark-making. As an alternative to fine brushes, they are great for pattern-making and decorative work on smaller pieces of paper. For younger children, tape a pop stick to one end of the cotton buds to create handles that are easier to control. You can also create your own dabbing tools by attaching wads of stuffing and fabric to the end of a stick using a rubber band or elastic tie.

Wet on wet: Working on wet paper with liquid watercolours in an interesting technique to explore. To prepare the paper, dip it in a water tray, place on a drawing board, and use a clean sponge to gently wipe off excess water. A dab of paint will flow and spread across the wet paper in unpredictable and intriguing ways.

Brushes, painting tools, and equipment

Brushes are made from a range of sources and have either natural or synthetic bristles. Both come in a variety of sizes and are numbered to indicate the brush size (the smaller the number the smaller the brush size). Brushes also come in a range of shapes including flat, round, dagger, and fan. For everyday use in early childhood settings, a collection of different sized round and flat brushes is sufficient for children to work with as a single brush can produce a wide range of marks, lines, and shapes. As a general guide, offer children larger sized brushes for large-scale paintings, and a medium to smaller range for finer, more detailed work.

When purchasing paint brushes consider handle length, whether short or long. Brushes with short handles tend to be easier for young children to use, however it can be interesting to experiment with both. The most important characteristic of a paintbrush is its quality. Brushes that are stiff and unyielding are frustrating to use and significantly reduce the pleasure of painting. In contrast, quality brushes are a joy to paint with and produce better outcomes for painters of all ages and experiences. A good quality brush will keep its shape and last longer when cared for properly. However, soft, synthetic brushes are long-lasting, more affordable, more versatile for use with a range of paint types and much easier to clean than professional animal hair paint brushes.

Rollers: Painting with rollers enables children to cover large spaces with a relatively even coat of paint. They are particularly useful for painting mural backgrounds.

Homemade bush brushes: Try making your own brushes to explore diverse ways to create lines and marks on a paper surface. Collect small twigs and natural materials. Bunch a cluster of materials together and bind to a stick with rubber bands or twine to make a brush. Experiment with inks, dyes, or thinned tempera paints.

Easels: Portable standing easels vary in size so that children of diverse ages and heights can paint comfortably. The paper placed on an easel should be roughly at a child's eye level.

Painting palettes: A palette refers to the choice of colours used for painting as well as the tray, board, or plate used to hold and mix paints.

Painting with objects: From time to time children may be motivated to paint using other materials and objects such as balloons, string, fly swatters, kitchen utensils, and car wheels. While such novelty painting activities can be fun and may attract children into the art studio, we encourage critical reflection to ensure that entertainment is not the only reason such experiences are offered. Always focus on the learning goals and potentials of every experience.

Encounters with colour

Investigating colour theory and exploring how to mix and create new colours is a particularly fascinating experience, with endless possibilities for exploration and discovery. Such inquiry can greatly enhance children's experiences with paint and painting. Colour wheels and paint swatches from hardware stores are great visual resources to accompany colour explorations, as are flower petals, leaves, and collections of natural materials. A basic set of primary colours (red, blue, and yellow) will enable you to create secondary colours (purple, green, and orange). However, to mix a wider scope of colours, purchase a warm and cool version of each primary colour, along with black and white. To learn more about colour theory search online for many instructional websites and videos.

> Brush care: Always rinse brushes well after use and only leave them soaking in water if you can't wash them right away. Dry brushes flat to prevent water dripping into the metal joint (ferrule) with the wooden handle. When dry, store with the bristles upright. Also try to keep glue brushes separate from painting brushes.

Discovering the names of different colours, and even making up names for colours can be very engaging. Observations, discussions, and informal conversations about children's colour mixing are most important. For example, raise children's awareness of the variety and nuance of colour by describing colours as light/dark, warm/cool, shiny/matt, dull/bright, pale/dense, opaque/transparent or fluorescent, metallic, pastel, primary, secondary; just to name a few!

Colour mixing proposals:

- With younger children, offer two primary colours to paint with so that through the act of painting children discover that two colours create a new colour when mixed together.
- As children develop confidence with painting techniques, offer small amounts of primary colours on a mixing palette and support children to create their own secondary colours. By offering a warm and cool version of blue and yellow for example, children can mix an almost endless range of "greens" by varying the amounts of each colour in their mix.
- The addition of white paint to another colour enables the creation of tints (lighter shades and pastel colours), while the addition of black (or a colour from the opposite side of the colour wheel) creates darker shades of a colour for children to observe and enjoy the variations within individual colours.
- Explore making brown with a combination of all three primary colours, or by adding small amounts of black or blue to orange.

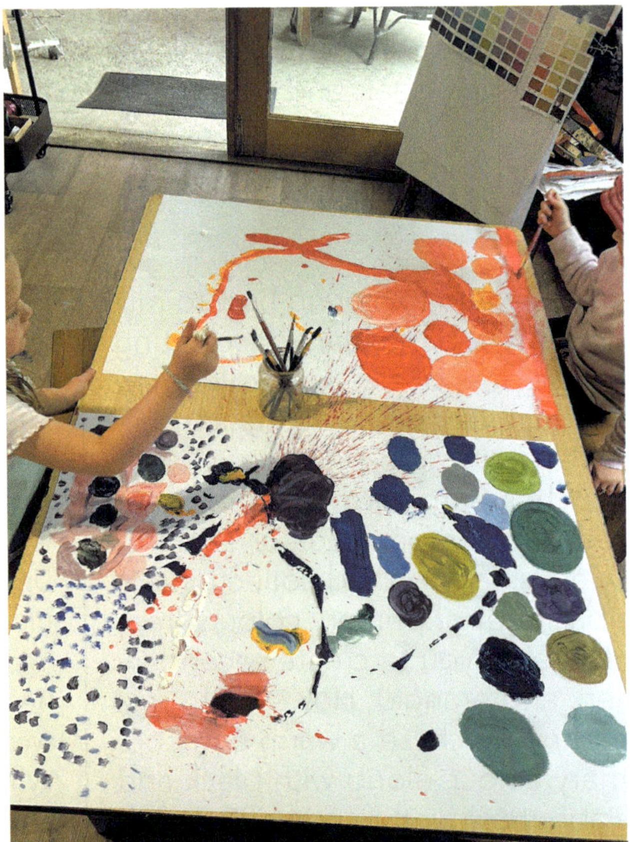

Figure P3C.5 Colour mixing is a fascinating experience that supports children's artistic knowledge, with colour swatches providing inspiration as children explore mixing and painting with cool and warm colours [Image: East Maitland Preschool].

- Curate and mix paints so that children can experience painting with earth colours, pastel colours, or a warm or cool palette of colours.
- Explore colour mixing using liquid watercolours. For example, watching liquid dyes flow and merge on absorbent paper (strong kitchen towel works well) is a mesmerising colour experience. Offer primary colours in jars and give each colour its own brush, eye dropper, or pipette. Carefully drip or dab each colour onto different areas of the paper. The colours will slowly spread to create new colours and intriguing patterns as they merge. To amplify this colour experience, work on a light table covered in a clear plastic sheet.

Additional painting ideas

Finger painting

Finger painting is an engaging sensory experience that gives children the opportunity to explore a very simple and direct form of mark-making. Without the need to control a painting tool, finger paint can be moved around and manipulated with hands and fingers. Children can use an isolated finger to draw images, lines, and shapes, or they can move all fingers in unison to make repetitions and symmetrical patterns. Colour, line, shape, texture, pattern, and movement can all be explored through finger painting, and because children can wipe everything out and start over, the process supports repeated experimentation with multiple possibilities. Be aware that not all children will want to participate in finger painting due to sensory issues or concerns about messy play. However, participating yourself and role-modelling positive encounters with finger paint may encourage children to join in.

To support children's engagement in finger painting:

- Offer smooth-flowing paint directly onto a table surface with enough space for children to move paint around using big body movements.
- Take photographs or time-lapse video to record children's actions and the mark-making techniques they have explored.
- Take a print of children's work onto large sheets of paper.
- Offer two primary colours to offer colour mixing exploration.
- Set up for success as outlined in the introduction to this section of the book by providing ready access to hand-washing and cleaning resources.
- The provision of water-resistant aprons will minimise clothing stains when finger painting on tables.
- It can be helpful when only two or three children participate at a time, to more easily manage, clean and reset the space in between groups.

Shape variations

Offering different sized and shaped paper is a great way to inspire new ideas for painting compositions. Provide triangles, circles, squares, or long strips of paper for painting at tables or easels.

Painting with water

For a no mess painting experience, offer children water buckets and thick brushes in the outside environment. Water will darken a surface like paint (although only temporarily) and children can enjoy the same skills of dabbing brushes into pots, applying the contents to a surface, and transforming a surface through their actions. Concrete and tiled pathways, wooden fences, large rocks, and brick walls are all good surfaces for painting with water.

Painting three-dimensional objects

Painting on a 3d form (e.g. boxes, cylinders, wood blocks, paper mâché sculptures) is very different to working on a flat surface and presents children with a range of challenges as they work from different angles to cover multiple or irregular surfaces.

Create underpaintings

Sometimes starting with a blank page can be daunting. Like masters of old, children can create underpaintings by adding paint to paper with sponges, rollers or large paint brushes. When dry the underpaintings can be drawn, painted, or printed on; with the layers of paint and marks creating interest and depth to children's work.

Multiple imaging

Make photocopies of children's drawings and offer them back to children to paint on. Try using liquid watercolours or watercolour palettes to create different effects and finishes.

Light on dark

Offer children a different aesthetic experience by painting with white and/or pastel-coloured paints on dark or black paper.

Observational painting

Experienced painters may enjoy the challenge of still life or portrait painting where they can use their observation skills to paint from life, rather than from their imagination and memory.

Murals

Murals provide opportunities for children to create collaborative artworks and work on a large scale. They are a great way to extend a group investigation or interest as they bring children together to share their experiences and

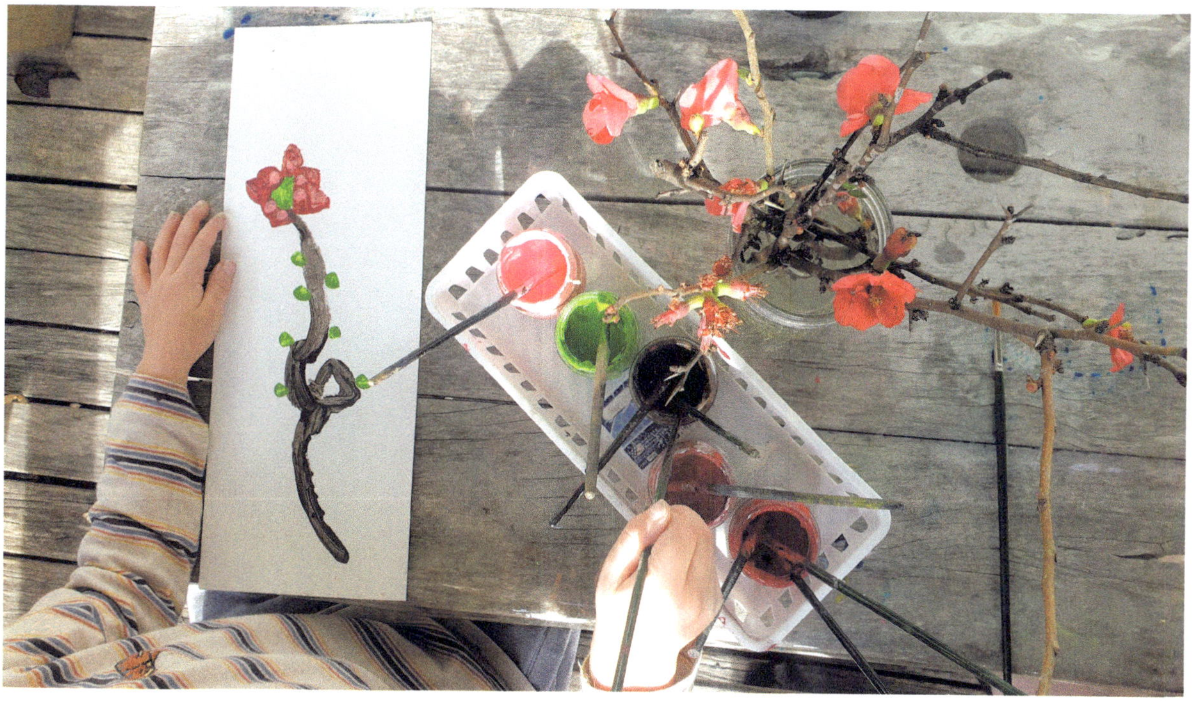

Figure P3C.6 When children are encouraged to observe closely, they learn to notice details, develop perception skills, and build aesthetic awareness [Image: Adrienne Wilkins, Sophia Preschool].

discoveries through artmaking. There are several ways to approach making a mural and a range of ways children can participate and contribute. Here are a few ideas:

- Talk to children about murals and the idea of making an artwork together.
- Provide large pieces of strong paper or cardboard on a table, floor space, or double easel. Rolls of paper, thick cloth, primed canvas, or sheets of clear plastic can also be used.
- Secure your chosen surface so it doesn't move around when children are working, and ensure there is enough space and enough paint for those participating.
- Offer the option to first draw ideas with a marker or oil pastels before adding paint.
- Individual drawings can be cut out and pasted onto a mural background.
- Older children may enjoy planning and working on their mural over a number of days, gradually completing a background before discussing and adding additional features. Organising ideas in this way can help ensure there is a space for everyone's contributions. New ideas can be integrated as the art-work evolves.

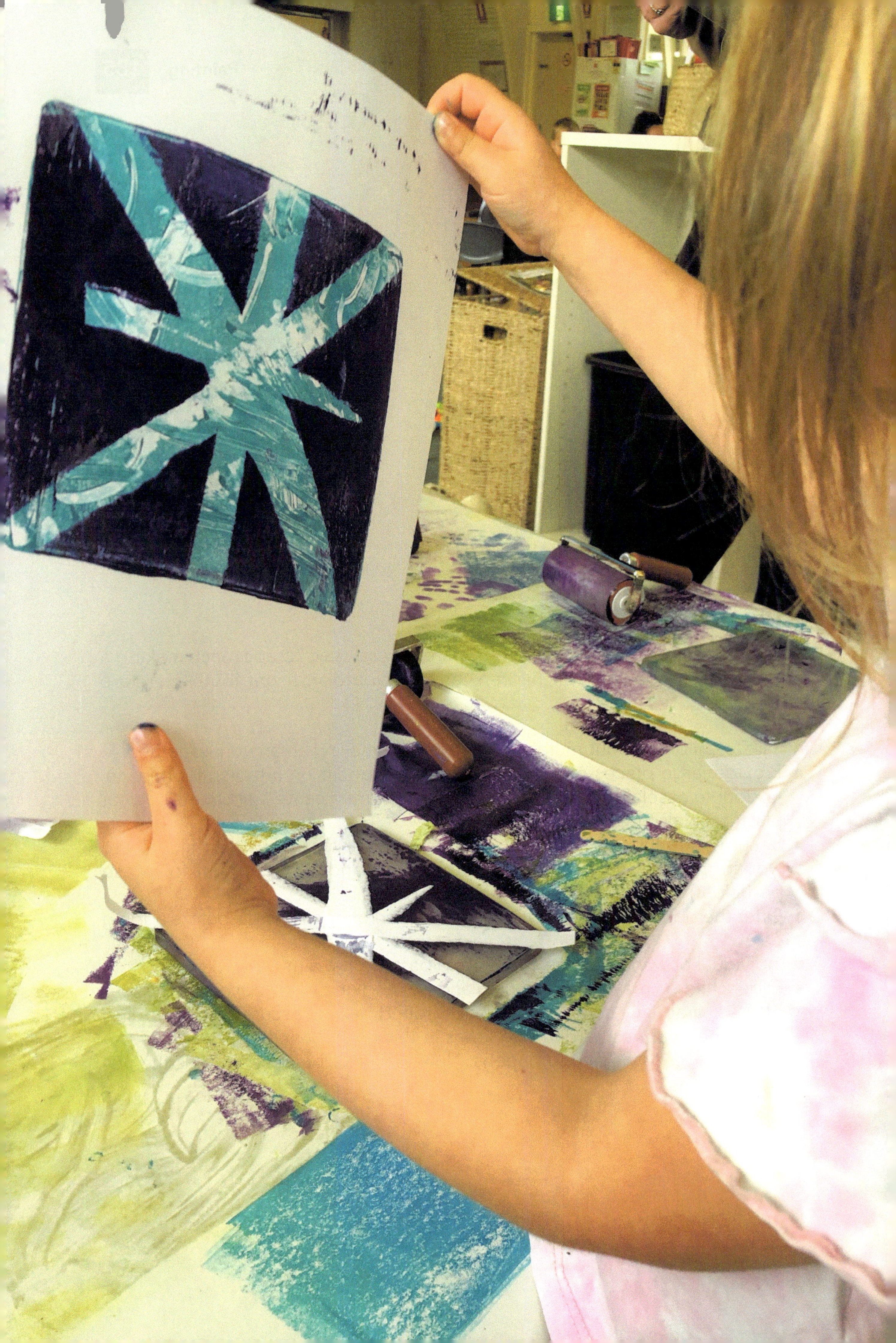

3.3 Printmaking

Printmaking is an art method where a design or image is transferred from one surface to another. The joy and wonder of printing processes and the resulting products are such a delight to share with children and feel like a kind of magic. This is because the process of applying paint to one surface and transferring it to another often produces an unpredictable result, which is only revealed when the print is "pulled" or "lifted." Children are very motivated by this "great reveal" and by the excitement of making images with unpredictable outcomes.

Introducing children to printmaking

Object printing is a simple and easy printmaking method to begin print explorations with children. The process involves dabbing an object into paint or ink and then printing it onto a surface such as paper or cardboard. Young children often discover and play with this basic form of printmaking spontaneously when they stamp their food-covered hands onto a surface or notice their footprints in sand. Adults can expand this exploration by providing a range of objects, textures, and shapes for children to print with. Ongoing experiences will provide children with opportunities to develop this printing skill and use it to explore their ideas for patterning, design, and image making.

Mono printing is another user-friendly printmaking method to explore with young children. This process starts with the application of paint or ink onto a flat surface, such as a table or sheet of strong transparent plastic (often called Perspex). Children then draw into the surface of the paint and/or arrange flat objects (such as leaves) onto the paint surface to create a design. When ready, a sheet of paper is placed on top, and pressure is applied (using hands, brayer or a roller) to transfer the image. The resulting print is a mirror image of the original design, and a unique "one -off" print. The process can end here, or when dry, a print can be used to overlay the next print and create a more complex design. There are so many possibilities for layering prints to create visually pleasing designs, especially when you curate the selection of colours and support children to develop their technical skills. Children may also like to use drawing or painting materials to rework or add details to their prints once they have dried.

Figure P3D.1 Lifting a gel plate print made by placing torn paper strips on the second purple paint layer keeps the first aqua blue paint layer visible [Image: Gai Lindsay taken at UOW Pulse Kids' Uni].

DOI: 10.4324/9781003561835-17

A range of other printmaking techniques such as lithography, etching, woodcut, and Lino printing can also be explored with young children by replacing traditional materials and surfaces with scratch foam and gel plates. These adaptations enable children to explore traditional printing processes without the use of specific engraving tools or a printing press.

Planning for success

When introducing different methods of printmaking to children, we recommend role modelling and demonstrating the printing techniques involved. Once familiar with the processes, children will be able to explore them with increasing independence. It is also beneficial to start with simple printing experiences and add complexity over time. For example, mono printing techniques can be introduced to children when they are finger painting on a table surface. Invite them to help you take a print of the patterns and marks they have made in the paint by placing a sheet of paper over the top. Show them how to apply pressure evenly over the paper surface and demonstrate how to carefully lift the paper from the corners to reveal the print. This works best when the paint layer is not too thick.

For each of the printmaking methods listed below, deconstruct the elements of the experience, scaffold the learning, and offer multiple opportunities for children to engage with the elements of the printmaking process. For example, before expecting children to create a multi-layered print, firstly offer them many opportunities to simply use brayers or rollers to spread ink or paint onto a surface.

Experimentation is the key with printmaking. Play with multiple ways to make marks and create layers of colour and pattern. Whether successful or not, even discarded prints and scraps of printed paper or fabric can be used for future artmaking. For example, you could use them as a base for drawing or as materials for paper and collage constructions. The more you play with printmaking techniques, the more you will discover how engaging, motivating, and joyful the process can be!

Setting up and cleaning up

As outlined in the Part 3 introduction and in the painting section, setting up for success includes thinking about protective clothing, work surfaces, table covers, and strategies to ensure smooth implementation and cleaning up. For most printmaking methods, setting up a table where children can stand for ease of rolling and pressing will support their success.

Involve the children in the care and cleaning of surfaces and printing tools. Wash printing plates and brayers in warm soapy water. Taking the time to remove paint and ink from your tools will make them last well.

Printmaking tools

- **Brayer** – A brayer is a firm rubber roller with a handle which is used in printmaking to evenly distribute ink or paint onto a printing surface. When using brayers with children, teach them to lay the brayer on its "back" so that the paint covered roller is facing upwards in between uses.

- **Baren** – A printmaking baren is a handheld, mushroom-ended tool. A baren is used to apply pressure and achieve even ink or pigment distribution when creating prints.
- **Plate** – A plate for printmaking is a flat surface made of materials such as wood, linoleum sheets, Styrofoam sheets, Perspex/acrylic sheets, and commercial or home-made gelatin plates (commercially known as gel printing plates). It is also possible to print directly from a smooth, even table surface, although this makes cleaning up more time-consuming. A textured printing plate can be made by collaging materials onto a piece of cardboard prior to applying ink or paint and printing the textures. Additionally, textured objects (e.g., plants, bubble wrap, kitchen tools) can be pressed into paint or ink that has been rolled onto a plate to create patterns and textures that can be printed.

Paint and ink options

Printmaking uses a range of paints and inks that are suited to different techniques and outcomes. For use in educational settings, the most common options are:

Acrylic paint can be effectively used for object printing, gel-plate printing, and screen-printing techniques. However, if using acrylic paint for mono-printing or even scratch-foam printing, be aware that the paint can dry onto the paper and cause rips when lifting the print. To spend more time on the process and avoid ripped paper accidents, use a slower drying acrylic paint (often called "open" acrylic paint) or mix a slow-drying medium or drying retarder into the acrylic paint. When selecting colours for your printmaking consider colour theory to mix colours and shades that will create harmonious, compilatory, or contrasting colour effects. Also be aware that some non-toxic acrylic paints are watery and translucent, so will not be as effective for printmaking.

Block printers ink is a thick, sticky ink used for printing techniques such as mono-printing from a Perspex sheet or a carved Lino or wood block. While these inks are dense, a very small amount goes a long way. Printers inks enable prints to be layered and lifted without the ink sticking to and ripping the paper during the process. Printers inks are available in black, white, and a range of primary and secondary colours. Specific colours and shades can be placed onto a Perspex sheet using a spatula or plastic spoon before rolling out a smooth layer. Once the brayer is smoothly coated with ink, it is rolled onto the printing plate prior to rubbing the plate and the painting surface together using the back of a wooden spoon or a baren.

Surfaces for printmaking

Prints can be applied to paper, cardboard, or fabric. The choice of surfaces to print on depends on the technique used and the desired purpose or result.

When simply focussing on the process and exploration of printmaking, any surface that will effectively reveal the shapes, colours, or textures of the print will work well. Choose a resilient paper that will withstand handling and pressure. As outlined in the introduction to Part 3, litho-paper is less likely to rip when manipulated to apply pressure and "lift" prints. However, with care you can experiment with a wide range of papers to achieve different effects. For example, printing onto tissue paper or rice paper (although more fragile) can result in beautiful thin painted papers that can be used for layered collage; similar to the artwork of Eric Carle in the children's book *The Very Hungry Caterpillar* (Carle, 1994). Printmaking can create wonderful wrapping paper, gift cards, artworks, decorated calico bags, placemats, or even designs on clothing or homewares like cushions or wall- hangings. The key to making a good choice of paper for printing with children is to test out the process yourself using a range of papers or fabrics to see which surface holds the paint most effectively and will stand up to repeated handling.

Types of printmaking

Object-printing

As outlined earlier, object printing involves applying paint to objects which are stamped onto paper, cardboard, or fabric to create a painted imprint of the shape and textures of the object. Object prints can be randomly applied or arranged in repeated patterns and designs. Acrylic paints or printmaking inks may be used to make object prints. When printing on fabric, the addition of a fabric medium to standard paint or ink will render the finished work washable and colour fast. To economically and efficiently apply paint to the printmaking object, spread and press a spoonful of acrylic paint onto a damp, flat kitchen sponge in a flat plastic container or tray. Press the printmaking object into the paint-filled sponge to gather the paint onto the object before pressing it onto the paper or surface to be printed. A layer of newspaper or a flat piece of foam placed under a plastic table cover helps objects to be pressed "into" the printing surface; enabling an even application of paint. While commercial rubber stamps can be used for printmaking, the creative use of natural or man-made objects and recyclables is limitless.

> **Examples of object printing items**: leaves, flowers, sponges, kitchen tools, potato mashers, toys, cardboard tubes, bottle lids, wooden building blocks, patterned meat trays, or moulded plastic packaging. Add patterns to flat wooden block surfaces by gluing textured items onto the block.

Scratch-foam printing

Scratch or draw marks using a pencil or pointed object into a thin, Styrofoam sheet before applying paint and making a print. Thin Styrofoam sheets

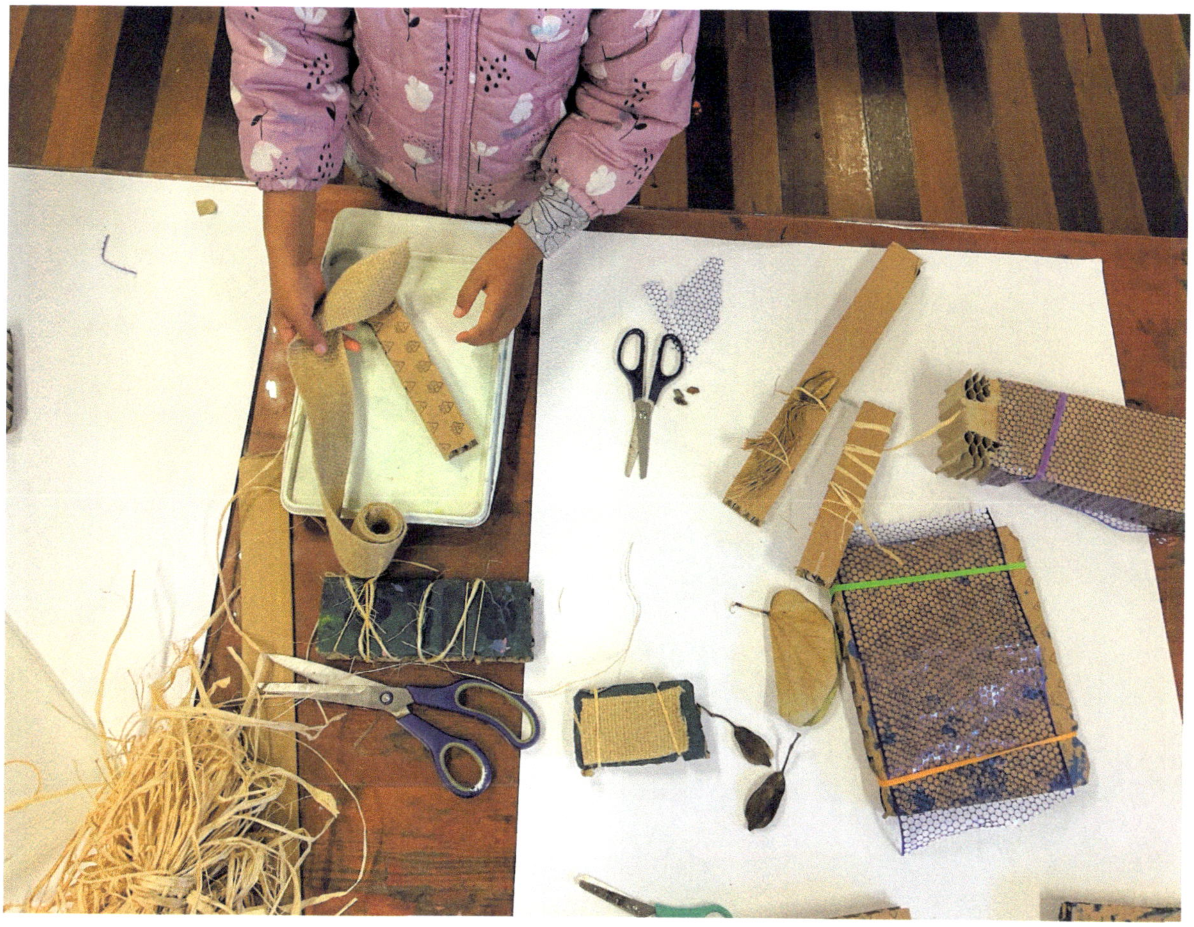

Figure P3D.2 Collect or make objects to use for printmaking. Any textured surface will create patterns in the paint or ink [Image: Maitland East Preschool].

(known as scratch-foam), can be purchased commercially or recycled from Styrofoam food packaging trays. Cut sheets into the desired size using scissors or a sharp blade and ruler. Smaller scratch foam pieces (about 5 x 5 cm or 3 x 3 inches) are manageable for children and produce a clean imprint of the scratched design. Apply acrylic paint to the scratch foam surface using a foam roller, paintbrush, or roll paint onto a flat surface using a brayer before transferring paint onto the scratch foam. Ensure the paint layer is thin and that the indented drawn lines remain paint-free. (If necessary, retrace the indented lines with a pencil to remove any excess paint). To create the print, either place the painted scratch foam surface paint side down onto paper or place the paper onto the painted surface and press and rub your hand or a rubber brayer firmly across the surface. Carefully separate the scratch-foam plate from the paper to lift the print.

Mono-printing with ink

Mono-prints are made by transferring this ink from a Perspex* sheet (or similar) onto paper, cardboard, or fabric. Block printer ink is a good choice for Mono-printing as it is a slow-drying ink that allows manipulation before printing.

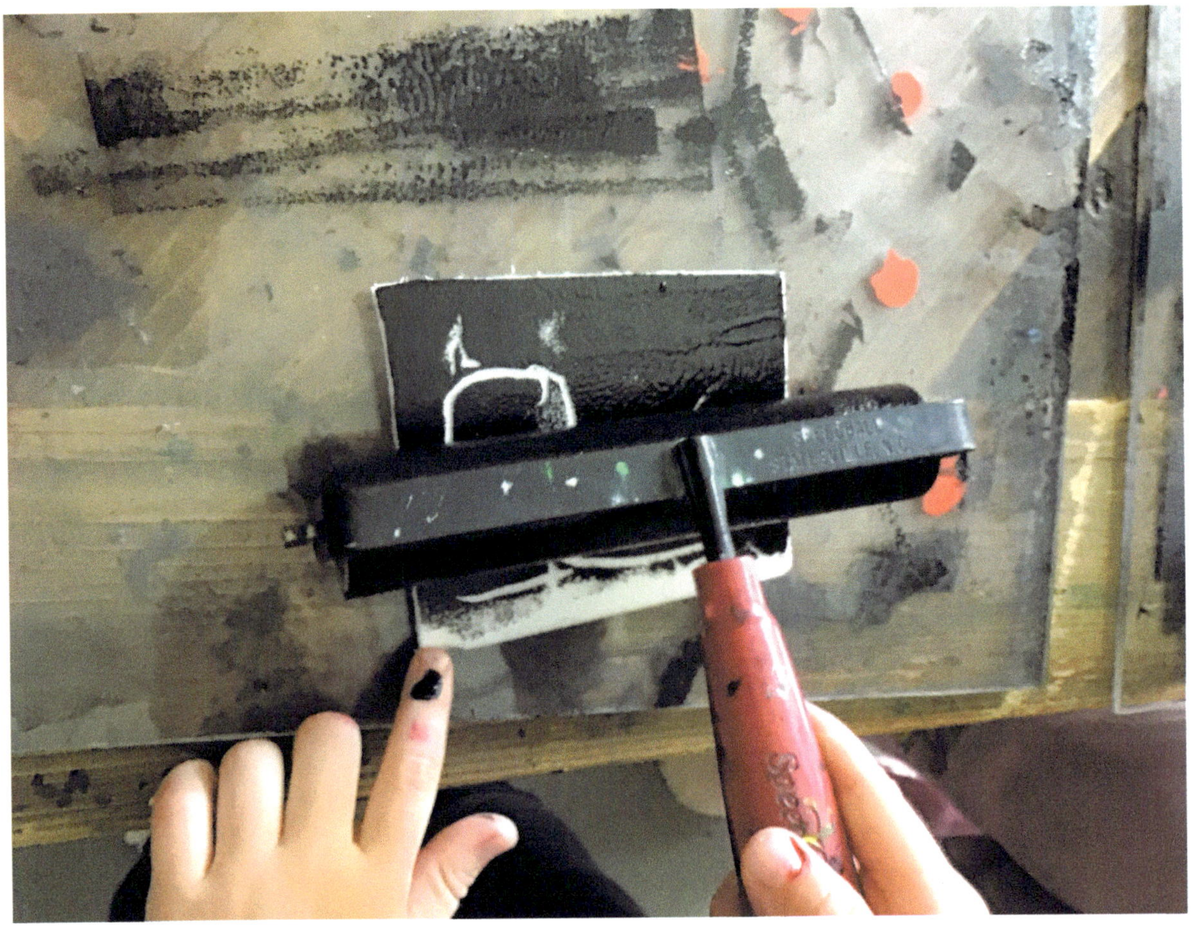

Figure P3D.3 Draw into scratch foam, apply acrylic paint with a brayer or foam roller and press paper onto the thin layer of paint to take a print [Image: Bomaderry Community Preschool].

Ink mono-print process:

- Spread about ¼ teaspoon of block ink on a Perspex sheet, rolling a brayer until a thin layer makes a light squelching sound.
- Optionally, place scrap paper on the inked surface and rub gently to lift excess ink, making the final print cleaner.
- Use drawing tools (e.g., matchsticks, ice-cream sticks) or fingers to make marks in the ink.
- Apply paper and "lift" the ink pattern by rubbing with your hand or firmly rolling with a brayer.
- Another option is to draw on the paper with a crayon, pencil, or even charcoal, which will lift the ink onto the underside of the paper wherever marks were pressed.
- Natural materials (e.g., leaves) can be placed on the inked surface for texture. Roll paper over them to create prints, or use the inked objects face down to print onto paper.
- Ghost prints can be made by lifting any remaining ink on the plate onto paper.

*Perspex = a solid transparent sheet of plastic

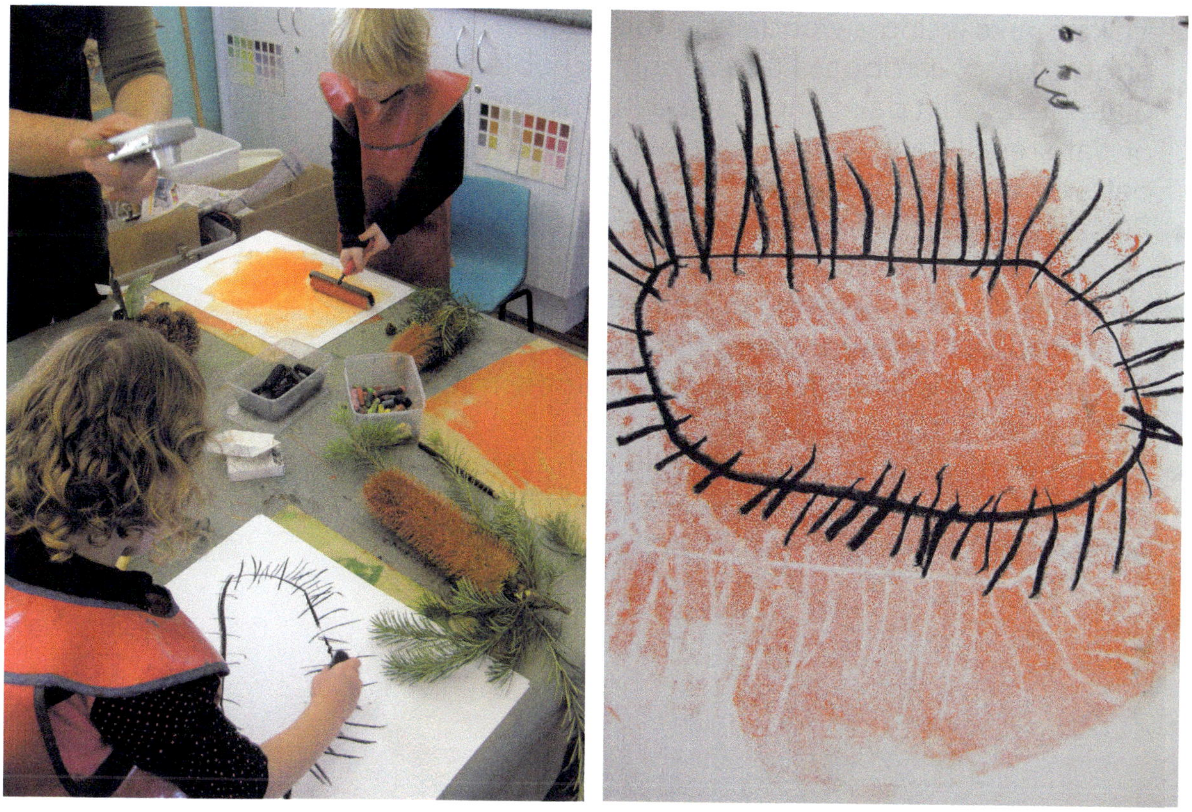

Figure P3D.4(a,b) Monoprints are unique every time. Drawing with charcoal on paper over an inked plate lifts the ink design. Flipping the paper creates fascinating secondary patterns [Images: Gai Lindsay, at Lyrebird Preschool].

Gel-plate printing

Like ink mono-printing, gel-plate printing also creates a unique monoprint. However, gel-plate printing uses acrylic paint rather than specialist printer's inks and is therefore more accessible for the classroom. Gel-plates can be handmade using glycerin, gelatin, and water, or you can purchase commercial gel-plates. Commercial gelatine style plates in a range of sizes enable the creation of very effective prints that dry quickly and allow single or multiple layers of paint application and pattern making. Be aware that water-soluble acrylics tend to be too translucent and may lack pigment and polymers to provide good coverage. Always test paints before use with children to ensure a satisfying experience and a solid application of paint to paper.

To make a gel-plate print:

- Position the gel-plate onto a sheet of paper. This not only provides a clean working surface, but helps to align the printing paper when making multi-layered prints.
- Place small dots (no more than about 1 teaspoon) of acrylic paint onto the gel-plate surface and use a brayer to roll and spread the paint out evenly (colours can be blended as part of the rolling out process).

- Make marks (using a wooden paddle pop stick or similar) or press items (e.g. bubble wrap, cardboard tubes, printing objects, natural items) onto the gel-plate plate to lift paint and make patterns. Ripped or cut paper, plants, leaves, or flat stencil items can also be added and left on the plate to create relief patterns and designs.
- Press paper onto the painted/patterned surface and rub across the whole area using your hands. (This process is a lovely, tactile experience!)
- Carefully lift/peel away the print (see Figure P3D.1).
- This process can be repeated to layer colours, patterns, and textures.
- A web search will reveal numerous demonstration videos to inspire multiple techniques and methods.
- Commercial gel-plates clean easily with water, sponges, and cloth rags. Dry with paper towels or fabric before smearing a little baby oil onto the surface and storing between sheets of paper.

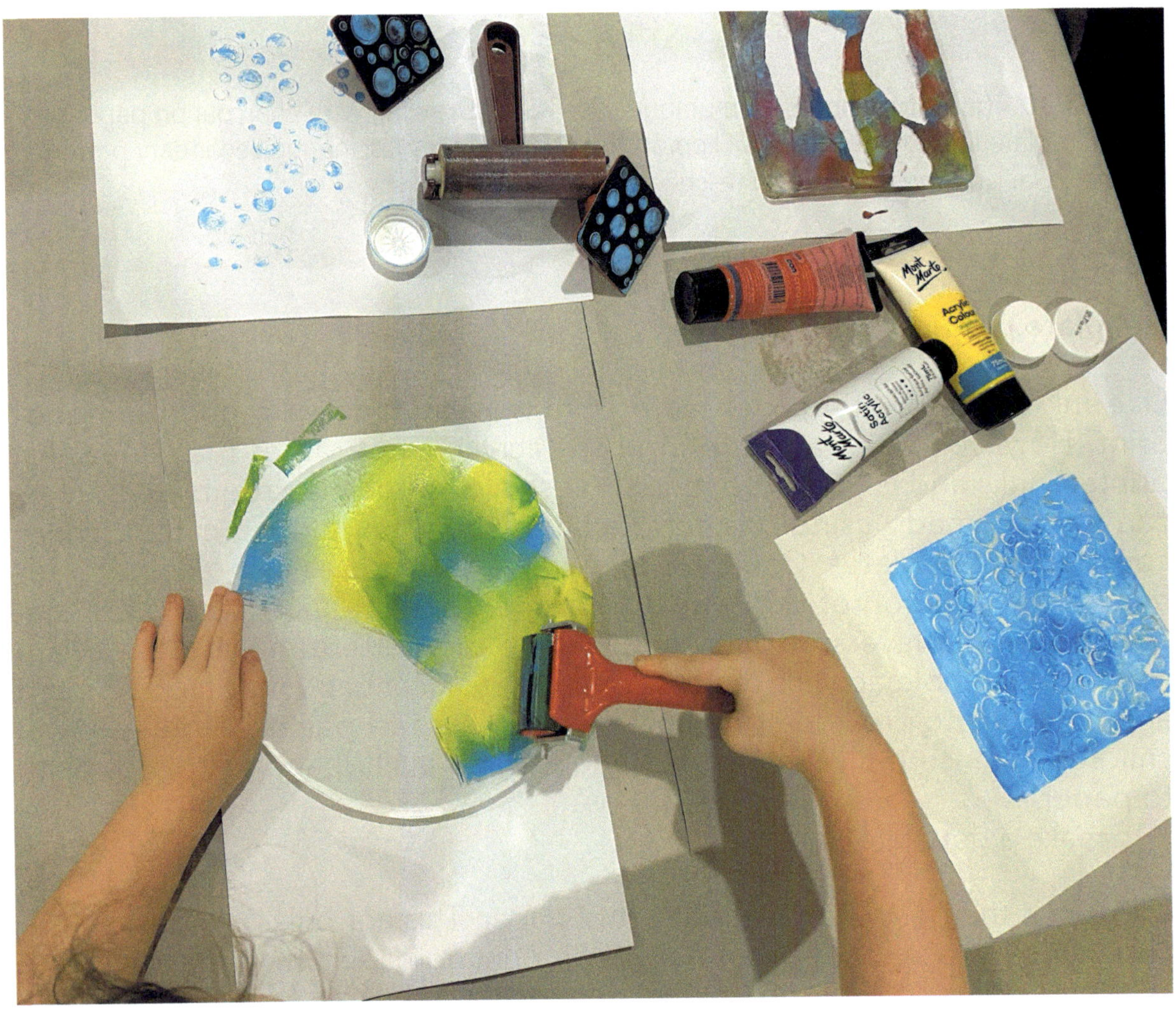

Figure P3D.5 Children delight in learning how to use gel plates, brayers, acrylic paints and object printing tools to create wonderful multi-layered prints [Image Gai Lindsay, at Dripstone Childrens Centre].

Other forms of printing to explore

The following forms of printmaking offer rich exploration potential. Although they require specialised tools and papers, they are still worth investigating if you are able to borrow or purchase the materials. An online search will provide an introduction for you to consider exploring screen printing and cyanotype prints.

Screen-printing: Paint is pressed through a screen (silk or synthetic) stretched tightly on a frame. A stencil placed under the screen surface blocks the paint application to create spaces of colour. For children, the application of a child-designed and cut paper stencil is most appropriate. Children respond enthusiastically to the process of dragging the paint across the screen surface using a squeegee (a printing frame-wide rubber blade attached to a handle) to reveal the negative space (non-application of paint) in the shape of their stencil.

Cyanotype prints: Also known as sun prints, cyanotypes are a photographic printmaking process in which objects are positioned onto chemically treated (light-sensitive) paper or fabric. Pre-coated papers can be purchased or you can access instructions to create your own treated papers or fabric. When exposed to an ultra-violet light source (usually the sun), a chemical reaction creates the cyan-blue background, and wherever the paper or fabric was covered the object remains white; creating a beautiful print.

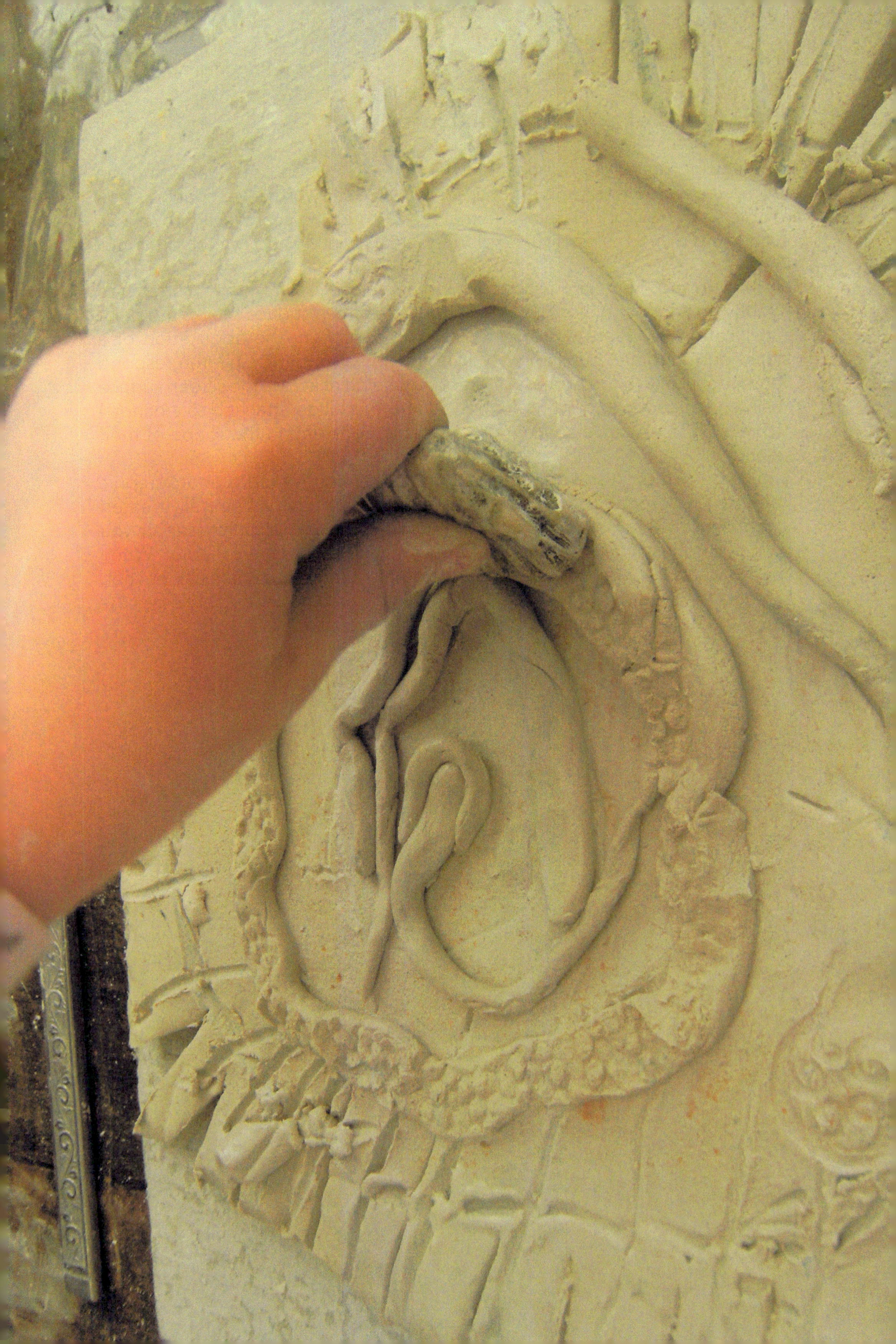

3.4 Clay

Clay is an ancient, organic material that has been used creatively by humans for thousands of years. As a natural, flexible material, clay has a density and texture that fascinates children, engages their curiosity, and fosters connections with the earth. Clay is a particularly valuable medium for open ended play and inquiry, as it offers children endless opportunities for manipulating, building, shaping, pattern making, constructing, and expressing their ideas in three dimensions. Because clay can be shaped, pulled apart, reshaped, and stored for later use, it is also a valuable medium for reinforcing sustainable practices.

Introducing children to clay

When presenting clay to children, ensure it is soft, flexible, and responsive to the touch. Clay that is too hard or too sticky is difficult to work with and will rarely hold children's attention. Good quality clay will also have "plasticity," which means it will bend, stretch and retain its shape when moulded. Be sure to offer children regular "meetings with clay" from an early age to offer them many opportunities to play, poke, squeeze, and become familiar with clay and the skills required to manipulate it. You can support children to develop clay skills and develop their confidence as sculptors by talking with them about their ideas, drawing attention to their discoveries and valuing their explorations. As the need arises, and you perceive that children may benefit from learning new skills, model basic rolling and joining techniques, or offer suggestions that will engage children in trial and error and help them resolve issues of balance, connection, pattern, or surface finishes.

Consider the following suggestions when introducing children to clay:

- Present clay in its packaging and support children to remove it from the wrapping.
- Take notice of children's initial reactions and document their ongoing journey of discovery.

Figure P3E.1 Clay's natural flexibility invites children to explore patterns, textures, and three-dimensional expression, fostering curiosity, and connections with the earth while supporting sustainable practice [Image: Gai Lindsay, Lyrebird Preschool].

DOI: 10.4324/9781003561835-18

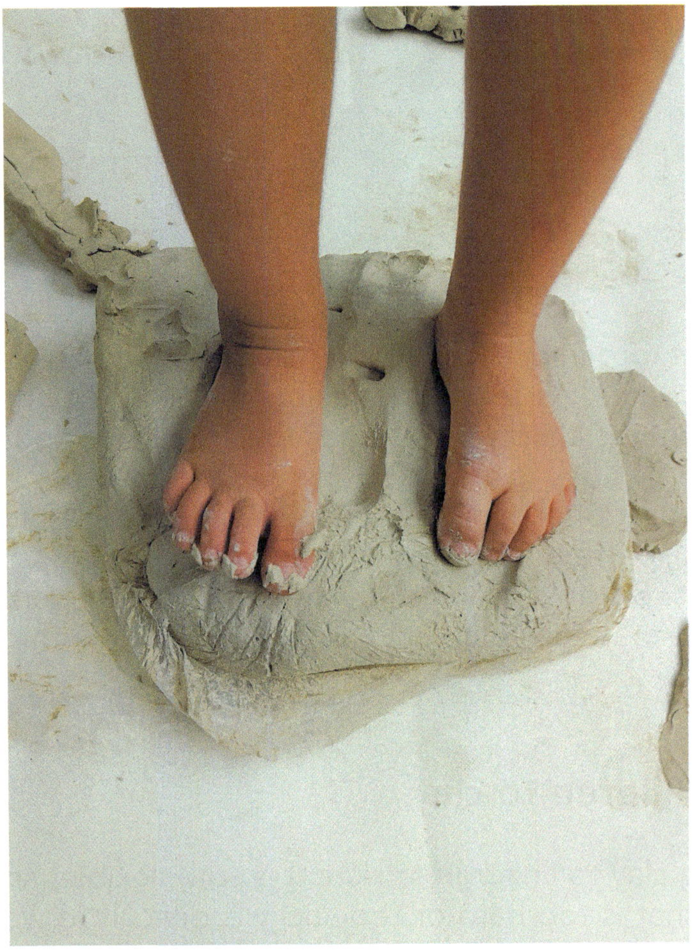

Figure P3E.2 From a young age, children can be introduced to clay through sensory and tactile explorations. With opportunities to experiment and play, they become familiar with the properties of clay and discover diverse ways to manipulate and shape it [Image: Carolyn Perwius. Saigon Kids Early Learning Centre].

- Explore clay with children by playing with it, role modelling a positive and experimental approach.
- Avoid the provision of tools and props in the early stages of clay exploration as hands are the best tools for "getting to know" clay.
- Manipulate clay by squeezing, poking, pummelling, and kneading it.
- Discuss how it feels and collaboratively discover the unique ways it can be shaped.
- Demonstrate and practice rolling balls and clay coils.
- Deepen children's knowledge by offering clay regularly over long periods of time.

Expressing and representing ideas

Like all art mediums, clay enables children to express ideas in visual form. As children squeeze, poke, and manipulate the clay, they may notice shapes and forms that remind them of something familiar; exclaiming for example, "Hey! Look! I made an ice cream!" (or a "snake," or whatever it is they see in the clay). Such exciting moments of unplanned discovery often lead children toward more intentional and purposeful clay manipulation.

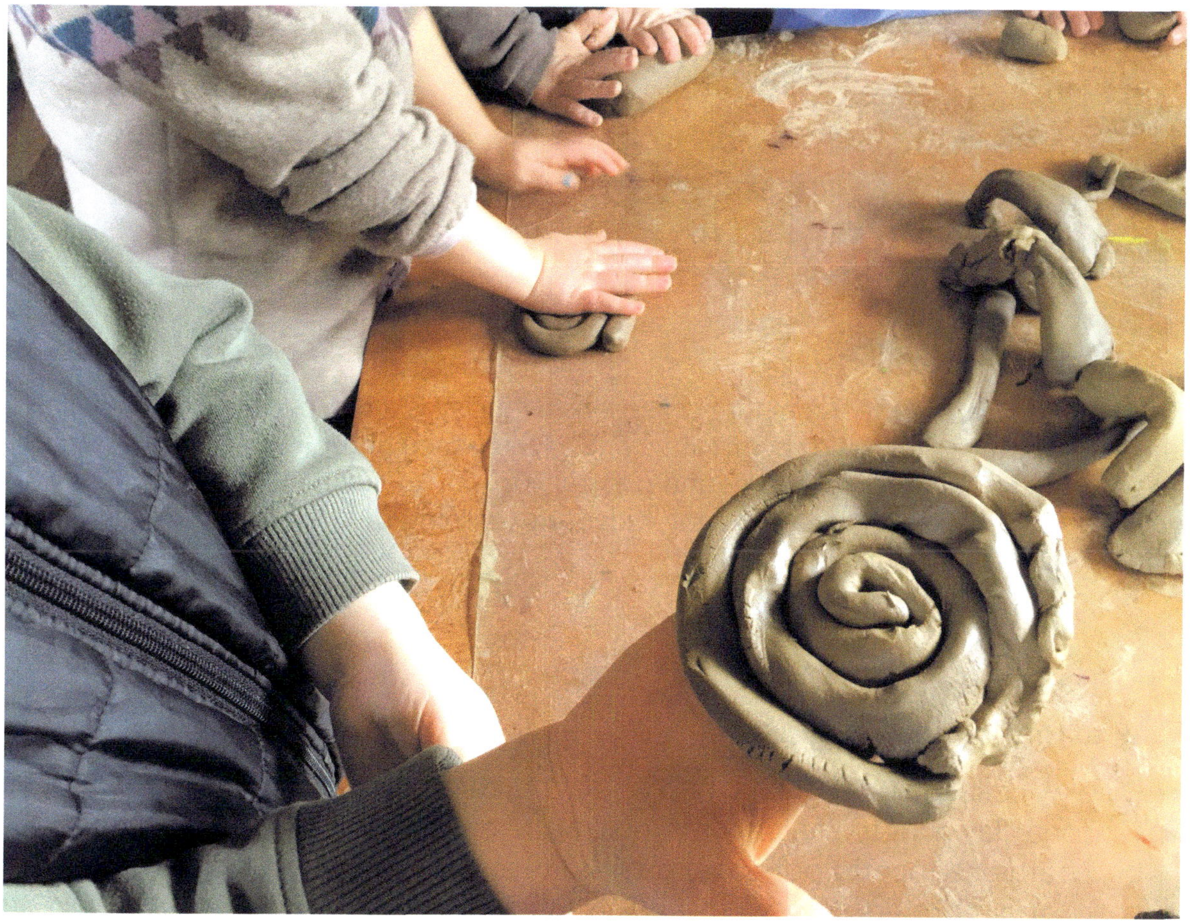

Figure P3E.3 Hands are the best tools for exploring clay. When children learn the basic skills of rolling clay into balls and coils, they can manipulate and combine them in endless ways [Image: Adrienne Wilkins, Sophia Preschool].

To facilitate ongoing clay learning, support children to:

- Learn about where clay comes from.
- Explore texture and mark-making by pressing, imprinting, scratching, and drawing into slabs of clay with a variety of clay tools and found objects.
- Smooth the clay surface by rubbing with a damp sponge or wet fingers.
- Create nature sculptures or mandalas with clay and stones, twigs, seed pods and shells.
- Explore making structures by manipulating coils into bridges, arches, and standing columns.
- Join clay pieces together using armatures or rough-up surfaces with scratching tools and "glue" together using slurry/slip (see terms and techniques).

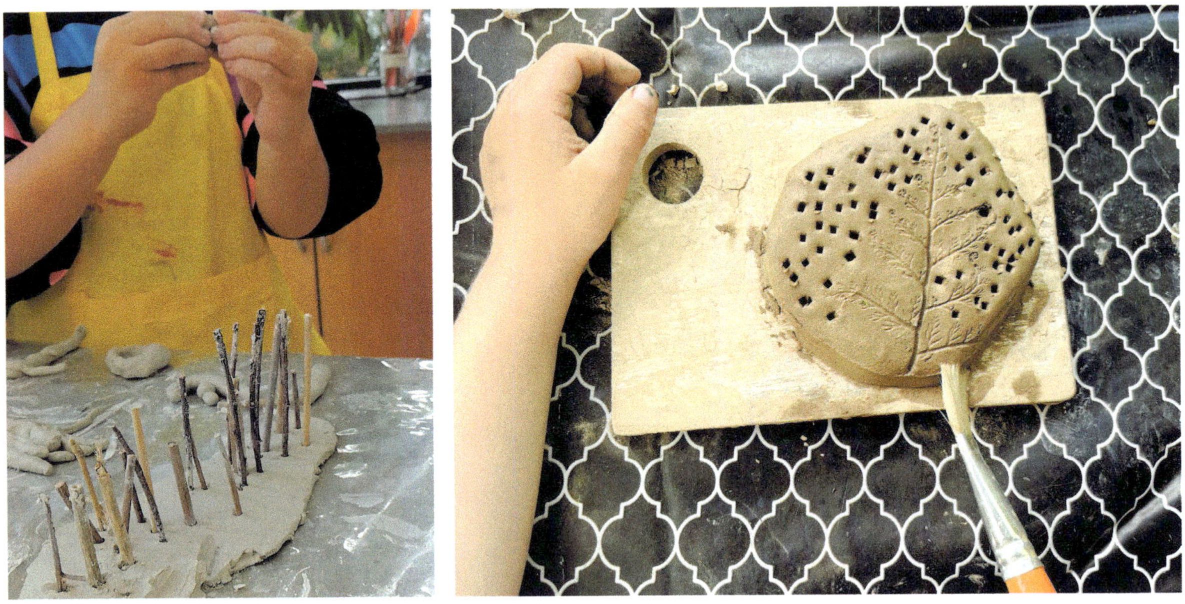

Figures P3E.4(a,b) Offering nature collections with clay is a wonderful way to inspire children's creative explorations. Smooth stones, twigs, seed pods, leaves, and shells can be used to create nature sculptures and pressed into clay to make imprints and marks [Image P3E.4a: Carolyn Perwius. Saigon Kids Early Learning Centre, Image P3E.4b: Adrienne Wilkins, Sophia Preschool].

Clay extension ideas:

- Display collections of glazed and unglazed ceramics.
- Go for a clay hunt to search for things made of clay/ceramics such as tea pots, bird baths, terracotta pots, and painted tiles.
- Learn about potters and ceramic artists in your community and via art books or online videos. Invite them to visit your school or organise a field trip to their studio.
- Try using a potter's wheel!
- Access a kiln to fire a special clay project (local potter or high school arts department).

Additional notes

Be aware that air-dried constructions can fall apart, especially when small pieces are not joined with expertise. You can seal air-dried clay items with paint and finish with a layer of matt or glossy sealant. If you plan to have clay pieces glazed and fired in a kiln, we recommend reaching out to a local potter or ceramic artist to develop your knowledge and expertise about the appropriate firing temperature and process for the type of clay you have used.

Unless you have access to a kiln and the expertise of a potter, glazing and firing are not necessary for children to benefit from playing and working with clay.

Rather than drying every item made with clay, document children's clay work in photographs. With practice and regular use, children will accept the ephemeral nature of playing with clay without focusing on creating an item to keep every time they experiment, explore and play with clay.

Setting up a clay work area

- Set up a clay table inside or outside.
- A large piece of thick canvas cloth or hessian clipped or tied onto the table is a good work surface as it makes cleaning up easy. The fabric base absorbs excess liquids and stops clay from sticking to the table.
- Alternatively, use plain Lino mats, wooden boards, and mats made from fibre cement sheeting as individual surfaces for children to work on. Cardboard squares and canvas boards can also be used, however cardboard will dry out the clay, and canvas boards will buckle and warp over time.
- A bench or table at children's height is ideal for offering buckets or bowls of water for handwashing and cleaning up. Clay that settles in the bowls can be strained and reused for slurry (see terms and techniques) or tipped out in the garden.
- Note: **It is important not to wash clay hands in the sink** because over time particles of clay can settle in the pipes and cause problems with the plumbing.

Useful tools and equipment

- Airtight containers for storing clay.
- Clay cutter for slicing pieces of clay from the block. Can be purchased or made by attaching a length of strong fishing line or wire to handles made of short lengths of wooden dowelling.
- Rolling pins (or thick dowelling) and two even lengths of flat wood for creating flat "slabs" of clay. Placed either side of the flattened clay, the flat wood lengths support even rolling of a slab.
- Jars with lids for storing thick sloppy clay (known as slurry or slip) and a collection of old paint brushes to apply it when connecting clay pieces.
- Small water bowls and sponges for smoothing clay.
- A set of tools for cutting, shaping, smoothing, or creating textures in clay. Sets of potter's tools can be purchased, but you can just as easily use butter knives, wooden skewers, and popsticks.
- Shells, pinecones, and seed pods for creating textures.
- Water buckets, a thick sponge and scrapers, or pallet knives for cleaning up.
- A large tarpaulin or thick plastic sheet to protect the floor under the work area can also be used with younger children to work with clay on the floor.

Safety considerations

Fine clay dust particles can be a health hazard if inhaled. When cleaning up the clay area, always wash your tools, equipment, and surfaces with a damp sponge, rather than sweeping it up with a broom. If using a drop sheet under a table, take it outside for cleaning to prevent clay dust from circulating indoors. Anyone with respiratory issues, should wear a face mask when cleaning up clay areas and tools.

Use these terms with children to introduce them to the world of clay artistry.

Armature: A support to help join or strengthen a sculpture, such as wire, sticks, or dowelling inserted into pieces of clay that stick out (such as arms or legs).
Coils: Lengths of rolled clay. Roll pieces of clay back and forth using the full length of flat hands and splayed fingers.
Glaze: A liquid coating applied to clay pieces to add colour and texture prior to firing.
Kiln: A specialist oven that fires and bakes clay at very high temperatures.
Slabs and tiles: A piece of clay rolled flat and cut into even shapes. To create uniform and flat slabs of clay, roll clay between two pieces of flat timber batting with a rolling pin or dowel.
Slurry/slip: A thick paste made by mixing clay and water and used to join pieces of clay together. Apply with an old paintbrush to scoured (roughed up) up pieces of clay before pressing together to join.
Wedging: The process of "throwing" and banging out air bubbles from clay.

Types of clay

There are several types of clay suitable for use with children:

Natural clays are formed in the earth from fine deposits of weathered rock. They vary in colour due to the amount of iron and mineral content accumulated during their formation. They range in texture from fine and smooth to gritty and grainy and have different levels of plasticity (flexibility and stretchability). The types of natural clay most suitable for use with children are *earthenware* and *stoneware clay*. Both types are versatile and easily shaped. Earthenware, such as terracotta and Raku clay, can be used on a potter's wheel or for hand-building. *Porcelain clay*, also known as Kaolin clay is a white, versatile, and pliant clay. However, its very fine texture can make it more difficult for beginners to use. Even though these clays are suitable for

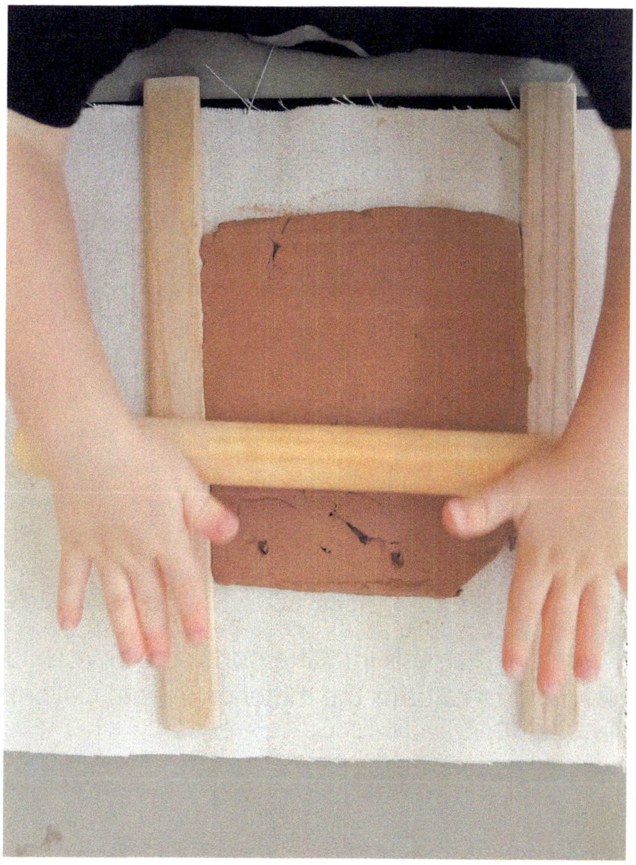

Figure P3E.5 Children can learn a range of clay skills and sculpting techniques. To create flat, uniform slabs of clay, roll clay between two pieces of flat timber [Image: Carolyn Perwius. Saigon Kids Early Learning Centre].

firing, for education settings they can be reused and recycled indefinitely (see tips for storage and recycling).

Paper Clay, a mix of natural clay and cellulose fibre, is often used for decorative work, sculpture, and tableware, because the mix of cellulose fibres offers more elasticity and strength while building. Paper clay can be bought ready-made, or made by mixing together clay slip and small amounts of paper pulp. Paper clay is fired the same way that the base clay is fired.

Air Dry Clay is designed to dry and set without a kiln. It is a natural clay mixed with additives such as cellulose fibres, corn starch, paper, or wood fibres that air dry slowly into a hard solid. Once dry, they can be painted and decorated with pens, ink, or acrylic paint. Such products are not food-safe or watertight, so should only be used for projects such as sculptures, candle holders, or jewellery.

Polymer Clay is a synthetic modelling clay used for making beads, jewellery, or small objects and is cured by oven baking. It is firm and can be very challenging for young children to manipulate. Note that it is a very expensive option for classroom use, perhaps best saved for special, small object projects.

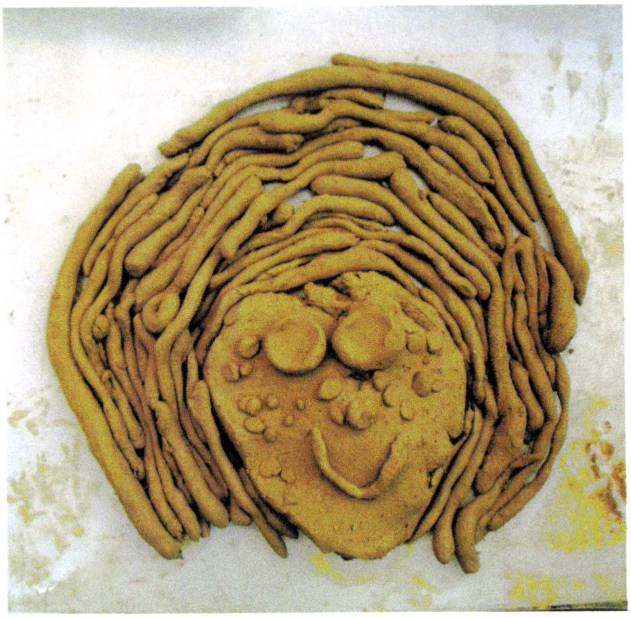

Figure P3E.6 Creating with clay, like this intricate portrait, allows children to explore complex designs while learning to care for the material [Image: Gai Lindsay, Child artist Josie Grootenboer, Lyrebird Preschool].

Caring for and storing clay

Clay will dry out when exposed to air, so it is important to keep it moist and stored properly. Learning to care for clay will engage children in sustainable practices and ensure you are able to use it for an extended period of time. When planning experiences with clay, factor in plenty of time for cleaning the area and storing clay as part of the experience, using the following tips as a guide.

- After opening a bag of clay and using a clay cutter to slice smaller pieces for use, reseal the block of clay in plastic wrap or a damp cloth and place in an airtight container.
- If clay becomes dry, rub and knead a little water into it.
- Rather than providing a bowl of water for dampening fingers and smoothing clay surfaces, place a slightly damp sponge in a flat-bottomed bowl or container for children to press and dampen their fingers on.
- To pack up, remove all foreign items from the clay and ask children to help you roll it into balls or cubes about the size of your fist.
- A fun and enjoyable alternative to rolling clay into balls is to wedge clay into a cube. This is done by throwing or forcefully banging clumps of clay onto the table surface, progressively creating a cube.
- Push a hole in the centre of the ball or cube with your thumb, fill the hole with water, and seal the hole by squeezing edges together. The water will absorb into the clay to keep it pliable.

- Store cubes in an airtight container wrapped in a damp towel or a soft plastic bag with no perforations. (If clay develops mould on the surface after a long period of storage, this can be safely scraped off.)
- For long-term projects, cover unfinished work with damp cloths or repurposed plastic bags. Covering helps to keep it damp and pliable, enabling children to return and build on their creations over time.
- If planning to keep children's work, either arrange to have the work glazed and fired, or place on firm squares of cardboard or plywood sheets to air dry.

Recycling clay

If you have hardened pieces of natural clay, it can be recycled using the following steps. Involve children in the transformation process.

1. Place the dry clay pieces in a tub or bucket and cover with water.
2. Leave for a few days before draining off excess liquid.
3. Store some of the muddy clay in glass jars with lids to use as slurry.
4. Let the mud clay dry out until you can knead it back into balls or cubes.

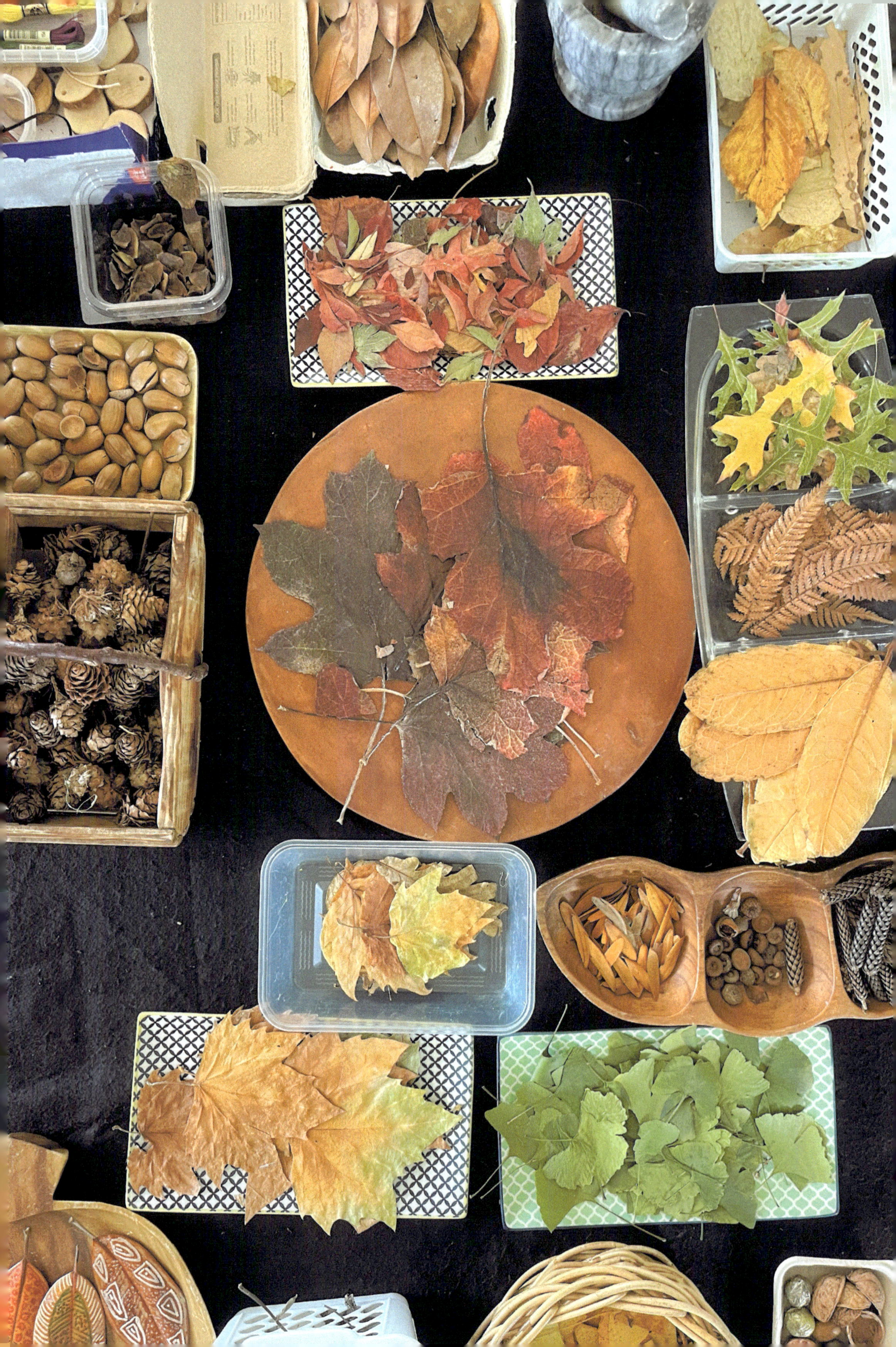

3.5 Ephemeral art and loose parts

Play with loose parts and collections of natural materials offers rich potential to provoke children's curiosity, imagination, and problem-solving. As an arts practice, ephemeral art is increasingly valued in education settings due to its alignment with sustainable values and its potential to foster children's creativity, possibility thinking and sense of ecological responsibility. Ephemeral art, also referred to as transient art, is unique because it only lasts for a short period of time. Traditionally, ephemeral arts practice utilised materials collected in the natural environment, in which the ephemeral artwork was created. However, loose parts, a term describing materials that afford multiple possibilities (Daly & Beloglovsky, 2014), have also gained popularity for ephemeral artmaking due to increasing awareness about the need for more sustainable approaches to both education and art. Collections of aesthetically interesting items can be sourced from both nature and from clean waste products from industry at very little cost. Creating an environment where collected materials are beautifully stored and presented offers children opportunities to explore visual concepts and designs, connect with nature, connect with each other, and represent their ideas visually.

The creative use of found materials sparks interest and curiosity; and the value of such experience is grounded in open-ended loose parts play and exploration (Daly & Beloglovsky, 2014). Sustained time to deeply explore materials provides children with opportunities to engage with creative processes that nurture divergent thinking and problem-solving. The inclusion of loose parts in learning environments invites collaboration between children, fostering relationships, social-emotional development, and the ability to negotiate and communicate (Daly & Beloglovsky, 2014). Every child can engage with loose parts in rich and meaningful ways because their multifaceted nature and lack of predetermined outcomes means they are inclusive of all children. For example, a child fascinated by categorisation may choose to sort and order a collection by size, while others may delight in counting and pattern-making.

Figure P3F.1 Ephemeral art with natural materials and loose parts fosters creativity, curiosity, and ecological awareness through open-ended exploration and collaboration [Image: Adrienne Wilkins, Sophia Preschool].

DOI: 10.4324/9781003561835-19

Introducing children to ephemeral art

Ephemeral art refers to an art process that is not permanent. It is the act of making designs and patterns out of natural or recycled materials which are then packed away or, in the case of natural materials in the environment, allowed to naturally decompose and return to the land. With intentional facilitation by educators, ephemeral art using collections of found natural materials is a practical and accessible art form to use during excursions or on return to the educational setting. Collecting materials and making ephemeral designs is a wonderful way to deepen children's connection to special natural spaces in your playground or community. Invite children to collect materials they find interesting or beautiful. Decide with children which items are appropriate and sustainable to collect and which items should not be collected (such as flowers or leaves still attached to their plant or shells still containing sea creatures!). Create patterns and designs using the collected materials, discussing colours, shapes, textures, and arrangements. If children are new to ephemeral artmaking, a mandala pattern (a circular, symmetrical

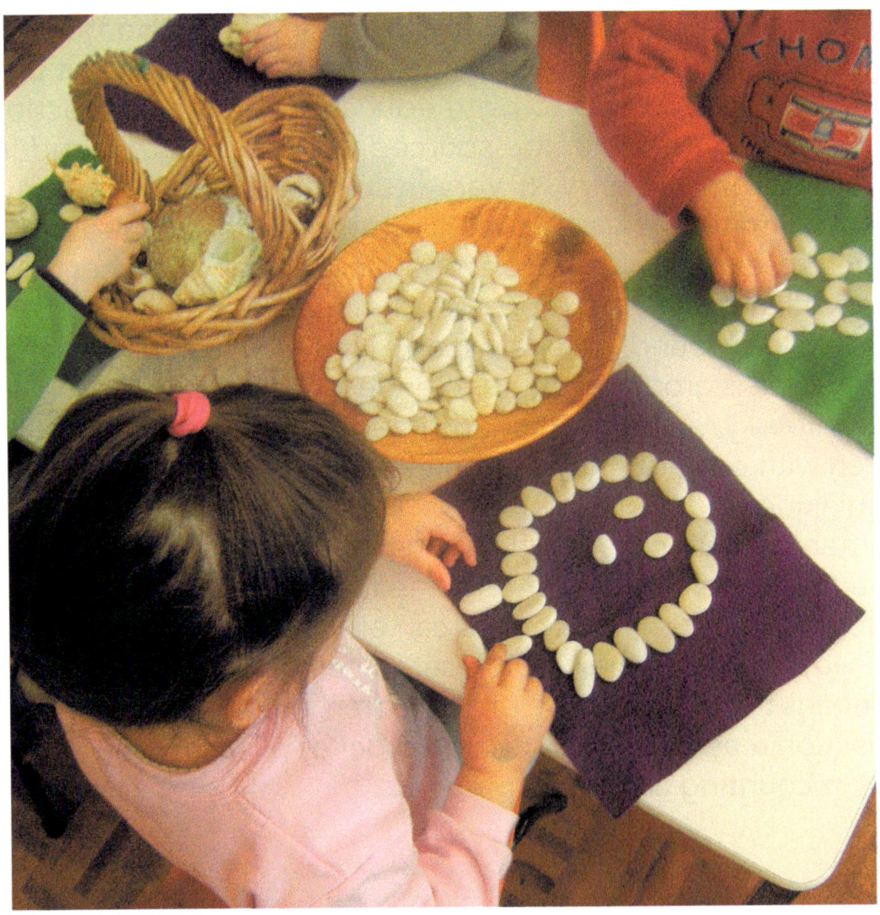

Figure P3F.2 Introducing ephemeral art begins with a small, curated selection of materials and intentional spaces for children to work. This thoughtful approach helps them learn the processes of collecting, arranging, and exploring patterns, fostering creativity and a deeper understanding of this transient art form [Image: Gai Lindsay, at Lyrebird Preschool].

arrangement of materials) can be an interesting starting point and children can collaboratively contribute to each layer as the mandala pattern expands.

Playing with, and collecting materials and objects fosters our human desire to collect, organise, design, and create. Ephemeral art creates an invitation to explore and design visual patterns in abstract ways rather than being limited by literal or representational art making. When ephemeral arts are created in the natural environment, the wind and the rain eventually deconstruct the art work. However, in educational settings, the ephemeral aspect of this art process invites children to select collections of materials and a surface to work on, create patterns and symbols, play, explore, and represent their ideas. To introduce ephemeral art exploration to children:

- Avoid overwhelming children with too many material options.
- Start with a small collection of loose parts and natural materials (e.g. a basket of smooth stones and shells).
- Provide extended periods of time for children to simply delight in lining up and sorting objects into categories.
- Play alongside children to model arrangements which may inspire children to attempt repeated patterns or circular mandala designs.
- Role model processes of examining and arranging materials; noticing shapes, colours, and textures, and deciding when the arrangement is complete.
- Articulate your own thought processes as you play and construct alongside children; including any decisions to adapt, rearrange and record the work with a photograph.
- Prior to sorting and returning materials to their storage containers, children's final design, and the process of building the ephemeral artwork, can be digitally recorded (photos or video).
- Demonstrate and role model the process of carefully sorting and returning items to their storage containers before leaving the space ready for others to use.

The value in gradually introducing a small collection of loose parts is that children will increasingly take ownership of caring for materials and spaces, and become familiar with the expectations for their use by following your guidance and modelling.

To extend children's engagement with ephemeral art making, engage children in collaborative loose parts play and ephemeral art projects to offer them opportunities for developing relationships, negotiation, and problem-solving. Foster children's confidence to select materials and document their designs (through photography and drawing), and provoke their thinking by introducing cultural designs such as mandalas or patterned tiles and mosaics. Visits to art galleries or engagement with artists who use loose parts and recycled materials can also inspire new approaches. Extend children's play by using the loose parts materials typically used for ephemeral art in other visual arts processes (e.g. collage, assemblage, woodworking). Although ephemeral art typically involves reusing loose parts and recycled materials, children's designs can be made permanent with the addition of adhesives like wire or glue.

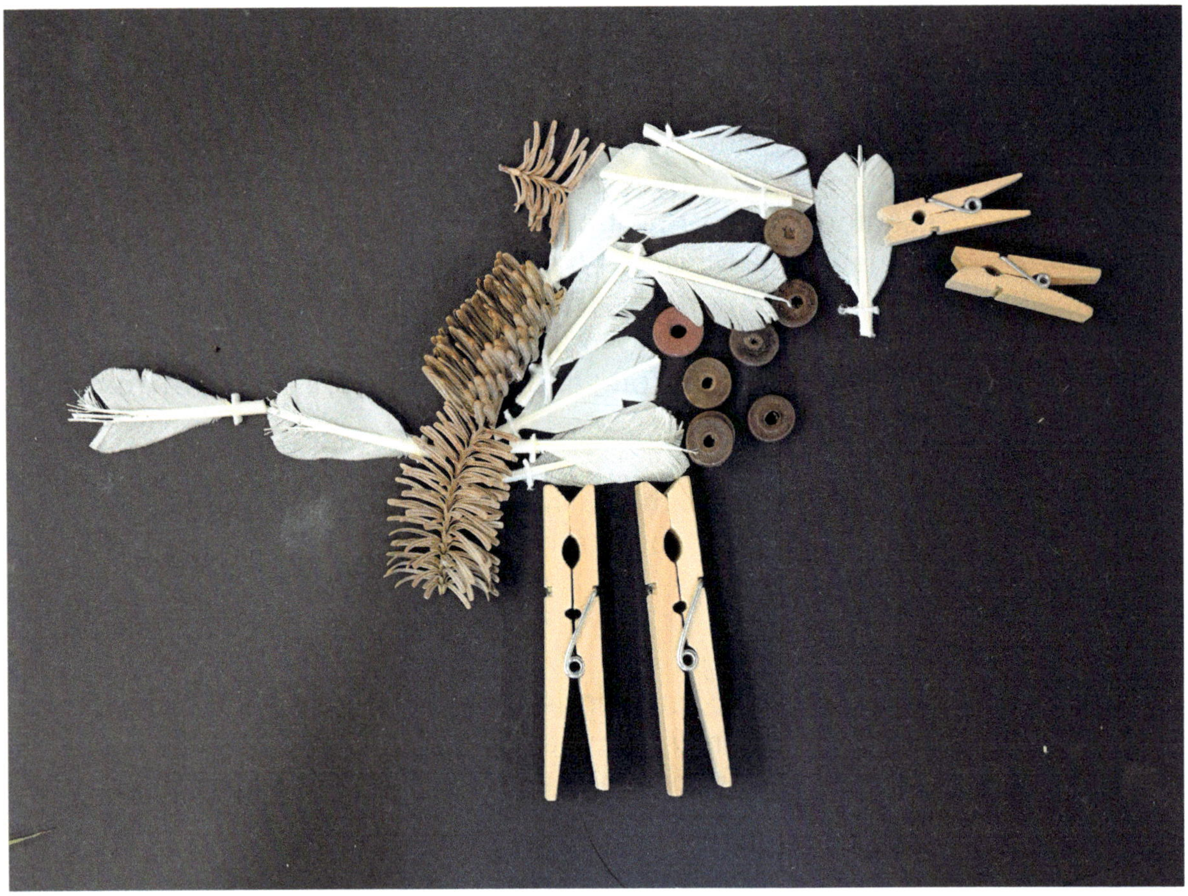

Figure P3F.3 Combining natural materials and loose parts, ephemeral art offers children a unique way to represent and explore their ideas [Image: Aurora International School of the Arts].

Collecting, maintaining, and storing collections

Creating a comprehensive collection of natural and manufactured materials for ephemeral artmaking takes time, but can start simply with just one or two sets of collected materials. Encourage children and families to collect loose parts and natural treasures from their homes, gardens, and during family outings. Loose parts are ideally sourced and collected sustainably from second-hand shops (e.g. beads, buttons, baskets for storage), recycled materials (e.g. bottle lids, metal washers, fabric, string), or sourced from the bi-products of industry (e.g. plastic objects, cardboard shapes). Some useful loose parts materials, such as PVC pipe, glass and stone pebbles or lengths of chain can be more difficult to source, raising the option to purchase loose parts from unexpected places such as the local hardware store. The Remida recycling centre in Reggio Emilia, Italy is an inspirational example of an industry partnership where pre-industrial waste, imperfect materials, and unsold stock are collected and aesthetically displayed as an invitation for educators and artists to use in their work; while promoting awareness around issues of sustainability

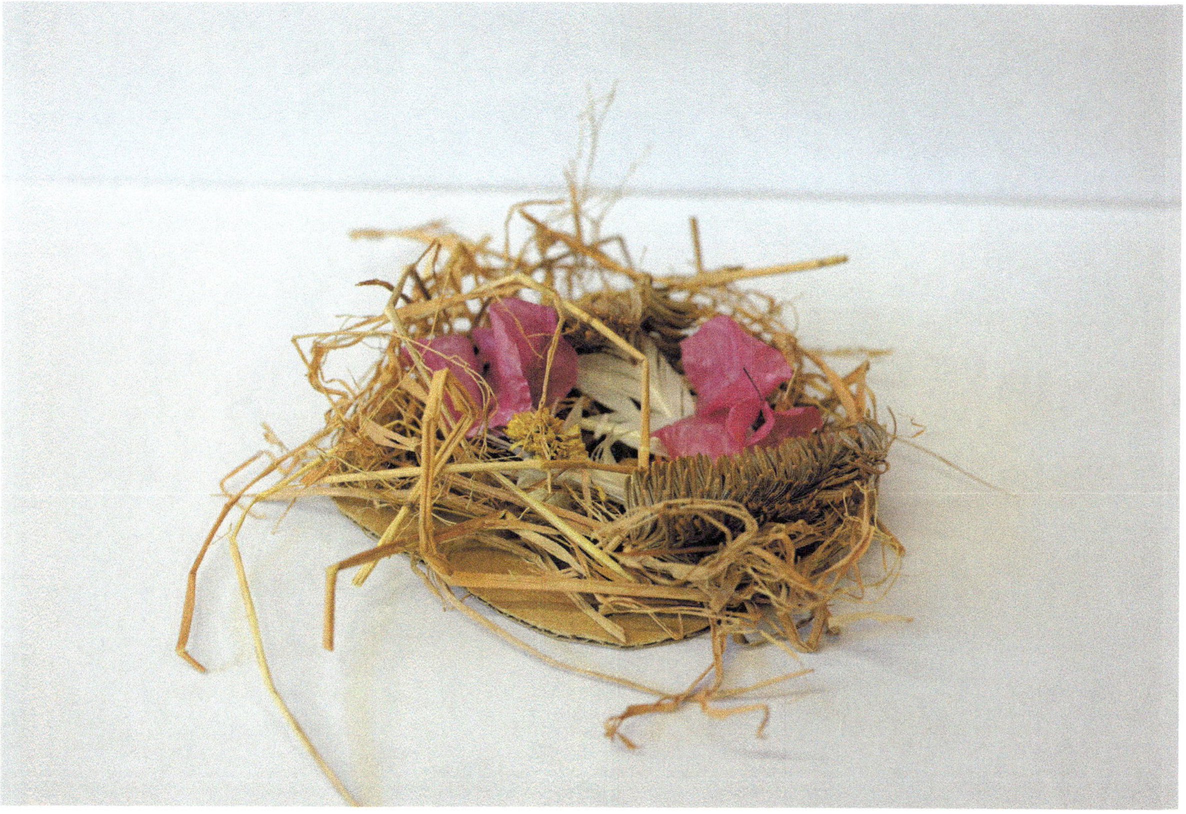

Figure P3F.4 Three-dimensional exploration in ephemeral art allows children to engage deeply with materials and ideas as they explore the possibilities of form and structure [Image: Aurora International School of the Arts].

(Ferrari & Giacopini, 2005). Seek out similar recycling centres in your community. No matter where you source your materials from, it is essential to ensure children's safety by carefully cleaning second-hand items, determining whether smaller items may present choking hazard risks, and removing sharp edges to minimise cuts or grazes.

Collecting natural materials from the environment, such as leaves, twigs, and shells, can yield beautiful collections for ephemeral artmaking, loose parts play, and other art methods such as collage. However, it is important to consider the negative environmental consequences when taking natural items from the environment. Avoid or minimise removing excessive materials from beaches, waterways, and forests. Engage in conversations with children and families to raise awareness about delicate ecosystems and open up dialogue regarding environmental responsibility and the materials that will and will not be included in natural material collections.

Organising and storing each collection in well-labelled containers creates a sense of visual order and communicates an important message that these carefully collected and organised materials are treasured artmaking resources. Invite children to look closely at each item and consider its unique qualities. Discuss the possibilities for including the material in a design or artwork.

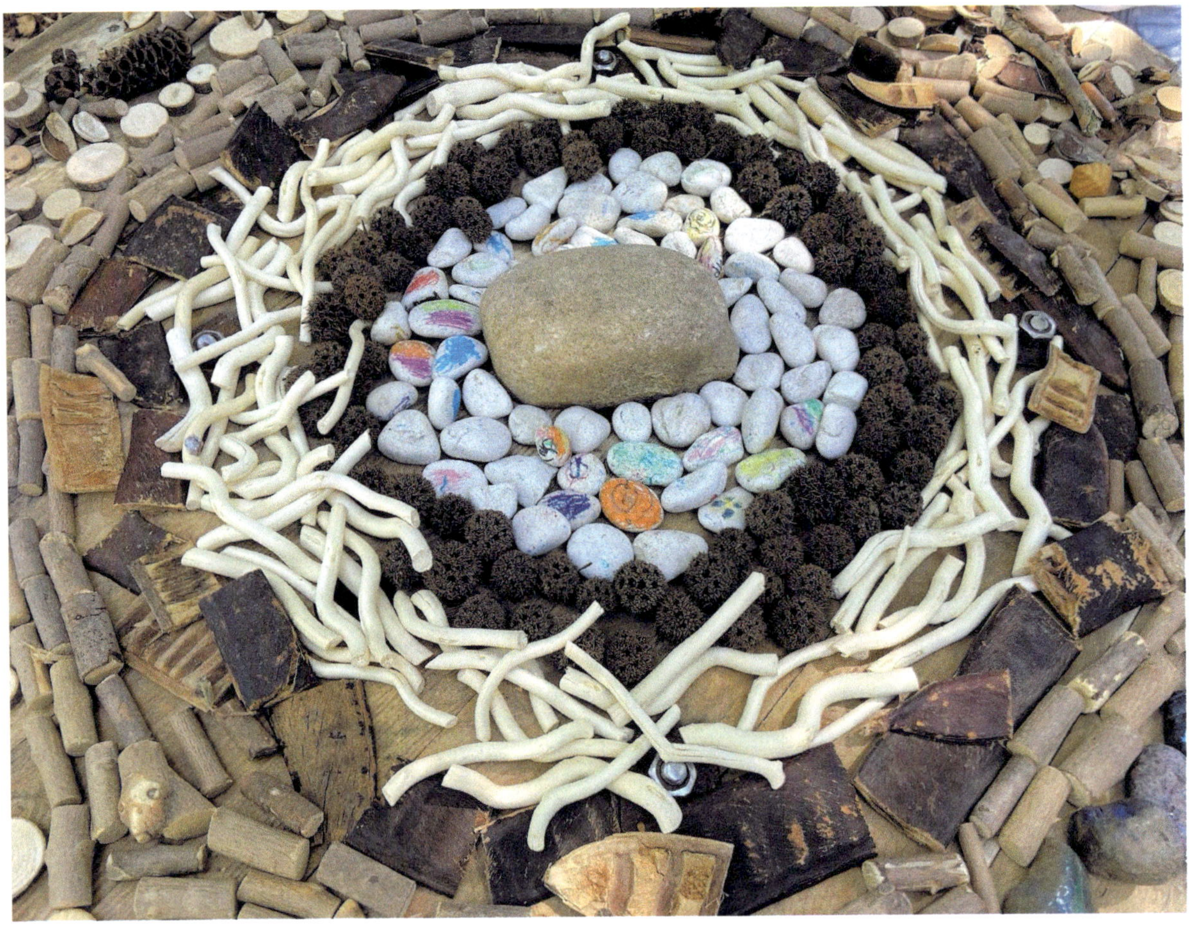

Figure P3F.5 Collaborative ephemeral art experiences foster a sense of community as children work together to create and contribute. This shared process encourages teamwork, communication, and a collective appreciation for creativity [Image: Frances Forshlager, The Nature of Creativity].

Ephemeral art spaces

Intentionally planned spaces for ephemeral and loose parts artmaking enrich children's experience. Set up away from high-traffic areas, a table or mat area positioned next to ephemeral and loose parts collections offer a rich invitation to play and design. If working on the floor, define an area for group work by providing cushions or carpet squares. For larger explorations, a large sheet or piece of fabric arranged in the space can be an exciting invitation for children to work collaboratively. Beyond art studio areas, collections of natural materials and loose parts are rich additions to any classroom area, such as in the construction area and outdoor spaces.

The following suggestions inspire the creation of spaces that will invite and delight:

- Add a lamp for added atmosphere and aesthetic appeal.
- Offer magnifying glasses to encourage close noticing and observation.
- Carpet or mats under the workspace prevent dropped items posing a trip or slip hazard.

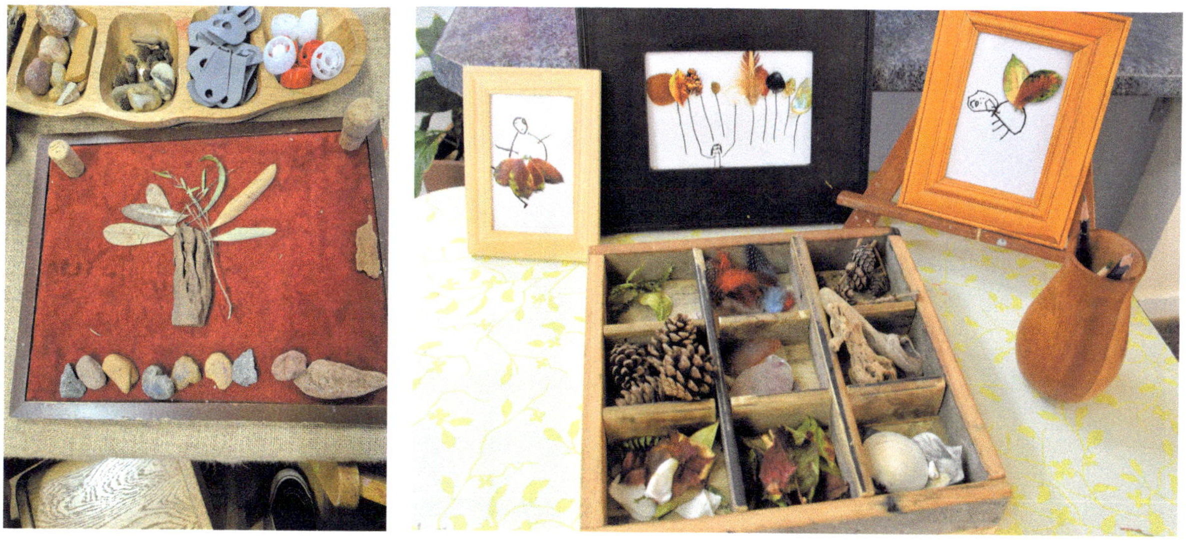

Figure P3F.6(a,b) Thoughtfully arranged environments, where materials are organised engagingly, invite creativity and exploration [Image P3F.6a: Maitland Preschool, P3F.6b: Sarah Probine].

- Lightboxes offer compelling spaces for collaborative work; with the added benefit of highlighting the details in translucent natural treasures.
- Offer a variety of surfaces to create designs on, such as circular placemats, old picture frames, squares of felt, carpet, and floor tiles.
- The inclusion of digital cameras provides children with the option to document their work prior to packing away.

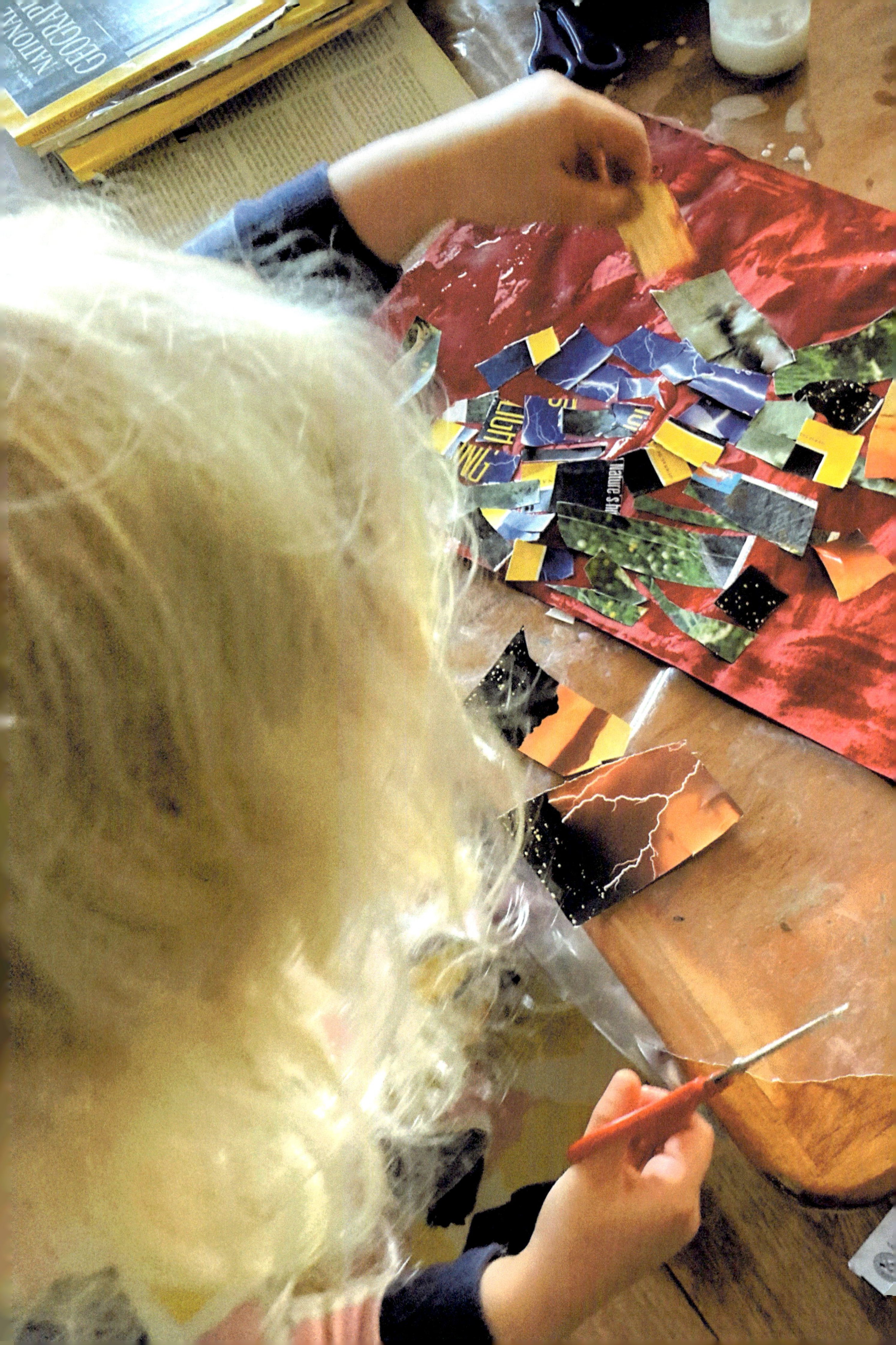

3.6 Collage and assembly

Collage is an exciting visual arts experience that provides children with a range of possibilities for image-making and creative expression. Using the three-step process of choosing a material, adding an adhesive, and attaching materials to a surface, collage brings together solid blocks of colour, patterns, and a range of shapes and textures to create a composition. This process is often described as "painting with paper," however, collage materials can expand beyond the use of papers to include a range of natural, man-made, and recycled materials.

Whether creating a collage with one material or many, collage experiences support children to engage in creative decision-making, develop a range of manipulative skills, experiment with everyday materials, and explore diverse approaches to picture-making.

Introducing children to collage

While any material can be used to make a collage, introducing children to a small range of interesting papers, glue, and brushes is a good place to start. Paper in its many forms offers enormous potential for patterning and picture-making. It can be cut, torn, rolled, folded, layered, arranged, glued, taped, stapled, painted, and drawn on; and this type of flexibility provides rich scope for exploration. To support children's engagement, encourage them to observe and discuss the qualities of the collage materials, and wonder together how they might be used. Be prepared for diverse responses to the materials, as some children may simply want to explore the glue without pasting any collage materials. Others may tear and cut paper, but show little interest in gluing their cut-out shapes onto a base. This time for exploring materials and tools is important for children's learning processes and unused materials can be collected for later reuse. To support children's artistic vocabulary, describe the colours and textures of materials, discuss shapes that are organic or geometric, and edges that are straight, bendy, or curved. Design and composition skills can also be practised before introducing glue by using collections of felt shapes or loose parts that can be arranged and rearranged onto a felt board.

The following suggestions for getting started will support children's ongoing engagement with collage materials:

- Start simply with a small selection of materials.

Figure P3G.1 Collage compositions can begin with a plan or emerge organically as children find inspiration in materials and follow their instincts for composition and design [Image: Adrienne Wilkins, Sophia Preschool].

DOI: 10.4324/9781003561835-20

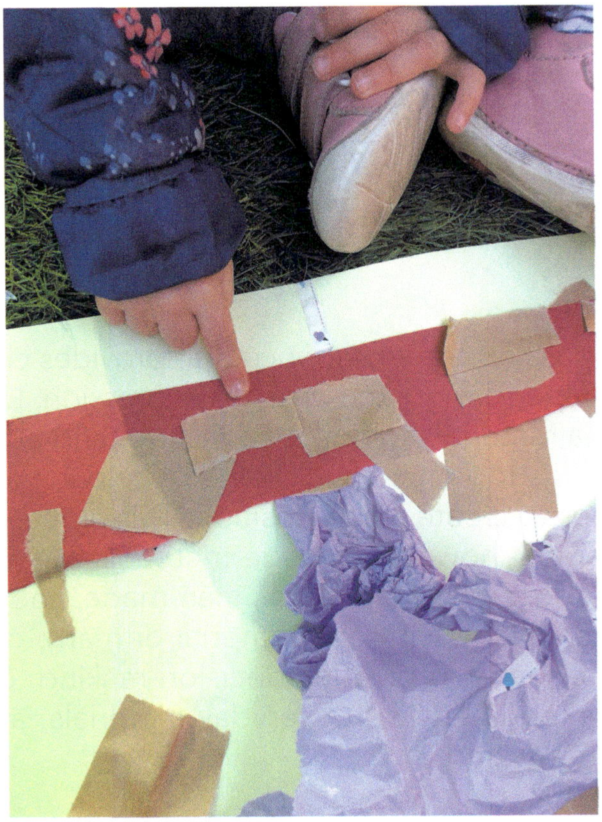

Figure P3G.2 Simple precut shapes and paper strips offer young children opportunities to explore collage composition in open-ended ways. Experienced collage makers may prefer to cut and tear their own paper for collage [Image: Gai Lindsay, at UOW Pulse Kids' Uni].

- Offer precut shapes and/or thick and thin strips of paper that can be applied in open-ended ways.
- Choose papers that can be easily cut or torn by children.
- Present materials attractively to create intrigue and appeal to children's curiosity.
- Offer a strong base or surface that will hold layers of glue and collage materials.
- Support children's spatial awareness and understanding of composition by commenting on their arrangements of materials (e.g. under, above, beside, in a row, in the corners, separate, overlapping).
- Observe, respond to, and affirm children's exploration of collage materials.
- Value children's ideas and offer suggestions to inspire ongoing exploration.
- Offer support and model skills as children encounter challenges.
- Collect, and recycle materials to foster sustainable practices.
- Offer repeated opportunities and time for children to build their skills with materials and tools. As children develop the skills to work with paper, scissors, and glue, a broader range of materials (e.g., staplers and tape) can be introduced to add complexity, provide challenges, and inspire new ways of thinking and working.

Curating materials

Thoughtfully collecting, organising, and presenting materials has enormous potential for inspiring children's engagement and participation in collage experiences. For example, curating papers into colour groups or according to texture (embossed, glossy, matt) creates visual appeal and can inspire children's choices

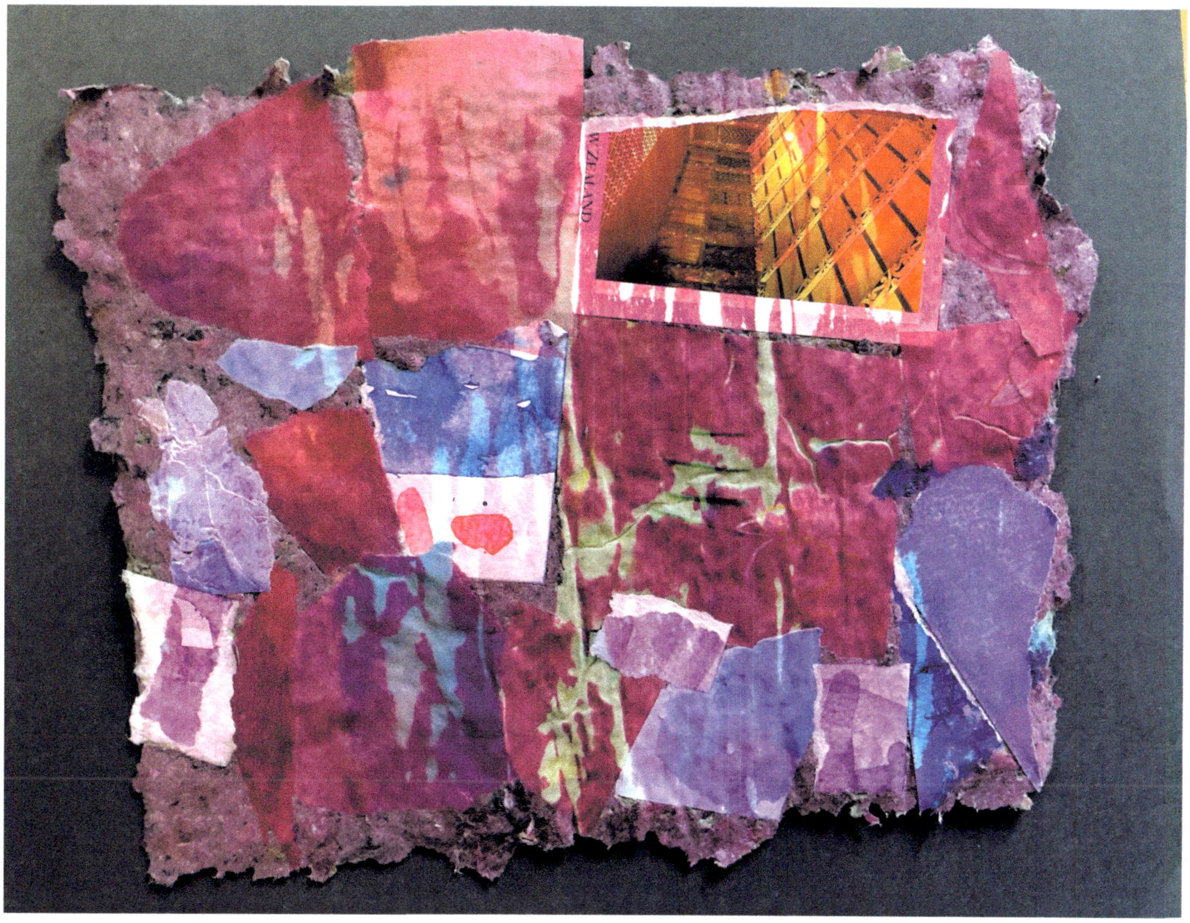

Figure P3G.3 Handmade papers, recycled paintings, and magazine cutouts create vibrant and eco-friendly paper collage artworks [Image: Adrienne Wilkins, Sophia Preschool].

for making collage designs. It is also important to offer materials that are open-ended and flexible enough to inspire multiple uses. For example, why offer plastic, stick-on eyes when children can draw or cut out their own? The use of novelty items such as pom poms, stickers, and foam shapes should be critically reflected on in terms of sustainability and their ability to be used in open-ended ways. To foster sustainable use of materials, collect and offer children recycles papers, discarded paintings, string, wool, fabric, and packaging materials. Light-weight, natural materials such as dried flowers, leaves, and sand can also be used in collage explorations.

COLLAGE MATERIAL SUGGESTIONS

Recycled wrapping paper and greeting cards, maps, magazines, paper doilies, fabric, wool, string, ribbons, match sticks, flat paddle pop sticks, buttons, feathers, seed pods, twigs, and sustainably collected natural items.

Scissors, glue, and brushes

Scissors: Use small scissors that fit children's hands well and support children to use scissors carefully and safely.

Glue: Wallpaper glue or cornflour paste will attach most papers onto cardboard or paper surfaces. A little PVA mixed with wallpaper paste creates a strong economical glue. For objects such as buttons, beads, fabric, match sticks, wool, string, and wood, use children's PVA or wood glue and a stronger support base. With supervision, children can learn to safely use low-temperature glue guns to attach heavier 3-D materials to an object or base. Be mindful that some children dislike the stickiness of glue on their hands. Therefore, keep cleaning cloths nearby for wiping fingers, hands, and brush handles to support all children to engage effectively. Alternatively, glue sticks are a good alternative for basic gluing tasks.

Brushes: Short-handled flat brushes are good for applying pastes and glues. Always wash them immediately after use or soak them in a little water until able to wash thoroughly with warm water and a mild detergent. If possible, keep glue and paintbrushes separate or use scruffier paintbrushes for gluing only.

Collage extension ideas

To extend children's collage explorations, consider the following ideas and teaching strategies:

- Research collage artists with children. Learn about and be inspired by the techniques and materials they use. For example, be inspired by the famous "cut-outs" of Henri Matisse or Eric Carle's illustrations to paint and prepare your own collection of collage papers.
- Offer different sized, shaped, and coloured backgrounds to vary visual impact and inspire new ideas for composition.
- Introduce paper-tearing techniques to inspire creative design. Organic and irregular shapes offer a contrast to sharp-edged geometric shapes and produce interesting visual effects.
- By adding a little glue to paint, flat collage materials can be adhered to paintings.
- Work socially and collaboratively to create large collage murals.
- Explore collage with a range of transparent papers on a light box covered with clear plastic.
- Explore folding and cutting techniques to help children create their own shapes, patterns, and repetitions.

Assemblage art and construction

Assemblage art offers children the opportunity to build on collage experiences and explore design through construction in three-dimensions. Through assemblage art processes, children are encouraged to see the extraordinary in everyday objects and materials, to rethink and reimagine them, and to explore their potential for transformation. Assemblage and construction materials (see Table P3G.1) can be creatively assembled, designed, and repurposed. As children encounter the challenges of arranging, balancing, and joining objects and materials; they are thinking imaginatively, encountering problems, persevering, developing problem-solving strategies, building spatial awareness, and using a range of manipulative skills.

Curating materials and tools

Assemblage artists draw from a range of sources and materials to create assemblages and installations.

Table P3G.1 Assemblage art collections

Paper-based materials	Cardboard boxes and cylinders, newspapers, magazines, paper bags, catalogues, old books, packaging inserts, egg cartons
Fabric	Old clothes, fabric scraps, wool, string, cord, ribbon
Plastic	Clear and coloured bottles, plastic cutlery, straws, bottle tops and lids, felt pen lids, toys, bubble wrap, fruit bags, tubing
Wood	Wood offcuts, cork, toys, curtain rings, beads, buttons
Metal	Foil, wire, old jewellery, buttons, keys, old CDs / DVDs
Natural	Leaves, pressed flowers, feathers, seed pods, sticks, shells
Other	Rubber, foam, broken crockery, industrial recyclables

Safety considerations

- Ensure the materials you collect for creative reuse are clean and have no sharp edges or points.
- Materials should be sturdy, odourless, and not produce dust particles when cut.
- Supervision is paramount when children are using tools, glue, and smaller items that may be a choking hazard.
- Store all tools out of children's reach when not being used.

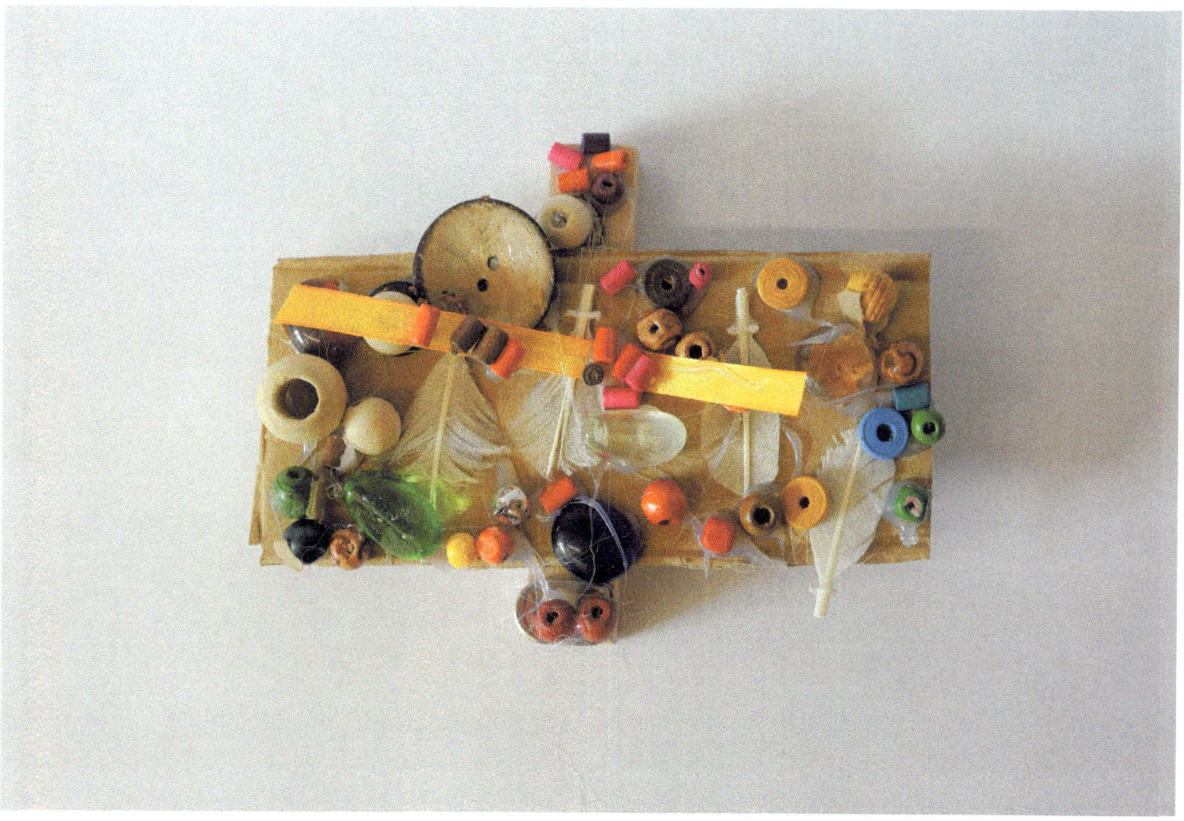

Figure P3G.4 Building on collage experiences, assemblage art provides children with opportunities to arrange and design using three-dimensional materials [Image: Aurora International School of the Arts].

Introducing children to assemblage art and construction:

Connecting assemblage and construction art to learning about sustainable practices and the environment is a great way to support children's interest and enthusiasm for reusing discarded objects. Inviting children and families to engage in the process of collecting materials for creative reuse is also an important way to motivate children's interest and involvement. As materials are brought into the classroom, involve children in sorting, storing, and even helping to clean them as necessary. Such processes offer children an engaging learning experience that supports them to become familiar with materials and their varied properties. Materials and objects can be sorted according to their attributes, whether sparkly, rough or smooth, or according to their material category (e.g. metal, wood, paper). Engage children in conversations about size, texture, colour, and shape, or wonder about the life and purpose objects had before they were discarded. For example, you might ask, "Where did this come from?" or "What might this have been used for?" Sorting together creates time for observing, feeling, describing, thinking, wondering, and sharing discoveries; while pondering what else materials might be used for or become.

Creating three-dimensional assemblages and constructions requires the use of tools and the development of skills to join materials together. Teaching techniques for cutting and joining materials with a range of tools and resources supports children's fine motor skills and ability to work independently. With

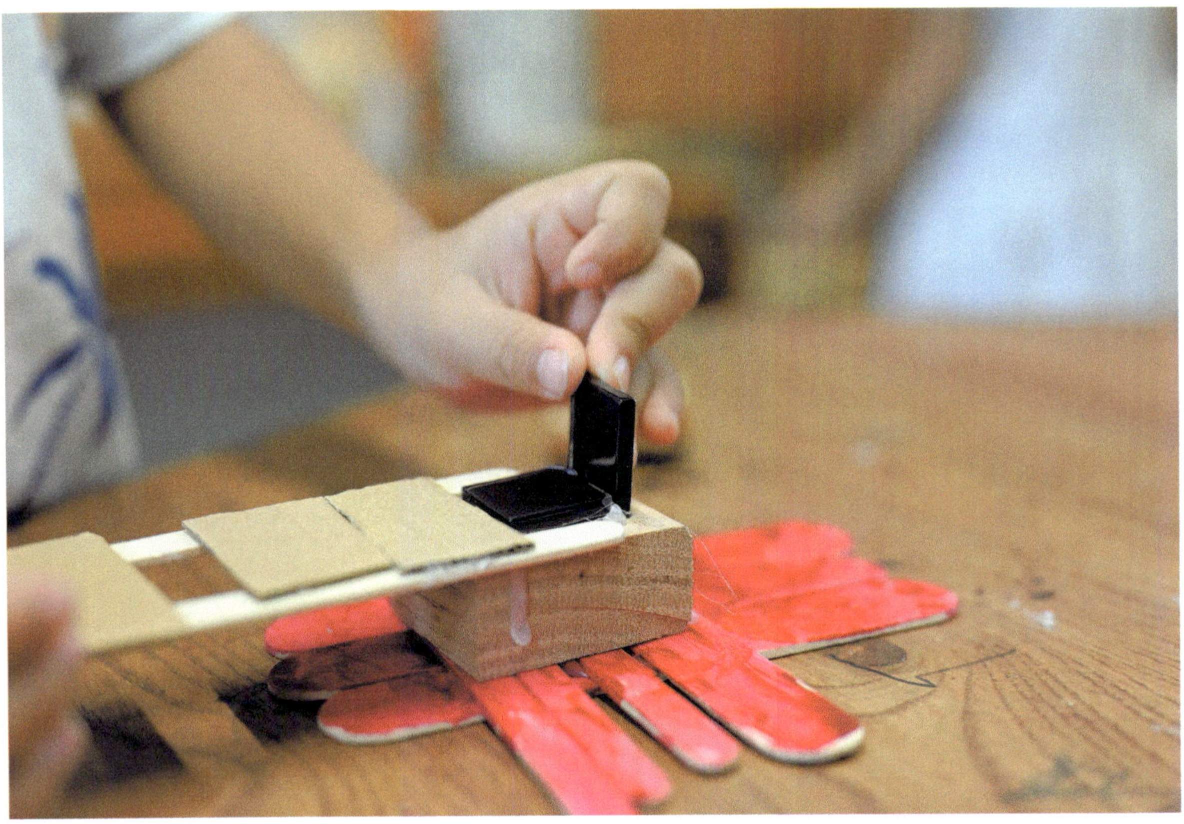

Figure P3G.5 Combining and transforming everyday materials involves creative thinking, problem solving, perseverance, and a range of manipulative skills [Image: Aurora International School of the Arts].

supervision and support, children can learn how to safely use cutting tools (scissors and child-safe cardboard cutting saws), glues, tapes, split pins, paper clips, and staplers. Depending on the materials being used and children's design and construction goals, clothes pegs, hole punches, bulldog clips, and fine wire are also useful tools for joining assemblage components.

Storing materials

Organising, storing, and displaying collections of collage and recycled materials is important to ensure easy access and to avoid clutter. To create a beautiful and inspiring display of materials, organise sorted items in containers on shelves. Larger materials require storage management as they are more difficult to store aesthetically. For example, stand cardboard tubing in a large pot and cut larger pieces of cardboard and paper into small pieces for easier storage. Search online to locate and visit local recycling centres to source and be inspired to collect and store materials in ways that inspire wonder and spark children's imagination.

Planning ideas and experiences

Like collage compositions, children's assemblage and constructions can begin with a plan or emerge organically as children follow their instincts for play and exploration. Experiences may extend on children's current construction play, or expand their interest in specific materials. For example, exploring construction and assembly with one material such as cardboard, or an attribute such as transparency can inspire interesting long-term inquiry.

There are multiple possibilities for creative assembly, and it is fun to experiment with different combinations of materials. To provide inspiration and contexts for working with found objects and materials:

- Curate and present varied combinations of objects and materials to children in interesting ways. For example, a collection of materials in shades of brown and taupe (e.g., shells, seedpods, matchsticks, and dried leaves) presented with timber offcuts may provoke aesthetic 3-D designs.
- Model and demonstrate strategies for joining materials.
- Introduce, discuss, and be inspired by images of assemblage art and sculptures.
- Broaden children's thinking and ideas through questions, suggestions, and prompts (I wonder what you might use for…?; I thought you might like to try….; I wonder what would happen if….?).

Construction and sculpture materials

The following materials, and associated tools and construction processes, can be explored separately or combined according to children's imaginations and the demands of the project. We suggest that children have many opportunities to get to know the properties and affordances of materials and tools separately, in order to build their material and technical knowledge and construction skills.

Cardboard, heavy paper, and recycled boxes can be cut, folded, reshaped, and stuck together to make and create three-dimensional constructions. Cardboard tubing and long, thin strips of cardboard can be cut and folded to add to constructions or to make props for imaginative play. Joined with glue, tape or even a glue-gun, cardboard and boxes, along with paper and other collage materials, offer endless possibilities for construction. As children develop skills and experience, combine boxes, cardboard pieces, paper, and cylinders with additional fabrics, papers, drawing, and assemblage materials to inspire children's constructions and designs.

Gathering and curating construction resources:

- Offer children neutral surfaces and boxes without text, logos, or images. Food packaging boxes, such as cereal and pasta boxes, can be opened at the seams, turned inside out, and taped back together to create a clean surface without advertising and perfect for drawing and collaging on. Boxes can also be wrapped in plain paper to create a "blank canvas" for drawing, painting, and collage work.
- Cut flaps from large boxes to create a collection of various-sized squares and strips of cardboard to offer with box construction.
- Score thick cardboard boxes and packaging to make it easier to cut or shape. Place a ruler parallel with the corrugation lines and use a knife or the blunt edge of a tool to create shallow cuts or indentations, before bending or cutting the cardboard along the scored line.
- Purchase tools designed specifically for children to safely cut and punch holes in cardboard boxes, making them ideal for creative and constructive play. Tools such as plastic safety saws, serrated safety-knives, hole punches, and child-safe screwdrivers offer safe and effective construction potential.
- Offer whole cardboard cylinders as well as cut cardboard rings of varying widths.
- Provide a range of strong masking and sticky tapes for joining cardboard items together.
- Strips of paper painted with PVA glue make excellent "joiners" to sturdily connect construction pieces and save on the overuse of masking tape.
- Provide floor space for construction with large boxes. Cover some boxes for painting or drawing on and leave others open for children to use in their own ways.
- Recycle magazines by rolling up the pages and taping them to make tubes. Paper tubes can be joined together to make shapes and three-dimensional free-form sculptures.
- Cut long strips of thick construction paper and experiment with ways to curl, roll, bend, fold, and join them together.

Wire sculpture offers a wonderful creative opportunity for children, combining tactile play, creative expression, and exploration of form and structure. Soft, pliable wire can be bent and shaped as sculptures or used as joiners and

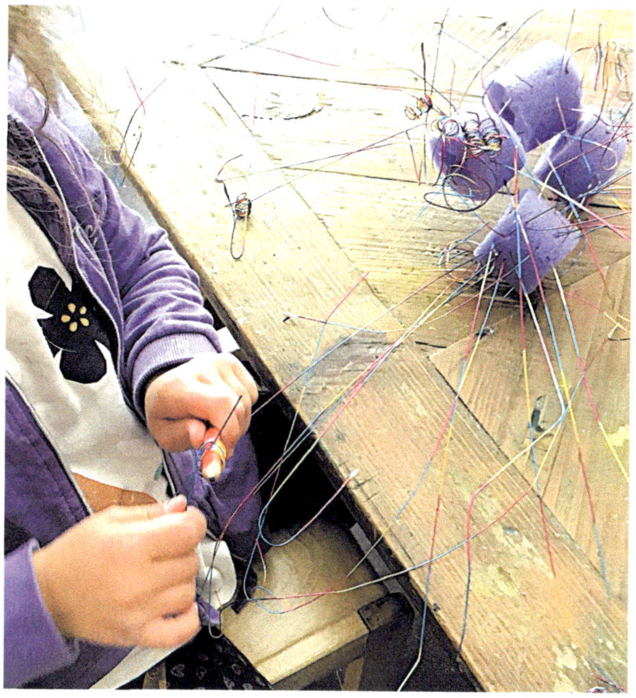

Figure P3G.6 Soft, pliable wire offers diverse possibilities for assemblage and sculpture. It can be shaped and manipulated as an independent medium, used as a joiner, or creatively combined with a range of recycled materials [Image: Bomaderry Community Preschool].

attachments on other construction projects. Soft, pliable wires (aluminium, copper) that are flexible and easy for children to manipulate are sold in rolls or cut lengths of florist wire and as shorter pipe cleaners. Garden supply stores stock PVC-coated gardening wires that offer rich manipulative potential. Fingers and basic tools, such as child-safe pliers, are sufficient for cutting and manipulating wire. Large alligator clips, cable ties, small spring clamps, and even cubes of clay will support children to secure and hold pieces of wire; freeing up their hands to manipulate and sculpt the wire pieces.

Softwood offcuts (source untreated timbers) are wonderful for assemblage, construction, and sculpture projects. Work on a stable base to attach flat sticks, wooden and glass beads, corks, and other collage materials. Materials can be joined with wood glue, wire, and woodwork tools. (For more detailed information about woodwork and carpentry, see the next section.) Projects can be embellished with paint, markers, and additional collage materials and objects.

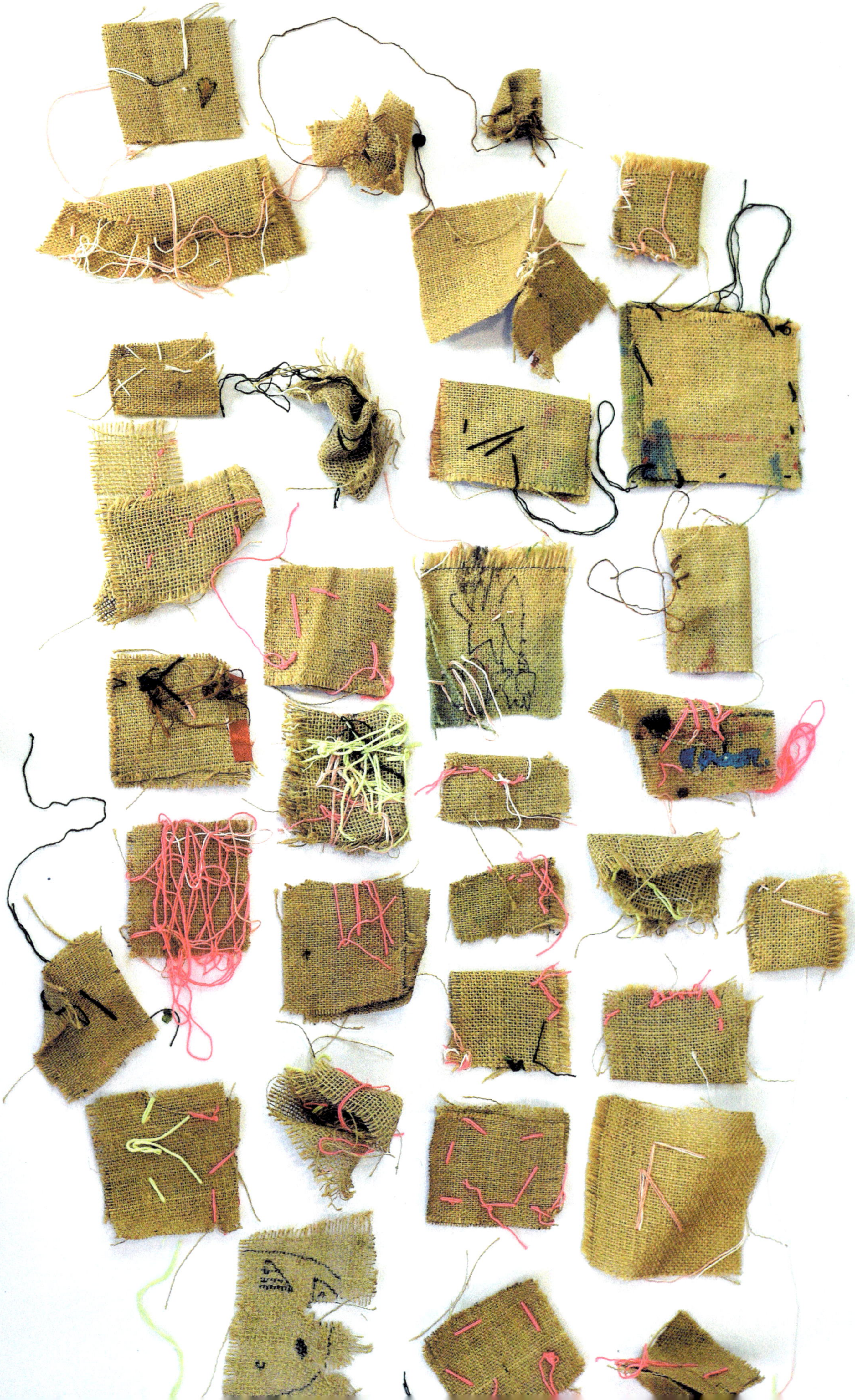

3.7 Traditional crafts and artisan processes

Crafting and artisan techniques hold an important place in society and should be included in the rich repertoire of arts techniques offered in your visual arts curriculum. As outlined in Chapter 8, many of the traditional crafts and artisan methods which used to be commonplace features in early years classrooms have all but disappeared from education settings, and have too often been rejected as too structured or instructional. In the desire to offer children completely open-ended arts experiences, the rich methods and techniques, not to mention the rich cultural traditions of craft and artisan work, have been denied to children. And yet, we believe these processes and techniques, when carefully planned to suit children's abilities and development, offer excellent learning potentials.

The intersection between visual arts and crafting methods can be blurred. While crafting methods are orderly and generally involve step-by-step processes, they can still be applied in open-ended, developmentally appropriate ways. As children build a repertoire of the skills, methods, and techniques associated with traditional crafts and artisan processes, they can use these materials and processes to express themselves in artistic, creative, and visually aesthetic ways; delighting in the joy of mastering processes and keeping alive traditions that have been passed down for generations through cultures, families and communities. Crafting methods and traditional techniques foster creativity and practical skills and build appreciation for both art-making processes and cultural heritage.

Introducing crafts and artisan techniques to children

When introducing craft and artisan processes to young children, the educator's role is to demonstrate and teach techniques; and be a supportive assistant when guidance or assistance is helpful. We emphasise that teaching children about the materials, skills, and processes associated with craftwork and artisan methods is NOT about showing them a finished product and expecting them to follow step-by-step instructions to replicate the product. That just leads to frustration and, more often than not, results in products largely constructed by adults. Instead, drawing inspiration from artisan and crafting traditions creates opportunities to

Figure P3H.1 Introducing children to sewing is effective when using smaller pieces of loose weave hessian because larger needles are easier for children to hold and manoeuvre through the fabric [Image: Aurora International School Of The Arts].

DOI: 10.4324/9781003561835-21

introduce children to beautiful materials, colours, and textures, while building their awareness of processes that centralise making, decorating and practical problem-solving. Additionally, traditional crafts often use sustainable materials which also encourages recycling and sustainable consumption.

Artisan traditions and crafts introduce children to a variety of life skills, many of which are being lost in family and community contexts. Taking the time to immerse children in traditional craft and artisan methods fosters a range of benefits, including:

- Sustained effort, concentration, and attention to detail
- Creative problem-solving, experimentation, and resourcefulness
- Patience and perseverance in spite of challenge
- Purposeful development of fine motor skills and hand-eye coordination
- Appreciation for cultural artistic expression
- Using language and new terminology to explain or learn processes
- Collaborating with others
- Using recycled and sustainable materials

Start with crafting or artisan skills already familiar to you. For example, if you knit, bring your wool and needles into the setting and introduce them to the children. While knitting may be too advanced a skill for most young children, introducing them to balls of wool and creating opportunities for children to sort, feel, and make patterns with wool scraps can be a great introduction to these materials. This can lead to opportunities to use wool for collage, sewing, threading, and weaving. Craft and artisan processes invite risk-taking and real-world skills and problem-solving.

No matter what the crafting or artisan process or technique may be, it is important for you to engage in research about the process before introducing it to children. Explore the traditions and history of the method by inviting local experts to demonstrate their craft to the children, providing both inspiration and a valuable learning opportunity for everyone involved. Play with materials and tools and as you do, think about how you can make the processes and materials accessible for the children you work with. Collect materials, tools, and equipment to regularly use with children, knowing that skills development takes time and practice.

Knowing the elements or pre-skills of a craft or artisan process will support you to intentionally scaffold the techniques and processes involved. Deconstruct a whole craft or artisan process into the pre-skills and concepts which make up the whole process and introduce it to children in stages to build their skills and knowledge of the materials, tools, and processes. For example, some (not all) of the pre-skills for sewing are:

- Playing with lengths of wool
- Snipping with scissors
- Developing vocabulary and body movements for "up," "down," "in," "out," "under," "over"
- Poking and posting into holes
- Pulling threads

The materials and tools used for artisan and crafting methods can be offered individually as stand-alone learning experiences to enable children at any age or stage of development to play with and explore. For example, before teaching the complex skill of paper folding, offer children repeated opportunities to explore many types of paper to learn about how to rip, scrunch, and bend it. Deconstruct learning experiences to support children to meet and engage with the elements and pre-skills that underpin more complex processes.

The rest of this section presents a brief introduction to a range of craft and artisan processes. Where relevant, we offer hints and tips to guide your planning and practice.

Sewing

Play with thread, fabric, needles, and scissors introduces practical sewing, stitching, and threading skills; supporting exploration of texture, colour, and pattern, not to mention focus, hand-eye coordination, and persistence. The following tips offer ideas and strategies:

- Before working with needles and thread to learn the "over-and-under" or "in-and-out" process of placing stitches into fabric, it is important for children to have many opportunities to play with the conceptual language and processes of threading. For example, provide large beads which can be "threaded" onto stiff chords or even wire.
- When selecting fabrics, choose open weave materials such as hessian to make pushing the needle through fabric much less frustrating.
- To secure and hold fabric, stretch it in a frame. Frames can either be individual and circular or larger to support a group of children to work communally. Another way to stiffen fabric for easy holding and handling is to apply iron-on wadding or stiffening to the fabric.
- While it is possible to buy plastic needles with large eyes (the hole at the end of the needle), large-eyed, slightly blunt steel needles are effective and resilient for threading and sewing purposes. Store needles upright in a piece of firm foam to keep track of the needles being used.
- If you have tried to thread wool through the eye of a needle, you know it can be challenging. Make a very handy needle threader (which children can use) by cutting a 3–4 cm long thin strip of paper which fits through the eye of the needle. Fold the paper in half and lay the end of the wool or thread between the paper fold. Pinch together to thread the paper through the eye of the needle; with the thread encased inside. (Thanks to Gai's great-grandmother Edna Budden, "Ma," for teaching her this technique!)
- Bring an electric sewing machine into the classroom. Children are fascinated by the process of pushing a pedal to create stitched lines to join fabrics together or make stitched lines. With support and risk management, children can learn how to use real machines, techniques, and skills.
- Play with fabrics to feel textures, sort colours, and make patterns.
- Explore fabric arts such as quilting, fabric collage, and clothing design.

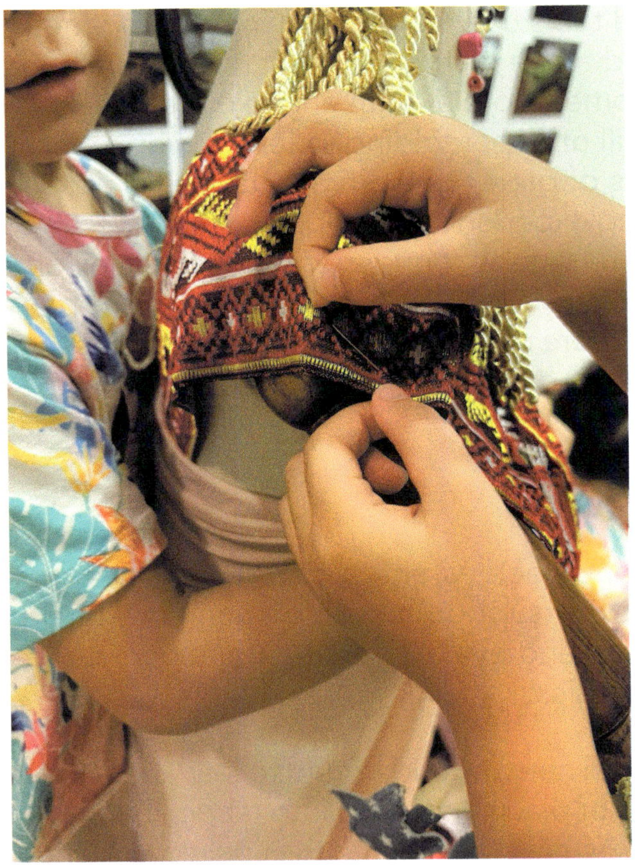

Figure P3H.2 Children capably hand-sew decorative fabric onto their costume design [Image: Aurora International School Of The Arts].

Weaving

Weaving involves passing threads, yarns, or materials over and under each other to create fabric, textiles, and mats. Vertical (warp) threads are tightly secured in place on a loom or framework, and horizontal (weft) threads are woven over and under the warp threads to create woven fabric. While children can learn about traditional tapestry weaving, where the colour and placement of weft threads build up an image or pattern, the concept to introduce to children should simply focus on the over-under manipulation of materials. Young children can delight in, and push and poke threads and materials into boxes or baskets as a first step of exploration, while older children can practice the process of weaving weft threads on a grid or vertical frame.

In educational settings, weaving can be done with paper strips, fibres (wool, string, rope), strips of fabric, plant matter, raffia, and recycled materials such as strips of packaging and plastic bags. You can also be creative with the objects upon which you weave. Instead of setting up vertical warp threads (which is more complex for you and the children), the under-over weaving process can be done on a fence, wire or plastic mesh, or a stand with vertical sticks attached.

Another traditional and simple form of weaving popular with children is God's Eye weaving (also known as Ojo de Dios). In some cultures, this method

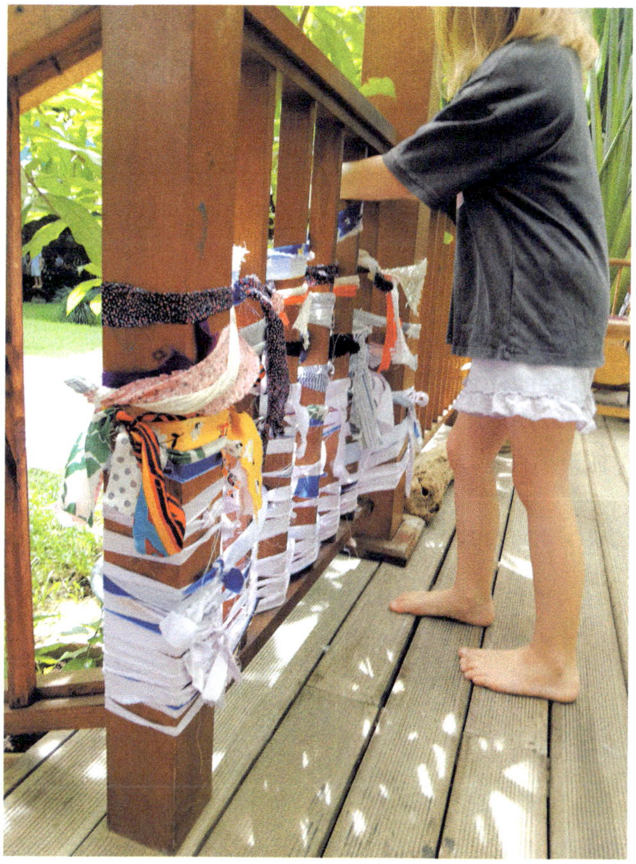

Figure P3H.3 Anywhere there are bars or mesh, like a fence or balcony railing, you can weave using recycled fabrics or plastics [Image: Carolyn Prawius at Saigon Kids Early Learning Centre].

symbolises protection and the watchful eye of a deity. Children enjoy this basic weaving technique for the beautiful colour patterns it produces when coloured yarns are wrapped around two crossed sticks to create diamond-shaped patterns.

Woodwork

Woodwork offers children rich, purposeful, and imaginative opportunities to experience the joy of construction with recycled and repurposed materials. Children are drawn to the real, "heavy" work of carpentry which requires strength and coordination (Morehouse, 2015). Construction with wood and collected materials introduces children to tools and techniques as they plan, solve problems, and implement safety protocols. Learning to manage risk is a feature of woodworking and builds children's agency and self-confidence. When children learn to connect pieces of wood and attach materials using hammers, nails, and other tools, they are translating their imagination and thinking into three-dimensional forms. As children measure, cut, sand, and assemble, they are developing hand-eye coordination, motor skills, spatial awareness, numeracy, and language; as well as fostering creativity, collaboration skills, and a sense of personal accomplishment.

To introduce woodwork in your setting, collect a set of tools and source a sturdy carpentry table. A stable, heavy woodworking table will better absorb the sounds and vibrations associated with hammering. Approach local builders and carpenters to source soft wood such as pine offcuts (from responsible forestation suppliers).

Essential tools include:

- Safety goggles
- Headphones for children with noise sensitivity
- Clamps to hold items firmly while children work
- Stubby-handled, well-balanced hammers
- Round nails (25mm) with a broad head.

Other tools to add to your collection may include:

- Pull-saws
- Sand paper
- Palm drills
- Screwdrivers and screws
- Measuring tools

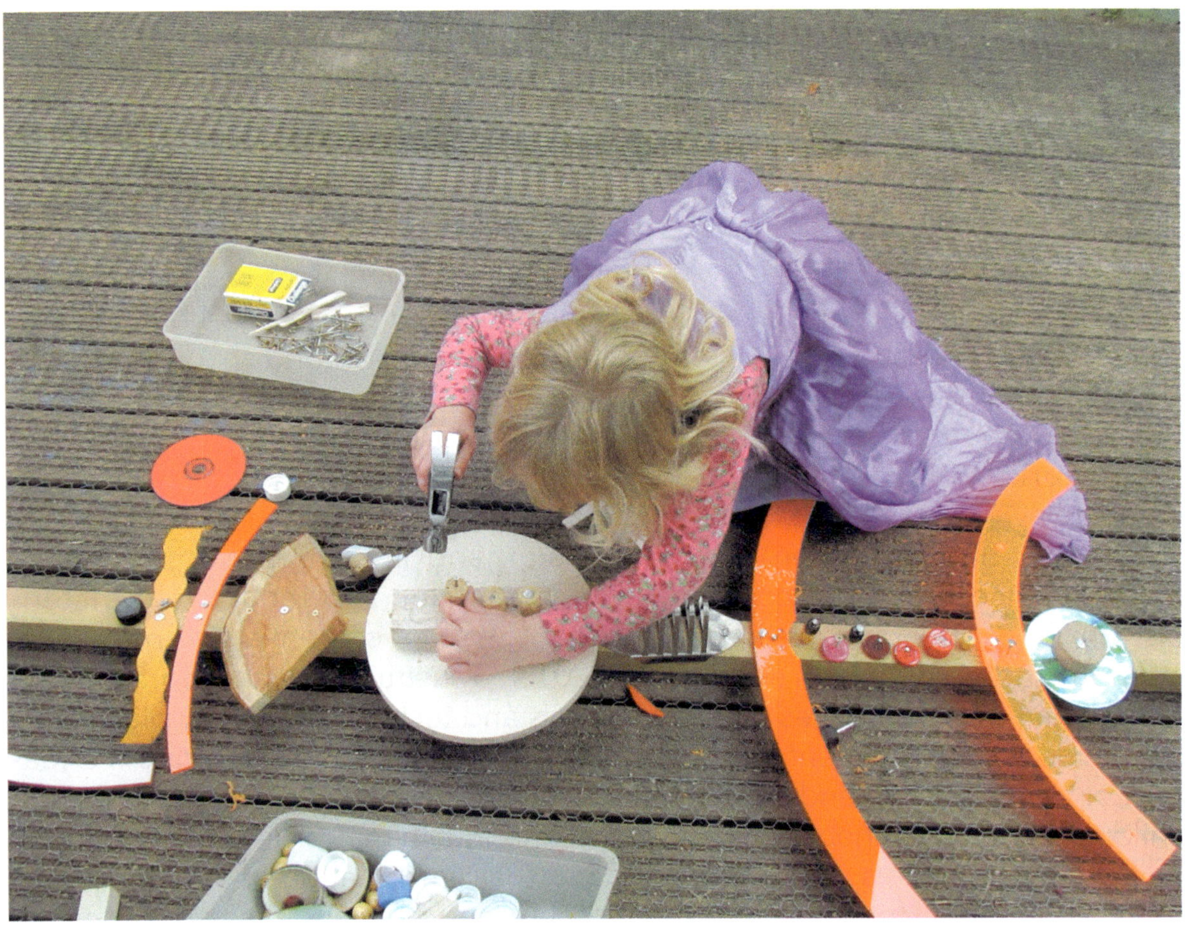

Figure P3H.4 Using wood offcuts and collected materials in carpentry fosters creative planning and problem-solving, enhancing children's agency and engagement [Image: Pete Moorhouse, Irresistible Learning].

- Nail pullers or claw hammers
- A large magnet or clean dustpan for picking up spilt nails
- Loose parts and recycled materials such as bottle lids and packaging materials
- Heavy pieces of leather, felt offcuts, and strips of heavy cardboard make great connectors and design elements.

Initially, children should simply be supported to become familiar with woodwork materials and processes. Avoid deciding or suggesting what children should make. Instead. Let them consider the affordances of the materials. If children want to simply enjoy the challenge and satisfaction of hammering nails, let that be the focus until they are ready to progress. When learning to hammer, small cubes of foam (or thick cardboard or packaging) into which the nail is pressed will hold the nail upright for hammering and prevent accidents.

When children decide they want to attach plastic lids to a piece of wood or even make a specific design, avoid taking over, but do stay present as children decide on and try out their strategies. To support authentic learning, and to manage risk, offer suggestions or techniques to build children's woodworking skills and knowledge. For a range of excellent resources we encourage you to access the website of friend and colleague Pete Moorhouse (see reference list).

Cultural artisan traditions

Respond to your local community and cultural groups to introduce children to cultural and artisan crafts, such as making kites, lanterns, baskets, feltwork, and beadwork. Such crafts and artisan techniques maintain connections with cultural traditions and skills passed down through communities and families. Identify local craftspeople to demonstrate their craft to children and to raise your own awareness about cultural and artisan processes. A visit to your local markets will raise awareness about the craft-makers and artisans in your community. Additionally, families in your setting may know, or even be, local craftspeople and artisans

Be aware of the risk of tokenism. For example, many educational settings make folded paper lanterns for Chinese New Year. Rather than choosing simplistic techniques (which have little to do with lantern festivals that occur in many Asian cultures), learn how real paper lanterns are made and then interpret and adapt the materials and techniques to support an arts experience for children that draws upon those traditions. Remember, you can be inspired by an art or craft process, without replicating a specific product. Create opportunities for children to meet materials, play with them, explore them, and perhaps implement artisan processes relevant to their interests, development, capabilities, and cultures.

Paper crafts

There are many paper crafts that can be adapted for exploration with children. Most people have fond memories of making paper planes, folded paper fans, and paper mâché creatures. Young children can engage with these processes

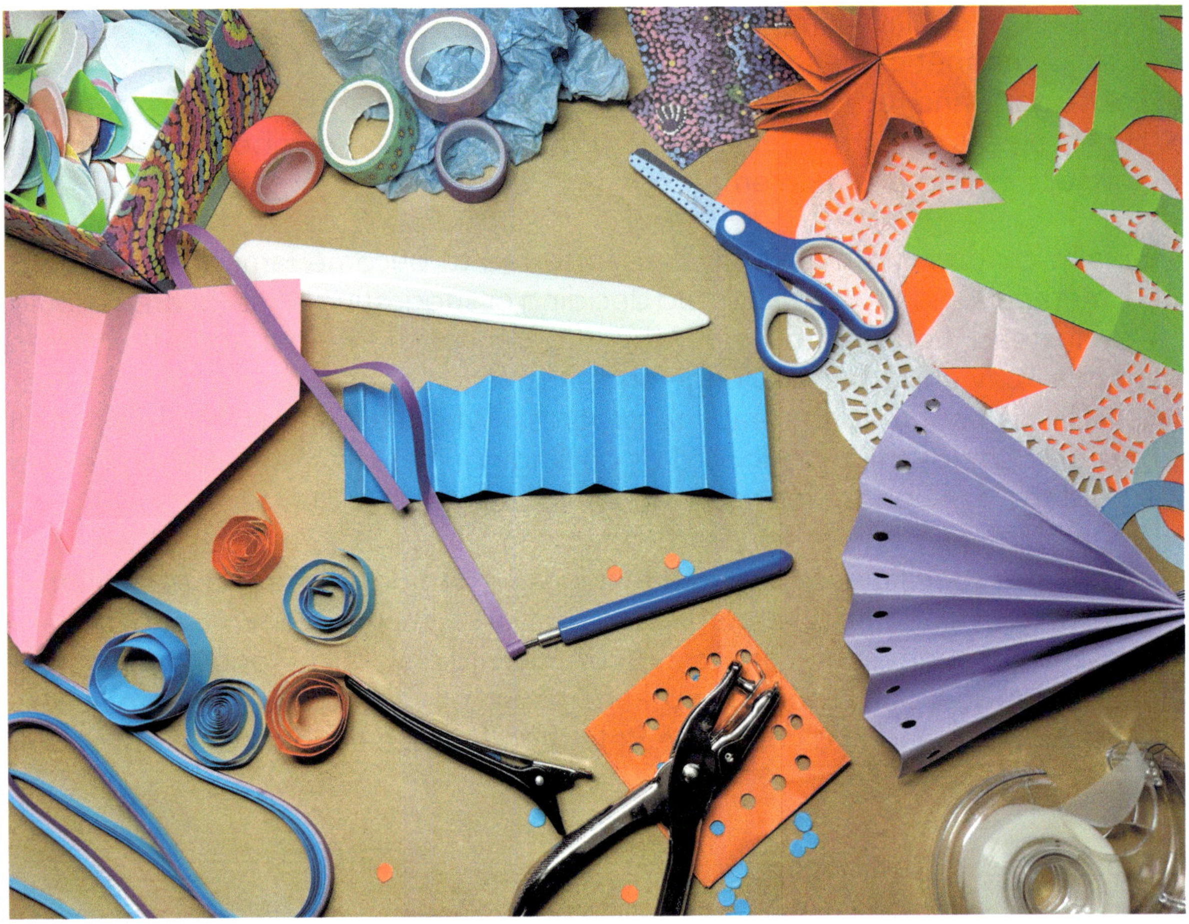

Figure P3H.5 Explore the versatility of paper with folding, cutting, quilling, holepunch and various paper craft tools [Image: Gai Lindsay].

and with the preliminary skills and explorations that precede being ready to complete more complex paper crafts.

Children of any age can explore, sort, and play with the properties of a range of paper types. Scrunch, rip, and cut paper with scissors. Explore how to bend and fold it. Wet paper and observe how the texture and properties change. As children change the properties of paper using scissors, glue, and hole punches they are not only developing fine motor skills, hand-eye coordination, and spatial awareness, but more importantly they are developing an awareness of their ability to change and alter a material through their own efforts and exploration! A good starting point is to collect and get to know the properties of a range of papers, and cardboard types and build a collection of papers and paper craft tools. Consider the following papercraft options and adapt them to cater to the experiences and interests of the children you work and play with:

Paper making: To make paper with children, shred recycled paper (you can also add plant fibres) and soak in water to create a pulp. Spread the pulp evenly on a fine mesh screen, drain the excess water, press it flat, and let it dry completely to form a new sheet of handmade paper.

Papier mâché: Mix equal parts of plain flour and water to create a paste. Tear strips of absorbent paper (butchers, newspaper, and tissue paper) and dip them into the paste before layering them over a mould. An alternative to using balloons is to make 3-D shapes using scrunched paper wrapped in tape, or use cardboard to make a sphere or other shape (do an online search for plenty of inspiration). Let the layers of paper mâché dry completely before painting the finished piece.

Quilling: Quilling involves rolling very narrow strips of paper into coils and shaping them into decorative designs. A quilling tool has a short-rounded handle with a thin slotted tip for holding and rolling the paper strips. These can be purchased commercially or home-made (an online search will provide sources and instructions). You can even improvise and use fine hair clips to hold and wrap the paper into coils. Children delight in the process of making springy coils, which can be arranged and glued onto a surface.

Origami and paper folding: While the precision and patience required to create traditional origami animals and shapes may be overly challenging for very young children, they will still be fascinated to learn about (and perhaps imitate) paper folding processes. The opportunity to play with, fold, and bend paper is well within children's range of capability. As children develop their capacity to fold paper and follow instructions, introduce simple origami projects. Provide children with sheets of coloured paper to fold paper fans. Fold the paper into quarters prior to snipping and cutting around the edges to create cut-out radial patterns and snowflake designs. Introduce basic paper plane making to integrate STEM learning with the arts. Some children may ask adults to do all of the folding for them, and while that can be a fun game, it can disrupt children's potential to learn new skills. Persist as a supporter, modeller, and guide for children, without taking over and doing all of the work! Consistently communicate your expectation that children are capable of learning new skills and take the time to slow down and encourage children in the process.

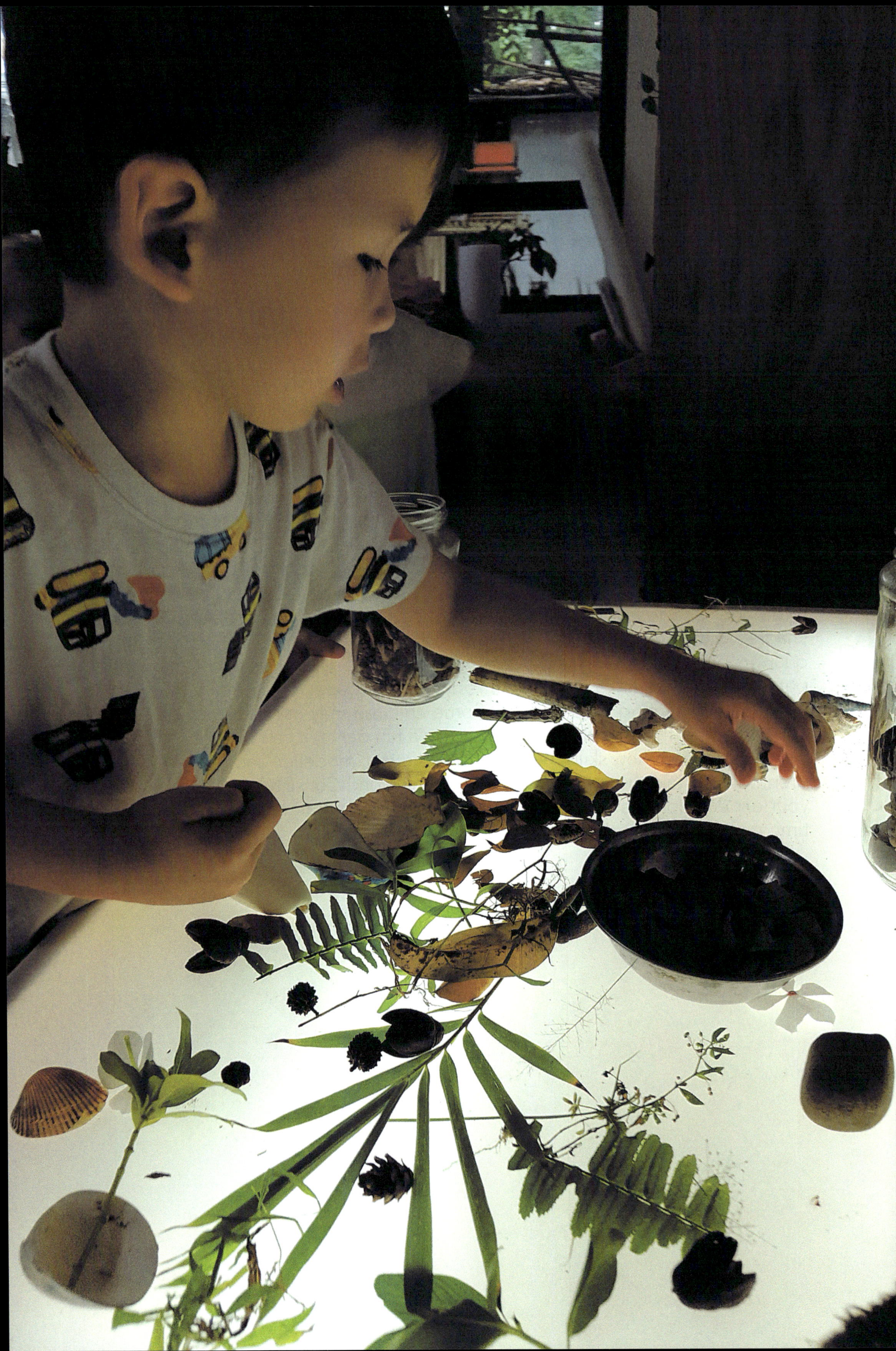

3.8 Photography, light and lenses

Technology offers many exciting possibilities to combine visual arts exploration with scientific inquiry, creative exploration, and meaningful connections across the curriculum. While play with light and the installation of environmental fairy lights has become popular in early education settings, it is worthwhile to appreciate the learning potential of technological tools rather than using them for aesthetic purposes only. Taking a superficial approach to light and lens technologies neglects their potential as tools for inquiry, exploration, and deep learning.

Digital technologies continue to evolve rapidly. Instead of identifying specific animation and drawing applications available in the market, this section focuses on the benefits of using various readily available technology tools. These tools support children with observing, exploring, and creating diverse opportunities for creativity, image-making, and aesthetic research. We explore how photography, video, projectors, light tables, microscopes, and a range of everyday technologies can foster children's curiosity, expand their understanding of the world, and enrich their art-making practice. Additionally, we encourage you to investigate the range of creative possibilities afforded by drawing apps and digital animation programmes used on tablets and computers; while being cautious to avoid applications that are formulaic rather than open-ended and creative.

Photography and digital imaging

Photography is a powerful tool for making children's interests visible (Moorhouse, 2018). Photography and digital storytelling offer children visual tools to communicate their interests and tell their stories. Acting as a lens for how children see the world, children's photographic images provide insights about what fascinates them and what they think is interesting. Photography, applied as a unique visual artform with children, offers the potential to include children's images in documentation, learning stories, and exhibitions. When combined with other visual arts media such as painting, drawing, printmaking, collage, and sculpture, photography offers endless opportunities for creative image-making

Exploring photography with children is rich with potential for creative expression and learning. Engaging with the language of photography invites children to:

- slow down
- observe closely

Figure P3I.1 A child examines and arranges natural materials on a lightbox, a rich opportunity for aesthetic research [Image: Carolyn Prawius, Saigon Kids Early Learning Centre].

DOI: 10.4324/9781003561835-22

- be present in the moment
- connect with their environment
- explore the world from multiple perspectives
- engage with what they are seeing in new ways
- learn responsible care for and use of a camera or tablet
- learn technical skills and master the languages of technology
- engage in decision making
- develop agency

Introducing photography to children

Children can learn photography skills and utilise photographic media for exploring their environment and documenting their play, observations and interests. Before introducing photography to children, discuss the need to care for the camera or tablet. Establish child-determined rules for their use, such as careful walking and wearing a wrist or neck strap. Discuss the need to respect others' privacy and build a culture of gaining permission before taking photos of children or their work. Moorhouse (2018) reminds us that it is essential to gather parental (and children's) permission if images are going to be shared in documentation, publications, or online.

Introduce a range of low-tech tools to encourage close observation, focus skills and new ways of looking at the world. For example, support children to explore looking through magnifying glasses, kaleidoscopes, binoculars, microscopes, telescopes, fish-eye lenses, door peepholes, and even cardboard sheets with small shaped peepholes to frame a view. Children can also learn to focus on objects by looking through cardboard tubes or a drink bottle with the base cut

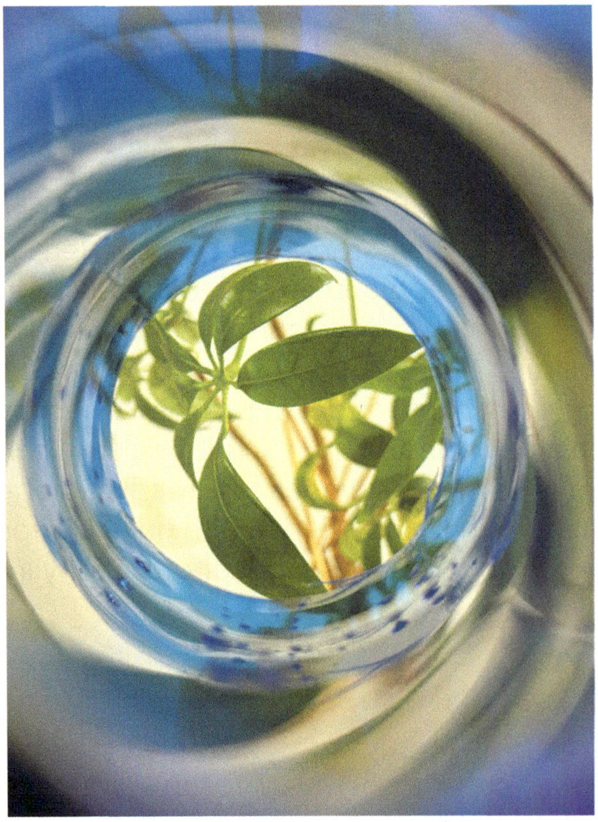

Figure P3I.2 Teach children how to focus on the subject of their photo and create a fascinating image, by looking at objects through a recycled plastic bottle or tube [Image: Gai Lindsay].

off. Such resources enable play and exploration opportunities that encourage children to look, notice, and experience the focus of their attention in new ways.

It is important not to assume that children have prior knowledge of photographic technologies and processes; while appreciating that some children will already be experts! Intentionally teach children how to turn photographic devices on and off (e.g. icons to press on a tablet), how to take a photo, how to hold the device still, use focus and zoom functions, and how to view and delete images. If sharing a device, develop protocols for recording the photographer who creates a series of images during their turn. For example, teach children to take a selfie (self-photograph) before taking their photos so that the images following the selfie are attributed to a particular child photographer.

To extend children's engagement with photography:

- Explore the work of photographic artists
- Discuss images in books and magazines
- Visit a photographic exhibition
- Teach children how to aim at and frame the subject of a photograph. Create a photography treasure hunt by taking photos of objects throughout your setting and challenging children to find and take a matching photo of the object. This will encourage children to consider their camera positioning and perspective.
- Tape a cardboard tube or a plastic bottle mouthpiece around the camera lens to create a tunnel vision view of a focal point. Magnifying lenses can also be clipped to the camera lens on tablets or phones, creating incredible zoom and magnifying functionality.

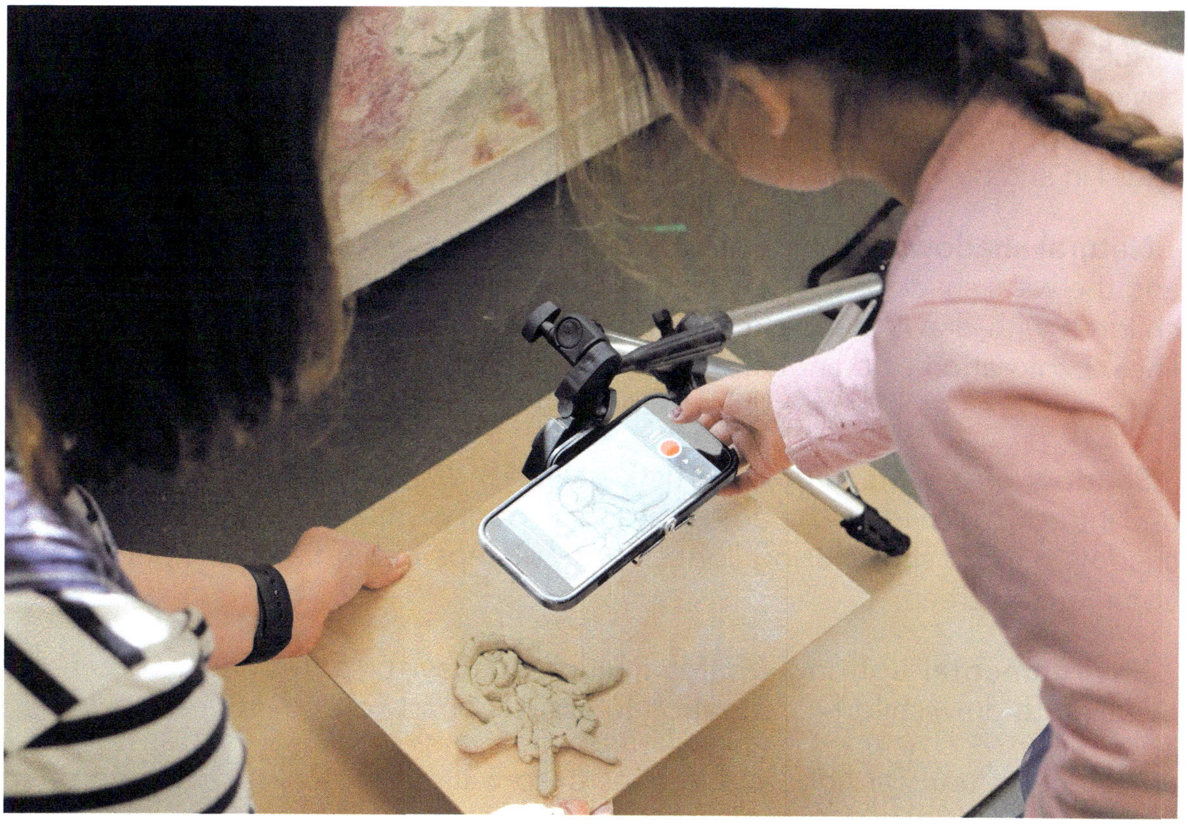

Figure P3I.3 Creating a synergy between an ancient art material and digital art, a stop-motion application tool captures images of Isla's clay figure to produce an animation [Image: Bomaderry Community Preschool].

- Partner with children to look at, appreciate, and discuss the photos they have taken to inspire conversation and facilitate opportunities for children to tell their stories.
- Challenge children to explore portraiture and diverse subject matter such as buildings, landscapes, shadows, colours, patterns, or shapes in the environment.
- Explore photo editing functions to play with visual effects such as colour saturation and pixelation, or explore how images look when converted to black and white.
- Print children's photographs to use for bookmaking, storytelling, collage, and painting projects. (Black and white images make a great base for drawing and painting.)
- Photography can also extend children's play with other art forms. For example, images of children's ephemeral art can be placed over an inked monoprint plate and traced to lift an imprint of the drawn lines, or an image placed under a gel-plate can inspire and suggest hand-painted designs and colours.

> "Children view the world in unique ways and the camera allows them to capture (their) perspectives" (Pete Moorhouse, 2018).

- Explore the use of time-lapse and video functions in camera apps to make stop-motion-style animations. There are many online instructions to guide your selection of applications and processes.

Encounters with light and shadow

Playing in a darkened space with jewel-like colours and shafts of light that illuminate objects and faces poses a wonderful aesthetic experience. As children play with light and shadows, they are supported to explore cause and effect, and engage in joyful and sensory-rich learning. Light and shadows can be found naturally in the environment or purposely created using projectors, light tables, lamps, torches, and fairy lights. Consider safety risks such as heat and light damage to children's eyes and skin and prevent fire hazards by turning off unattended electrical appliances.

Natural shadows offer many opportunities to pay attention to light, shadow and the ways shadows move when the sun gradually changes position. Provide children with drawing tools (chalk, markers, etc.) to trace shadow shapes and lines. Exploration of cyanotype prints (see printmaking section) is a way to use the sun to create object and plant silhouettes.

Shadow play with puppets artistically extends play with light and shadow and introduces children to traditional artisan puppet-making techniques. Create shadow puppet shows using light boxes or lamps behind a fabric, paper, or a commercial screen.

Environmental lighting creates inviting spaces for artmaking and can be installed to draw children's attention to objects or artworks of interest.

Projectors transfer light and images onto walls or other surfaces and offer exciting ways to play with scale, colour, light, and shadow. An online search will present you with a range of current digital, laser, and LED projectors to enable the projection of document cameras, photographs and videos.

These tools offer the potential to immerse children in embodied encounters with images that align with current projects or interests, and enable us to create rich immersive playscapes. For example, projecting a skyscraper or mountain image onto a wall enables children to become giants as they stand in front of and within the projected image. You can also project live video of children's play on a wall to support children to witness and be immersed in their own play and construction by connecting a camera device or laptop camera to a projector. The projector also transforms small objects into large projected images. Try projecting daisies, insects, or other objects of interest onto a wall to enable children to examine, dance in, or even trace their lines and finer details. Playing with scale is an exciting process that will engage children's curiosity, encourage them to see things in new ways, and inspire their hypotheses and research.

Overhead projectors (OHP) and document cameras are also excellent tools for use in children's learning environments. While rarely used for their traditional purpose, this technology can be repurposed to enable children to explore their ideas for composition with transparent colours and shapes. Children can also explore silhouettes and shadows when they place solid objects onto the clear projector surface. Effective results can also be achieved by connecting a digital projector to a document camera on which selected objects are arranged. By manipulating shapes, colours, light, and shadow, children can

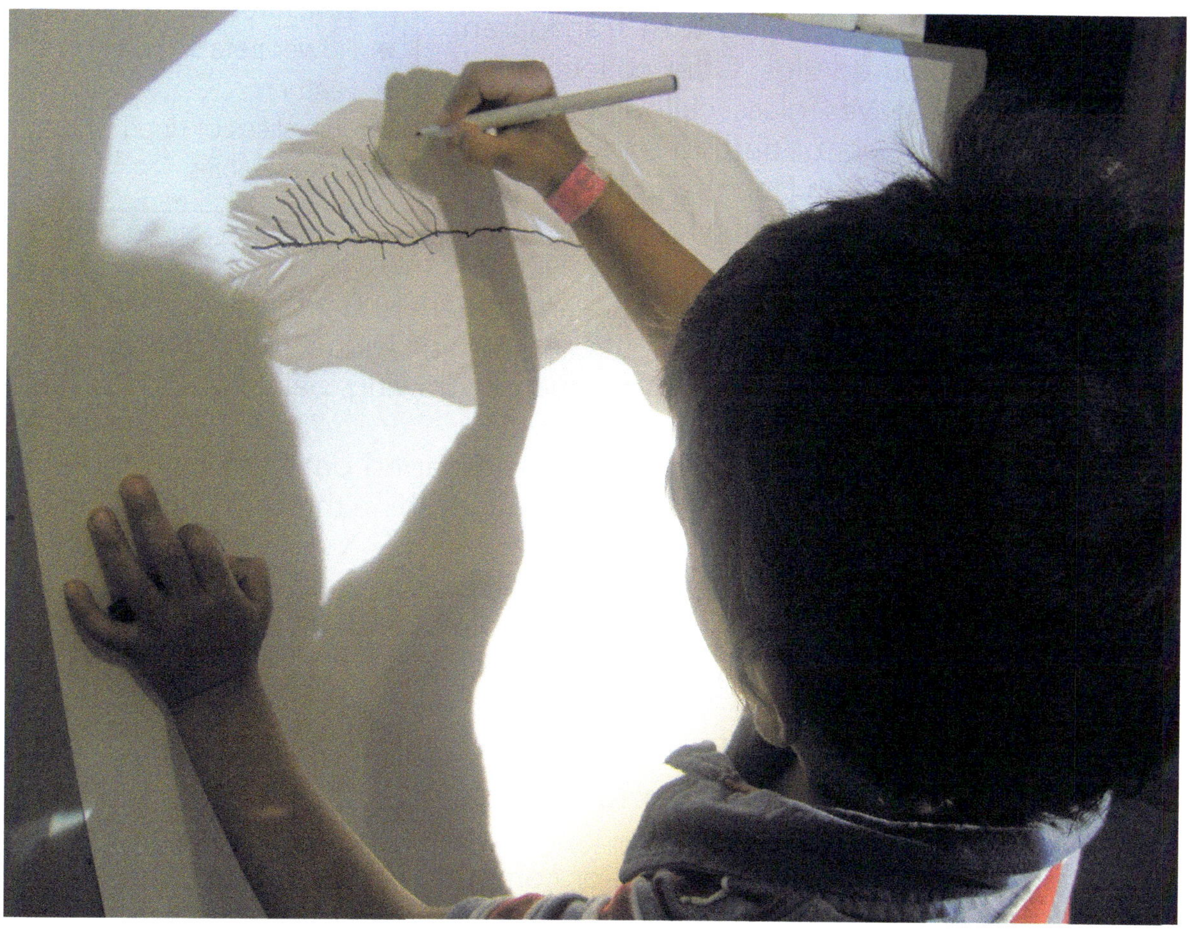

Figure P3I.4 An OHP projection of a feather provides an interesting and detailed object for tracing [Image: Gai Lindsay, Lyrebird Preschool].

create ephemeral art and patterns on the projector or document camera surface, and see their designs in a new light as they are projected onto a screen or wall. To extend this experience, you could place a large sheet of paper on the wall so that children can trace their designs and then paint them. Children's drawings can also be transferred onto transparent paper and projected onto a wall to create an enlarged version of their work.

Suggested items to collect and use with projectors and light boxes:

- Cellophane
- Transparent buttons/beads
- Plastic bottle caps (opaque and translucent)
- Plastic lids (from jars or containers)
- Bases of coloured plastic bottles
- Sea glass, seashells and stones
- Cut glass dishes and crystals
- Wire for bending and construction
- Reflective papers, plastics, and fabrics
- Leaves (dry or fresh to observe veins and structure)
- Flower petals
- Feathers
- Thin slices of dried fruits or vegetables

Light tables or tablets are flat, illuminated surfaces traditionally used to trace, edit, or design using transparent or translucent materials. In education settings they are increasingly used to create aesthetic playscapes where loose parts are used to play, arrange, and create patterns. They emit light from beneath a heavy-duty plastic surface, enabling the user to place items like paper, transparent film and other interesting items on top; offering highly engaging, backlit visual arts experiences. Consider some of the following to enrich your use of the light table with children and create artistic magic!

- Go beyond pattern making with transparent commercial-coloured tiles. Offer collections of objects such as leaves, glass, cellophane, transparent buttons, lace, or netting to add variety and inspire exploration (see the Ephemeral Art and loose parts design section for material curation and collection ideas).
- Paint and draw on the light table using arts materials. Cover the surface with a clear plastic cloth to protect the lights and electric wiring. The light table can enhance and extend artwork methods such as drawing, painting, collage, and clay work.
- Place various materials (plastics, fabrics, and paper) onto the light table to explore how materials block (opacity) or let light shine through (transparency) to different degrees.
- Introduce shiny objects like CDs, foil, or metallic surfaces to reflect light from torches or lamps. Use mirrors on the light table to explore reflection, symmetry, and light angles.

Everyday technology arts extensions

Technology isn't limited to electronics or computer-based devices, but can be any tools that make everyday tasks easier or more efficient. Collect common tools such as staplers, hole punches, photocopiers, scissors, compasses, rulers, kitchen

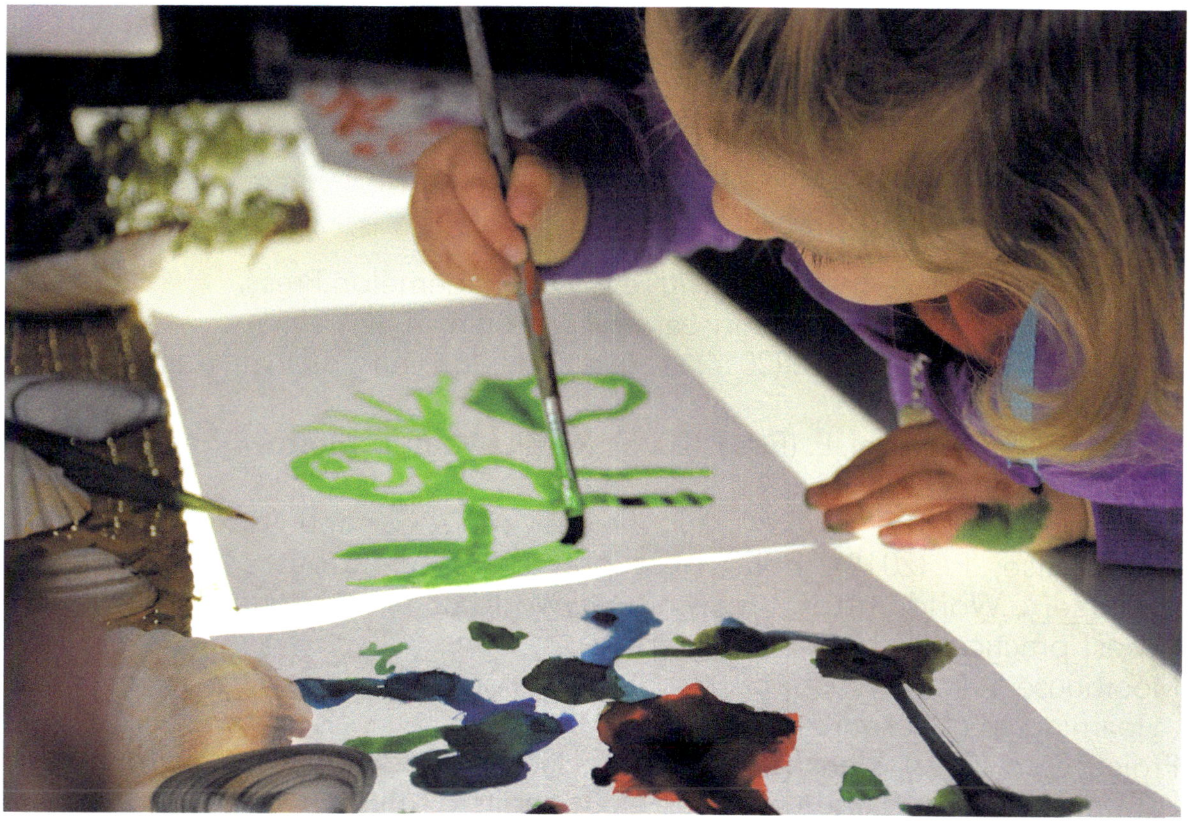

Figure P3I.5 The light table provides a luminous quality to dyes on paper, transforming a simple painting experience into something rather magical [Image: Sarah Probine].

utensils, and glue guns to consider how children can play with, and extend their creative use of materials using such tools. Here are just a few ideas to get you started:

- Photocopy children's drawings to provide child-designed colouring-in using a range of arts materials.
- Use a photocopier or printer to create images of objects, keys, cutlery, leaves, and hands. These images can be used as collage materials or positioned on a blank piece of paper to inspire drawing or painting experiences.
- Stencils for printmaking can be made by cutting shapes or punching holes in sheets of plastic (such as plastic folder dividers).
- Children can make their own "glitter" or collage materials using a hole punch on coloured paper, metallic wrap, and dried leaves.
- Children will delight in making a drawing robot using loose parts and a battery-operated motor or electronic toothbrush (search "drawbot" online for instructions).

References

Brooks, M. (2022). *Authentic art with children*. Pademelon Press.

Carle, E. (1994). *The very hungry caterpillar*. Puffin.

Daly, L., & Beloglovsky, M. (2014). *Loose parts: Inspiring play in young children* (Vol. 1). Redleaf Press.

Ferrari, A., & Giacopini, E. (Eds.). (2005). *REMIDA day* (L. Morrow, Trans.). Reggio Children.

Moorhouse, P. (2015). *Woodwork in the early years*. Community Playthings.

Moorhouse, P. (2018). EYFS best practice - All about... photography. Nursery World. https://www.nurseryworld.co.uk/content/features/eyfs-best-practice-all-about-photography/

Moorhouse, P. (n.d.). *Woodwork resources*. Irresistible Learning. https://irresistible-learning.co.uk/resources/

Project Zero. (2003). *Eight habits of mind*. Harvard Graduate School of Education. https://pz.harvard.edu/resources/eight-habits-of-mind

Reggio Children. (2005). *Remida day*. Reggio Children.

Weissman Topal, C., & Gandini, L. (1999). *Beautiful stuff!: Learning with found materials*. Davis Publications Inc.

Index

Note:- page references in *italics* denote figures, in **bold text** denotes tables.

9781032911960